Stock Market Investing, Options, Forex, Swing and Day Trading for Beginners:

5 in 1

The MOST COMPLETE COURSE on How to Become a Profitable Investor, TRADE FOR A LIVING & Build PASSIVE INCOME

Matthew Douglas

2

Options Trading for Beginners: CRASH COURSE

The Beginner's Guide to GET STARTED, Make a Living, CREATE WEALTH and Passive Income from Home. Investing and MAKING PROFIT with Options and Day Trading.

Matthew Douglas

Table of Contents

Introduction

Most people who invest in the stock markets do so with the desire to have safe investments that will grow over the long term of 5,10 and even 30 years. Others prefer a more active approach that lets them make money over shorter time intervals, even weeks. Or they want a hedge, neutral strategies, or even the ability to bet against a company in the belief its stock will decline. All of this action occurs in the options market, which is an exciting way to take a more active interest in stocks. Before we look at day trading, we will provide a quick review of the concepts of options.

Options are admittedly tricky. This is for the simple reason that historically, the economy deals with absolutes. When you look at the way that economies have risen and formulated, it's always been based on the trading of commodities - commodities being defined as the result of a form of labor to turn a raw resource into something else. A commodity could be anything from a wooden table, which is the result of the labor which went into developing that table from the wood and using the screws to put it together, to the wood which defines that table in the first place, which is the result of the labor of harvesting the raw resource of lumber and wood from forests. In this respect, commodities are what have made up the bulk of the economy.

Money has had quite a long journey itself. Social economies started from the concept of barter. One thing was traded for another thing and the economy existed within a system of absolutes. I have a bushel of apples, which I am willing to trade another person who has a bucket of goat's milk. In this respect, commodities were traded absolutely without the need for a mediator. Money slowly became introduced into the equation.

The line between commodities traded for a requisite value, as in the barter system, and the first early` money systems can be very blurred. After all, this is all just a method of trading the unwanted for another unwanted. However, the concept of a "coincidence of wants" would pop up, which is essentially the concept that things don't always follow a linear timetable. Certain things which would be normally traded for another will often spoil one before the other. This led to the need for an intermediate commodity, and thus the idea of commodity money - money with an intrinsic value representing a given exchange value - was born.

The first conceptions of money were instilled in the usage of early coinage. This popped up in Mesopotamia rather early in its history. A certain amount of gold or similarly precious metal would stand in for a certain amount of grain within a local granary, generally barley. However, more standardized mediums of exchange which would find themselves useful and in demand year round, such as but not limited to copper, gold, silver, and wine. The linguistic impact of these specific means of exchange continues to persist elementally within modern language and culture. Take, for example, the French word argent, which can mean both silver, about the element and the metal, as well as money, as in the phrase "gagner d'argent" meaning "to be paid" or, literally, "to win money".

Over time, money came to be represented through paper. This practice has its roots in China, where the usage of paper to represent arbitrary values of other things such as gold would pop up. This practice would eventually spread. Paper money generally first came to European culture through the Scandinavian countries where ore was abundant and carrying metal with you would prove to be very heavy and cumbersome. Instead, exchange notes representing these same quantities were substituted, which began the journey of money as we know it today.

The thing which happened with money represents another ideal entirely which ties very heavily back to the development of options trading, and which is a fundamental lesson in what options are and how and why they're used. The development of money represented an essential separation: the separation between the finite and the abstract. The finite barter economy where tangible goods were swapped with and for tangible goods represented an ideal that would end up to have a great many essential problems entangled with it. Among these is the notion of the coincidence above of wants. To develop the concept of year round exchange, it was necessary to form an essential detachment between the tangible good to be exchanged by, as stated, the development of a third variable, a third mediator commodity which replaces the finite qualities of other tradable commodities in favor of infinite qualities such as tradability and a sense of vague value - a mutable definition of immutable usefulness, such that in the currency's vague value an infinite set of possible solutions can be derived from its very use.

As a result of this development of vague values and finite tradability of an item with theoretically infinite value came the essential detachment I've been speaking of, the boundary of where the tangible real use value - the perceived value of a commodity and its usefulness insofar as the person who is buying and selling it perceives it - of a given object is translated into a demonstrable exchange value expressed solely through the usage of currency. This detachment can best be referred to as the transition of comparing two items' subjective use values to the linear development of items receiving objective exchange values through the usage of market mechanisms.

Options trading represents a necessarily similar detachment: options represent a given exchange value of an object. The necessary promise that an object can be bought and sold at that given value at a future date. It's a binding securities contract that allows you to say ahead of time what value you are willing to buy or sell an object for.

This is important to realize because this central concept of options trading is the historical point at which these two notions of use value and exchange value began to separate. The entire idea of options trading specializes in the separation of the tangible notion of a commodity from the intangible selling price of a commodity. I'll say it this way: let's say that you have a bushel of corn. As last reported, a bushel of corn costs approximately $3.65. By next season, this cost could go up, or it could go down. The bushel of corn is still going to represent the same quantity and the same weight of corn in the next season: that amount of that commodity will be the same, and that commodity will still be the same as it is at the time of the contract. However, the given exchange value of the corn will indeed be different, assuming non-vacuum conditions because economics doesn't, and never has, existed within a vacuum. The price will go up, or the price will go down. What exactly happens depends highly upon the market forces which are at work. But, the price will most definitely not be the same.

An option contract takes this variable aspect - the notion of shifting exchange values - and makes it an absolute. An options contract says that, regardless of the economic "weather", the commodity will sell for a given price on a given date, flat, period, full stop. Note that it's also important to remember that there are also stock options, which function similarly to commodity options but instead act as a means of.

There's a bit more to it: options mean that the buyer or seller of the commodity has the option, or the choice, to buy or sell the commodity for that value. It doesn't mean, however, the obligation; the buyer or seller is under absolutely no obligation to purchase or sell the stock at that price, the options contract merely means that the possibility is, in fact, there.

Options have a long history, and are the most prolific of any securities in human history. There's reason to believe that they're the first securities system developed in human history. They have their roots in even early human society.

The first recorded instance of the usage of options was when Greek great Thales of Miletus decided to take advantage of the olive harvest. The story goes that Thales had caught wind of the prediction that the next season would garner a far larger olive harvest than the usual.

Before the harvest, he sought out the exclusive right to olive presses come harvest time. When the olive harvest came around and the size of it was indeed much bigger than usual, he took advantage of his rights to the olive presses to rent the presses out at a higher rate since the demand of use was far greater due to the far larger harvest.

Options have had a nominal use ever since the notion of markets and monetary exchange. Their tens of hundreds of years of usage have built them to be a very usable and successful market instrument in speculating and hedging (we'll talk more about what they mean in just a second). However, they've had quite a bumpy road to get where they are today. The biggest example of options and futures being quite risky is in the Dutch tulip market bubble, largely regarded as one of the first, if not the first, major speculative bubble in human history.

Essentially, what happened was that tulips were incredibly valuable in Europe, especially the Netherlands during the time after it had recently established sovereignty from Spain and found itself having a huge amount of trade fortunes known primarily as the Dutch Golden Age, wherein the Netherlands found itself being cast as the epicenter of the East Indies trade that dominated Europe; during this time, one voyage alone would often be able to yield profits as high as four-hundred percent.

During this time is actually when tulips gained status as a very high-end luxury item.

To understand how this entire process works, you have to understand the cultivation process for tulips. Tulips are generally grown from their bulbs and spread by way of tulip seeds and tulip buds. When a given tulip bud grows up to be a flower, the original tulip bud disappears, with a copycat bud and several other buds. These actually - if properly taken care of and cultivated - will spread to produce new tulips. The process for a seed to grow into a bulb will take about 7 to 12 years, which is quite a long time.

Given that these were the most vivid, colorful, and beautiful flowers in Europe, they began to be highly sought after. The time to grow a tulip on one's own was far too long, so many opted to instead by the already grown tulips from others, specifically the tulip bulbs which would flower in the dormant period from early summer to early fall.

The flowers would continue to grow and grow in popularity as a result of their high social status. Because of this, professional tulip growers began to pay more and more for certain tulip bulbs with certain coloration patterns that made them even prettier than normal. As time went on, the price of these tulips went up as well, but since the demand for those tulips went up, the price of normal tulip bulbs went up. After a while, tulip bulbs of any sort were selling for absolutely absurd amounts.

What is an option

An option is simply a contract between two parties which is based on an underlying asset. You can create an options contract for any type of asset, but our focus is on options contracts for stocks. They are called options because one party of the contract will have the option to buy or sell stocks depending on whether certain conditions are met.

An option is a type of derivative. While they've been around for a long time, the general public didn't become aware of the concept of derivatives until the 2008 financial crash, when a particular type of derivative, mortgage-backed securities, caused financial havoc when huge numbers of bets went bad at the same time. A derivative sounds fancy, but all it means is that it's an asset whose value depends on the value of something else. In the case of options, the options contract is based on the value of the shares of stocks that the contract is based on.

One option contract represents 100 shares of stock. The contract will cost the buyer a much smaller sum than it would cost to buy the shares of stock. In a sense, an options contract is a bet that the stock will move in a certain direction over a given period. That is why they can be used for speculation. Like most contracts, an options contract has an expiration date or "expiry". In the United States options can be exercised on or before the expiration date, if the agreed-upon condition is realized. In Europe, they can only be exercised on the expiration date.

There are, of course, only two ways a stock can move, and so there are two types of options contracts. These are:

· A call: this is a bet that the stock will rise in price on or before the ending date of the contract.

· A put: this is a bet that the stock will decline in price, on or before the ending date of the contract.

For a call, the condition that the contract is based on is that the price of a share of stock will go up past an agreed upon price per share, which is called the strike price. When it does, the buyer of the option can exercise their right to buy stock shares from the seller (or writer as they are called) of the call option. That is, they can "call it in". If the share price goes above the strike price, the writer or seller of the call contract must sell the shares if the buyer chooses to exercise their right to buy them.

This is true no matter how high the stock price has risen. So, suppose that the strike price for ABC stock was set at $67 when the contract was entered into by the two parties. Second, we'll assume that at that time the share price was $65. If the share price rises to $68 a share, the owner of the shares must sell them if the buyer wants to exercise their option (to buy the shares). This is also true if the share price rises to $100.

The seller of the contract takes a bit of risk. They can't lose money, but they might miss out on a big move in the share price of the stock, and hence miss out on a big profit they could have had.

Why bother? The reason is that the buyer can buy the shares at the strike price. If the shares have risen to $100 a share, the buyer can buy the shares from the seller of the options contract at $68 per share, and then immediately turn around and sell them for $100 a share, making a quick profit of $32 per share! Of course, that is a quote of gross revenue, there are some fees involved and a commission to the broker, but in the end, the buyer would make a substantial profit in this scenario.

Now you may be wondering why the person selling the contract would bother. The reason is that they can charge a non-refundable fee for entering into the contract. This fee is called the premium. If you're selling calls, you get to keep the premium no matter what. In many cases, the share price will never exceed the strike price, so they get to keep the premium and the shares. If it does exceed the strike price, they get to keep the premium, and even though they may have missed out on some profit they could have had, they will probably earn a bit of profit on the shares they sold anyway. For the seller, it's a win-win deal. This kind of option contract is known as a covered call.

Covered calls provide one option strategy, which is to generate income from your shares.

Premiums are small, as compared to the price of the underlying stock. The risk to the buyer of the call is relatively small, and they get the chance to control shares of stock for a certain time without actually owning them. Of course, to exercise your option, you will have to have the capital on hand or access to the capital to buy the shares to make your quick profit. Many people, however, don't even do that and they simply trade options (that is you get the contract, and then sell it on the options markets before the expiry).

Options contracts are for 100 shares each. Premiums will usually be pretty small, so say $1 per share, so you can buy the options contract for 100 shares for $100. If it doesn't work out for the buyer, they lose a relatively small amount of money compared to the large funds that would be involved buying the stock. From the buyers perspective, it gives them the ability to speculate on the markets for relatively small sums of money and without actually owning the stock. Then if their speculation proves right, they can exercise their options and buy and sell the shares of stock.

When you read about options, they are typically described in some fancy sounding language. It will make sense now that you've seen how a covered call works. For a call, an option is a contract giving the owner the right, but not the obligation, to buy shares of stock at a fixed price over a specific, limited period. Typically, options contracts last a few months, but you can also buy weekly, which last a week on Fridays. There are also quarterly which expire the last business day at the end of each quarter. Also, for long term considerations, you can buy LEAPS which is typically a period over a few years.

Now let's take a look at the other type of options contract, which is known as a put. A put gives the buyer the right to sell the underlying stock at an agreed-upon price on or before the expiration date. Again, the put contract is sold for a premium and the pre-agreed upon share price is known as the strike price. When a trader buys a put, the bet is that the price of the stock will go below the strike price over the lifetime of the contract. Let's illustrate with an example.

Joe buys a put contract for XYZ Company. At the time that he buys the put contract, XYZ is trading at $100 a share. The premium for the contract is $2, so he buys it for $200. The strike price is $90.

Joe believes or has heard that some bad news will come out about XYZ, or maybe he is simply bearish about the market at large. Then before the contract expires, the bad news does come out. The share price drops to $60. Now Joe can exercise his right in the contract.

He buys 100 shares on the stock market at $60 a share. The seller of the put contract must buy the shares from Joe – at the strike price. So, the seller buys 100 shares of XYZ stock at $90 a share, and Joe walks away with a $30 per share profit (less the premium fee and brokerage commission).

The seller of the put got a raw deal, they probably doubted the news would drive the stock price that low, and so made a bet it wouldn't to get the income from the premium. Even though they lost their bet they get to keep the premium, so they aren't out. They also have the 100 shares of XYZ, and who knows, maybe things will turn around in the future.

These are dramatic examples designed for illustration. Most of the time stock probably won't move that much, although options traders try to look for volatile stocks that are moving a lot. Sellers will probably try and sell more stable stocks, so they won't risk as much.

If the share price of stock never goes above the strike price in the case of a call or goes below the share price in the case of a put by the expiration date, the option expires worthless. The seller of the option walks away with their premium and in the case of the call, keeps their shares, and in the case of a put, has no obligation to buy shares. The buyer of the option loses only the premium when it expires worthless (note that the buyer never gets the premium back under any circumstances).

Trading Options

Now like anything else, you can buy and sell an option itself. What is an option worth? The premium! Depending on various factors, the premium can go up or down. The person who buys the options contract is the owner of the contract. The seller still has their obligation, if the share price meets the required conditions against the strike price in the contract. You probably have a good idea of what a share or stock of a company is. To keep it simple, a single share represents a solitary unit of ownership in that company. Companies will offer their shares for sale to raise some capital for themselves. These shares, or equities, are going to be listed as well as traded on the stock exchange amongst interested traders.

21

In the stock exchange, a lot of things can go on. You will notice that there are going to be many high profile shares that trade in huge volumes. These also may have some derivatives that are associated with them. A derivative is a contract that can occur between at least two parties, and sometimes more, in which the contract will derive its value from an underlying security, such as an index or a stock.

The most commonly traded derivatives that you can find on the stock market will be options and futures. We won't spend a lot of time on futures in this guidebook, but they are often easier to understand than options, but they often have less flexibility and will carry more risk with them.

Regular people believe that options trading is risky. It's a recognition for being unsafe, but this is a misconception about choices trading. Although it might be accurate that options trading is risky, it could be extremely profitable if you are built with superb trading skills and techniques. Like every other form of offline or maybe online trading, it includes uncertainty and risk. Uncertainties and risks in trading options are better in case one does not have any notion of what he's doing. An alternative is an arrangement whereby one grants another the best to purchase and sell off a thing down the road. In the situation of Dow index future choices, when one purchases a Dow call alternatives this entails they're purchasing the right/privilege to buy that underlying Dow future at a definite cost in a particular time down the road. This definite cost is known as "strike price" while the particular time is known as the "expiration date". This particular trading may additionally be known as when one investor purchases a put, they're essentially promoting the industry because a call fundamentally purchases the industry. In much the same, when an investor offers a put, they're purchasing the industry since promoting a call essentially sells the industry. To have that opportunity to purchase an alternative in this long term, investors pay a so called "premium." In case the marketplace doesn't make the strike cost of the possibility, subsequently that option will likely be seen as useless on the expiration date. Additionally, if the marketplace doesn't get to the strike cost of the choice on the expiration date, it makes sense the investor is going to be issued the underlying future in which particular hit selling price.

The owner of the option is considered to be long in the position. If you are short on the position, you've sold an option you didn't own at the time of sale.

The buyer of an option has three possible outcomes:

· They can hold the option until it expires, and the strike price is not exceeded, so the option expires worthless.

· They can sell the option at some point before it expires. In this case, you are said to "close out your position".

· They can exercise their rights under the option. This means you will buy the underlying shares of stock or sell the underlying shares of stock, for a call or a put, respectively. The buyer of the option is the person with the right but not the obligation to buy or sell the shares. The seller of the option contract (also sometimes called the writer) must buy or sell the shares. Their possible outcomes are:

· You can buy the option back and close out your position.

· Take "assignment", which means buy or sell the shares as required if they have met the condition set by the strike price.

· If the strike price condition isn't met, you let the contract expire worthlessly, and keep your premium.

Of course, remember that in all cases the seller always keeps the original premium.

An option can be in the money or out of the money. If an option for ABC stock has a strike price of $50 and shares of ABC stock are trading for $55, it is in the money $5. If the shares are trading for $47, the option is out of the money $3.

For a call, it works oppositely, since you earn money as the buyer of the option if the stock falls below the strike price. For ABC, a put option with a strike price of $50, if the stock price is trading at $55, the option is out of the money $5. On the other hand, for a put contract, if it's trading at $40, the option contract is in the money $10.

The intrinsic value of an option is the amount that it is in the money.

We also need to know the so-called time value of the option. This is the difference between the intrinsic value and the premium per share paid for the option. That is:

à Time value = premium paid − value in the money

If you paid $7 for an XYZ option and it's in the money $2, the time value is $7 - $2 = $5.

When an option is out of the money, it has no intrinsic value. So the time value is given by the premium paid, but it declines at increasing rates as the expiration date gets closer. The options contract will be worth less and less to a potential buyer since its likely to expire worthlessly.

When you look at an options ticker, it will include the premium (the cost of buying on a per share basis) and the expiration date. Options also have a deliverable, which is the amount of the underlying that will be bought or sold if the option is exercised. Typically, this is 100 shares of the stock. The multiplier defines the net credit or debit to your account if the option is exercised (or assigned, in the case that you are the writer of the option).

A few more things to be aware of as a buyer include:

· Break-even point: This is the strike price + option premium.

· Maximum loss: Premium paid for the option.

Long vs. Short

There are four basic options available:

· Long call: this is the right to buy shares. This means you are bullish on the stock, that is you expect its value to increase, possibly by a large amount.

· Long put: this is the right to sell shares of stock. You're bearish on the stock, but it's long because you expect to profit from the options contract by selling the shares at the strike price which is higher than the share price on the market.

· Short call: An obligation to sell a stock. You're bearish on the stock, and don't believe the share price will increase enough to beat the strike price. It can be covered, meaning that you already own the shares (lower risk) or naked, which means you don't own the shares when you write the contract (high-risk trade).

· Short put: This is an obligation to buy shares of stock. You're bullish on the stock and believe the share price will stay above the strike price.

Now let's size up potential profits and losses for the different options.

Long Call (role: buyer)

For our long call, let's assume we have:

Long 1 ABC Aug 50 Call @ $1

This means the option contract is for 100 shares (the value 1 = 100 shares, or one option contract) of ABC stock. The option expires the third Friday in August. The strike price is $50, and the premium is $1. This is a low-risk strategy with your only risk limited to the premium, with high potential upside (thought the probability of going above the strike price may not be high). It's also low risk for the seller since they keep the premium and the worstcase outcome is selling the shares at the strike price which was higher than the price of the shares at the time the contract was written, but lower than the market price at the time of sale.

For the buyer of this contract:

· The maximum loss is limited to the premium, which is the quoted price multiplied by 100 for the total number of shares, or $1 x 100 = $100.

· Maximum gain: Theoretically unlimited, depending on how much the share price exceeds the strike price.

Short or Naked Calls (role: seller)

We began our discussion with covered calls. In that case, as the seller of the option, the call was "covered" by the underlying stock. A naked call is one that is uncovered. That is, you write call options without owning the underlying stock. Remember for a call option, if you are forced into an assignment, you must sell the underlying shares. With a naked call, you face potential losses since you don't own the shares when you write the call. On the market, naked calls are known as "shorts". The ticker might look something like this:

Short 1 ABC Jun 25 Call @ $2

This tells us that the option contract expires the third Friday in June. The strike price is $25, and the premium is $2.

In this case:

· The breakeven point is strike price + option premium = $25 + $2 = $27.

· Maximum gain is 100 shares x premium = $200.

· Maximum loss is unlimited, depending on how high the stock goes because you would have to buy the shares if assigned. Since this is high risk and you'd need the capital available to take care of the deal if the need arises, brokerages assign levels to options traders to determine whether they are allowed to participate in such high-risk trades. When you open an account to trade options, you'll need to know your assigned level to determine which types of trades you can make.

Short Puts (role: seller)

A short put, like a naked call, is a risky trading strategy and you'll be required to have capital available to risk. This is a small possible gain with a large possible loss option. Consider the following put:

Short 1 ABC Jul 30 Put @ $2

This option expires the third Friday in July, has a strike price of $30 and a premium of $2.

· Maximum gain: $2 premium x 100 shares = $200.

· Maximum loss: ($30 strike price - $2 premium) x 100 = $2,800.

· Breakeven: ($30 strike price - $2 premium) = $28.

Long Put (role: buyer)

For a long put, we're betting that the stock price will drop below the strike price. This is a lower risk strategy than a short put for the buyer. If the price fails to drop below the strike price, then you're only out the premium. Of course, to exercise your right to sell the shares, you'll have to have access to the capital necessary to buy them. We'll say our example is:

Long 1 ABC Sep 40 Put @ $3

The contract expires on the third Friday of September. The strike price is $40, and the premium is $3, so the cost to buy the contract is $3 x 100 = $300.

· Maximum loss: The maximum loss is the premium cost, so $3 x 100 = $300.

· Maximum gain: The maximum gain is given by (strike price – premium) x 100 = ($40 - $3) x 100 = $3,700.

· The breakeven point is strike price minus the premium, or $40 - $3 = $37.

So this is a lower risk strategy – since the maximum loss is much smaller than the potential gain.

For now, that is all we need to know about options. Our next step is to learn some of the basics of day trading.

Chapter 1: The Trader's Psychology

The point of the book is to make you aware of everything that is involved, but we have to remember that the mindset is going to be the thing that holds the key to our success. This isn't true just with stocks and options trading, but with life in general.

The Basics of Trading Psychology

Fear

Fear can be one of the most dangerous weapons that we use against ourselves. It holds us back from things we want and makes us push away the things that we need. If you let fear control your life, you'll never really be in charge of any of your thoughts or emotions. Fear can make us nervous, grumpy, and even sick. Almost as bad as this, it can make us lose a ton of money.

Those going into options trading need to make sure that they don't allow fear to hold them back. Though you have to be cautious, you should understand that you can't be too afraid from making a move you might actually trust. Know the difference between being smart and safe, and blinded by worry.

Looking at the Analysis

It's important to understand how to perform a proper technical analysis not just to determine the value of a certain option, but also to make sure you don't scare yourself away with any certain number. You might see a dip in a chart, or a price projection lower than you hoped, immediately becoming fearful and avoiding a certain option. Remember to not let yourself get too afraid of all the things you might come across on any given trading chart. You might see scary projections that show a particular stock crashing, or maybe you see that it's projected to decrease by half. Make sure before you trust a certain trading chart that you understand how it was developed. Someone that wasn't sure what they were doing might have created the display, or there's a chance that it was even dramatized as a method of convincing others not to invest. Always check sources, and if something is particularly concerning or confusing, don't be afraid to run your own analysis as well.

Hearing Rumors

If you are someone that hangs around with other traders, maybe even going to the New York Stock Exchange on a daily basis, there's a good chance you are talking stocks with others. Make sure that any "tips" or "predictions" you hear are all taken with a grain of salt. Tricking others into believing a certain thing is true about different stocks and options can sometimes dapple into an area of legal morality, but it's important to still make sure you don't get caught up with some facts or rumors that have been twisted.

You should only base your purchases on solid facts, never just something you heard from your friend's boyfriend's sister's ex-broker. While they might have the legitimate inside scoop, they could also be completely misunderstanding something that they heard. Before you go fearfully selling all your investments from the whisper of a stranger, make sure you do your research and make an educated guess.

Accepting Change

As animals, us humans are constantly looking for a constant. We appreciate the steadiness that comes along with some aspects of life because it's insurance that things will remain the same. Sometimes, we might avoid doing something we know is right, just because we are too afraid to get out of our comfort zone. Make sure that you never allow your own fear of change hold you back.

Sometimes, you might just have to sell an old stock that has been gradually plummeting. Maybe you have to accept that an option is no longer worth anything, even though it's been your constant for years. Ask yourself if you are actually afraid of losing the money, or just dealing with the fear.

Greed

Greed can be one of the biggest issues that certain traders run into. The reason we're doing this in the first place is for money, and some people think that's greedy enough. While we do need money to feed our family, pay off debt, and just have some cash to live from day-to-day, there are other sources of income than stocks. Still, you get the opportunity to make big money just from money that you already have. If you are good enough at trading, you can even make it your fulltime job.

To ensure that you are trading for the right reasons, always ask yourself questions. Why do you need to take such a big risk? Is it worth sacrificing money that could go towards a vacation? Are you making these decisions to feed your family, or are you doing it, so you can go on a self-indulgent shopping spree?

It's true that we deserve to have some "me time," and we all should spoil ourselves every once in a while, as we can't depend on other people to always do that for us. However, greed can really be a downfall if we're not careful.

Know When to Stop

Knowing when to stop can be the most challenging part of life. It's so hard to say no to another episode when your streaming service starts playing the next one. How are we supposed to say no to another chip when there are so many in the bag? Sometimes, if you see your price rising, you might just want to stay in it as long as you can. In reality, you have to make sure that you know when it's time to just pull out and say no.

If you wait too long, you could end up losing twice as much money as you were expecting to make. This is when the gambling part comes in and things can get really tricky. Make sure you are well versed on your limits and that you are not putting yourself in a dangerous position if you don't trust your own self-control.

Accept Responsibility

Sometimes, we don't want to have to admit that we're wrong, so we'll end up putting ourselves in a bad position just to try to prove it to someone, even just ourselves, that we were right. For example, maybe you told everyone about this great investment you were going to make, sharing tips and secrets with other trader friends about a price you were expecting to rise.

Then, maybe that price never rises, and you are left with just the same amount that you originally invested. You were wrong, but you are not ready to give up yet. Then, the price starts rapidly dropping, but you are still not ready to admit you are wrong, so you don't sell even though you start losing money. You have to know when to just accept responsibility and admit that you might have been wrong about a certain decision.

Pigs Get Slaughtered

This is a common saying in the stock market world. It means that pigs, anyone who becomes too greedy, will get destroyed by the stock market because of their blind desire to make money. Make sure that you are not a pig. In order to avoid always wanting more and having a mentality that puts pressure on doubling profits, make sure you keep track of just how much you've been making.

This might include just some notes in your journal about how much money you've made so far. You'll want to continually look at how much money you've made to make sure that you keep perspective on how far you've come, rather than continually looking to the future and worrying about how far you have to go. Remember that any sort of significant fortune takes time to build.

Though you might hear some stories about people that made thousands over night from a great tip, remember that this isn't common. You very well could be the next person to get a huge sum of money from a small investment in a quick way, but you can't allow yourself to bank on this.

Discipline

Having a good knowledge and understanding of different stocks and options is important, but discipline might be the most crucial quality for a trader to have. Not only do you have to avoid fear and greed, but you have to make sure to stay disciplined in every other area.

On one level, this means keeping up with stocks and staying organized. You don't want to just check things every few days. Even if you plan on implementing a longer strategy for your returns, you should still keep up with what's happening in the market daily to make sure that nothing is overlooked.

On a different level, you have to stay disciplined with your strategy. Decide where personal rules might bend and how willing you are to go outside your comfort zone. While you have to plan for risk management, you should also plan that things might go well. If the price moves higher than you expected, are you going to hold out, or are you going to stay strict with your strategy?

Stick to Your Plan

If you don't stick to the right plan, you might end up derailing the entire thing. You can remember this element in other areas of your life. You can be a little lose with the plan, but if you go off track too much, what's the point of having it in the first place? If you are too rigid, you could potentially lose out on some great opportunities, but too lose can make everything fall apart.

Prepare for Risk Management

Aside from just knowing when to pull out to avoid being greedy, you also need to make sure that you are doing it, so you don't end up losing money. Have plans in place for risk management and make sure that you stick to these in order to ensure you won't be losing money in the end.

Determine What Works Best

The most important aspect in a trading mindset is remembering that everyone is different. What works best for you could be someone else's downfall and vice versa. Practice different methods and if something works for you, don't be afraid to stick to that. Allow variety into your strategies, but be knowledgeable and strict with what you cut out and what you let in. Identify your strengths and weaknesses so that you can continually grow your strategies and always determine how you can improve and how you can cut out unnecessary loss.

Things That Distinguish Winning and Losing Traders in Options Trading

As an options trader, you need to know how to calculate and find the break-even point. In options trading, there are basically 2 break-even points. With short term options, you need to make use of the commission rates and bid spread to work out the break-even point. This is if you intend to hold on to the options until their expiration date.

Now if you are seeking short term trade without holding on to the options, then find out the difference between asking price and bid price. This difference is also known as the spread.

Embrace the underlying stock's trend

As an investor and trader in options, you need to consider the trend of the underlying stock as your friend. This means that you should not fight it. Basically, if the stock price is headed upwards, you should find a strategy that is in tandem with this movement. If you oppose it, you are unlikely to win.

Similarly, if the stock is on a downward trend, then do not oppose this movement but try and find a strategy that will accommodate this trend. You need to understand however that this saying is intended to guide you but is not necessarily a rule. This means you apply it even while you consider all other factors. For instance, the major news may have an immediate effect on the price trend of a stock or shares.

As a trader, you should learn to jump successfully on a trend and follow the crowds rather than go to extremes and oppose it. Most amateurs who see an upward trend often think the stock is about to level out. However, the reality is that the momentum is often considered a great thing by seasoned traders. Therefore, do not try and oppose the trend because you will surely lose. Instead, try and design a strategy that will accommodate the trend. In short, the trend is always your friend, do not resist as momentum is great.

Watch out for earnings release dates

Call and put options are generally expensive with the price increases significantly if there is an earnings release announcement looming. The reason is that the anticipation of very good or very bad earnings report will likely affect the stock price. When this is an underlying stock in an options trade, then you should adjust your trades appropriately.

Once an earnings release has been made, then options prices will fall significantly. You need to also watch out very carefully for this. The prices will first go up just before the earnings are released and then fall shortly thereafter. It is also possible for call options prices to dip despite earnings announcements. This may happen if the earnings announced are not as impressive as expected.

As an example, stocks such as Google may rise insanely during the earnings announcement week only to dip significantly shortly thereafter. Consider Apple shares that were trading at $450 at the markets. Call options with Apple as the underlying stock were trading at $460. However, the market had targeted a price of $480 within 3 days, which did not happen. This costs investors money. Such underlying assets are considered volatile due to the high increase in price, rapid drop shortly thereafter and a related risk of losing money.

Traps to Avoid On Expiration Day

The ease of the guidelines for participation and the aggressive marketing brings a lively interest of people for the binary options trade. Some greedy brokers take advantage of this desire that touches an audience of new private investors, mostly beginners. The most frequent abuses or frauds found are:

- The impossibility of withdrawing your money: here the fraudulent binary options broker prevents any withdrawal, or does not accept withdrawals until a minimum level is reached in the account.

- Fraud in the bank card: once the bank details are sent (by phone or after a first deposit) withdrawals are made from the clients' account without their authorization.
- An offer of "bonus" is offered to the clients, the company commits to credit in the customer's account the same amount as this deposit. The client then learns that the bonus is not granted until "bet" at least x times its amount (20 to 30 times in the cases cited).
- Fraud in managed accounts: training offers are proposed and a "coach" is assigned to the client. Very often, the coach proposes to the debutants to be advised by telephone in their bets. When the first losses occur, the coaches advise the client to place supplementary funds to "redo". When losses accumulate, "the coach becomes unplayable or gives the only explanation that a bad operation is the source of the losses."
- Conditions of trade impossible to achieve: the broker demands the investor to make positions more than x days in the month. Maybe even more than the number of days worked in the month.
- Withdrawal penalty: the broker applies significant "charges" from 10 to 50% to dissuade the investor from recovering their money. Generally, the merchant has no knowledge of this information until the day he tries to withdraw his funds and has a hard time finding this information before.

On the other hand, if the most serious companies propose access to a market resulting from supply and demand, the majority is happy proposing over the counter products (without going through a stock market). The prices are then decided either by the company itself, which acts as a counterpart for its own account and has an interest in the client losing, 5 either by an affiliated company or friend.

The first thing that we need to do when setting up our own accounts with options trading is to make sure that we are prepared mentally to handle all of this. Options trading is a great investment tool and if you use it in the proper manner, you can make a lot of money in the process. With that said, there are some risks, and you need to take the right steps from the beginning to determine how to get started. Because of this, some of our first tips are going to explore how you can prepare yourself mentally to become a successful options trader. Some of the things that you can do to accomplish this include:

Tip 1: Find a Broker

One of the first things that you should do when trying to get yourself set up for options trading is to find a broker to invest with. A broker is going to be your best friend right from the very beginning. They will determine the fees that you have to pay for each trade that you do. They will answer your questions as you go along. They will provide you with the platform that you will use when you utilize their services as well.

Picking out a good broker is so important when you are trying to see some results with options trading. When you are searching for a good broker, make sure that you spend some time discussing their fees and what services that they offer. You will be amazed at the different prices that each one is going to suggest for the same kinds of services, and it is always better to know this ahead of time. If someone offers a higher price but also has more services for that price, it is worth considering them. But if a broker has a higher price and fewer services, it is fine to go with someone else and take a better deal.

Once you have an idea of the fees you will be paying with each broker and how much value they will provide to you, it is time to move on to asking them some questions. Go in with a list of questions that you have and make sure they all get answered. Discuss how the fees are, how much they are able to help you with the trades, how the platform works, what kind of assets they offer for options trading and more.

You should feel fully confident with the broker you wish to work with. There are many brokers out there, but not all of them are going to offer the services that you want, some may not be able to answer your questions, and others just may not put you at ease like you want. After interviewing a few different brokers, you should have a good idea of who you would like to work with on all your trading endeavors and you can choose to go with them.

One thing that you should consider when you are looking for a broker. Many of these brokers will allow you to take a practice run or two on one of their demo accounts. This can benefit you in a few ways. First, it gives you the opportunity to try out the platform that the broker is offering and see if it is the right one for you. If you feel that something is off with the platform or it just isn't working well for you, at least you will know this ahead of time.

Another benefit of trying a demo account, if it is offered, is that you get a chance to try out a few of your trades ahead of time, to see how they work and determine if you actually know what you are doing, and if you are using the strategies in the proper way, before you enter the market. If you find that some of your trades aren't going well, you can then re-evaluate your plan and work from there.

Once you have picked out the broker you would like to work with, it is time to set up your account. Check and see if there are any minimum amounts that you need to put in your account to get started and then deposit the amount that you want to have. Some people add in all of the capital that they want to save for the investment into the account right away, and others will just put in the amount they need for that particular trade. Check and see what the rules are with your broker.

Once your money is in the account, you can start to do your research and determine which trades you want to use. You will want to make a trading plan ahead of time, one that outlines your risks, that says what strategy you want to use, and the entry and exit points that you should use and more. This helps you to see what steps you should take in order to start the trades and see the success right away.

After doing your research and setting up the plan, you can give the broker your orders. This tells them what securities to purchase, how many, for what price, and some of the other requirements that you set out. Then stick with the trading plan to make the best decisions to make the trade work out in your favor.

Tip 2: Have some confidence in your trading strategy

As a new trader, you need to spend some time thinking about the trading strategy that you want to use. This particular plan is going to encompass everything that you have already learned about trading, about the markets, and how to apply all of the different techniques. After you sit down and think about the trading approach that you want to work with, then it is time to implement it. Not only do you need to have a plan written out and ready to go though. You must also have the right confidence in this strategy to ensure that you will implement it and get the full benefits from it.

Because of this, no matter what kind of trader you are, always consider the reasons as to why you are taking on this particular type of trade, why you have chosen a certain amount of funds for that trade, and what the profit targets are for this trade. Ideally, the trading strategy is also going to include some reasons as to why you have taken a particular trade.

No matter how tempting it may be to do this, never proceed with a new trade before all of this information is established. Once you have established a reason why you want to go into a particular trade. From there, you can set up a profit target and the right risk parameters to see some results.

For example, you may write out a plan where you have decided that the if the market does move to point A, then you are going to count your losses and then move yourself on to the next trade. But, if the market instead moves to point B, then you are going to take the profits and will strategize on the following trade you want to do. This is an approach that is known as plan your trades then trade your plans. It is always a good idea to stay disciplined with your trades and then stick to the plan as much as possible. If you are able to maintain this approach, then you are establishing a great foundation for options trading and seeing results.

Tip 3: Be Comfortable with Your Trading Capital
There is no trader out there, whether it comes with options or another security or investment opportunity, who wants to lose money. If they did, they wouldn't waste their time even trying to invest or trade. However, most options trader understand that it is possible to trade options and make money sometimes, and lose money the other times.

Basically, if you get into the options market and you are not ready to accept the risk that you may lose money, then you are going to start trading on your emotions. And trading on your emotions is a terrible thing to do. Once this happens, you may as well just throw your money in the trash. Emotional trading is going to throw discipline out of the window and you will stand no chance of performing as expected.

Before you enter the market, knowing that it is possible that you could lose money and with the idea that your emotions should be kept away, make sure that you are comfortable with the amount of capital that you are trading. There are different rules out there to help you determine how much you should invest and risk. Many experts recommend you stick with about two percent of your total account.
What this means is that when you enter into a trade, you should never risk more than two percent of the total account. This way, if you do lose money, you won't risk the whole account, and you can still have some capital set aside to help you move on to a new trade, without wiping it all out. You can choose to go with

a different set amount on any trade, but making sure that you set this amount in the beginning and then stick with it, can really go a long way in helping you to do well with your trades, can keep your emotions out of the game, and ensures that you don't wipe out your account on one trade.

Tip 4: Keep Your Expectations Realistic

It is easy to get caught up in the idea of doing options. You are excited to jump right in. And maybe you have heard about others who jumped into the market and saw a lot of success in the process. They made a lot of money and did really well with this kind of market. It is good to have some excitement when you first get started, but this doesn't mean that you can run with reckless abandon and just go into the market without having some realistic expectations.

There are going to be some really good trades. And then there are going to be some really bad trades. And as a beginner, you are more likely to run into the bad trades as you learn the ropes and how to make it all come together. The best thing that you can do in this situation is make sure that your expectations are realistic the whole time, and to not get carried away.

Remember that you should never let your emotions take over or take control over what you are doing with your trades. When you forget to keep your expectations realistic, you are letting the emotions come into play. When you start with trading, think that it is possible you will lose a few trades, and then work on a trading plan that helps to avoid this as much as possible. Just realize that all beginners are going to lose some money, and then work on a program and a plan that can help you avoid this.

Tip 5: Your Psychology Is Important

The way that you handle the market is going to be so important. In fact, the psychology that you have going into the trade is going to be your foundation. It doesn't matter if you are a commodities, options, or stock trader. The conditions in the market that you pay attention to are never constant, and there are a lot of changes. And there are times that even with the best preparation and understanding of the market, you will end up losing money. Because of this, it is important that you have a strong foundation that will help you face all of the challenges that the market may and will bring your way.

There are a lot of bad things that can happen in the market, and in 2008 (along with many other times) those things did occur. For example, there are bailouts from the government, housing crisis, the dot-com bubble, and more. Many times these can be seen and the more advanced traders will get out of the market with time to spare. But there are times that even the experts get caught up, and then they lose money in the process.

However, traders need to have a nice strong foundation to help them weather through these storms. These storms are going to happen, no matter how much you work to try and avoid them. Traders who are able to keep their emotions out of the game, who can keep their levels of risk down to a minimum, and who can pick themselves back up after a loss are the ones who are going to be the winners overall.

Getting started with options trading can be really difficult to work with. You must make sure that you are able to set up your account the proper way, and that you know what to expect with all of the different aspects. But if you are able to get your psychology in the right place, find a good broker, and have the right amount of capital in place, you are going to see some amazing results.

Chapter 2: Options Contracts for Beginners

With this chapter, we will introduce the idea of options contracts and the way they're used in the stock market. In the introductory discussion of ours, we'll focus on the most essential way to get involved in options, which involves buying options contracts based on bets you make on whether future stock prices will rise or perhaps fall. Eventually, we will see that you can also write or perhaps sell options contracts and that the contracts are traded on the markets.

What's an Options Contract?

An options contract sounds fancy but it is a very easy concept.? It is a contract. Which means it is a legal agreement between a seller and a buyer.? It allows the purchaser of the contract to purchase or perhaps dispose of an asset with a fixed amount.? The purchase is optional? so the buyer of the contract doesn't have to purchase or even sell the asset.? The contract has an expiration date, so the purchaser? in case they decide to exercise their right? must make the trade on or perhaps before the expiration date.? The purchaser of the contract pays a non refundable fee for the contract.

While the focus of the book is actually on options contracts related to the stock market, some options contracts occur in every aspect of daily life as well as real estate and speculation. A basic example illustrates the idea of an options contract. Suppose you're itching to get a BMW and you have decided the model you want must be silver. You drop by a local dealer and it turns out they do not have a silver model in stock. The dealer claims he can get you one by the end of the month. You say you will take the automobile in case the dealer can get it by the very last day of the month and he will sell it to you for $67,500. He agrees and also requires you to put a $3,000 deposit on the automobile.

If the very last day of the month arrives as well as the dealer has not produced the automobile, then you are freed from the contract and get a refund. In the event he does produce the automobile at any particular date before the end of the month, you've the choice to purchase it or perhaps not. In case you wanted the automobile you can purchase it, but of course, you cannot be made to purchase the automobile, and perhaps you have changed the mind of yours in the meanwhile.

The right is there but not the obligation to purchase, in short, no pressure in case you decided not to push through with the purchase of the automobile. In case you choose to let the opportunity pass, nonetheless, since the dealer met the end of his of the bargain and produced the automobile, you lose the $3,000 deposit.

With this situation, the dealer, who plays the role of the writer of the contract, has the obligation to follow through with the sale based upon the agreed upon price.

Assume that when the automobile arrives at the dealership, BMW announces it'll no longer make silver automobiles. As a result, prices of new silver BMWs that were the last ones to roll off the assembly line, skyrocket. Other sellers are selling their silver BMWs for $100,000. Nevertheless, since this dealer entered into an options contract with you, he should sell the automobile to you for the pre agreed price of $67,500. You choose to get the automobile and drive away smiling, knowing you saved $32,500 and selling it at a benefit in case you needed to.

The situation here's capturing the essence of options contracts, even in case you have never thought of haggling with an automobile dealer in those words.

An alternative is in a sense a sort of bet. In the illustration of the automobile, the bet would be that the dealer can produce the exact automobile you would like within the specified period and at the agreed price. The dealer is betting too. His bet is the fact that the pre agreed to price is a great one for him. Naturally, if BMW stops making silver automobiles, then he has made the wrong option.

It can work the other way too. Let us say that rather than BMW deciding not to make silver automobiles anymore when your automobile is being driven onto the lot, another automobile crashes into it. Now your silver BMW has a small dent on the rear bumper with some scratches. As a result, the automobile has immediately declined in value. But in case you want the automobile, since you have agreed to the options contract, you must pay $67,500, even though with the dent it is only really worth $55,000. You can walk away and lose your $3,000 or perhaps pay what's now a premium price on a broken automobile.

Another example which is often used to explain options contracts is the purchase of a house to be constructed by a developer under the agreement that certain conditions are met. The customer will be expected to put a non refundable down payment or perhaps deposit on the house. Let us say that the developer agrees to build them the home for $300,000 provided that a new school is built within five miles of the development within one year. Thus, the contract expires within the first year. At any time during the year, the customer has the choice to go ahead with the building of the home for $300,000 if the school is built. The developer has agreed to the cost regardless of what. Therefore if the housing market in general and the building of the school, in particular, drive up demand for housing in the area, and the developer is selling new homes which are now priced at $500,000, he's to sell the home for $300,000 because that was the cost agreed to when the contract was signed. The home buyer got what they wanted, being within five miles of the new school with the home price fixed at $300,000. The developer was assured of the sale but missed out on the unknown, which was the skyrocketing price resulting from increased demand. On the other hand, when the school is not built and the buyers do not exercise their option to purchase the home before the contract expires at one year, the developer can pocket the $20,000 cash.

What's an options contract on the stock market?

An options contract on the stock market is somewhat related to the fictitious situation we just described with the automobile. In the case of the automobile, we saw that unforeseen events can make the bet made by the buyer and the automobile dealer profitable or perhaps not. The same principle happens in the stock market. Obviously in the case of the automobile, the customer is merely hoping to get the automobile they want at what they perceive to be a bargain

48

price. However, if BMW stopped making silver automobiles, they could sell it to a third party and then get yourself a white one from the dealer. Nevertheless, typically, the customer wants the automobile. Which is not the case when it comes to options with stocks.

On the stock market, we're betting on the future price itself, and the shares of stock will be bought or perhaps sold at a profit if things work out. The main factor is the buyer of the options contract isn't hoping to get the shares and hold them for a long time period like a regular investor. Rather, you are hoping to create a bet on the cost of the stock, secure that price, and then have the ability to trade the shares on that cost regardless of what happens on the real markets. We are going to illustrate this with an example.

CALL Options

A call is actually a kind of option contract that provides the choice to buy an asset at the agreed upon amount at the designated deadline or time. The reason why you will do this's whether you felt that the cost of a given stock would increase in cost over the specified time period. Let us illustrate with an example.

Suppose that Acme Communications makes cutting edge smartphones. The rumors are actually which they are going to announce a new smartphone in the next 3 weeks that's likely to take the industry by storm, with customers lined out the door to make preorders.

The present price that Acme Communications is actually trading at is actually $44.25 a share. The present pricing of an asset is actually termed as the spot price. Put another way, the spot price is actually the real amount that you will be having to pay for the shares as you will purchase it from the stock market today.

No one actually knows whether the stock price is going to go up when the announcement is actually made, or even if the announcement will also be made. But you have done the research of yours and are reasonably confident these events are going to take place. You have to to estimate just how much the shares are going to go up and based on the research of yours you think it is going to shoot up to sixty five dolars a share by the end of the month.

You enter into an options contract for hundred shares at one dolars per share. You pay this fee to the brokerage that's writing the options contract. In total, for hundred shares you pay hundred dolars.

The price which is actually paid for an options contract is actually hundred dolars. This price is known as the premium. You do not get the premium back. It is a fee that you simply pay no matter what. When you create a profit, then it is all good. But in case your bet is actually wrong, then you will lose the premium. For the buyer of an options contract, the premium is the risk of theirs.

You will need to set a cost that you think will be lower compared to the level to which the cost per share will rise. The cost that you agree to is known as the strike price. For this contract, you set the strike price of yours at fifty dolars. Remember, exercising the right of yours to purchase the shares is optional. You will just purchase the shares in case the cost goes high enough that you will make an income on the trade. If the shares never exceed fifty dolars, say they reach forty eight dolars, you're not required to purchase them. And why would you? As part of the contract deal, you would be expected to purchase them at fifty dolars.

We will say that the contract is actually entered on the 1st of August, and the deadline is actually the third Friday in August. When the price goes higher compared to your strike price during that time, you are able to exercise the option of yours. Let us say that as the deadline approaches, things go basically as you planned. Acme Communications announces the new phone of its, and the stock starts climbing. The stock price on the real market (the spot price) goes up to sixty dolars.

Now the seller is needed to sell you the shares at fifty dolars a share. You purchase the shares, after which you are able to quickly get rid of these at optimal amount or a quality, or perhaps sixty dolars a share. You try to make a profit of ten dolars a share, not taking into account any commissions or perhaps fees.

The Call Seller
The call seller who enters into the options contract with the buyer is actually obligated to sell the shares to the buyer of the options contract at the strike price. If the contract sets the strike price at fifty dolars a share for hundred shares, the seller must sell the stock at that price even if the market price goes up to any higher price, such as seventy dolars a share. The call seller keeps the premium. Thus, if the customer does not exercise the option of theirs, the call seller still gets the cash from the premium.

Derivative Contracts
You most likely heard about derivatives or perhaps derivative contracts during the 2008 financial crisis. While they could be designed in complex ways, the idea of a derivative contract is pretty easy. This means that the contract is actually based on some underlying asset. For an options contract, the asset is actually the stock that you agree to buy or even sell. The contracts themselves can and are actually bought and sold. That's exactly why you might have read about folks trading in derivatives. The stock which is the topic of an options contract is known as the underlying.
Thus, in case you buy an options contract using the Apple stock price as a basis, the term underlying would be applicable to the stock from Apple.

Profits from the Call
Remember the brokerage may have some extra fees. Nevertheless, using our numbers remember we paid a premium of one dolars per share, and the strike price was fifty dolars. Computing for profit is among the basics when it concerns trading. It's where profits are actually determined and forecasted for future options to buy or even sell.

The profit per share was: Profit = sixty dolars? (fifty dolars one dolars) = nine dolars per share
The contract was for hundred shares, so the total profit will be ninety dolars.
What happens if the strike price is not reached?
The strike price is actually the essential piece of info you have to keep in mind when trading options. In the event the strike price is not reached, then the alternative will simply expire and be worthless. The distinction between the current market price or perhaps the strike and spot price price is actually a degree of the profit per share that you'll make.

For instance, hundred dolars is actually the cost of the stock, as well as the strike price is actually seventy five dolars, then the profit (disregarding fees) will be twenty five dolars. If the strike price was ninety five dolars, then the profit per share would only be five dolars. While the pay off from a strike price which is closer to the actual market price is actually smaller, it is very likely to pay off than a strike price that predicts a big action.

Why purchase a call option
The main reason that you buy an options contract is to reduce the risk of yours. When you buy an options contract, the only money you are putting at risk is actually the premium. In the case of the hypothetical example of ours, that's hundred dolars. If the stock does not surpass the strike price, you are able to just walk away from the deal and just lose the hundred dolars.
You can, of course, buy the stocks outright and hope to profit. In order to buy hundred shares, you will have to invest substantially more money:
Hundred x $44.25 = $4,425.
If the stock goes up value, then you will make money.
Nevertheless, suppose that your hunch about the markets was wrong. Maybe Acme Communications, instead of announcing

a new phone which will be in demand that is high, instead reveals that their next phone will be postponed for a season. Should you choose to unload the stocks you bought for $4,425, you'll just get $4,000, and you will have lost $425.

On the other hand, you are able to see exactly how you reduced the risk of yours by buying a call option. If so, you will not exercise the right of yours to buy the stock and just lose the premium. The total loss of yours will be hundred dolars.

The Flexibility of Options

In normal stock trading, you are betting on one direction, that the value of the stock is going to go up with time. And you are battling the opposite, hoping to stay away from losses in case the stock declines.

Options open the door to making a profit when stocks decline in value. Needless to say, it depends on being in the position to make the correct call, but in case you bet on a stock losing value and you are right, you are able to make substantial profits. Timing and the size of the trade of yours will be important too, and you will have to remain focused on the strike price and the current market price of the underlying.

Put Options

A call option is the choice to purchase a stock in case it gets to the strike price. Now let us look at the opposite situation. A put is actually an option contract just where you find the right but not the obligation to sell a stock before the contract expires. Going back to the previous example of ours, suppose that Acme Communications looks to be heading to the stock and bad times is actually trading at $44.25 a share. Your bet is actually it is going to decrease to at least thirty five dolars a share, so you buy a put option with a strike price of thirty five dolars a share. If the bet of yours that the stock is going to decline in value and you are right, let us say it drops to thirty dolars a share, then you are able to make a five dolars per share profit on the sale. If the stock meets the strike price, the seller of the put is actually obligated to buy the stock at that price tag. Put simply, despite the fact that the stock has dropped in value to thirty dolars a share on the market, they need to purchase the shares from you at thirty five dolars a share.

Let us suppose that instead it only drops to thirty eight dolars a share. With this situation, you do not have to sell and just walk away from the deal having paid the premium. And so once again, as was the case with a call option, the premium is actually the only cash you risk as to the customer.

The seller of a put option must buy the stock from you at the strike price in case you exercise the option of yours. In the event the strike price is actually thirty five dolars but for some reason, the stock crashes to one dolars, the seller of the put must buy the shares from you at thirty five dolars.

Why Buy a Put Option?
The solution is actually simple? when you buy stocks the typical way, you do not make some money from the declining values of stocks. You lose money. With a put option, it provides you with the possibility of betting on the stock losing value.

Summary: Buyers of Options

The buyer of an options contract :? Must pay the premium. This's non refundable, so the premium is actually the minimum level of capital you invest and is actually the total amount you risk.? You're not required to buy or perhaps sell some stock even when the deadline arrives.? You've bought the right to buy and / or sell the stock.? When you buy a call, then you've the choice to buy the expiry of the agreement. When you get a put, you've the choice to sell the stock when the expiry arrives. The choice to sell only falls in instances when there's a marked difference between the market price and your own strike price; with the market price being too low.

Summary: Sellers of Calls and Puts

Eventually we will see that you might wish to sell options and there are many good reasons for doing so. Today, we will simply summarize the basic principles.? The seller of an options contract will hold the premium no matter what. Thus, if the customer does not exercise the option of theirs, you have the premium as profit.? If the buyer of a call option exercises the option of theirs to buy the stock, you need to sell it to them at the strike price. Thus, if the strike price is actually forty dolars but the current market price is actually sixty five dolars, you're missing out on a big profit per share. Nevertheless, as we will see later this can still be profitable.? If the buyer exercises the right of theirs on a put contract, you have to pay for the stock from them at the deadline.

Number of Shares

The number of shares in one options contract is actually hundred shares. Typically, traders are going to trade multiple contracts. To you will get the profit per share and then calculate total profit as (profit per share * hundred shares * # of contracts).

Now let us get acquainted with the industry jargon so you are able to have a much better understanding of what's going on when you start trading.

Chapter 3: Binary Options Trading

One of the options trading methods that have been very popular in recent times is binary options. While many options traders associated gambling to binary options, it is very clear that many people have little to no knowledge about what binary options are and how to trade them. Today, there are millions of people who trade binary options without an understanding of how it works. They are lured by greed and the desire to make money quick. While the binary option is a high-risk options trading, many people increase their own risk and blow off their trading capital through their ignorance of the trade. So, the first thing you want to do is to make sure you know what binary options are, where to trade them, and how to trade them.

What Are Binary Options?

Binary options are exotic options whose payoff is based on a "Yes" or "No" predictions. This is the reason it is called binary option: you have only two options for wining, either a "Yes" or a "No." Unlike other options trading methods, you stand a chance to make money when your predictions are right and then you lose the money you invested when your predictions are wrong. It is a "something or nothing at all" type of options trading.

Usually, the binary options of the U.S. offer a fixed monetary return to the trader when the underlying prediction regarding the option is right. In the U.S., binary options are usually traded with a minimum of $ 100. Non-U.S. traded binary options offer a percentage amount when the predictions are right. The most important factor is to read, analyze, and understand the dangers of working with the binary option before diving into the trade.

Here is a sample scenario dealing with binary options: Will the price of an underlying security (gold, silver, stock, index etc) be above $ 1,200 by 5.pm?

A binary option for an underlying asset may be trading at a bid price of $ 36 and an offer price of $ 40.00 at 3.pm. If you want to buy the binary option, then you will have to pay an amount of $ 36.00. If you want to sell, then you will sell at $ 40.00.

If the asset's price is above $ 1,200 by 5 pm, the binary option will expire in the money, and you'll be entitled to $ 100.00. Your profit margin will be $ 64 (gain minus cost of binary option). However, if its value never went above $ 1200, the binary option will expire out of the money, and you'll earn $ 0.00.

How to Spot Scam Binary Option Brokers

The world of binary option is full of scams and fraudulent brokers who simply want to make money off investors and novice traders. In fact, there are myriad of stories of people whose funds have been locked with scam binary options traders who have used seductive schemes to lure people to trade and lose their hard-earned money.

If you want to trade binary options, you have to first of all, differentiate between the scam brokers from the real ones. If you don't, you'll find yourself being trodden by sharks and wolves. So, how do you spot a scam binary options broker?

Scam Binary Options Software: This is the first scam that many scam binary options brokers use. They say on their website that they have trading software that ensures you make a profit through every trade. You will make consistent wins; all the trade is risk-free.

Trading Bonus: They even provide you with a trading bonus to get started with. They claim they provide you with a specific amount of money to get started and test the system for yourself. This lures people to invest with their own money.

Fake Testimonials: They provide you with testimonials of people who have used their scam trading software to make a sum only in a short time. Don't fall for this scam, all those testimonials are fake.

Huge Deposits: They require you to make a huge deposit with them to use the software to earn money. If you fund your trading account with the money, you'll be absolutely scammed and never be able to access the funds again.

Fund Withdrawal Issues: When you win as they rightly said, you can't withdraw your funds. You can try as hard as you can, but that's not going to work. Their email address can't be accessed. When they realize people know their domain name, they shut down their website and build another one with a new domain name.

Basic Steps for Binary Options Trading

Trading in binary options might be different from other types of options. The most common type is the fixed return option, where you can trade in stocks, indexes, commodities, and currencies. The following are the steps to take to get started in trading in binary options the right way:

1. Select a broker(s)
This is the most important step. You have to choose a broker that is licensed to provide binary options brokerage offers. Skip the scam brokers and look for the credible brokers. You can also use multiple brokers. Some of the known binary options brokers are Expert Options, iQ Trading, 24 Option, and Binary Options Auto Trading.
2. Register and make a deposit to start trading

After you have read and analyzed the broker carefully, the next step is to follow the steps outlined to register on the trading platform. By registering, you can now get access to the members-only trading area. This should be followed by making a deposit on the platform to start trading. You need at least $ 100 to get started.

3. Select your asset class and trade type

What do you want to trade? You have to select the asset class: foreign currency, stock, index, commodities, and so forth. Once you're done, you can then determine your trade. There are various types of binary options offered by brokers: high low/call put, one-touch, no-touch, 30 seconds, and boundary options.

4. Determine the amount to invest

How much do you want to invest in the trade? For example, if you're trading high low/call put, you can select call when you think that the price of an underlying asset will rise. If that happens, you will be entitled to win the stated amount for the option. When the never happens, you'll lose. This also applies to put options.

5. Determine your win/loss

The exciting thing about binary options is that you can win hundreds of dollars in a few minutes if your predictions are right. For instance, if your trade has a payout promise of 90% for $ 100 investment, you can stand the chance of winning $ 90 in a short period of time.

But, you can also lose. This is the reason it is advisable to only invest money you can afford to lose in all options, including binary option. Don't get too greedy and dip all your trading capital into a binary options trade. You'll risk being wiped out of the market completely.

Chapter 4: Stock Options Trading

Stocks are the most volatile and commonly traded financial instrument in the market. Every year, millions of people trade directly in stocks. When the market goes against them, they lose their investment capital. This is why trading stocks through options have been embraced by the high seasoned investor, as well as the beginner investor. Stock options trading provides the opportunity to invest in stocks that will generate better profits without directly risking a lot of money in the trade. While losses are limited to the amount of money used to pay for the option, many people have come to love stock options trading.

How Stock Options Works

In the world of stock options, there are three most important indicators for profit: "in the money" (ITM), "out of the money," (OTM) and "at the money" (ATM).These three indicators are the main profit signals in stock options trading.

Call Options

Let's look at this example: you bought 200 shares of Apple (NYSE: AAPL) stock, trading at 200 per share a year ago. The entire transaction cost you$ 4,000. After three months, you realized that the price of Apple stocks has risen to $ 205 per share due to technical and fundamental factors. So, you wanted to profit from the bullish market while holding your position. You decided to write a call option and sell them to Kim.

For the stock option to make a profit, the strike price of the call option must not get past the price of the stock; the bigger the difference, the better. This occurrence allows the stock option to have intrinsic value; it means it is "in the money" (ITM). In this case, you'll make a profit from the premium amount collected and still have the value of the stock increase.

However, when the stock falls in value, it would be logical for Kim to exercise her right to "call" option, thereby buying the shares at the predetermined strike price.

On the contrary, if the call option's strike value remains higher than the stock option on the date of expiration, the situation is described as "out of the money" (OTM). This means the option is worthless at the expiration date. There is another scenario possible, and that is breaking even. That is, both the stock and strike prices have the same value as the contract matures. Of course, you wouldn't be trading just to break even.

Covered Call

Since you already own the shares of Apple in your brokerage account, you can use the covered call options trading strategy to earn premiums while assuming the risk of the stock options trade. But you need to know and understand the market. If you want to place the call before purchasing the stock, that will be a naked call, which is only recommended for professional/seasoned stock options traders.

Put Options

Let's look at this example: you bought 200 shares of Apple (NYSE: AAPL) stock, trading at 200 per share a year ago. The entire transaction costs you$ 4,000. After a month, you realized that the price of Apple stocks has fallen to $ 190 per share due to economic and fundamental factors.

However, you decided to sell the put option to Kim in order to make money since you expect the stock price to fall again. Well, if it is a put option, the strike price is probably still higher than what Apple stock is trading at to be tagged "ITM" (thus, this allows you to collect the premium paid for the option and still hold onto the stock).

Again, the underlying stock's value has to surpass the value of the strike price in order for the options contract to be OTM (that means Kim will lose the premium). When both prices are at the same level at expiration, the stock option will be ATM.

Protective Put

The market has changed completely, and the stock of Apple has just been falling. You're afraid you might lose the value of your shares. So, you wanted to hedge your stock while maintaining your position and, therefore, buy a protective put option. The protective put hedges your stock from losing its value due to the bearish market. When the market goes down further, you will benefit because you've hedged your stock.

Key Tips for Stock Options Trading

Before you trade in stocks, you want to get yourself acquainted with the rules of the game. Understanding how stock options work and how to trade them will give you the edge against those who simply jump in the game without anything in mind.

You can either use put, call, or a combination of these options to trade in a market. Complex stock options strategies, such as married put, iron condor, and all others make use of a combination of call and put options.

The amount of money paid to purchase the underlying stock is known as the premium. The premium serves as incentive of an investor to take on the risk for selling the stock via the option. It generates income for the stockholder.

Every stock option, either put or call is made up of 100 shares of stock. That means if you want to place a 5 call option, you'll need to purchase 500 shares of the underlying stock before opening the trade.

Determine your minimum loss and maximum gains before entering the trade. This will help you avoid gambling and know whether the odds are in your favor or against you. And when you had a loss, cut your losses and move onto the next thing.

A good trading plan plus the commitment to homework are the keys to making it in stock options trading. You have to do your homework and stick to your trading plan for options trading. This is how to increase your gains.

Options Trading Strategies for Beginners

The misconception about Options Trading is that it is very difficult to understand, but that is simply not the case. As we discussed in the above chapters, using options trading an investor can generate great amounts of profits from small initial investments with minimum risks. Options are powerful and flexible and can prove to be extremely beneficial if properly used. The way to do that is to gain knowledge about the working and fundamentals of options trading before starting the actual trade. We have also discussed that in options trading, we can combine various strategies to generate an optimized strategy to help us make the best out of options trading. Let us learn about these strategies in this chapter.

Covered Call
The covered call strategy generates profits through the means of premiums. There's a term called "Long" for covered call. This term is used to denote the purchase of assets with the optimism that the value of said asset would rise in the future. Selling call option on this long position enables the investors to generate recurring incomes. Covered calls are neutral in nature and it is estimated that for the duration of call option on an asset, the price of the asset will change only minutely, be it high or low. Covered calls are also known as buy-write. Although covered calls provide generous income on short terms, with some patience it can help the investors to generate income as a chain of premiums. If the investor is willing to wait out, they can choose to keep the underlying assets and not sell them even in the case of a small depression, elevation or inactivity, this works as a protection scheme on long asset position and generate income in premiums. A disadvantage is

that if the price of the underlying stock exceeds the price of the option, then the investor has to give up the gains on stocks.

Covered call being a neutral strategy means it is not optimal for investors who are very brutish in terms of earning. It is suggested that such investors keep the stock on hold and not exercise the write option as if the asset price goes up; the option takes the profit on the asset. Also, if the stocks take a big hit and the estimated loss is going to be too great for recovery from premiums using the call option, the investor should sell the stocks.

Two terms are used for keeping track of profit and loss in this strategy, these terms are:

The maximum loss- It is calculated by removing the amount received as premium from the purchasing price of the underlying asset.

The maximum profit- it is calculated by calculating the total of strike price of short call option and premium received and then subtracting the purchasing price from it.

Married Put
Married put acts like a safety net in the field of options trading. The investor who is holding a long position has to purchase the at-the-money put option to prevent themselves from taking a big hit if the stock prices fall.

Married put is also known as synthetic long call. Some people may think married put to be similar to covered put, but that is not the case. Married put is optimal for those bullish investors who are wary of probable loss in near-sightedness. Another benefit of implementing the put option is that with this option, the investor gets to enjoy the benefits exclusively available to stockowners such as voting rights and receiving dividends. So is not the case if the investor has invested in a call only option. Same as the covered put, married put strategy can allow the investors to reap unlimited benefits generated from the initial investment in the underlying stocks. The only deductions from the profit will be the investment used for buying premium of the put option. There's a stage called breakeven at which the price of the underlying asset exceeds the price paid for the options premium. It is after this stage that the profit begins to generate.

Another new term called Floor is used, which is referred to the difference between the actual price at which the underlying stock was purchased, and the strike price of the put. The exercise of a put options falls under the category of married put only when both the assets and the put option is purchased on the same day. The broker is then informed to deliver the bought stocks when the investor exercises their put option.

The question that now arises is when to use this strategy?

As mentioned in the first line of this concept, married put acts like a safety net or insurance for the investors and that is how it should be addressed, not as a money-reaping strategy. The price paid for purchasing premium of put is dedicated from the total profits. This strategy should be used to act as a protection of stocks for short terms so as to counter the probable dip in the stock prices. This gives the investor some sort of reassurance knowing that the chances of loss have been diminished and they can continue to trade.

Bull Call Spread

Bull Call Spread is ideal for use when a hike in the price of the underlying stock is estimated in the near future by the investor. In Bull Call Spread, the investor has to purchase two specific call options on the same underlying asset and within the month of contract expiration. These two call options are at-the-money call option and out-of-the-money call option. Upon beginning the trade, the Bull Call Spread takes a debit from their account, which is known as bull call debit spread.

The cost of implementing bullish options of the trade are eliminated by the sale of out-of-the-money call option.

The total profit is calculated by taking the difference between the strike price of the call options and the bull call debit that was taken at the beginning of the trade. Maximum gain is said to be reached when the price of the underlying assets exceeds the strike prices of the two calls.

Similarly, the maximum loss is calculated by the addition of all the costs incurred in the form of commissions and premiums. An investor faces maximum loss when the prices of the underlying assets fall near to the date of expiration and is either less than or equal to the higher strike price of the two calls.

A few terms are associated with Bull Call Spread, which are as follows:

• Break-even point: In the Bull Call Spread, The breakeven point is calculated by the addition of prices of the total premiums purchased and the strike price of the long call.

• Intense Bull Call Spread: Intense Bull Call Spread is determined by subtracting the lower strike price of two call options from the higher one. The investor can reap maximum profits only when the stock prices elevate by a significant margin.

What makes Bull Call Spread alluring to the traders?
There are a number of advantages of the Bull Call Spread strategy that attract the options traders. These advantages are:

1. There is a certain limit to the loss. Bull Call Spread prevents the investors from facing too huge losses. Bull Call Spread generates higher returns from the initial investment than other strategies in which only call options are purchased.
2. More profits are generated when the price of the underlying assets do not rise above the price of the out-of-the-money short call option.

3. Call options can be bought at a lower price than the strike price.

What are the downsides of Bull Call Spread?
Since Bull Call spread generates more profits than the strategies in which only call options are bought, it means there are more purchases in this strategy than other strategies which means cost paid as the commission is higher. Bull Call Spread generates no profits if the price of the underlying asset exceeds the price of the out-of-the-money call option.

What additional steps can you take in Bull Call Spread to strengthen your position?
a. When the prices of the underlying assets are speculated to elevate above the strike price of the short call option, the investor can choose to implement the buy to close option on the out-of-the-money short call and then short it to again establish another out-of-the-money call. Another alternative to that is the investor may just exercise buy to close on the out-of-the-money short call option and leave it at that to reap benefits from the long call option.

b. In a situation where the prices of the underlying assets are not expected to change majorly, the investor can implement an out-of-the-money call option at a higher strike price, this transitions the Bull Call spread position to Long Call Ladder spread and the break-even point is decreased.

c. The investor can also transition into Bear Call Spread by closing the long call option. This is ideal for when the price of the underlying stock is speculated to turn back upon reaching the strike price of the short call. The transition has to be done as soon as the price of the underlying stocks becomes equal to the price of short call.

Bear Put Spread
This strategy is adopted in the situations where a drop in the price of the underlying asset is expected. Bear Put Spread consists of buying put options at a specific strike price and selling an equal number of puts at a lower strike price which share the same expiration date.

67

Two components make up the Bear Put Spread which are-
1. A short put having a low strike price.
2. A long put having a higher strike price.

Both of the puts share the same underlying assets and same expiration date. In the Bear Put, profits are achieved where there is a depression in the underlying stock prices.

These two components affect the profit and losses in these ways:
1. It limits the profits when the strike price of the short put having a lower strike price is higher than the price of the underlying stock.
2. It limits the loss when the strike price of the long put having a higher strike price is lower than that of the underlying stock.

Additions steps that can be taken for Bear Put Spread to strengthen your position
1. When the price of the underlying stock is expected to fall below the price of short put having a lower strike price, the investor is suggested to implement the buy to close the short put option and in return sell it to buy an out-of-the-money put option. Similar to Bull Call spread, the investor can opt for an alternative where he just implements buy to close on short put option and keep the long put as it is to reap the profits.

B) If a halt or a moderate drop is expected in the price of the underlying stock when it becomes equal to the price of the underlying stock, the investor can transition to Bull Put Spread by closing out of the Long Put option and purchase out-of-the-money put options.

What makes Bear Put Spread appealing to the investors?
There are a number of attractions that allure the investors. They are:
1. The most appealing feature of the Bear Put Spread is that it limits the risk of loss. This reassurance convinces the investors to try it out. The total amount paid for

purchasing the put options in Bear Put Spread is lower than the price of a single put purchased independently because the capital spent for purchasing the long put option having higher strike price is compensated from the sale of the short put option having a lower strike price.

2. The price of shorting the assets is controlled by the cost of Bear Put Spread, which greatly reduces the risk. In case of a hike in the stock prices, the risk will become marginal in selling short stocks.

3. Bear Put Spread is commended to reap good profits when a depression in the price of the underlying stock from the date of the trade up to the date of expiration of the contract is speculated by the investors, but this fall in prices should not be too huge, as no additional benefits will be rewarded.

Drawbacks of the Bear Put Spread

A. The profit is limited if the price of the underlying assets goes lower than the price of the out-of-the-money options. No additional benefits will be rewarded.

B. The cost incurred in paying commissions is higher than the cost of outright purchasing single put options.

Protective Collar

Protective Collar is a strategy that is used for protecting the investment when the market becomes unstable and is susceptible to unexpected drops in stocks prices. Protective Collar provides downside protection that means it lowers the chances of losing the investment.

A Protective Collar consists of two components, which are:

1. Buying a put option to control the downside risk of underlying assets.

2. A call option is exercised to pay the capital to purchase the stocks. A covered call and long put position are joined together to perform this function.

It is through this pairing of the long put and short call option with their corresponding strike prices that this strategy acts as a protective Collar around the underlying stock. The two components share the same expiration date, purchased on the same underlying stock and are generally of the out-of-the-money options type.

To provide a collar of protection from the downside risk, we can work with the assumption that the strike price of the second component i.e., Call option exceeds the strike price of the first component i.e., put option. Let us understand this with an example.

Assume that the sale price of an asset is 60$, a put option with a strike price of $55 and a call option with a strike price of 65$ is purchased on this asset. This call option bought for $65 then serves as the protective Collar for the stock gains.

Optimal situations for implementing protective Collar
Protective Collar strategy is the most optimal for reducing the downside risks and at the same time not costing too much for providing this safety. This is done by exercising OTM calls on the protective puts, as puts are expensive to be purchased outright.

Limitations of Protective Collar
A single strategy cannot provide all kinds of benefits, and like each other strategy Protective Collar has its drawbacks too. The Protective Collar strategy puts the primary focus on the protection from downside risk while the upside is pretty much given up. It is optimal for as long as the strike price is falling, but as soon as the price starts rising the Protective Collar loses its appeal and all the profits beyond the strike price are wasted. In other words, it is good for the situations in which the price of the stocks start falling after rising continuously for a long time.

How does Protective Collar act as a hedge against Taxation?
As we have learned the major advantage of Protective Collar is its capability of providing protection from downside risks, but

its advantages are not limited to only that, it has one another advantage.

Consider a case in which the price of the underlying stock is increasing at a rapid pace. Now the investor speculates two different scenarios, either the stock price will go even higher or the market will have a depression and the prices will fall. What would the investor do in that case? He/she has the option to sell the stock at the current price and wait for some time before purchasing it back and if the luck is on their side, they may even be able to purchase it at a strike price even lower than the price it was bought at before. But here's the catch, doing this may cause your profits to attract the taxes. The other major advantage of Protective Collar is that it saves your profits from this taxation by forming a hedge against the taxation by giving security against the drop in the market prices. Taxation will only be a problem if the investor decides to sell the stock and earn profits that way.

Long Straddle

The Long Straddle strategy generates profits from the shift in the price of the underlying asset, the shift can either be a decline or rise in the price, but it will only generate profits if it's marginal. The profit is generated when corresponding to the same underlying stock having the same expiration date, the investor purchases a long call and a long put on it. The profit generation possibilities are equal for the shift of the price of the underlying stock in either direction, though it is required that the shift manifested in the market should make the market go from a state of stability to instability.

The factors that cause this instability is usually something major such as something to do with elections, market laws, some government action or a major news. Bullishness and beariness are two reasons that form the instability in the market. Bullishness is when the market is under the threat of falling stock prices and beariness is when the market is speculated to face a rise in the stock prices. The beariness and bullishness counters each other to create instability in the market. However, the investors are not aware of the real cause of the instability and thus cannot determine whether it was the beariness or the bullishness. Long straddle is optimal in such conditions as in Long Straddle the profits are generated both from bullishness and beariness of the market. It still does not guarantee 100% profit as the market may not sway in the manner it is expected to.

It is a gambling game as the investor can only forecast and not be completely sure of the turn the prices of the underlying assets may take in the market. A new term introduced here is called Implied Volatility. Implied Volatility, as the name suggests is used to imply or predict volatility of the market in the near future and then accordingly pricing the options. A rise in the Implied Volatility while using Long Straddle strategy can generate profits, while a decrease in the Implied Volatility corresponds to a decrease in the value of the options.

To get rid of the risks resulting from the direction of the flow of Volatility in market, the investor can opt for buying both call and put options on the same underlying stock.

Calculation of losses and profits for Long Straddle
The alluring feature of the Long Straddle strategy is that the extent to which a risk can lead to losses is contained while the extent to which profits can be generated is unlimited. Such as, for when the price of an underlying asset hits rock bottom i.e., zero, the profit generated is given by subtracting the Premiums paid for the options from the strike price of underlying asset.

Consequently, the maximum risk is generated by the addition of the prices of the put and call options.

The formulas for calculating profits for rising prices and falling prices are given in the following ways:

- When the shift in the prices of the underlying assets in the market is upwards, the profit is calculated by subtracting the sum of the cost of premiums and the strike price of call option from the actual price of the underlying stock.
- When the shift in the prices of the underlying assets in the market is downwards or decreasing, the profit is calculated by subtracting the sum of the cost of premiums and the cost of the underlying stock from the strike price of the put option.
- The Maximum loss caused is given by the addition of all the commissions and premiums paid by the trader. Technically a loss is generated when the price of the underlying asset becomes equal to the strike price of the options.

Plus Points of Long Straddle

1. As we discussed above, the best and most unique feature of the Long Straddle is that it generates profits regardless of the direction of the shift in the market prices. There is equal potential for reaping benefits in both directions.
2. The market is influenced by a large number of factors such as news reports and federal laws. Knowing these can give us an idea of the direction of shift in the market prices.
3. The maximum loss in Long Straddle is not as drastic as it could be i.e., it limits the risk of the loss.
4. The potential of generating profits is limitless when the direction of the shift in the market prices remains same for a considerable amount of time.

Drawbacks of Long Straddle

1. Since profits are generated from the shift in the direction of the market prices, loss is generated when there is no shift in the prices of the underlying stocks.
2. When there is a drop in Volatility of the put and call options, loss occurs.
3. The cost of paying commissions by the traders is higher than direct purchase of options.

73

4. Loss also occurs if the current price of the underlying stocks becomes higher or lower than the strike price and does not touch any of the upper or lower break-even point.

Long Strangle

For the above strategies we have studied so far, all the call and put options were written on the same underlying stock having the same strike prices and the same expiration date, but the Long Strangle has a stark contrast in comparison to them. In the Long Strangle the underlying stocks and the expiration dates of both the put and call options remain the same, but their respective strike prices are different.

The principle of Long Strangle is similar to that of Long Straddle where profits are generated when there is a shift in the prices of the underlying assets, but the direction of the shift is not known or does not matter.

There are two types of strangles namely Long Strangle and Short Strangle.

The Long Strangle consists of two steps:

a) Purchasing an out-of-the-money put option.

b) Purchasing an out-of-the-money call option.

Both of the options are responsible for generating their share of the profits. The profit generation is distributed among both of the options in a way such that when the price of the underlying stock is continuously rising, the call option generates profits and when the price of the underlying stock is going down. Thus the potential for generating profits is unlimited.

In contrast to Long Strangle, the Short Strangle consists of the selling of both the call and put options previously purchased. Short Strangle does not offer unlimited profits and the maximum profit that can be generated is calculated by subtracting the cost of trading from the premium earned from shorting the two options.

A Long Strangle is made up of two major components that are a long put option having a lower strike price and a long call option having a higher strike price. The expiration date remains the same, but the strike price of the two components are different although they still are purchased on the same underlying stocks.

The potential of the profits when the prices of the underlying assets are rising is infinite as they can continue to keep rising without reaching a limit, although for the downward shift in the prices of the underlying stock, there is a limit to how low the stock prices can go which is zero, therefore profit potential is limited for falling prices.
The loss is generated when there is no shift in the prices of the underlying assets i.e., the market remains stagnant. If this remains the situation when the expiration date is reached and the stock prices remain equal to the strike price, loss occurs. The loss is calculated by the addition of all the capital paid for commissions and the premiums purchased by the traders.

The factor that causes this behavior of profit generation from the shift in the direction of the prices of the underlying stock is the Volatility of the market. The more volatile the market is, the more profits Long Strangle will generate. Profits occur when the price of the underlying stocks break through the upper or lower break-even points.

Long Call Butterfly Spread

Long Call Butterfly Spread differs from all the previous options strategies we have learned so far in the sense that the previous strategies only consisted of two components, but Long Call Butterfly Spread works with three. They're exercised in the following order:

1. Firstly the investor purchases a call option for a low strike price.
2. The investor sells two call options for a higher strike Rice.

3. The investor purchases another call having an even
    more expensive strike price.

The strike prices of all the call options written on the same
underlying stock are different, but the expiration date remains
the same. The potential profit in the case of Long Call Butterfly
Spread is limited when the price of the underlying stock is
found equal to the strike price of the short call on the date of
expiration.

The maximum profit is calculated by subtracting the lowest
strike prices from the in-between strike prices and then
further subtracting the total cost incurred in terms of
commissions and premiums and other things from the
previous result.

The maximum risk occurs when at the day of expiration the
strike price is either reaching past the highest strike price or
the lowest strike price. Whichever constraint is breached, the
maximum risk occurs. The maximum risk is calculated by the
addition of all the costs incurred in realizing the Long Call
Butterfly Spread position.

Speculating the state of the market

Long Call Butterfly Spread yearns maximum when the price of
the underlying assets is the equivalent of the center strike
price on expiration date, therefore, the state of the market is
judged by how close or far the price of the underlying assets is
from the center strike price. The forecast the market would
either be neutral or there will be an expected increase in the
market stock prices. The forecast is thus dependent on the
center strike price in the following ways-

1. The forecast is said to be neutral when there is no
    change in the price of the underlying stocks. In Long
    Call Butterfly Spread, the forecast is neutral for the
    price of the underlying stock being equal or very close
    to the center strike price during the time of trade
    initiation.

2. The forecast changes to bearish when the price of the underlying asset is less than the center strike price during the time of the trade initiation.

Drawbacks of Long Call Butterfly Spread

1. Long Call Butterfly Spread is inferior from the Long Straddle and Long Strangle strategies in the sense that both the previous strategies had unlimited potential for profit generation, but Long Call Butterfly Spread has limited potential for profits.

2. Since there are more steps involved in the establishment of Long Call Butterfly Spread position, the cost of premiums and the commissions that the traders have to pay is also more than other strategies.

Iron Condor

When the market conditions are less volatile and the investor wants to implement a strategy with lower chances of risks, Iron Condor strategy is optimal. Iron Condor is famous among the veteran traders who have good experience with Options Trading. The word Condor is in reference to a bald large sized vulture, which resembles the profit/loss graph of the Iron Condor strategy.

The Iron Condor strategy combines the powers of two vertical spread strategies we studied previously namely Bear Call spread and Bull Call Spread. There are four contract options for these two vertical spreads with unequal values of strike prices while the expiration date remains the same for all.

Iron Condor position is established by selling and buying put and call options in the following manner where the investor has to first sell an out-of-the-money call and an out-of-the-money put option and at the same time buy an out-of-the-money call and an out-of-the-money put option.

The strategies we previously studied such as the Long Strangle and Long Straddle generate maximum profits when the market is in a volatile state and the prices of the underlying stock never seems to be stable. But what about when the market conditions are not volatile enough? Iron Condor is ideal for those situations when the price of the underlying stock is not expected to show much change as it can generate much more net profit as compared to other strategies in such a state.

It is important to note that the cost paid for commissions by the traders is high in the case of Iron Condor as there are 4 different option contracts.

Maximum profit potential is generated at the beginning of the Iron condor establishment. Profit is reaped as a result of less volatile state of the prices of the underlying assets in the market.

On the other hand, the maximum potential loss is calculated by the given formula:

Max potential loss = (Strike price of one spread - Strike price of another spread) x size of contract - Premium received
Plus points of Iron Condor
1. We have a way of calculating the maximum loss and profit potential prior to their occurrence.
2. Iron Condor is modifiable in the way that it can be transitioned into other strategies.
3. A transition can be made into the Bull Put Spread by closing out the call options when the price of the underlying stock rises and seems to continue for a considerable amount of time.
4. A transition can be made into the Bear Put Spread by closing out the call options when the price of the underlying stocks decreases and seems to continue for a considerable amount of time.
5. The net credit generated is much more than the net debit spent on the spread.

Limitations of Iron Condor
1. As it was mentioned earlier, the investors prefer Iron Condor with enough experience in the Options trading.

It can be too complex for the investors who trade at lower levels.

2. The cost of the commissions is high because of the multiple number of call and put options.

Iron Butterfly

The strategy is known as Iron Butterfly because the shape of the profit/loss diagrams for this strategy resembles a Butterfly. There are two kinds of spreads for Iron Butterfly which are- Long Iron Butterfly Spread and Short Iron Butterfly Spread.

Long Iron Butterfly Spread

The Long Iron Butterfly Spread is made up of 4 components and requires the investors to purchase Bear put and Bull call spread. The strike prices of the Long put and Long Call are equal and share the same expiration date, but the distance between the strike prices is equal. In contrast to Iron Condor strategy, which was net credit oriented, Long Iron Butterfly Spread strategy is net debit oriented.

It shares more similarities with Iron Condor in the sense that the potential of profit is not unlimited, along with limited maximum risk. Also, the strategy is not ideal for uninformed traders as the strategy is quite complex in comparison to other strategies.

And since this strategy includes four different spreads and three different strike prices, the amount paid by the traders is also quite high which can only be compensated with timely and appropriate buying and selling of options.

Calculating maximum profit and losses for Long Iron Butterfly Spread

Maximum profit is calculated using this formula:

Profit = (Highest strike price - middle strike price - lowest strike price) - cost of the commissions and premiums paid by the trader

The profit is generated using different spreads in different scenarios in the following ways-

1. For the Bear put spread to achieve maximum profit, the prices of the underlying stock should remain less than even the lowest strike price when the expiration date arrives as a result of which the all the calls expire and the put options are still of in-the-money type.

2. For the Bull Call spread to achieve maximum profit, the prices of the underlying stock should be even greater than the highest strike prices when the expiration date arrives as a result of which all the calls expire and the call options are still of in-the-money type.

Maximum risk or maximum loss for Long Iron butterfly Spread can be calculated by combining the costs of all the debits incurred in the establishment of this position. This situation arises when the strike price of the underlying stock is the same as the center strike price of the long options such that when the date of expiration arrives, all the debits the trader paid for establishing the Long Iron Butterfly Spread are lost in the process and no profits are generated.

There are two break-even points in Long Iron Butterfly Spread, one known as the upper break-even point and the other one called lower break-even point. The upper break-even point is that point at which the stock price can be generated by calculating the sum of the net debit paid and the center strike price. The lower break-even point is that point at which the stock price can be generated by subtracting net debit paid from the center strike price.

Short Iron Butterfly Spread
The number of components in Short Iron Butterfly Spread remain the same as Long Iron Butterfly Spread. What actually changes is the type of bear spread and bull spread options. In

the Long Iron Butterfly Spread where we purchased a Bull call and a Bear put spread, we now purchase a Bull Put and a Bear Call spread.

The other aspects of the calling options remain same as Long Iron Butterfly Spread which are- same expiration dates, equidistant from each other and also sharing the exact same strike prices. The Short Iron Butterfly Spread differs from the Long Iron Butterfly Spread in the sense of orientation. While the former is net credit oriented, the later was studied to be net debit oriented. The risk/reward ratio of Short Iron Butterfly Spread is the same, as that of Long Iron Butterfly Spread and the complexity of the strategy also remains the same.

The calculation of maximum profit and risks also differ from the Long Iron Butterfly Spread. Here maximum profit is reaped at the condition that when the date of expiration arrives, the stock price is found equal to the strike price of the short options as a result of which the options expire generating no gain of their own. The actual calculation is done with the help of this formula:

Profit = Net credit - Cost paid by the traders in the form of commissions

Maximum loss occurs in Short Iron Butterfly Spread when the price of the underlying stock is beyond any of the highest or lowest strike price i.e., Stock price > Highest strike price or Lowest strike price > Stock price. It is calculated with the help of this simple formula-

Maximum loss = (Center strike price - Lower strike price) - Net credit

Maximum risk leads to two different scenarios:
1. For the Bull Put spread to achieve maximum loss, the prices of the underlying stock have to be less than even

81

the lowest strike prices when the date of the expiration arrives as a result of which the call options expire and the put options are of in-the-money type.

2. For the Bear Call spread to achieve maximum loss, the prices of the underlying stock have to be higher than even the highest strike prices when the date of the expiration arrives as a result of which the put options expire, but the call options are of in-the-money type.

3. The break-even points of Short Iron Butterfly Spread are the same as we discussed above. The upper break-even point is reached when the price of the underlying stock can be calculated by the addition of center strike price and net credit. The lower break-even point is reached when the price of the underlying stock can be calculated by subtracting the net credits from the center strike price.

Chapter 5: Forex Options Trading
Instead of trading currencies directly to avoid high potential risks, you can also trade them via options. A Forex option is a derivative of Forex /currency trading. It is also important to know that forex options trading is simply a combination of traditional options and currency. All the terms and principles of options trading apply; the only that changes is the financial instrument.

What Is an FX Option?

An FX option acts the same way as any other options contract, except you are trading currencies. Here, you (buyer) have the right to purchase an underlying currency and hold on to it for a period at a price determined with the seller (the strike price). Again, the strike price is set when the contract is drawn. It is also important to note that the owner of the FX option has the right to exercise or not to exercise the option at maturity, while the seller is bound to sell the underlying currency to the FX trader. The amount of money paid to buy the option is also called the premium.

There are a lot of factors that come into play when trying to calculate the premium price of an FX option. But, most often, experts use a statistical or probability assumption approach to help figure it out. In FX option, a premium means two main things for both parties involved in the trade: an opportunity risk for the selling party if the other party exercises the right and buys the underlying security.

At the other end, it represents the opportunity to own the underlying currency at the contract's predetermined strike price. Upon maturity, where it was profitable, the holder of the FX option enjoys the privilege of garnering from the trade an intrinsic value for the currency. This value depends on the correlation between the currency's price and the option's strike price, and the time value can be measured by the difference between the premium and the said intrinsic value.

Why FX Options?

There is time value for any options purchased by the buyer at a premium price. The risks associated with forex trading stem from volatility, expiration time, the price of the underlying currency, and the interest rate differentials. The premium paid for the option is sometimes very high. The option contracts cannot be resold or re-traded.

The benefits of FX options cannot be underestimated. They help reduce the potential risk of buying a currency pair;

traders can trade in currencies through the options contract without necessary gaining ownership of hundreds of the currency pairs.

FX Options are also used to hedge trading positions in the forex trading market. This prevents losing the value of the underlying currency when the value goes up. Unlike the cash or futures market, it does not involve the immediate settlement of transactions. An FX option is also used as a form of hedge to prevent losing the value of a currency pair when the market is generally falling in value.

Types of Options

Basically, there are two types of FX options trading available in the market. To do well in the current market, it is essential to understand and know how these forex options trading works.
1. Traditional FX Options
This is known as the vanilla FX options type, involving both call and put options. As usual, this right goes without any obligation.

For example, A EUR/USD option would provide the buyer with the right to sell €1500 and buy $ 1000 on January 2. The strike price for the option is EUR/USD 1.50. The holder of the currency pair will incur revenue in this trade if its exchange rate is not more than 1. 50.
The underlying contract will expire in the money and generate profit. Let's say that the EUR/USD has fallen to 1.00. The profit derived from the FX option will be as follows: (1.50 − 1.00) x 1,000 = 500. In this case, the holder is benefitting from the fall in currency rate.
The buyer of the option will have to tell how many options contracts they want to buy, pay the premium for the contract, and hold onto the contract until it gets in the money before exercising the due rights to buy or sell the underlying

currency. The only loss here is the premium paid for the option when the option expires without any of these options exercised.

2. Sing Payment Options Trading (SPOT)

Single payment options (SPOT) operate just like a binary option, offering the buyer an all or nothing type of offer for placing and making associated deals. Traders receive payouts based on the probability of a prediction about current prices in the future being right or wrong.

When you expect the market to rise up, you place a call option. When your prediction comes through, then you will win the agreed profit set forth for the option.

Losses are made when the prediction for the FS options are wrong. Premium payments for SPOT are often higher than the traditional options trading for currencies. It's highly advisable that traders understand the risks and rewards associated with this type of options trading before engaging in it.

Where to Trade Forex Options

If you are looking to trade in forex options, you have to research many retail forex brokerage firms to check whether they provide that service. Due to the recent losses that many traders have been having when trading forex options, many brokers have decided to ensure that only traders with capital protection are allowed in order to cap the risks of enormous losses, especially with SPOT.

There are some brokerage firms that provide access to the option and future exchanges, while others simply provide you with an OTC contract. Prior to signing on any broker platform, ensure you examine the fees and deposit requirements for trading. Check out the CBOE to learn more about the market before placing a trade on the platform.

Chapter 6: All About Buying Covered Calls
The answer is yes, there are some serious benefits to be had when you buy covered calls, but it's a little different than selling these bad boys, so here, we'll go into deeper detail about buying covered calls, and why it may be beneficial to you.

What is Buying a Covered Call

Buying a covered call means that you're buying a stock at a certain price. For example, let's say that you are looking to buy some IBM stock. Instead of writing to get it at a certain price, you are buying it from the trader at a certain price, when the stock falls below a certain level.

So let's say the IBM stock is trading at $45 currently. You buy a covered call that says the stock will be sold at $40 a share. So, the stock goes up to $47, and you get that stock for $40, and essentially, you're saving $700 on the stock price. If it goes down to $39 somehow, you can't exercise this, and then, you end up losing out on the premium, whatever that may be.

The benefits of Buying Covered Calls

There are a few major benefits of buying covered calls, and here, we'll discuss how these purchases can benefit you.

First and foremost, if you're an investor looking to have more stock under your belt, you will want to buy covered calls. While you will have to pay a fee for those options, here is the thing: if the stock is predicted to drop super low, you can nab this up. At this point, you can have it under your belt for a fraction of what it might be otherwise.

Selling stock usually is a bit pricier than the covered call option, and if you're looking for options to nab this stock, then this is something you should consider.

What many don't realize, is that while yes, the investor can make some serious bank selling these, buying these from right under their noses has benefits too. When you buy them, you own them, which means you can do whatever you want with them.

So, that brings us to the second point. One way to invest in a smart manner is to buy the stock for cheap, and then turn around and then sell covered calls to this for a higher price. That way, you get the options fee from the next person, and you also can cash in on this.

That is the third benefit of this. You can cash in on this stock at any time too. So, let's say that the stock falls, you buy it for the covered call price, let's say the covered call price is .37 per share, so 370 dollars. If you then see the stock price immediately go up to say .50 a share, so 500 if you sell it, there you go, you made a 130-dollar profit. You also can cash in on the dividends of your stocks too.

There is also another benefit to buying covered calls: the type of stock you're getting. These stocks aren't just sitting in limbo not doing a darn thing. Instead, they are fluctuating a lot, and this will, in turn, mean that you can potentially cash in on this, or even sell more covered calls based on what you're doing. You will realize over time that the stock you get with this is actually very volatile compared to others, or it has a lot of impact on our economy somehow. These are also industries that won't be leaving anytime soon, such as energy industries.

Buying covered calls also adds to your portfolio. If you want to be taken seriously as an investor, I do suggest that you start adding to your portfolio. This will, in turn, showcase to other investors, and even your broker, your potential. You also can sell these at any time, net the cash, put it in the options account, and it could help you potentially get to level 5 on investment.

So yes, buying is a great way to essentially set yourself up for success. While you have heard a lot about how selling essentially puts you in control and generates a great retirement, you can really take advantage of buying too when it comes to options trading. Covered calls are bought for a reason, and while you may not see the advantages now, there are quite a few advantages that are ready to be exercised.

All About Open Interest

Let's talk about open interest. This doesn't count every buy and sell contract, but instead, this is a picture of the trading activity on the option, and whether the money is flowing about, and if the underlying stock is increasing, or decreasing under it all.

So what does that mean? Well, open interest is one of the data fields that you see when you look at the option, and that also includes the bid price, ask price, the implied volatility, and the volume too. Many traders ignore this, and this is actually a really bad thing to ignore.

Why is that? Well, essentially it doesn't update during the trading day, and you may not realize it, but sometimes this causes contracts to be exercised without you knowing it.

Let us use an example. You have 1000 shares of stock ABC, and you want to do a covered call, selling 10 of these calls, and you essentially would enter this into open. It is an open transaction and add 10 of these shares to the open interest. You're essentially entering the transaction to buy from closed, and that would decrease the open interest of this by 10 as well.

So let's say you are buying 10 of the ABC calls to open, and the other will buy 10 calls to close, the same number, so it won't change.

But why does this matter? Well, if you're looking at the total open interest, you won't know immediately whether the options are sold or bought, and this is why many ignore this. But, the truth is, this also has important information, and you shouldn't assume there is nothing there. One way to use this is to look at the volume of the contracts that you trade. When this starts to exceed the existing open interest, it does suggest that trading in that option is super high, which means lots are acting on it. You should potentially act on this if you feel that you're going to get a profit from acquiring that underlying stock.

Let us take another example. You see the open interest on a stock, such as maybe IBM, is 12,000. This does suggest that the market in this is active, and there might be investors that want to trade at this point. You see the bid price is just $1, and the option is $1.06, which means you can buy one call option contract at the price that is mid-market.

But, let's say that the open interest is like 3. This is practically no activity on those call options, and there isn't a secondary market because people aren't interested, so you will struggle to enter and exit this at a reasonable price.

Let us take maybe looking at say GameStop for example. After their recent reports, their stock is probably at an incredibly low open interest. That means you shouldn't try to act on that. But, Apple is currently putting out more products and is getting ready to shell out more flagship products, so their stock has a huge open interest on it, and that means, you should potentially consider entering and exiting it, and possibly buying covered calls on that stock for a good price.

Open interest doesn't get updated as much, but it is still of an important case to understand, and it can affect you rush in and approach a trade. It gives you a good indication of the overall trading volume on the stock; which makes it very significant.

The Risks of Covered Calls

With buying covered calls, you essentially are betting that the stock will go high enough that you can get it at the price you're trying to get it for. That is your number one risk.

But, how is that a risk? Well, whenever you're buying a call, you have to pay the person who is putting out the covered call a fee. Now, this fee may be a little bit; it may be a few hundred dollars.

In essence, you're betting that the stock will go up high enough that you can get that stock from them.

Now, let's take, for example, you see the stock currently at 100. Let's say the covered call is for 105, and you decide you want to get an options contract for that. So, you choose that, the time that elapses happens, but the stock never reaches 105, and it stays at 103. Well, unfortunately, you just lost out on some cash there because of that, because you were betting on t to go up so you could get a deal, and unfortunately, that didn't happen.

The thing with buying covered calls, is you need to make sure that you're getting stock that is going to increase within that timeframe, is at a price that you're willing to pay, and has a chance of potentially netting you a profit. If it does have all three of these then get into it and take that risk. But, what can be worrisome is how much you can potentially lose.

For example, let's say that you are interested in getting a stock that has the potential for growth. You decide to purchase some of the stock from investor X. Investor X has a covered call written out where you'll pay .95 per share, so after 100 shares, it's 950 dollars. You decide you go for it, and you get that 300-dollar fee paid to him. Swell, right?

Well, unfortunately, that stock does not increase. It doesn't decrease either, it just stagnates. You thought you had a chance to do this, but then, it ends up potentially doing nothing to help you. Lo and behold, you just lost that 300 dollars, the investor gets to keep that, and their shares too.

If you do that five times, with five different stocks, that's $1500 right there down the drain. So remember that when you're looking into covered calls because this can potentially wreck you if you aren't careful.

Finding the Right Stock and Strike Price for a Covered Call

So how do you find the right stock for this? Well, again you want to find a stock that is going to have enough volatility where it will get to the price that you want it to be, pays decent dividends, and also is a field that will actually be around for a while.

One that currently is thriving is DSL actually. You may think that it isn't going to do as well, but it still holds an impressive number of dividends. That means if you can find stocks that are being sold, that have the potential to possibly change the game for the better later on, and also are worth investing in, you should do that.

You should look for a stock that you have a feeling you can easily get too. If there are a lot of open interests on the stock, I do suggest possibly taking your time and putting effort into that. You'd be amazed at the difference it can make.

You should also look at the different healthcare industries and service industries. What people don't realize, is that healthcare investors actually have a lot of good value to them. Shares for that can actually be quite high too, which means you can get instant payouts with a lot of these.

Options traders that buy calls also should be looking at the way the strike price is. You want a call that's right near a price of the stock, but a little bit higher. It actually should be something that is almost incremental, and you want to look at a stock that has enough volatility that it's actually moving about, but you have a chance to make some serious cash.

The goal for options traders that buy is they are buying a stock, hoping to get a 100% gain in a month. So you want that stock that you know, super fast, is going to net you some serious value.

While those stocks that are chugging about might seem like a good idea if your goal is to purchase and then net the dividends, though not every investor like this will want that end goal. What you want instead, is the ability to quickly turn around, net profits, and do so in short order.

You also want to look for calls that are quick, ones that don't have a lot of time value added to that. Why is that? Well, the longer you hold it, the lesser the value.

Whenever you buy call options, you're not only getting the share price higher to make money, and you need it to do so in a short timeframe. So that means you need to be watching the clock — options decay in value, which is bad for buyers. While the sellers love that, and they'll try to make an option continue on for time immemorial since they already got their cash, you need to work fast. You need to make sure that it's got a short expiration date but has the potential to hit that level. So you want something that is volatile, that has a life to it, and potential especially if you plan just to net those dividends of the stock itself, and overall is quick.

When it comes to the strike price, always try to shy towards the lower level of this. The lower it is, the better, because that will mean that you're going to get the right results from this, and ultimately can help you net a profit.

How to Buy a Successful Covered Call

So let's talk about how you buy a covered call and a stock that you want to have. How do you do it? Well, the answer is simple.

First, you must take a look at the stock that you want to buy, the shares, and what you're going to need to pay, especially against those premiums.

So, let's say you want to buy stock with Ford, because hey, Ford is releasing a new engine and car set, and you have a feeling it will increase in price. You can do this with Apple as well because there are rumors the MacBook Pro 2019 is coming out next month or something. Lots of people like to jump on the apple covered calls right before the reveals of their iPhones. So you log into your account, and from there look for the stock that has a price in the range that you want. You want the strike price to be a decent amount, such as maybe 14 dollars a share per 100 shares. Now, when you're inside, you choose the call that you want to buy, and maybe you choose that call option and look to see how many days this will go. You should from there, choose the option to get this call. Once you're going to do there, if you're going to right click, and choose what you want to do with the covered stock and choose that you want a contract for this one. You may be taken at this point to the page to fill out the information, and you should from there, look to see what your cost basis is going to be, and the amount that you're going to pay. You should look for a decent price on the shares, and make sure that you're not letting them fall too much.

If the stock is falling, do not take it. That's a sinking ship, and you can say goodbye to that. But, once you choose this, you then will start to look at the stock, and once you see that the shares are at a higher price than what you bought the covered call for, you can then log in, and choose to exercise this.

At this point, once you've exercised it, the investor will be obligated to sell you the option, and from there, you can now buy the covered call option that you want at the price that is listed.

Now, let's take the flip side. Suppose maybe you didn't see the trends changing all that much, and it became a stagnated stock. Unfortunately, the longer you hold out, the less fluctuation is going to happen on the stock. Your goal is to get out of there as fast as possible. The problem is, over time, that stock will stay at that range. You want to invest the moment you know there is a big change.

So yes, right before the Apple reveal will be great, the stock goes up, you cash in on that option immediately. But, let's say that it's been a slower month, and you end up not doing anything with it. Well, the investor you bought it from will get to collect it.

Now, if you invested in say, GameStop which is currently struggling, and then, you notice that even with the summer releases nothing happens, you're basically just paying someone a few hundred for a stock that's a sinking ship. Remember that and try to avoid the sinking ships as much as possible.

When you get the stock, however, you can always trade it again for a higher right, open up your own covered calls on it (with the risk of losing the stock of course) or just cash in on those dividends. Remember, once you get it, you do have the power to do what's best for you.

Chapter 7: Starter Strategies to Try

While the early days of your options trading career are likely to consist of a persistent feeling of information overload, there are certain areas where you don't have to worry about learning too much from scratch too soon. Specifically, there are numerous different basic strategies that you can use as a way of focusing on the types of skills you are learning in a productive direction. When it comes to planning out your ultimate rates of success, it is important to keep in mind that while the following strategies are certainly going to help you to improve your overall success rate, it is still never going to be a sure thing. No matter how good at trading options you are, losing out on a trade that appeared to be a sure thing is always going to be a part of the process.

The buy-write: This strategy is also known as a covered call and it is ideal if you are unsure about a specific underlying stock because it lets you buy in with confidence regardless of the current market conditions. How it works is that after you purchase the underlying stock in question, you go ahead and create a call that is set to the number of the underlying shares of stock that you now own. This is a great option if you are going to be otherwise occupied in the near future and don't want to worry about the underlying stock as you know that you will still be seeing the benefits of premiums if nothing else. It will also help you to protect investments that were made on a longer time frame as you will know that you will be able to hold onto a profitable sale price if nothing else. This strategy can be especially useful when paired with LEAPS, funds that were purchased via a margin and index futures as well as traditional stocks.

For example, in order to use this strategy successfully, you would start by purchasing a single option in a given underlying stock which will cost you $38 and then sell it at $48. Meanwhile, you would pay $1 for the call and then be able to go about your business knowing that you were going to make $100 even if the market doesn't move. This, in turn, moves the cost of each share up to about $47 which means that if the stock drops a second time the shares will stay where they are at which means your $100 premium is quite secure.

Long combination: Also known as the synthetic long stock strategy, the long combination is utilized by purchasing a call and a put with the same details at the same strike price. You will want the underlying asset price to be quite close to the strike price when you pull the trigger. This is a bullish strategy and the short put is uncovered which leaves you with a significant amount of risk if things go wrong. As such, this strategy is only recommended when the indicators you favor show that the market is likely to move in the way you expect.

This strategy is known as the synthetic long stock due to the fact that the risk and reward are nearly the same as the more common long stock strategy. Additionally, if you hold onto the position until it expires you will likely end up purchasing the underlying asset anyway. Specifically, if the underlying asset ends up higher than the strike price then you will want to exercise the call. Meanwhile, if it is below the strike price it is very likely that the put will be assigned which means you will still need to purchase the asset.

With that being said, there is no limit to how much you want the underlying asset to move once you have set up this strategy, the more positive momentum it has the more money you stand to make. The maximum amount you can expect to lose if things don't go according to plan is limited to the amount of the strike price plus the net debit or minus the net credit.

In this case, purchasing the call will give you the right to purchase the underlying asset at the strike price. Selling the put at the same price then obligates you to purchase the underlying asset at this price if you find yourself in a situation where the option is assigned.

Risk reversal: This is a hedging strategy that involves selling a call and buying a put option. This then mitigates the risk of downward price movements that are unfavorable while limiting the total potential for profit from any upward movements that occur. If you are trading in the forex market then the risk reversal is the difference in volatility between the put and the call.

If you are short on an underlying instrument then hedging with this position involves implementing a long risk reversal via the purchase of a call option. You would then write a put option on the same underlying asset. On the other hand, if you are long on an underlying asset then you would short the risk reversal to hedge the position via the writing of a call and the purchasing of a put option related to the same underlying asset.

Fibonacci strategy: To utilize this strategy, you can use any chart that you see fit as long as it contains either a run up or a run down in price as well as multiple retracements. Next, all you need to do is to begin drawing Fibonacci lines on the chart. If you draw Fibonacci lines on a strong down trend then you will want to start from the high point on the chart and then move towards the lowest swing point, otherwise, the inverse is true. With this done all you need to do is to determine the confluence points that can come from any Fibonacci level be it 38 percent, 50 percent, 62 percent or 79 percent.

To utilize Fibonacci extensions with this strategy, the basics are going to be largely the same. You are simply going to choose a chart that catches your eye and then add in Fibonacci lines, except this time you will want Fibonacci extensions enabled as well. You will then look for the points of confluence where the lines overlap to determine what a likely entry point is going to be.

Fibonacci numbers are exceedingly useful as they naturally reflect the psychology of the traders in the market. One of the most useful times to utilize Fibonacci levels is when it comes to determining the resistance and support of markets that are currently ranging. It doesn't matter if it is long or short, a range will eventually break because a market cannot stay in an indecisive position forever.

In order to determine how a ranging or sideways market is going to break then all you need to do is determine the range on the timeframe you prefer and then determine the low and the high of that range. If the Fibonacci levels indicated that the price is going to break above the range then an uptrend is likely to form and if it breaks below the range then a downtrend is likely to form.

Call front spread: The call front spread strategy allows you to purchase a call that is at the money or slightly below the money at a discounted price compared to purchasing the option on its own. Furthermore, the ultimate goal is to gain the call at the first strike price for a credit or only a small debit by selling a pair of calls at the second strike price. Both strike prices will use the same month of expiration.

It is important to keep in mind that there is a very large ceiling for risk in this scenario as if the underlying stock moves more than you have anticipated by a large margin there is nothing protecting your existing interests. As such, you should only try this strategy if you feel only a little bullish as you want the underlying stock to move to the second strike price but then stop completely. If you are not quite as sure what the strength of the market is going to be, the skip strike butterfly call is more appropriate.

For the best results, you are going to want to see the underlying stock price rise a small amount from the first strike price to the second. This will cover one of the calls that you sold while leaving the second one open to generate more reward, or risk if things do not work out in your favor. As such, it is important to keep a close eye on the underlying stock to ensure that unexpected moves aren't quickly countered and also by having an ironclad stop loss in place, just in case. This risk can further be mitigated by using it with index options as opposed to traditional options because indexes are even less volatile than

98

individual underlying stocks with low volatility because various price movements tend to cancel out major movement in either direction.

Straddle: The straddle can be used to either go long or short. The long straddle can be extremely effective if you feel as though the price of a given underlying asset is going to move significantly in one direction, you just don't know what direction that will ultimately be. To utilize this strategy, you will need to purchase a put and a call, both using the same underlying asset, strike price, and timeframe. After the long straddle has been created successfully you will be guaranteed to generate a profit if the price in question moves in either direction before it expires.

On the other hand, if you are interested in utilizing a short straddle, you will instead want to sell a call and a put with the same costs, timeframe and underlying asset. This will allow you to profit from the premium, even if everything else doesn't turn out as well as you may have liked. This guaranteed profit means that this is a particularly useful strategy if you don't expect to see movement very much in either direction before the option expires. Nevertheless, it is still important to remember that the chances that this strategy will be successful are directly related to the odds that the underlying asset is going to move in the first place.

Long strangle: To make use of a long strangle, you will need to purchase a call and a put that is based on the same underlying asset along with the same maturation level. They will need to have different strike prices, however. The strike price for the call should be above the price for the put and both should start at a point that is out of the money. This is an especially useful strategy if you expect the underlying asset to move a good deal but are unclear as to which direction it will choose. When utilized correctly, you will be practically guaranteed to make a profit after the related costs have been taken into account.

Functionally, a strangle is similar to a straddle except that it is often cheaper to execute on as you are buying into options that are already out of the money. As such, you can typically pay as much as 50 percent the cost of a straddle for a strangle which makes it even easier to play both sides of the fence. Typically, a long strangle is more useful than a short straddle because it offers up twice the premium for the same amount of risk.

Butterfly spread: A butterfly spread is a mixture of a bear spread strategy and a more traditional bull strategy which also makes use of a total of 3 strike points. To start with, you will want to purchase a call option at the lowest price possible. From there, you will want to sell two calls at a price that is higher along with a third call that is even higher still. The goal here should be to ensure that a range of potential profits are possible at prices that are within the current trend.

Positioning your options in this manner will allow you to create a potentially "neutral" position for yourself where you will be able to make money within the butterfly as long as the price of the underlying security stays within a range that is below as well as above the current market price. Remember, an underlying security is the option that you're either looking to purchase or sell, it's not the share of the company itself. The point of the basic butterfly spread is to create a sort of profit range so that there is not merely one certain price on which a share must fall in order for you to be profitable. By creating a range of numbers that will lead to success, you have a higher likelihood of walking away with a profit than you would if you were to only purchasing or sell one put or call and hope for the best.

Another critically important factor that you need to be thinking about as you pick out options with the proper strike prices for your butterfly is that these prices should be the same distance from the middle strike price at which you are selling stocks. For example, let's say that you decide to sell two options at a strike price that's set a sixty-dollars. If you made the decision to purchase this middle-of-the-road strike price, then you're going to have to purchase one option on either side at fifty-five dollars and sixty-five dollars, respectively. This way, the investor (you) will profit from the transaction as long as the underlying asset's price stays between fifty-five and sixty-five dollars. If the underlying asset price ends up being exactly on either of these numbers, then the investor is going to realize the maximum level of loss; however, any money amount between these two numbers would lead to some sort of profit for the investor.

Chapter 8: Fundamental & Technical Analysis

Technical Analysis

When working with technical analysis you are always going to want to remember that it functions because of the belief that the way the price of a given trade has moved in the past is going to be an equally reliable metric for determining what it is likely to do again in the future. Regardless of which market you choose to focus on, you'll find that there is always more technical data available than you will ever be able to realistically parse without quite a significant amount of help. Luckily, you won't be sifting through the data all on your own, and you will have numerous technical tools including things such as charts, trends, and indicators to help you push your success rates to new heights.

While some of the methods you will be asked to apply might seem arcane at first, the fact of the matter is that all you are essentially doing is looking to determine future trends along with their relative strengths. This, in turn, is crucial to your long-term success and will make each of your trades more reliable practically every single time.

Understand core assumptions: Technical analysis is all about measuring the relative value of a particular trade or underlying asset by using available tools to find otherwise invisible patterns that, ideally, few other people have currently noticed. When it comes to using technical analysis properly you are going to always need to assume three things are true. First and foremost, the market ultimately discounts everything; second, trends will always be an adequate predictor of price and third, history is bound to repeat itself when given enough time to do so.

Technical analysis believes that the current price of the underlying asset in question is the only metric that matters when it comes to looking into the current state of things outside of the market, specifically because everything else is already automatically factored in when the current price is set as it is. As such, to accurately use this type of analysis all you need to know is the current price of the potential trade in question as well as the greater economic climate as a whole.

Those who practice technical analysis are then able to interpret what the price is suggesting about market sentiment in order to make predictions about where the price of a given cryptocurrency is going to go in the future. This is possible due to the fact that pricing movements aren't random. Instead, they follow trends that appear in both the short and the long-term. Determining these trends in advance is key to using technical analysis successfully because all trends are likely to repeat themselves over time, thus the use of historical charts in order to determine likely trends in the future.

When it comes to technical analysis, the what, is always going to be more important than the why. That is, the fact that the price moved in a specific way is far more important to a technical analyst then why it made that particular movement. Supply and demand should always be consulted, but beyond that, there are likely too many variables to make it worthwhile to consider all of them as opposed to their results.

Chart Patterns to Be Aware Of

Flags and Pennants: Both flags and pennants show retracement, that is deviations that will be visible in the short term in relation to the primary trend. Retracement results in no breakout occurring from either the resistance or support levels but this won't matter as the security will also not be following the dominant trend. The lack of breakout means this trend will be relatively short term. The resistance and support lines of the pennant occur within a larger trend and converge so precisely that they practically form a point. A flag is essentially the same except that the resistance and support lines from the flag will be essentially parallel instead.

If you are looking for them, both flags and pennants are more likely to be found in the mid-section of the primary phase of the trend. They can last up to two weeks before being absorbed back into the primary trend line. They are typically associated with falling volume which means that if you notice a flag or a pennant and the volume is not falling then you are more likely actually seeing a reversal which is an actually changing trend instead of a simple retracement.

Head Above Shoulders Formation: If you are looking for indicators of how long any one particular trend is likely to continue, then looking for a grouping of three peaks in a price chart, known as the head above shoulders formation, can indicate a bearish pattern moving forward. The peaks to the left and to the right of the primary peak, also known as the shoulders, should be somewhat smaller than the head peak and also connect at a specific price. This price is known as the neckline and when it reaches the right shoulder the price will likely then plunge noticeably.

The inverse head and shoulders (or head and shoulders bottom) is a sign that the price of the security in question is about to rise in the face of an existing downward trend. It typically forms at the lowest overall price of the trend.

Based on the analysis of the peak-and-trough pattern from the Dow Theory, an upward trend is then seen as indicative of a series of successive rising troughs and peaks. Meanwhile, a downward trend is indicative of a series of lower peaks and deeper troughs. If this is the case, then the head and shoulders pattern represents a weakening of an existing trend as the troughs and peaks deteriorate.

The head and shoulders top forms at the peaks of an upwards trend and signals that a reversal is often forthcoming through a process of four steps. The first of these starts with the creation of the far-left shoulder which can be formed when the cryptocurrency reaches a new high before dropping to a new low. This is then followed by the formation of the head which occurs when the security reaches an even higher high before retracing back to the low found in the left shoulder. Finally, the right shoulder is formed from a high that is lower than the high found in the head, countered by a retracement back to the low of the left shoulder. The pattern is then completed when the price drops back below the neckline.

In both instances, the price dipping below the neckline signals the true reversal of the trend in question which means the security will now be moving in the opposite direction. This breakout point is often the ideal point to go either short or long depending. It is important to keep in mind, however, that the security is unlikely to continue smoothly in the direction the pattern suggests. As such, you will want to keep an eye out for what is called a throwback move.

Gann: While not universally trusted, Gann indicators have been used by traders for decades and remain a useful way of determining the direction a specific currency is likely to move next. Gann angles are used to determine certain elements of the chart include price, time and pattern which makes it easier to determine the future, past and even present of the market as well as how that information will determine the future of the price.

While you could be forgiven for thinking they are similar to trend lines, Gann angles are actually a different beast entirely. They are, in fact, a series of diagonal lines that move at a fixed rate and can likely be generated by your trading program. When they are compared to a trend line you will notice the Gann angle makes it possible for users to determine a true price at a specific point in the future assuming the current trend continues at its current strength.

Due to the fact that all times exist on the same line, the Gann angle can then also be used to predict resistance, support and direction strength as well as the timing on bottoms and tops as well. Gann angles are typically used to determine likely points of support and resistance and it is easy to get started with as it only requires the trade to determine the proper scale for the chart before drawing in the relevant Gann angles from the primary bottoms to the tops.

Essentially, this means that they make it less complicated for the trader to properly frame the market and thus makes it easier for them to predict the way the market is likely to move in the future based on the way it is currently moving in the predetermined framework. Angles that indicate a positive trend determine support and angles that show a downward trend outline resistance. This means that by understanding the accurate angle of a chart, the trader can more easily determine the best time to buy or sell far more simply than what could otherwise be the case. When utilizing Gann angles it is crucial that you keep in mind all the different things that can potentially cause the market to change between specific angles.

Cup and handle formation: The cup and handle formation most commonly appears if given security reaches a peak price before dropping off significantly for a prolonged amount of time. Sooner than later, however, the security will rebound, which is the perfect time to buy. This is an indicator of a trend that is rapidly rising which means you are going to want to take advantage of it as soon as possible before you miss out.

The handle will form on the cup when those who purchased the security at the previous high-water mark and couldn't wait any longer begin to sell which makes new investors interested who then begin to buy as well. This type of formation does not typically form quickly, and indeed, has been known to take a year or more to become visible.

Ideally, you will then be able to take advantage of this trend as soon as the handle starts to form. If you see the cup and handle forming, you will still want to consider any other day to day patterns that may be interfering with the overall trend as they are going to go a long way when it comes to determining the actual effectiveness of buying in at a specific point.

Trend lines

Trend lines represent the typical direction that a given underlying asset is likely to move in and, thus, can be very beneficial for traders to highlight prior to trading. This is easier said than done, however, due to the high degree of volatility that assets of all types experience on a regular basis. As such, you will find it much more useful to consider only the highs and lows that the underlying asset experiences as this will make it far easier to determine a workable pattern. Once you have determined the highs and the lows for the underlying asset it then becomes much easier to determine if the highs are increasing while the lows are decreasing or vice versa. You will also want to remain alert to the possibility of sidewise trends, where the price doesn't move much of anywhere, as this is a sign that you should avoid trading for the time being. When watching the trend lines, you will likely notice that the price movement of a given underlying asset tends to bounce off the same high and low points time after time. These are what are known as resistance and support levels and identifying them makes it easier for you to determine the supply and demand of the coin in question. The support level is the level that the price is unlikely to drop below because there are always going to be traders who are willing to buy at that point, driving demand back up. Once the price reaches the point where traders feel the price is unlikely to go any higher, they start to sell, and a level of resistance is created.

Moving averages: The most commonly used confirmation tool is one that is referred to as the moving average convergence divergence or MACD for short. This tool measures the amount of difference that there is between two averages that have been smoothed to minimize ancillary noise.

The difference between the two results is then further smoothed by the process before then being matched against the moving average that it relates to as well. If the resulting smoothed average is still greater than the existing moving average, then you can be sure that the positive trend you were chasing actually exists. Meanwhile, if the smoothed average ends up below the existing moving average than any negative trends will be confirmed instead.

The moving average convergence divergence indicator is a type of oscillating indicator that primarily moves between zero and the centerline. If the MACD value is high then you can assume the related underlying asset is nearly overbought and if the value is low, then the stock is nearly oversold.

The MACD chart is typically based on a combination of several EMAs. These averages can be based on any timeframe, though the most common is the 12-26-9 chart. This chart is typically broken into multiple parts, the first of which is the 26-day and 12-day chart. Mixing up the EMAs will allow you to more accurately gauge the level of momentum that the trend you are tracking is experiencing.

If the 12-day EMA ends up above the 26-day EMA, then you can assume the underlying stock in on an uptrend and the reverse indicates a downtrend. If the 12-day EMA increases more quickly than the 26-day EMA then the uptrend is going to be even more well-pronounced. However, if the 12-day EMA moves closer to the 26-day EMA then you can safely assume that it is starting to slow, and the momentum is waning, which means it is going to take the trend with it.

The MACD uses the EMA by considering the difference between them once they are plotted out. If the 26-day and the 12-day are the same, then the MACD equal out to 0. If the 12-day ends up at a higher point than the 26-day then you can assume the MACD is positive, if not, it will be negative. The greater the difference between the two, the greater the difference between the MAACD line and zero.

The Different Types of Charts Used in Technical Analysis

Technical analysis is all about the price chart which is a chart with an x and y axis. The price is measured along the vertical axis and the time is measured via the horizontal axis. There are numerous different types of price charts that different types of traders prefer, these include the point and figure chart, the Renko chart, the Kagi chart, the Heikin-Ashi chart, the bar chart, the candlestick chart, the line chart, and the tick chart. However, the ones you will need to concern yourself with at first are going to be included in any forex trading platform software and are the bar chart, the candlestick chart, the line chart, and the point and click chart which is why they are outlined in greater detail below.

Line chart: Of all the various types of charts, the line charts is the simplest because it only presents price information in the form of closing prices in a fixed time span. The lines that give it its name are created when the various closing price points are then connected with a line. When looking at a line chart it is important to keep in mind that they will not be able to provide an accurate visual representation of the range that individual points reached which means you won't be able to see either opening prices or those that were high or low prior to close.

Regardless, the closing point is important to always consider which is why this chart is so commonly referred to by technical traders of all skill levels.

Bar chart: A bar chart takes the information that can be found in a line chart and expands upon it in a number of interesting ways. For starters, the chart is made using a number of vertical lines that provide information on various data points. The top and bottom of the line can then be thought of as the high and low of the trading timeframe respectively while the closing price is also indicated with a dash on the right side of the bar. Furthermore, the point where the currency price opened is indicated via a dash and will show up on the left side of the bar in question.

Candlestick chart: A candlestick chart is similar to a bar chart, though the information it provides is much more detailed overall. Like a bar chart it includes a line to indicate the range for the day, however, when you are looking at a candlestick chart you will notice a wide bar near the vertical line which indicates the degree of the difference the price saw throughout the day. If the price that the stock is trading at increases overall for the day, then the candlestick will often be clear while if the price has decreased then the candlestick is going to be read.

Point and figure chart: While seen less frequently than some of the other types of charts, a point and figure chart has been around for nearly a century and can still be useful in certain situations today. This chart can accurately reflect the way price is going to move, though it won't indicate timing or volume. It can be thought of as a pure indicator of price with the excessive noise surrounding the market muted, ensuring nothing is skewed.

A point and figure chart is noticeable because it is made up of Xs and Os rather than lines and points. The Xs will indicate points where positive trends occurred while the Os will indicate periods of downward movement. You will also notice numbers and letters listed along the bottom of the chart which corresponds to months as well as dates. This type of chart will also make it clear how much the price is going to have to move in order for an X to become an O or an O to become an X.

Trend or range: When it comes to using technical analysis successfully, you will want to determine early on if you are more interested in trading based on the trends you find or on the range. While they are both properties related to price, these two concepts are very different in practice which means you will want to choose one to emphasize over the other. If you decide to trade according to trend, then you are more interested in going with the flow and choosing stocks to trade while everyone else is having the same idea.

The Benefits of Technical Analysis in Options Trading

Rather than construct long-winded paragraphs that elaborate on the benefits of options trading, I've decided to forego the long discussion and, instead, include a simple but hopefully comprehensive list that advises readers about the many spectacular benefits they stand to gain by pursuing options. Keep in mind, though, that all of the following benefits won't come immediately, and for some traders, may never come, even. The benefits you receive from options trading depend upon your approach, your experience, your patience, and your dedication, so it's a nearly impossible task to predict which ones will grace your presence. But because you're a beginner trader, simply becoming familiar with the possible benefits of options trading is enough, at least in regards to your initial 48 hours of trading. (Because let's face it, you probably won't experience many of these benefits within your first 48 hours of trading. Many will come for sure, just not so soon).

Here's the list of options trading benefits that you can peruse on your own time:

- Call and put options, along with strike prices and premiums, allow traders not only to take calculated risks, but to have an idea of worst case scenario situations at all times. This lets you plan ahead, to gather some sort of idea for what to expect, and to prepare yourself for whatever situation you're confronted with.

- Options have "leverage," which means buying options can help an investor earn more per dollar than buying equity on a stock.
- Risk is significantly reduced with options—any potential for monetary loss is limited to the premium/strike price, so you won't be entirely affected if assets experience a dramatic loss in market value.
- Beginner options trading strategies are easy to learn and easy to understand, which means even beginner options traders can find relatively immediate and meaningful success when they begin trading.
- Option trading is highly flexible, especially when you start trading with different options forms—you can customize options contracts, select strike prices, and even decide expiration dates and cycles for investments.
- There are an array of financial resources, materials, tools, and mobile applications readily available at your fingertips, for little to no cost. In addition, there are a series of high-quality, local brokers and brokerages across the country who are happy to assist, advise, consult, and work for you. (Plus, you have the option to decide whether an online brokerage or human broker is the right financial advisor or tool for your personal financial situation).

Technical Analysis Secrets to Become the Best Trader

Here are some helpful tips and advice that should guide you as you trade online in options.

1. *The price of any stock can move in 3 basic directions*
These directions are up, down and no movement at all. Depending on the kind of call that you have, you can leverage

111

from this movement to make a profit or at least avoid incurring losses.

Plenty of first-time traders and investors assume that prices of securities will go either up or down. However, this is a wrong school of thought because sometimes there is no movement at all in the price of stocks and shares. This is a very important fact in the world of options trading.

Plenty of real-life, practical examples show a particular stock or share did not move significantly for quite a lengthy period. For instance, the KOL share traded within a $4 range for a total of 23 days. If you had invested money in either a call option or a put option through this stock, you would have lost money.

According to seasoned traders, chances of making a profit with a call or put option are hardly ever 50% but only 33%. This is likely due to the fact that stock price movements are random. You will eventually realize that 33% of the time, stocks rise, 33% of the time they dip in price and another 33% of the time they stay the same. Time will more often be your worst enemy if you have a long put or call option.

A purchase of a call option is usually with the hope that prices will go up. In the event that prices do rise, then you will make a profit. At other times the prices will remain the same or even fall. In such events, if you have an out-of-the-money call, the option will most likely expire, and you will lose your investment. In the event that the price remains stagnant and you have an in-the-money option, then you will at least recoup some of the money you invested.

There will be times when frustrations will engulf you. This is when you just sit and watch prices start to skyrocket just a couple of weeks after the options you purchased had expired. This is often an indicator that your strategy was not on point and you did not give it sufficient time. Even seasoned traders sometimes buy call options that eventually expire in a given month and then the stocks prices rise sharply in the following month.

It is therefore advisable to purchase a longer-term call option rather than one that expires after a single month. Now since stocks move in 3 general directions, it is assumed that close to 70% of options traders with long call and put options suffer losses. On the other hand, this implies that 70% of option sellers make money. This is one of the main reasons why conservative options traders prefer to write or sell options.

2. Before buying options look at the underlying stock's chart

Basically, you want to find out as much information as possible about the performance and worth of an underlying stock before investing in it.

You should, therefore, ensure that you take a serious look at the chart of the stock. This chart should indicate the performance of the stock in the last couple of days. The best is to look at a stock's performance in the last 30 and 90 days. You should also take a look at last year's performance.

When you look at the charts, look at the movement of the shares and try note any trends. Also, try and observe any general movement of the shares. Then answer a couple of questions. For instance, is the stock operating within a narrow range or is it bending upwards or downwards? Is this chart in tandem with your options trading strategy?

To identify the trend of a particular stock, try and draw a straight line along in the middle of the share prices. Then draw a line both above and below so as to indicate a channel of the general flow of the share.

Chart readings and buying call options

Let us assume you wish to invest in a call option. Then you should ask yourself if the stock price is likely to rise and why. If you think the stock will rise and trade at a higher level, then you may be mistaken, unless something drastic happens or new information becomes evident. New information can be a shareholders meeting, impending earnings announcement, a new CEO, product launch and so on.

If there is a chart showing the presence of support at lower prices and stock prices fall to that level, then it may be advisable to buy call options. The call option will be a great bet when prices are down because prices will very likely head back up. However, never allow greed to occupy your mind. When you see a profit, take and do not wait too long.

Chart readings and buying put options

Now supposing the stock chart indicates a solid resistance at a higher price. If the stock is beginning to approach this higher level, then it is possible that the price might begin to move in that direction as well. So as the price moves, expect to gain small but significant profits. Avoid greed so that anytime the stock price falls simply move in and make some money.

Chart readings for purchase of call and put options

Now, if your chart readings indicate that the shares are within the lower levels of its range, then it is likely that daily changes in price will send it towards the middle of the range. If this is so, then you should move in and make a profit as soon as the price tends upwards. Even minor profits such as buying at $1 and selling at $1.15 means a 15% profit margin.

3. Find out the break-even point before buying your options

Now you need to identify a call option that you wish to invest in, especially after studying its performance on the market. Before buying, however, you should work out the break-even point. In order to find this break-even point, you will have to consider things such as the commissions charged and the bid spread.

It is very important that you are positive the underlying stock of your options will move sufficiently so as to surpass the break-even point and earn a tidy profit. You should, therefore, learn how to work out the break-even point in options trade.

How to Apply Technical Analysis

Investors and traders can earn money from the price movements of stocks without the need to buy them. Although options have been around for quite some time now, not everyone has them in their investment portfolio. They believe that options are risky and very difficult to understand. They fail to realize that options have a better risk/reward ratio over stocks. Risks are reduced and profits are multiplied. Still, a lot of investors ignore options because their value depreciates with time. However, there are certain scenarios, where trading options has become a better alternative than trading stocks because of the significant increase in the risk/reward over the long term.

A Long Term Equity Anticipation Security is a type of options which can be held for a long time. It can be in the form of index or stock which can expire in 9 months or even in 2 years. This option was introduced in 1990 at the Chicago Board of Trade to encourage investors to include options in their investment portfolios. In some cases, the breakeven point and carry cost of a LEAPS option may be higher than a stock but the former has a significant lower risk than the latter. One very obvious disadvantage of LEAPS is that it can expire worthless. On the other hand, a stock still has some value even if the market is down. But, the risk can be easily mitigated by buying a deep-in-the-money LEAPS option. If the LEAPS option is further in-the-money, it is less probable for the market price to move below the strike price. Therefore, the option will just expire worthless. Each scenario must be evaluated depending on its case.

Furthermore, a LEAPS option is beneficial when expecting smaller movements in the price of safer indexes or stocks. As an illustration, a regular stock may offer 5% annual return, which is small for a traditional investor. However, a LEAPS option may multiple the 5% percentage to make it more profitable. This strategy is popularly used for expensive stocks which don't offer a lot of earnings. In general, a LEAPS option can offer investors a safer and more profitable method of investing on long term price movements without the need to put in a lot of cash. Although it doesn't provide a perfect investment scenario for every situation or portfolio, it can be used effectively to generate more profits while assuming minimal extra risks.

In some cases, options can be very profitable because they are able to reduce risks. In some instances, human emotion can also be eliminated from the trading equation because options offer a more defined strategy while requiring less capital from the investor. A technical trader can focus in either breakdowns/breakouts or trading ranges to generate profit from options trading.

A breakout trader assumes a lot of risk when he buys a stock because technical patterns dictate that volatility is impending. He invests in a stock because he is hoping that he is correct in predicting the price direction. This action is risky in itself. A backspread limits possible losses while ensuring unlimited potential to generate a profit. If the market price falls, the investor can even make a profit. However, it is good to remember that the possibility of a loss can occur when the stock moves sideways. As such, the trader must ensure that his breakout pattern is correct. He can actually use a put or call option without hedging. For breakout traders, he must ensure to buy more time when purchasing short term options. Although he may predict a breakout the following week, he may still need additional time for it to transpire.

A trend trader, on the other hand, assumes a risk when he buys a stock because he is relying that the strong trend will continue over the long term. If the trend slows down, opportunity costs are lost. A trend reversal will result to a loss. A trader can use LEAPS if he's confident that the trend will continue because the options can expire worthless if the price goes below the strike price. Selling a surrogate covered call option is another viable solution for neutral to bullish trend traders who want to make a profit over the short term. By writing a covered call option, the trader can generate a profit through the premium even if the price of the underlying asset goes up to the strike price. However, if the price of the underlying asset declines, he can lose the stock and get only the premium. Therefore, the solution is to use LEAPS instead of the actual underlying asset to write a covered call.

Fundamental Analysis

While it should come as no surprise that you are going to need to gather as much data as possible in order to make the best trades, regardless of what market you are working in; it is important to keep in mind that if you don't use it in the right way then it is all for naught. There are two ways to get the most out of any of the data that you gather, the first is via technical analysis and the second is via fundamental analysis. As a general rule, you will likely find it helpful to start off with fundamental analysis before moving on to technical analysis as the need arises.

To understand the difference between the two you may find it helpful to think about technical analysis as analyzing charts while fundamental analysis looks at specific factors based on the underlying asset for the market that you are working in. The core tenant of fundamental analysis is that there are related details out there that can tell the whole story when it comes to the market in question while technical analysis believes that the only details that are required are those that relate to the price at the moment. As such, fundamental analysis is typically considered easier to master as it all relates to concepts less expressly related to understanding market movement exclusively. Meanwhile, technical analysis is typically faster because key fundamental analysis data often is only made publicly available on a strict, and limited, schedule, sometimes only a few times a year meaning the availability for updating specific data is rather limited.

Fundamental Analysis Rules

The best time to use fundamental analysis is when you are looking to gain a broad idea of the state of the market as it stands and how that relates to the state of things in the near future when it comes time to actually trading successfully. Regardless of what market you are considering, the end goals are the same, find the most effective trade for the time period that you are targeting.

118

Establish a baseline: In order to begin analyzing the fundamentals, the first thing that you will need to do is to create a baseline regarding the company's overall performance. In order to generate the most useful results possible, the first thing that you are going to need to do is to gather data both regarding the company in question as well as the related industry as a whole. When gathering macro data, it is important to keep in mind that no market is going to operate in a vacuum which means the reasons behind specific market movement can be much more far reaching than they first appear. Fundamental analysis works because of the stock market's propensity for patterns which means if you trace a specific market movement back to the source you will have a better idea of what to keep an eye on in the future.

Furthermore, all industries go through several different phases where their penny stocks are going to be worth more or less overall based on general popularity. If the industry is producing many popular penny stocks, then overall volatility will be down while at the same time liquidity will be at an overall high.

Consider worldwide issues: Once you have a general grasp on the current phase you are dealing with, the next thing you will want to consider is anything that is going on in the wider world that will after the type of businesses you tend to favor in your penny stocks. Not being prepared for major paradigm shifts, especially in penny stocks where new companies come and go so quickly, means that you can easily miss out on massive profits and should be avoided at all costs.

To ensure you are not blindsided by news you could have seen coming, it is important to look beyond the obvious issues that are consuming the 24-hour news cycle and dig deeper into the comings and goings of the nations that are going to most directly affect your particular subsection of penny stocks. One important worldwide phenomenon that you will want to pay specific attention to is anything in the realm of technology as major paradigm shifts like the adoption of the smartphone, or the current move towards electric cars can create serious paradigm shifts.

Put it all together: Once you have a clear idea of what the market should look like as well as what may be on the horizon, the next step is to put it all together to compare what has been and what might to what the current state of the market is. Not only will this give you a realistic idea of what other investors are going to do if certain events occur the way they have in the past, you will also be able to use these details in order to identify underlying assets that are currently on the cusp of generating the type of movement that you need if you want to utilize them via binary option trades.

The best time to get on board with a new underlying asset is when it is nearing the end of the post-bust period or the end of a post-boom period depending on if you are going to place a call or a put. In these scenarios, you are going to have the greatest access to the freedom of the market and thus have the access to the greatest overall allowable risk that you are going to find in any market. Remember, the amount of risk that you can successfully handle without an increase in the likelihood of failure is going to start decreasing as soon as the boom or bust phase begins in earnest so it is important to get in as quickly as possible if you hope to truly maximize your profits.

Understand the relative strength of any given trade: When an underlying asset is experiencing a boom phase, the strength of its related fundamentals is going to be what determines the way that other investors are going to act when it comes to binary options trading. Remember, when it comes to fundamental analysis what an underlying asset looks like at the moment isn't nearly as important as what it is likely to look like in the future and the best way to determine those details is by keeping an eye on the past.

Quantitative Fundamental Analysis

The sheer volume of data and a large amount of varying numbers found in the average company's financial statements can easily be intimidating and bewildering for conscientious investors who are digging into them for the first time. Once you get the hang of them, however, you will quickly find that they are a goldmine of information when it comes to determining how likely a company is to continue producing reliable dividends in the future.

At their most basic, a company's financial statements disclose the information relating to its financial performance over a set period of time. Unlike with qualitative concepts, financial statements provide cold, hard facts about a company that is rarely open for interpretation.

Important statements

Balance sheet: A balance sheet shows a detailed record of all of a company's equity, liabilities and assets for a given period of time. A balance sheet shows a balance to the financial structure of a company by dividing the company's equity by the combination of shareholders and liabilities in order to determine its current assets.

In this case, assets represent the resources that the company is actively in control of at a specific point in time. It can include things like buildings, machinery, inventory, cash and more. It will also show the total value of any financing that has been used to generate those assets. Financing can come from either equity or liabilities. Liabilities include debt that must be paid back eventually while equity, in this case, measures the total amount of money that its owners have put into the business. This can include profits from previous years, which are known collectively as retained earnings.

Income statement: While the balance sheet can be thought of as a snapshot of the fundamental economic aspects of the company, an income statement takes a closer look at the performance of the company exclusively for a given timeframe. There is no limit to the length of time an income statement considers, which means you could see them generated month to month, or even day to day; however, the most common type used by public companies are either annual or quarterly. Income statements provide information on profit, expenses, and revenues that resulted from the business that took place over the specific period of time.

Cash flow statement: The cashflow statement frequently shows all of the cash outflow and inflow for the company over a given period of time. The cash flow statement often focuses on operating cash flow which is the cash that will be generated by day to day business operations. It will also include any cash that is available from investing which is often used as a means of investing in assets along with any cash that might have been generated by long-term asset sales or the sale of a secondary business that the company previously owned. Cash due to financing is another name for money that is paid off or received based on issuing or borrowing funds.

The cash flow statements are quite important as it is often more difficult for businesses to manipulate it when compared to many other types of financial documents. While accountants can manipulate earnings with ease, it is much more difficult to fake having access to cash in the bank where there is none that really exists. This is why many savvy investors consider the cash flow statement the most reliable way to measure a specific company's performance.

Finding the details: While tracking down all the disparate financial statements on the company's you are considering purchasing stock in can be cumbersome, the Securities and Exchange Commission (SEC) requires all publicly traded companies to submit regular filings outlining all of their financial activities including a variety of different financial statements. This also includes information such as managerial discussions, reports from auditors, deep dives into the operations and prospects of upcoming years and more.

These types of details can all be found in the 10-K filing that each company is required to file every year, along with the 10-Q filing that they must send out once per quarter. Both types of documents can be found online, both at the corporate website for the company as well as on the SEC website. As the version that hits the corporate site doesn't need to be complete, it is best to visit SEC.gov and get to know the Electronic Data Gathering, Analysis, and Retrieval system (EDGAR) which automates the process of indexing, validating, collecting, forward and accepting submissions. As this system was designed in the mid-90s, however, it is important to dedicate some time to learning the process as it is more cumbersome than 20 years of user interface advancements have to lead you to expect.

Qualitative Fundamental Analysis

Qualitative factors are generally less tangible and include things like its name recognition, the patents it holds and the quality of its board members. Qualitative factors to consider include:

Business model: The first thing that you are going to want to do when you catch wind of a company that might be worth following up on is to check out its business model which is more or less a generalization of how it makes its money. You can typically find these sorts of details on the company website or in its 10-K filing.

Competitive advantage: It is also important to consider the various competitive advantages that the company you have your eye on might have over its competition. Companies that are going to be successful in the long-term are always going to have an advantage over their competition in one of two ways. They can either have better operational effectiveness or improved strategic positioning. Operational effectiveness is the name given to doing the same things as the competition but in a more efficient and effective way. Strategic positioning occurs when a company gains an edge by doing things that nobody else is doing.

Changes to the company: In order to properly narrow down your search, you will typically find the most reliable results when it comes to companies that have recently seen major changes to their corporate structure as it is these types of changes that are likely to ultimately precede events that are more likely to see the company jump to the next level. The specifics of what happened in this instance are nearly as important as the fact that statistically speaking, 95 percent of companies that experience this type of growth started with a significant change to the status quo.

Chapter 9: Maximize your Profits

Now it is time to move on to some of the steps that you can take in order to maximize your profits with the help of options. Options are a great way to earn a profit because they allow you a way to reduce your exposure and the amount of risk that you take on, while increasing the amount of profits that you could potentially make. some of the tips that you can use to help maximize your profits while options trading includes:

Tip 6: You can profit no matter the market situation
One of the first things that you will notice when you are working in the options market is that you can actually benefit from any situation in the market when you work with options. Most of the strategies that work with this investment vehicle are carried out by combining the different option positions, and sometimes they will even use the underlying position of the stock. Basically, you can use either different trading strategies, or work with a few together, to profit no matter what market situation is going on.

When you enter into the market with options, you always stand to make a huge amount of profits, while still keeping your risk to a minimum. Ordinary stock trading isn't as reliable and it comes with a lot more risk. The most crucial aspects of options trading is to know when you should enter a trade and how you should exit it. Knowing how and when to exit will ensure that you keep any losses to a minimum and that you can increase your profits as much as possible.

You will find that options strategies are considered one of the most versatile when it comes to the financial market. They are going to provide investors and traders alike with a lot of profit making opportunities, and there is a limited amount of risk and exposure present. This is one of the main reasons that a lot of investors like to take some time and invest in options instead of the other asset choices.

Since you are able to profit no matter what the market situation is doing, this gives you a lot of freedom when working with options. But it also means that you may have to learn a lot more strategies than usual. You should learn at least a few strategies for a rising market, for a stagnant market, and for a down turn market. This will ensure that you are ready to go no matter which way the market is heading.

While the ability to make a profit in any kind of market is a great thing and can open up many new opportunities to make money compared to just investing in the stock market, it does make things a bit trickier to work with. You have to understand where the market is going, you have to know which strategies work for the different market directions, and you have to be ready to switch back and forth depending on how the market is doing.

Tip 7: Take advantage of the volatility of options to make a profit

Options have some similarities to stocks, but they are a bit different. And one place you will notice these differences is with the time limit. Stocks can be held for as short of a time period, or as long of a time period, as you want, but options have an expiration date. This means that the time you get to do the trade is going to be limited. And as a trader, missing this window is going to be a costly mistake, one that you need to avoid if at all possible. If this chance is missed, then it may be a very long time before you see it again.

This is why it is never a good idea to work with a long-term strategy wen you are trying to trade with options. Strategies, such as working with the average down, are seen as bad choices for options trading because you simply don't get the right time frame to see them happen. Also, make sure that you are careful about margin requirements. Depending on what these are, they could have a big impact on the requirements for the amount of funds you are able to invest.

There are also times when multiple factors may affect a favorable price. For instance, the price of the asset you choose may go up, which is usually seen as a good thing. But, it is possible that any of the accruing benefits could be eroded due to other factors, such as volatility, time decay, and dividend payment. These constraints mean that you need to learn how to follow some of the different strategies for profit-taking.

Tip 8: Always set a profit taking stop loss

The next tip that you should follow is to set up a profit taking stop loss. You can set up a stop loss at about five percent. This means that you want it to reach a target price of $100 if the trailing target is gong to be $95. If the upward trend does continue and the price gets to $120, then the trailing target, assuming the 5 percent from before, is going to become $114. And it would keep going up from there, with the amount of profit that you wish to make in the process.

Now, let's say that the price is going to start to fall. When this happens, you will need to exit and then collect the profits at this level, or the trailing target that you set. This ensures that you get to enjoy some protection as the price increases, and then you will exit the trade as soon as the price starts to turn around. The thing that you need to remember here is that the stop loss levels should never be too high or too low. If they are too small, you will be kicked out of the market too soon in most cases. But if they are too large, they will make it impossible to enjoy profit taking.

Tip 9: Sell covered call options against long positions
Selling options Is an income generating process that is pretty lucrative. Depending on the amount of risk that you take and what kinds of trades you decide to do, you could easily take home more than two percent in returns each month. However, this is not the only method you can use in order to make it rich on the market. You can also go with something that is known as

a naked puts and sell these. This is similar in a way to selling stocks or shares that you don't actually own.

When you go through the process of selling a naked put options, you will be able to free up some of your time to do more. Stock trading allows you to have an opportunity to sell stocks of shares that you don't already own, and then you can earn a profit. This will free up your capital, allowing you to invest it or trade with it indefinitely.

To make this method work, it is best if you work with stocks that you already understand well, or those that you wouldn't mind actually owning. This way, you know when there are any major changes to the stock and you can make some changes to the way you invest before the market turns and harms your profits. There is still a level of hedging that is associated with this options trading method, so you must always be on the lookout for that.

Tip 10: Pick the right strategy

And often the one that you pick will lead you to finding the right options to sell. Some of the options trading strategies are going to work in a downturn, some are going to work the best in an upturn, and some do well when the market is more stagnant. When you pick out a strategy, you will then be able to choose the options that fit in with that strategy the best.

With that said, there are a few guidelines that you can learn to follow when it is time to purchase an option for trading. Following these guidelines will make it easier for you to identify the options that you should choose in order to make a good profit. Some of the guidelines include:

Determine whether the market is bullish or bearish. Also, make sure that you determine whether you are really strongly bullish, or just mildly bullish. This can make a difference in how the market is doing and which assets you would like to work with.

Think about how volatile the market is right now and how it could affect your strategy with options trading. Also, you can think about the status of the market at the time. Is the market currently calm or is there a lot of volatility that shows up? If it is not very high, then you should be able to buy the call options based on the underlying stock, and these are usually seen as relatively inexpensive.

Consider the strike price and the expiration date of any options you want to trade in. If you only have a few shares at this time, then this may make it the best time to purchase more of the stock or asset.

Your overall goal of working with the options trading market is to make as much profit as possible. No one goes into the market, or any kind of investment, with the idea that they want to lose money. But if you follow some of the tips above, you will be able to maximize your profits and see some great results.

Chapter 10: Speculation

Two of the biggest reasons why an investor might be interested in trading options in the first place is because of the factors of speculation and hedging. This chapter will focus on how exactly speculation and hedging work within the broader scope of options trading. You may find yourself in a position where you are already using these tactics in your trading life, but you should still read this chapter so that you can find new ways to use these techniques in a way to expand your current trading strategies. If you are already using these strategies in your current options trading strategies, it's probably best to think of this chapter as one that can deepen your understanding of these concepts and hone concepts with which you may already be familiar.

What is Speculation?

The first concept that we're going to discuss is speculation. Speculation in the broadest sense is the process that an investor takes on a stock with the expectation that there is a high potential to lose large amounts of money extremely quickly. The concept of speculation is largely the reason why options trading has the reputation of being one of the riskiest ways that you can invest your money. While this concept of trading is certainly risky in nature, it's important to understand that the money that is anticipated to be lost is typically seen as being won again in even larger amounts once the options have reached their maturation. It's important to understand that it can sometimes be difficult to decipher whether or not the intention behind the motivation to conduct a trade can be considered speculative or not. Some factors that can distinguish a speculation from a typical investment include the amount of leverage that is involved in the transaction, how long the investor plans to hold the stock, and the nature of the asset as a whole.

Options in general are considered be pretty speculative in nature because prior to purchasing an option you have to choose which direction you're going to purchase the asset as well as how much the price is going to increase or decrease over a certain period of time. Of course, due to the risky nature of options trading in general you might be asking yourself why people even engage in the act of speculation to begin with, it being regarded as such as a risky endeavor. The biggest reason why investors are most interested in options and speculation is that the risks are usually outweighed by the rewards. Especially if you can speculate well, then it's likely that you are going to be great at options trading.

One of the biggest reasons why options are speculative is because of the high levels of leveraging that often accompanies speculation. With options, you are able to purchase stake in something that is much cheaper than purchasing a regular stock at its full market price. This leveraging against the price of the entire stock is what largely allows an investor to own a *position* in the stock, rather than the entire stock itself. Let's take a look at an example. Let's say that there is an investor who is looking at a particular stock that costs fifty-dollars per share. This is a hefty sum of money, especially because this particular investor only has two-thousand dollars to spend on investments at this particular moment in time. You have two options here. You can either decide to purchase forty shares of this particular stock at the fifty-dollar going rate, or you can instead purchase options of the stock. If you decide to engage in the latter, this means that you will be purchasing one-thousand options shares of the stock instead of only forty. Of course, options are going to amplify both the losses and the gains that you're going to see

What is Hedging?
When you hedge an option, what you're essentially doing is providing yourself with security in other investments that are already in your portfolio. If we look at an example, this concept will become more accessible to you. For example, let's say that you own some stocks. They're high priced, and you really have no idea of knowing whether or not they're going to appreciate over the long-term; however, you know that you want to stick with this stock for the long-term because this is part of your long-term investment strategy. Instead of simply hoping for the

best even though you know that company in which you've invested is going through a rough patch, you are looking for more security. You decide that you're going to invest in an option, but in a way that counteracts the decisions that you've made regarding the activity that you've already invested in with the long-term stocks that you already own. Let's take a look at this concept on a more in-depth level, because whether you are aware of it or not, hedging is considered to be an advanced options trading strategy, even though the concepts within it are fairly straightforward.

How to Hedge an Option

Some common examples of hedging include taking out insurance that will minimize your income's exposure to risk in the unfortunate event of your death and paying money back in monthly sums rather than in one huge payment over a period of time. While these are great examples of hedging because you are able to see how leveraging is working on a smaller scale, the big stock market players see hedging a bit differently. To conglomerates such as the New York Stock Exchange, hedging is a bit different in the sense that it is typically used in a way that will counter the potential for competitors within an industry to cause you to lose money. Let's look at an example for this concept. Let's go out on a limb here and say that the Q-Tip industry has suddenly revolutionized itself. You are interested in getting in on this action, so you decide to invest in a company called Waxless. You think that everything is sound with your investment and you are sure that the Q-Tip industry's technology is going to skyrocket in value, only you come to find out that this "revolution" was not that great of an invention and the technology is actually causing people to have negative side effects. Due to these revelations, you come to find out that Waxless may have not been the best investment choice after all; however, you're willing to see things through a bit longer and see how the industry ends up doing in the long-term. In this situation, you are actually finding out that the Q-Tip industry is quite volatile in nature.

132

In an attempt to counter this volatility, you decide that you're going to purchase a stock in a competing Q-Tip company that is called EarDry. EarDry has adapted the technology that Waxless initially came out with, and there is some controversy in the industry about whether the Waxless technology or the EarDry technology is superior. Because you have decided to invest in EarDry *and* Waxless, you are putting your investments in a good position. Rather than only investing in one type of technology within the same sector of business, you decide to put some money into both. This way, in the event that one goes under, you will still have some security in the other methods. As one falls, it's likely that the other will rise and become the superior product on the market.

Hopefully through the example above, you have a better idea of how hedging works and how you can take advantage of it for yourself. The truth is, every type of investment should have some sort of hedge to go along with it. The real estate industry is known for its hedging tactics, as is the mortgage business as well. Let's take a look at some of the advantages that hedging can bring to the table for you, so that you can see why so many people use options in this manner.

Hedging Advantage 1: The Transfer of Risk

One of the biggest reasons why using options as a way to hedge is because of the ability for the hedge to transfer and diminish risk. Not only can hedging help to alleviate the stress that risk plays on your portfolio as a whole, but it can also serve to pacify other stressors of life as well. For example, if you're planning on opening a new business or own a home, hedging the risk that is associated with these sometimes-volatile ventures can help to bring you greater overall security. Of course, it's certainly important to understand that hedging should not be used in a way that's going to seek to alleviate the risk that's involved with betting everything that you own, but it is a way to compliment riskier options investment behavior.

Hedging Advantage 2: The Ability to Use Forward Contracts

In addition to diminishing some of the risk that is involved in trading options and using the technique of hedging, another advantage the hedging can provide the advanced options trader is the ability to engage in forward contracts. Forward contracts are pretty similar to options in the sense that they are obviously contracts, but they are also only good for a specific period of time. Unlike options, which are typically domestic in nature, forward contracts allow an investor to trade overseas and through international currency. If you're not currently using forward contracts as a way to hedge some of the risk that's involved when trading foreign currency, it might be a good idea to consider doing so. The idea is that while it may cost more to participate in the foreign market with a forward contract, you are offsetting this cost over the long-term.

Hedging Advantage 3: Currency Declination

Lastly, another advantage that hedging can offer an options trader again deals with a situation where he or she is trading options on the foreign market. Investors who are holding options in foreign markets often run the risk of having the currency decline while the options shares are still in their possession. It's important to understand that an option that is being used in conjunction with a foreign currency will only outperform the foreign currency if the *foreign currency* declines in relation to the dollar. While it's certainly a good idea to consider investing in foreign currency as a way to both diversify your portfolio and use hedging to your advantage in the greatest possible manner, you have to make sure that you understand how the foreign currency is going to operate under all different types of circumstances.

Chapter 11: Develop your Exit Strategy

If you find that you're more of a "fast-and-loose" stock market investor, rather than the type of person who meticulously acts only after weighing the pros and cons of each potential outcome, then there might be a chance that you do not even currently have an options trading exit strategy in place. This chapter will take you through the different types of exit strategies that are available to an options trader, and hopefully make you realize some of the reasons as to why exit strategies are extremely important, regardless of the specific type of stock that you're trading.

Why is an Exit Strategy Important?

Firstly, it's important to understand that some of the biggest reasons why investors need an exit strategy are emotional in nature. Factors such as greed, fear, and even the rush of the investment game itself are some of the circumstances that can take hold of an investor and cause him or her to make rash and otherwise inadvisable decisions with their money. Due to the fast-paced and sometimes one-sided nature of options trading, it is one of the most susceptible areas of the stock market to an investor's emotional wear-and-tear. Additionally, another important reason why every investor should be considering an exit strategy is because of the fact that it helps with money management. Again, being an expert at managing your money is another area where many options traders fail at the task at which they're trying to accomplish. These are two of the most important factors that you need to keep in mind when you're developing your options strategy, especially because you may not even be realizing how these factors are currently influencing your options trading decisions, for better or for worse.

Exit Strategies and Timing for Options Traders

One of the reasons why options trading is unique is because it requires investors to think about how time in influencing the value of an investment. Each option is going to mature and expire, and the reality is that time is going to cause the value of the option to deteriorate as the maturation date grows nearer and nearer. It's never a good idea to decide on a whim that it's the right time to sell or purchase a new option. Instead, consider setting time stamps for yourself along the life of the option that will indicate whether or not it's time to sell. If you set specific intervals along the life of the stock, you'll be able to look at the option more objectively than otherwise might be possible. Doing this and sticking to these guidelines for each option that you purchase or sell will help you to become more emotionless and less logical in your trading patterns.

Rolling an Option

In addition to thinking about the constrains of time in the most objective way possible, another good tip for developing an options trading exit strategy is to partake in what's known as "rolling out". If you were to do this, you would first decide to close your options that are currently open under a particular underlying asset. Instead of being done after this, you would open new options within the same underlying asset, only with different terms than the ones that you previously sold. Essentially what you are doing is moving your options to a new strike price, without losing out on the gains that you can make from selling entirely. More specifically, this means moving your options so that they are either positioned vertically or horizontally. If you ultimately decide that you're going to move them vertically, this means that you're going to renew your options within the same month under the same underlying stock. If you ultimately decide that you're going to move your options horizontally, this means that you're going to renew them within a different month. Of course, when you roll an option you also have the ability to partake in both types of this movement, buying some vertically and others horizontally.

Rolling an Option Before the Expiration Date

It should be obvious to you by now that time is a unique indicator of worth for an option. This being the case, the rolling option exit strategy attempts to use time decay to its advantage rather than to its detriment. Broadly speaking and depending on the time that the specific option has until expiration, there are certain times and days that are more significant than others from the perspective of how much an option is worth. The chart below should help to clarify this point:

As you can see from the chart above, the option begins to lose its value more quickly as it heads towards day sixty, and then decays even more rapidly around day thirty. When a person who is holding an option sees this deceleration, it might be within the parameters of his or her exit strategy to even go ahead and roll their option over before the expiration date has come to fruition. This way, they are leaving themselves and their money open for a situation to occur where they can potentially earn back some of the money that they've already paid to hold the option. You might be wondering whether or not there are times when an investor will decide that he or she is not going to use the rolling exit strategy, but it appears that this does not happen very often. The idea behind avoiding rolling over an option is that the investor is for some reason under the impression that the stock is going to appreciate more prior to the expiration date. Of course, there are some instances where this does in fact seem to be the outcome, but from a general perspective an option is going to lose value towards the end of its life, rather than see appreciation at the end of its tenure.

Chapter 12: Common Mistakes to Avoid

Options are one of the greatest wealth building tools, and a quick way to lose all your trading capital. Options can fall to zero or go up 1000%, and you must have a plan for either possibility. By deploying small amounts of capital and capturing full moves in your favor, they can a good asymmetric risk management tools and keep you from over leveraging your account.

Here are the biggest and most common pitfalls that new option traders encounter.

New option traders buy far out of the money options without understanding how the odds are stacked against them. If the Delta is only .10 on your option, then you have less than a 1 in 10 chance of your option expiring in the money Even if you get a move in your favor, your far out of the money option won't increase in value until the Delta expands enough to overcome the time decay.

It takes a large move in price to increase the value of out of the money options. The odds of it expiring in the money must increase enough to drive up the contract price. New option traders often become frustrated when price moves in their favor and their out of the money option goes down in value. In most instances this is gambling and not trading. Always try to be the casino and not the gambler.

It's not wise to trade illiquid options because you can lose 10% or more of your capital at risk entering and exiting your trade if the volume doesn't tighten the spread. Do research to see how much it will cost you to get in and out of the trade before you get started. Option spreads of .10 to .50 are preferable. A .10 bid/ask spread on an option will cost you $10 to get into the trade and then $10 to get out. A 100 share contract times .10 cents a share equals $10 each way. This is a $20 round trip, in addition to your commission fee, and this only covers one contract. A $1 bid/ask spread will cost you $100 in slippage to get in and then $100 or more to get out of one contract. This is an operating expense that adds up over time. The moment you enter a one contract option with a $1 bid/ask spread you are already down $100 in slippage. I only trade in the most liquid option contracts I can find, and stay away from the low volume markets that will slowly eat away at my trading capital.

Look for options that are in line with your trading time frame. Give your trade enough time to work. If you plan on Apple going to $110 in 2 months, then don't buy a weekly $110 strike call, because it will run out of time and expire worthless. Instead, buy a two month out call option that won't expire before your trade has time to work. You must be right about the price *and* time period; just one or the other is not good enough to be profitable.

One of the most important things to remember is that the implied volatility that is priced into options above the normal time value before earnings announcements or an uncertain event. The Vega premium disappears after the event comes and goes. For example, if an at the money weekly Apple call option and put option are trading at $10 above normal time value on the day an earnings announcement, the day after that $10 in Vega value will be gone. The trade is only profitable if intrinsic value of the option going in the money of the strike price is more than enough to replace the lost Vega value.

When trading through a volatile event like earnings, you must be right about the magnitude of the price; the direction alone is not enough. Buying options through earnings has a low probability of success because the option sellers give themselves a lot of Vega value to cover their risk. Because of this, it's very difficult to overcome the Vega collapse. Many will opine about the few times the move was not priced in, but that is an uncommon event.

There are two ways to use options to capture a simple price move. Option traders must understand that to make money in out of the money options they must be right about price, the time to get to the price, the magnitude of the price move, and if the price rises enough to overcome the cost of Theta and Vega above the strike price. However, with in the money options, you take on the risk of intrinsic value and you only need be right about the direction. In the money options have little Theta or Vega value, they are almost all intrinsic value and have high Deltas of over .90. With the right liquidity and going deep enough, in the money options can be used like synthetic stocks with less risk.

Don't risk more than you would when trading stocks. I advise never to risk more than 1% of trading capital on any one trade, and the same applies to options. If you can only trade 100 shares of Apple, then only trade one Apple in the money option contract. If your trading capital is large enough to handle trading 1000 shares of Twitter in your normal stock trading account, then trade 10 contracts of Twitter options. Don't trade too large with options. They can double and triple in price, but they can also go to zero. Options can move so fast that they are difficult to implement effective stop losses. It's much easier to have option trades be all or nothing trades with very small positions. With weekly options, a 50% stop loss on an option is the best you will be able to manage. Stop losses must be on the chart of a stock where they have value, and not at a random option price decline level. That's why I prefer all or nothing option trades.

Unlike stocks that are ownership in a company, options are derivatives of stocks and are contracts that will expire. They are not assets, they are bets. Options are a zero-sum game; there is a winner for every loser. To be on the winning side you need to trade with the odds in your favor. If you are a seller of premium, sell the deep out of the money options that have little chance of being worth anything. Option buyers can buy to open the in the money options in the direction of the current market trend. Option premium sellers can sell to open put options under the support of the hottest stocks during bull markets, and sell calls on the stocks in down trends.

Avoid the temptation of selling puts on junk stocks and calls on monster stocks in strong trends because this can be very dangerous. Don't buy low probability far out of the money lottery tickets, and then sell. Don't cap your upside on a hot stock by selling a covered call, instead buy a call option and get the upside for a small investment of capital. Be on the right side of the probabilities, manage your risk, and you will do very well over the long-term.

Chapter 13: Risks That You Need to Avoid
Understanding Options Risks

Options trading process does carry some risks with it. Understanding these risks and taking mitigating steps will make you not just a better trader but a more profitable one as well. A lot of traders love options trading because of the immense leverage that this kind of trading affords them. Should an investment work out as desired, then the profits are often quite high. With stocks, you can expect returns of between 10%, 15%, or even 20%. However, when it comes to options, profit margins in excess of 1,000% are very possible.

Basically, these kinds of trades are very possible due to the nature and leverage offered by options. A savvy trader realizes that he or she is able to control an almost equivalent number of shares as a traditional stock investor but at a fraction of the cost. Therefore, when you invest in options, you can spend a tiny amount of money to control a large number of shares. This kind of leverage limits your risks and exposure compared to a stock investor.

As an investor or trader, you should never spend more than 3% to 5% of your funds in any single trade. For instance, if you have $10,000 to invest, you should not spend more than $300 to $500 on any one trade.

Also, as a trader, you are not just mitigating against potential risks but are also looking to take advantage of the leverage. This is also known as gaining a professional trader's edge. While it is crucial to reduce the risk through careful analysis and selection of trades, you should also aim to make huge profits and enjoy big returns on your trades. There will always be some losses, and as a trader, you should get to appreciate this. However, your major goal as a trader should be to ensure that your wins are much, much larger than any losses that you may suffer.

All types of investment opportunities carry a certain level of risk. However, options trading carry a much higher risk of loss. Therefore, ensure that you have a thorough understanding of the risks and always be on the lookout. Also, these kinds of trades are very possible due to the nature and leverage offered by options. A savvy trader realizes that he or she is able to control an almost equivalent number of shares as a traditional stock investor but at a fraction of the cost. Therefore, when you invest in options, you can spend a tiny amount of money to control a large number of shares. This kind of leverage limits your risks and exposure compared to a stock investor.

Time Is Not on Your Side

You need to keep in mind that all options have an expiration date and that they do expire in time. When you invest in stocks, time is on your side most of the time. However, things are different when it comes to options. Basically, the closer that an option gets to its expiration, the quicker it loses its value and earning potential.

Options deterioration is usually rather rapid, and it accelerates in the last days until expiration. Basically, as an investor, ensure that you only invest dollar amounts that you can afford to lose. The good news though is that there are a couple of actions that you can take in order to get things on your side.

- Trade mostly in options with expiration dates that are within the investment opportunity

- Buy options at or very near the money

- Sell options any time you think volatility is highly priced

- Buy options when you are of the opinion that volatility is underpriced

Prices Can Move Pretty Fast

Options are highly leveraged financial instruments. Because of this, prices tend to move pretty fast. Basically, options prices can move huge amounts within minutes and sometimes even seconds. This is unlike other stock market instruments like stocks that move in hours and days.

Small movements in the price of a stock can have huge implications on the value of the underlying stock. You need to be vigilant and monitor price movements often. However, you can generate profits without monitoring activity on the markets twenty-four hours a day.

As an investor or trader, you should seek out opportunities where chances of earning a significant profit are immense. The opportunity should be sufficiently robust so that pricing by seconds will be of little concern. In short, search for opportunities that will lead to large profits even when you are not accurate when selling.

When structuring your options, you should ensure that you use the correct strike prices as well as expiration months in order to cut out most of the risk. You should also consider closing out your trades well before expiration of options. This way, time value will not dramatically deteriorate.

Naked Short Positions Can Result in Substantial Losses

Anytime that your naked short option presents a high likelihood of substantial and sometimes even unlimited losses. Shorting put naked means selling stock options with no hedging of your position.

When selling a naked short, it simply implies that you are actually selling a call option or even a put option but without securing it using an option position, a stock or cash. It is advisable to sell a put or a call in combination with other options or with stocks. Remember that whenever you short sell a stock, you are in essence selling borrowed stock. Sooner or later, you will have to return the stock.

Fortunately, with options, there is no borrowing of stock or any other security.

Chapter 14: Tips for Success

Know when to go off book: While sticking to your plan, even when your emotions are telling you to ignore it, is the mark of a successful trader, this in no way means that you must blindly follow your plan 100 percent of the time. You will, without a doubt, find yourself in a situation from time to time where your plan is going to be rendered completely useless by something outside of your control. You need to be aware enough of your plan's weaknesses, as well as changing market conditions, to know when following your predetermined course of action is going to lead to failure instead of success. Knowing when the situation really is changing, versus when your emotions are trying to hold sway is something that will come with practice, but even being aware of the disparity is a huge step in the right direction.

Avoid trades that are out of the money: While there are a few strategies out there that make it a point of picking up options that are currently out of the money, you can rest assured that they are most certainly the exception, not the rule. Remember, the options market is not like the traditional stock market which means that even if you are trading options based on underlying stocks buying low and selling high is just not a viable strategy. If a call has dropped out of the money, there is generally less than a 10 percent chance that it will return to acceptable levels before it expires which means that if you purchase these types of options what you are doing is little better than gambling, and you can find ways to gamble with odds in your favor of much higher than 10 percent.

Avoid hanging on too tightly to your starter strategy: Your core trading strategy is one that should always be constantly evolving as the circumstances surrounding your trading habits change and evolve as well. What's more, outside of your primary strategy you are going to want to eventually create additional plans that are more specifically tailored to various market states or specific strategies that are only useful in a narrow band of situations. Remember, the more prepared you are prior to

145

starting a day's worth of trading, the greater your overall profit level is likely to be, it is as simple as that.

Utilize the spread: If you are not entirely risk averse, then when it comes to taking advantage of volatile trades the best thing to do is utilize a spread as a way of both safeguarding your existing investments and, at the same time, making a profit. To utilize a long spread you are going to want to generate a call and a put, both with the same underlying asset, expiration details, and share amounts but with two very different strike prices. The call will need to have a higher strike price and will mark the upper limit of your profits and the put will have a lower strike price that will mark the lower limit of your losses. When creating a spread it is important that you purchase both halves at the same time as doing it in fits and spurts can add extraneous variables to the formula that are difficult to adjust for properly.

Never proceed without knowing the mood of the market: While using a personalized trading plan is always the right choice, having one doesn't change the fact that it is extremely important to consider the mood of the market before moving forward with the day's trades. First and foremost, it is important to keep in mind that the collective will of all of the traders who are currently participating in the market is just as much as a force as anything that is more concrete, including market news. In fact, even if companies release good news to various outlets and the news is not quite as good as everyone was anticipating it to be then related prices can still decrease.

To get a good idea of what the current mood of the market is like, you are going to want to know the average daily numbers that are common for your market and be on the lookout for them to start dropping sharply. While a day or two of major fluctuation can be completely normal, anything longer than that is a sure sign that something is up. Additionally, you will always want to be aware of what the major players in your market are up to.

Never get started without a clear plan for entry and exit: While finding your first set of entry/exit points can be difficult without experience to guide you, it is extremely important that you have them locked down prior to starting trading, even if the stakes are relatively low. Unless you are extremely lucky, starting without a clear idea of the playing field is going to do little but lose your money. If you aren't sure about what limits you should set, start with a generalized pair of points and work to fine tune it from there.

More important than setting entry and exit points, however, is using them, even when there is still the appearance of money on the table. One of the biggest hurdles that new options traders need to get over is the idea that you need to wring every last cent out of each and every successful trade. The fact of the matter is that, as long as you have a profitable trading plan, then there will always be more profitable trades in the future which means that instead of worrying about a small extra profit you should be more concerned with protecting the profit that the trade has already netted you. While you may occasionally make some extra profit ignoring this advice, odds are you will lose far more than you gain as profits peak unexpectedly and begin dropping again before you can effectively pull the trigger. If you are still having a hard time with this concept, consider this: options trading is a marathon, not a sprint, slow and steady will always win the race.

Never double down: When they are caught up in the heat of the moment, many new options traders will find themselves in a scenario where the best way to recoup a serious loss is to double down on the underlying stock in question at its newest, significantly lowered, price in an effort to make a profit under the assumption that things are going to turn around and then continue to do so to the point that everything is completely profitable once again. While it can be difficult to let an underlying stock that was once extremely profitable go, doubling down is rarely if ever going to be the correct decision.

147

If you find yourself in a spot where you don't know if the trade you are about to make is actually going to be a good choice, all you need to do is ask yourself if you would make the same one if you were going into the situation blind, the answer should tell you all you need to know.

If you find yourself in a moment where doubling down seems like the right choice, you are going to need to have the strength to talk yourself back down off of that investing ledge and to cut your losses as thoroughly as possible given the current situation. The sooner you cut your losses and move on from the trade that ended poorly, the sooner you can start putting energy and investments into a trade that still has the potential to make you a profit.

Never take anything personally: It is human nature to build stories around, and therefore form relationships with, all manner of inanimate objects including individual stocks or currency pairs. This is why it is perfectly natural to feel a closer connection to particular trades, and possibly even consider throwing out your plan when one of them takes an unexpected dive. Thinking about and acting on are two very different things, however, which is why being aware of these tendencies are so important to avoid them at all costs.

This scenario happens just as frequently with trades moving in positive directions as it does negative, but the results are always going to be the same. Specifically, it can be extremely tempting to hang on to a given trade much longer than you might otherwise decide to simply because it is on a hot streak that shows no sign of stopping. In these instances, the better choice of action is to instead sell off half of your shares and then set a new target based on the updated information to ensure you are in a position to have your cake and eat it too.

Not taking your choice of broker seriously: With so many things to consider, it is easy to understand why many new

148

option traders simply settle on the first broker that they find and go about their business from there. The fact of the matter is, however, that the broker you choose is going to be a huge part of your overall trading experience which means that the importance of choosing the right one should not be discounted if you are hoping for the best experience possible. This means that the first thing that you are going to want to do is to dig past the friendly exterior of their website and get to the meat and potatoes of what it is they truly offer. Remember, creating an eye-catching website is easy, filling it will legitimate information when you have ill intent is much more difficult.

First things first, this means looking into their history of customer service as a way of not only ensuring that they treat their customers in the right way, but also of checking to see that quality of service is where it needs to be as well. Remember, when you make a trade every second count which mean that if you need to contact your broker for help with a trade you need to know that you are going to be speaking with a person who can solve your problem as quickly as possible. The best way to ensure the customer service is up to snuff is to give them a call and see how long it takes for them to get back to you. If you wait more than a single business day, take your business elsewhere as if they are this disinterested in a new client, consider what the service is going to be like when they already have you right where they want you.

With that out the way, the next thing you will need to consider is the fees that the broker is going to charge in exchange for their services. There is very little regulation when it comes to these fees which means it is definitely going to pay to shop around. In addition to fees, it is important to consider any account minimums that are required as well as any fees having to do with withdrawing funds from the account.

Find a Mentor: When you are looking to go from causal trader to someone who trades successfully on the regular, there is only so much you can learn by yourself before you need a truly objective eye to ensure you are proceeding appropriately. This person can either be someone you know in real life, or it can take the form of one or more people online. The point is you need to find another person or two who you can bounce ideas off of and whose experience you can benefit from. Options trading doesn't need to be a solitary activity; take advantage of any community you can find.

Knowledge is the key: Without some type of information which you can use to assess your trades, you are basically playing at the roulette table. Even poker players show up to the table with a game plan. They can adapt to the circumstances and learn to read other players. That way, they can tell the contenders from the pretenders. Options trading is no different. If you are unable to use the information that is out there to your advantage, then what you will end up with is a series of guesses which may or may not play out. Based purely on the law of averages you have a 50/50 chance of making money. That may not seem like bad odds, but a string of poor decisions will leave you in the poor house in no time.

So, it is crucial that you become familiar with the various analytics and tools out there which you can use to your advantage. Bear in mind that everyone is going to be looking at the same information. However, it is up to you to figure out what can, or might, happen before everyone else does. This implies really learning and studying the numbers so that you can detect patterns and see where trends are headed, or where trends may reverse. The perfect antidote to that is vision and foresight. Practice building scenarios. Try to imagine what could happen is trends continue. Or, what would happen if trends reversed? What needs to happen in order for those trends to continue or reverse?

When you ask yourself such tough questions, your knowledge and understanding begin to expand. Your mind will suddenly be able to process greater amounts of information while you generate your own contingency plans based on the multiple what ifs. That may seem like a great deal of information to handle, but at the end of the day, any time spent in improving your trading acumen is certainly worth the effort.

Conclusion

A real options trading professional uses reasonable cash the board system on each trading chance, weighted against the potential danger of non-execution. This implies a real option dealer will never put all his money into one significant out of the cash position! Practical options trading professional uses exchange investigation strategies dependent on demonstrated procedures to put the chances of execution to support them and never treat each exchange as a 50/50 wager. Real options trading professional compute the measure of options influence to be utilized on each, so his portfolio is never over-utilized. A practical option trading professional don't hope to become wildly successful on his next exchange, and he isn't going for one tremendous grand slam yet a progression of little successes that in the end includes. A real option trading professional never enable one misfortune to clear out his portfolio since he approaches the market with deference realizing that regardless of how much investigation has been led, there is dependably an opportunity that the market will neutralize him.

The next step is to step up your dedication to options trading! It's safe to say that if you already trading, there are probably things that you could be doing to take your options trading to the next level. Contrastingly, if you have not yet started to trade options, it's time to get in the game! Both the beginning strategies in my first book about options trading and this book have definitely armed you with enough information to get started. The next step is to get into it. Even if this means that you're still not quite ready to begin options trading, you can still start to do more than simply read a book. For example, maybe this means that you set up meetings with a few brokers and compare commission costs, or maybe it means that you find a way to start trading in real-time via an application of some sort. The exact degree in which you want to pursue the options trading path is up to you, as long as you take the next steps towards making serious money!

The thing that matters is in ATTITUDE. Attitude oversees choices and activities. Any individual who approaches option trading with the "make easy money" attitude will likewise before long get themselves "getting-more unfortunate speedier" necessarily in light of the fact that these punters planning to "become showbiz royalty" on their next exchange, thoroughly rejects any similarity to a transfer the board system, completely thrown away reasonable investigation for a 50/50 "wager" and remove absolutely silly from the cash positions that either become showbiz royalty or lapse totally useless!

Introduction to Day Trading

Day trading entails buying and selling of stocks within the same day. It enables you grow your income through making profit from stock price changes that occur during the day. To successfully engage in day trading, it is important to understand how it works. This trading strategy allows you to maximize on the volume and volatility of stocks to generate income. It presents you with vast opportunities to make money from average amounts of capital. You can make profit both from the downward and upward movement of prices, which is a good thing.

As a day trader, you engage the services of a broker to purchase stock then sell it at a profit. Most of this happens during morning hours when the stock market is still volatile. This book outlines several important aspects of day trading. It highlights all the requirements for day trading and what you need to do once you start the business. It also informs you of the different strategies you can use in day trading, the common mistakes people make when engaging in the trade as well as the tips you should use to succeed in the trade.

While going through the book, you will learn how to enter and exit trades and how to reduce the risks associated with this short-term trading technique. The book also provides you with guidelines necessary for day trading different financial instruments such as options and futures. If you study it keenly, you will attain your financial goals more quickly as you upgrade your knowledge of the trade. Ideally, this book serves a as a great asset to new day traders as well as those who are experienced in the trade.

There are plenty of books on this subject on the market, thanks again for choosing this one! Every effort was made to ensure it is full of as much useful information as possible, please enjoy!

Chapter 1: How to be a Successful Day Trader

Being a day trader can be an extremely stressful job and it is not the sort of career that will appeal to everyone. The funds which you are investing and can potential lose are your own; a bad day on the markets can hurt you mentally and financially making it very difficult to return to your home office the next day and carry on. Before you decide to undertake day trading for yourself it is advisable to see if you have the following traits; you will be far more likely to be successful if you do:

- Experience

The more knowledge and experience you have of the stock market the better you will understand the principles and fundamentals of day trading. Whilst having experience of working in the stock market will be beneficial it is not essential. What is essential is an experience of completing detailed research. This requires patience and dedication and it the cornerstone to becoming a successful day trader. If you do not have the patience to complete the research then you will never gain a true understanding of the markets.

• Finance

As opposed to a trait this is a resource which will prove to be very useful. Day trading with finances you already have available will make it easier and more palatable to absorb any loss. However, many traders will not have reserves of cash with which to start trading. If this is the case you will need to arrange a line of finance. Borrowing to speculate in the stock market is a risky proposition, but it is better to have a reasonable amount of funds available in order to make a wide range of small trades; this will increase your likelihood of success.

• Discipline

It is very easy to get carried away when you are on a roll and add more funds or extend the trade. However, this can be counter- productive; it is essential to have a plan and stick to it. Doing this requires discipline but this is important to ensure you do not lose money unnecessarily. There is no place for emotions when day trading, each trade should be based on your research and knowledge of the market. If you decide to close all deals at the end of each day, which is the best route to take, then you should do so. This may sometimes lead to not having made as much funds as you could have, but it will also prevent unexpected and unaffordable losses. When you are trading you must be focused completely on trading; there is no room for anything else.

- Computer knowledge

Trading from home will require you to use a computer. You will need to research companies and market sectors; you will also need to be comfortably loading new software, including live feeds to your computer. Some day traders even operate several computers and monitors to ensure they have all the information they need displayed in front of them. To be able to do this properly you must be comfortable with your computer and what it is capable of; you do not need to be a computer programmer!

- Preparation

Research is a key component to becoming a good day trader; however, it is also essential to be prepared for any scenario. You will need to be able to absorb the latest information from a variety of sources and decide which information is relevant and genuine. It is often the case that people do not fully understand the stock market and will issue warnings which are unnecessary. Of course, there are also times when the warnings signs should be heeded.

Being prepared means having your plan, knowing where you are going and watching the market constantly. You will then be prepared to react to any situation and take the appropriate action.

- Commitment

A day trader will spend a lot of their time pouring over the internet; researching price trends or patterns in the market. Many days can be tedious; in fact there is very little glamour in day trading, particularly if you do it from home. It takes time, patience and commitment.

This is particularly important when dealing with a declining market. In this scenario many people are eager to sell and minimize their loss, being committed and sticking to your plan will enable you to capitalise, even in a falling market. As well as being committed to the markets and finding the best way forward, you will need to be able to stick to your opinion; no matter how many people challenge it.

- Decisive

Whether prices are rising rapidly or sinking you need to be able to make a decision and follow it through. This is not the type of business to be in if you are constantly second guessing yourself or are wary of committing to a decision.

Research and a plan should enable you to see the best way forward at all times; even if it means taking the facts that you know and making an educated guess. Once you have made a decision follow it through; this does not mean you will always make the right decision. However, if you do make the wrong one then you should be willing and able to stop your course of action and move to a better path.

• Support Network

Day trading from home can be a lonely experience; you will spend many hours by yourself researching and making purchases or sales. You will be reliant on your own judgment and can easily become absorbed in the buying and selling process. The adrenaline rush when you pick the right shares and they do well; is amazing. But, the opposite is also true; the days when trades do not go well can be disappointing and even soul destroying. This is when it is essential to have a good support network which will not criticise; they will simply be there to support you and ensure you move past the disappointment. They are an essential part of your team as they enable you to focus on moving forward; in fact, the most important role of your support network is to ensure you remember that you are trading to live; not living to trade.

• Open-Minded

Finally, it is essential to be open-minded. All the research and planning in the world will not prepare you for every eventuality; there is always something unexpected which occurs. It is essential to be open to any new experience or information received and be able to evaluate this; if necessary adjusting your plans accordingly.

There are many factors which can influence a day trade and, as more people attempt to trade on the markets from the comfort of their own home; there will be new ideas and techniques. Not all of these will work, but being open to any change in market factors will enable you to successfully adapt your technique and continue to trade.

It is possible to improve the skills described in this book, therefore, no matter how good you already think your skills are, there is no harm in practicing and improving your approach.

How to Get Started in Day Trading

Having made the decision to become a day trader you may be wondering how to move into your new career. It is important to remember that day trading is not a get rich scheme; as well as having researched the markets and developed an understanding of how they work; you will need to develop a strategy that you believe will work best. Before you start trading you must have studied the markets and understand what you are doing. There are a variety of different types of trading styles, these are explained in the next chapter; it is possible to mix and match any of the styles providing you understand the concepts first. To get started you will need the following:

- A computer

Trading on the stock market is possible without a computer, but you will expend the majority of your energy and resources on the telephone, dealing with brokers and attempting to secure a price for your trade that matches the information you have to hand. In reality, to trade from home you will need a computer; a desktop or laptop is fine. Although it is possible to use any computer, the best option would be to choose one with as large a hard drive as possible, at least three or four gigabytes of RAM and the best processor you can comfortably afford. The size of the screen and the resolution is also especially important. Ideally your computer will be able to output to several monitors at the same time.

- Telephone

This is an essential, although hopefully rarely used part of your kit. A day trader will buy and sell shares and commodities themselves. You computer will allow you to link directly with your brokerage account and make these transactions. However, there are times when your internet service has been disrupted and even your back-up service is off-line.

Should this happen and you need to sell or cancel a trade it is essential that you have quick and easy access to a phone. You will not need, or want to use your telephone to continue trading but you must be able to end a trade as soon as possible, if necessary.

A landline is perfectly acceptable, although it may be affected by the same problem which has disrupted your internet. This is when it is useful to have a cell phone available, especially if you are out and working away from home.

- Trading software

To connect with the stock market and start buying and selling shares you will need to use dedicated software. This will enable you to connect to the market in real time and buy or sell your shares. All software options will display the current price and some of the software will even display the recent price movements. In general the trading software is supplied by the brokerage you choose; it should be free of charge when you sign up for an account. The software will link through your brokers account and can even be integrated with your own programs or a third party provider; if you have some computer programming knowledge.

The majority of brokerages will also provide a free trial of the product. This is an excellent way of testing out the software and, using the demo mode to practice making trades on the market. This will allow you to become familiar with the software before you start trading and give you the opportunity to test out your strategies.

- Charting Software

As its name suggests, this piece of software will allow you to monitor the price of any stock, commodity and option. You should be able to see current prices and track trends. This will assist you in deciding when to purchase and when to sell your options to maximise your profit. There is a huge range of charting software available and it is best to try a demo of several different products before you choose one. It will become your most used tool!

For this reason it is essential that you choose one which is easy for you to read and access; generally the more expensive the software, the more features it will have. When first starting up, you should be happy with the more basic version. It is possible to download a demo and test the product out before committing to anything.

- Internet Access and a back-up plan

To connect to the stock market and your broker it is essential to have internet access. This should be reliable access with a reasonable download speed. Providing you have access of at least 256 kilobytes per second you will have no issue obtaining the information you need to make trades in a timely manner. A faster internet connection may be beneficial; if only to speed up the loading of your charts and data.

Even the best internet connection in the world is likely to have an issue from time to time. This could be an issue if you need to end a trade and cannot afford to wait. It is, therefore, essential to have a back-up plan in place. This may involve visiting a friend's house, a local cafe or even using your cell phone as a wireless hub and connecting via the data package associated with your mobile.

Whichever option you choose it will allow you to end any or all trades until the internet is restored and you can restart trading.

- Day Trading Brokerage

It is possible to trade without using a brokerage. However, this involves creating an account with each of the stock markets to enable you to trade. This is why the majority of day traders set up a brokerage account; it enables you to trade on any market. As a day trader you will need to create an account with a direct access broker as their systems will allow you to interact directly with the stock markets.

As you start to look for the right brokerage you will realise that there are literally hundreds of different ones. Some of these will specialise in offering services to the internet based home day trader, others will offer the lowest commission rates possible. It is best to choose the one that deals with the markets you intend to use first and one which is recommended by a friend or is well established with a good reputation.

- Market Data

Your market data, the information on current prices and volume of shares available, must be accurate and up to date. Many day traders use the market data provided by their brokerage. This data is usually provided for free and is posted in real time; meaning that you are looking at the same figures as though you were stood in the stock exchange.

It is possible to set up an account with a dedicated market data supplier, this will provide you with all the data you need plus some extras, such as price history and trends. As you become more experienced in day trading you may find it beneficial to have several sources of data. You cannot have too much information!

The more experienced you become in day trading the more diverse your interests will become and you may find it advantageous to have several computer screens, each one displaying different market data, you may even need to have several computers to enable fast processing of all the information and allow you to make the right trades. The decision as to which approach is best for you will be partly controlled by the amount of time you have spare and your ambitions as a day trader.

In order to understand Day Trading, it is important to know what it is not. Day Trading is not investing, which, in simple words, is the process of purchasing a stake in an asset with the hope of building a profit over time. Time, in this case, is subjective; however, investors can hold on to an asset for years or even decades.

Investors usually invest in organizations that pay off debts, make good profits, and have a good range of popular products and/or services. On the other hand, Day Trading is the process of purchasing and selling assets within the same day, often using borrowed funds to take advantage of small price shifts in highly liquid indexes or stocks.

How Day Trading Works

There was a time when the only people able to trade in financial markets were those working for trading houses, brokerages, and financial institutions. The rise of the internet, however, made things easier for individual traders to get in on the action. Day Trading, in particular, can be a very profitable career, as long as one goes about it in the right way.

However, it can be quite challenging for new traders, especially those who lack a good strategy. Furthermore, even the most experienced day traders hit rough patches occasionally. As stated earlier, Day Trading is the purchase and sale of an asset within a single trading day. It can happen in any marketplace, but it is more common in the stock and forex markets.

Day traders use short-term trading strategies and a high level of leverage to take advantage of small price movements in highly liquid currencies or stocks. Experienced day traders have their finger on events that lead to short-term price movements, such as the news, corporate earnings, economic statistics, and interest rates, which are subject to market psychology and market expectations.

When the market exceeds or fails to meet those expectations, it causes unexpected, significant moves that can benefit attuned day traders. However, venturing into this line of business is not a decision prospective day trader should take lightly. It is possible for day traders to make a comfortable living trading for a few hours each day.

However, for new traders, this kind of success takes time. Think like several months or more than a year. For most day traders, the first year is quite tough. It is full of numerous wins and losses, which can stretch anyone's nerves to the limit. Therefore, a day trader's first realistic goal should be to hold on to his/her trading capital.

Volatility is the name of the game when it comes to Day Trading. Traders rely on a market or stock's fluctuations to make money. They prefer stocks that bounce around several times a day, but do not care about the reason for those price fluctuations. Day traders will also go for stocks with high liquidity, which will allow them to enter and exit positions without affecting the price of the stock.

Day traders might short sell a stock if its price is decreasing or purchase if it is increasing. Actually, they might trade it several times in a day, purchasing it and short-selling it a number of times, based on the changing market sentiment. In spite of the trading strategy used, their wish is for the stock price to move.

Day Trading, however, is tricky for two main reasons. Firstly, day traders often compete with professionals, and secondly, they tend to have psychological biases that complicate the trading process.

Professional day traders understand the traps and tricks of this form of trading. In addition, they leverage personal connections, trading data subscriptions, and state-of-the-art technology to succeed. However, they still make losing trades. Some of these professionals are high-frequency traders whose aim is to skim pennies off every trade.

The Day Trading field is a crowded playground, which is why professional day traders love the participation of inexperienced traders. Essentially, it helps them make more money. In addition, retail traders tend to hold on to losing trades too long and sell winning trades too early.

Due to the urge to close a profitable trade to make some money, retail investors sort of pick the flowers and water the weeds. In other words, they have a strong aversion to making even a small loss. This tends to tie their hands behind their backs when it comes to purchasing a declining asset. This is due to the fear that it might decline further.

How to Start

People who want to start Day Trading should do several things to put themselves on the right path. Firstly, they need to step back and ask themselves whether this form of trading is really for them. Day Trading is not for the faint of heart. It requires a high level of focus and is not something people should risk their retirement plan to do.

Actually, beginners should consider opening a practice account before committing their hard-earned money. Reputable brokerage firms provide such accounts or stock market simulators to aspiring traders, through which they can make hypothetical trades and see the results.

In addition, aspiring day traders need to have a suitable brokerage account before they begin trading. Some brokers charge high transaction costs, which can erode the gains from winning trades. In addition, good brokers provide research resources that are invaluable to traders.

Aspiring traders who discover that Day Trading is not for them should do what smart investors do, which is engaging in long- term investing in a diversified fund or stock portfolio. They should regularly add more funds to their accounts and let the magic of growth expand their investment portfolio. This may not be as thrilling as Day Trading, but it is better than doing something that will clean out one's savings.

Consider Constraints and Goals

Before investing the time, energy, and effort in learning or creating and then practicing Day Trading, prospective day traders should consider their constraints and goals. For example:

1. Traders need to determine whether they have enough capital to engage in Day Trading. If they lack the capital, they should wait until they have it while they are learning about and practicing different trading strategies.

2. They should understand that achieving consistent gains takes several months to a year, even when practicing several hours each day. For those who practice intermittently, it will take longer to achieve success; therefore, prospective traders should put in the time and effort required to achieve their goals.

3. Once they start trading, they need to commit to trading for at least two hours a day, depending on their commitments.

4. Until their trading profits match or surpass their income, new day traders should not quit their day jobs. They also need to determine the ideal time of day to trade based on their other commitments. In addition, they should ensure that their trading strategy fits that time of day. Essentially, their trading strategy needs to fit their life.

5. People who want to venture into Day Trading need to determine whether they want to do it with the aim of quitting their regular jobs. To get to the point where they can replace their day jobs by Day Trading, prospective traders need to understand that they will probably need to practice and trade for a year or more, depending on their dedication.

Aspiring day traders should consider the factors above before investing their time and money in learning this line of trade.

Choose a Broker

While new traders are practicing and developing their trading strategies, they should set aside some time to choose a good and reputable broker. It may be the same broker they opened a demo or practice account with, or it may be another broker. Actually, choosing the right broker is one of the most important transactions day traders will make because they will entrust the broker with all of their capital.

Capital Needed to Start Day Trading

How much capital people need to start Day Trading depends on the market they trade, where they trade, and the style of trading they wish to do. There is a legal minimum capital requirement set by the stock market to day trade; however, based on the individual trading style, there is also a recommended minimum.

A day trader needs to have enough capital to have the flexibility to make a variety of trades and withstand a losing streak, which will inevitably happen. Traders also need to determine the amount of money they need, which requires them to address risk management. In addition, they should not risk more than 2% of their account on a single trade.

Capital is the most important component when it comes to Day Trading. By risking only 1% or 2%, even a long losing streak will keep most of the capital intact. For day traders in the United States, the legal minimum balance needed to day trade stocks is $25,000. Traders whose balance drops below this amount cannot engage in Day Trading until they make a deposit that brings their balance above $25,000.

To have a buffer, U.S. day traders should have at least $30,000 in their trading accounts. Stocks usually move in $0.01 increments and trade in lots of 100 shares; therefore, with at least $30,000 in their accounts, day traders will have some flexibility.

Day traders can usually get leverage up to four times the amount of their capital. A trader with $30,000 in his/her account, for example, can trade up to $120,000 worth of stock at any given time. Essentially, the trade price multiplied by the position size can equal more than the trader's account balance.

Day traders can trade fewer volatile stocks, which often require a bigger position size and a smaller stop loss, or stocks that are more volatile, with often require a smaller position size and a larger stop loss. Either way, the total risk on each trade should not be more than 2% of the trading account balance.

Day Trading Basics

Day Trading, on the surface, looks like it should be relatively easy. New day traders think it is all about making several simple trades as the price moves, making a little money, and repeating the whole process tomorrow. However, many dangers lurk in the Day Trading markets; unfortunately, a large percentage of new day traders are not aware of these dangers.

Some of the pitfalls for day traders include:

- Lack of Risk Management

Often new day traders often lack risk management protocols, which is a huge danger. Sometimes, they have an incomplete strategy for managing risk. Nevertheless, they are usually optimistic about their Day Trading abilities, which often causes them to overlook critical risk management steps. Establishing a basic risk management strategy involves the following steps:

- A Stop Loss

Traders should place a stop-loss order in each trade they make to control their risk. People who are starting out on Day Trading should limit their risk on each trade to 1% of their trading account balance. The difference between their entry price and stop-loss price, multiplied by their position size, is their risk.

• A Daily Limit

A daily-stop loss limit can help day traders by limiting how much money they can lose in a day. If day traders suffer multiple losing trades each day, they may still find themselves down more than 10% in a single day. A typical daily-stop loss limit should not be more than about 3% of a trader's account.

Therefore, if the trader loses 3% on any given day, he/she will stop trading for that day. As day traders develop a profitable trading record and gain experience, they can adjust their daily- stop loss limit to be equal to their average profitable trading day. By placing this limit, a typical winning day will recoup the losses from a single day.

Improperly Tested or Untested Trading Strategies

New day traders are often so eager to start trading and make money that they start using untested or improperly tested trading strategies with real money. Others, however, try out their strategies on demo accounts, and if they make a few successful trades, they immediately start trading with real money. Unfortunately, both of these approaches will probably lead to future disappointment.

Successful day traders, on the other hand, test their strategies on many different market conditions through demo trading to learn the pros and cons of their strategies before using them with real money. They demo trade for several months until they are comfortable with their Day Trading strategies before risking real capital with their strategies.

Broker

Choosing the right broker is one of the most important trades for a day trader. Day traders deposit their capital with their brokers, and yet some of them do not take the time to research their broker until a problem arises. Scam brokers, for example, can pop up anywhere.

Traders who find themselves working with such a broker will find it very difficult or even impossible to withdraw their money and any profits. Fortunately, scam brokers usually do not last long thanks to forum complaints. Therefore, a careful online search will reveal any problems with a broker.

A more subtle broker problem is constantly slow quotes. Day traders need direct and uninterrupted access to their broker, who then sends their orders to the appropriate exchange. They should test their broker's trading software because poor software will make it hard to execute trades in a timely manner.

Technology

No one is immune to technology problems. For example, computers can crash, power can go out, the internet can go down, and much more. Day traders cannot get out of a losing trade quickly if technology fails; therefore, they need to place a stop- loss order on every trade.

In addition, they need to program their broker's phone number into their cell phone and landline phone, so they can call them quickly in case of a problem. It is a good idea to have a mobile version of their trading platform on their internet-enabled mobile devices, which might still be operational if their computer crashes.

Order Types

The profits and losses day traders make come from the orders they place. Day traders should know their order types for getting in and out of a market order or a limit order. They also need to know how to set profit targets and stop-loss orders, both for going short and long.

For professional day traders, placing orders is automatic, like switching on a car's turn signal, when about to change lanes. Day traders who do not know their order types will have slow and clumsy trading or even place the wrong order type, which will cost them money.

It is normal for some trading mistakes to happen; however, compounding such mistakes with order-related trading mistakes is a recipe for disaster. Before they start trading, new day traders should know their order types.

Trader Personality and Tendencies

Another hidden danger for a new day trader is his/her personality and tendencies. In the beginning, Day Trading will be confusing, infuriating, and stressful in a way a new trader never thought it could. There are endless possibilities in the markets, and no one cares what anyone else is doing.

This freedom, however, can be unnerving and dangerous for many traders, which is why many of them lose money. When people are starting out, they do not know how they will react under different stresses and pressures. Some choose to quit, others to overtrade, and others still are too afraid to trade.

Many distractions keep people from staying focused and trading effectively. Traders should take a critical look at their personality to identify their shortcomings and then work to develop these six important Day Trading traits.

Day Trading Tools

For you to carry out day trading successfully there are several tools that you need. Some of these tools are freely available, while others must be purchased. Modern trading is not like the traditional version. This means that you need to get online to access day trading opportunities.

Therefore, the number one tool you need is a laptop or computer with an internet connection. The computer you use must have enough memory for it to process your requests fast enough. If your computer keeps crashing or stalling all the time, you will miss out on some lucrative opportunities. There are trading platforms that need a lot of memory to work, and you must always put this into consideration.

Your internet connection must also be fast enough. This will ensure that your trading platform loads in real-time. Ensure that you get an internet speed that processes data instantaneously to avoid experiencing any data lag. Due to some outages that occur with most internet providers, you may also need to invest in a backup internet device such as a smartphone hotspot or modem. Other essential tools and services that you need include:

Brokerage

To succeed in day trading, you need the services of a brokerage firm. The work of the firm is to conduct your trades. Some brokers are experienced in day trading than others. You must ensure that you get the right day trading broker who can help you make more profit from your transactions. Since day trading entails several trades per day, you need a broker that offers lower commission rates. You also need one that provides the best software for your transactions. If you prefer using specific trading software for your deals, then look for a broker that allows you to use this software.

Real-time Market Information

Market news and data are essential when it comes to day trading. They provide you with the latest updates on current and anticipated price changes on the market. This information allows you to customize your strategies accordingly. Professional day traders always spend a lot of money seeking this kind of information on news platforms, in online forums or through any other reliable channels.

Financial data is often generated from price movements of specific stocks and commodities. Most brokers have this information. However, you will need to specify the kind of data you need for your trades. The type of data to get depends on the type of stocks you wish to trade.

Monitors

Most computers have a capability that enables them to connect to more than one monitor. Due to the nature of the day trading business, you need to track market trends, study indicators, follow financial news items, and monitor price performance at the same time. For this to be possible, you need to have more than one processor so that the above tasks can run concurrently.

Classes

Although you can engage in day trading without attending any school, you must get trained on some of the strategies you need to succeed in the business. For instance, you may decide to enroll for an online course to acquire the necessary knowledge in the business. You may have all the essential tools in your possession, but if you do not have the right experience, all your efforts may go to waste.

Day Trading Pricing Charts

Charts are used by traders to monitor price changes. These changes determine when to enter or exit a trading position. There are several charts used in day trading. Although these charts differ in terms of functionality and layout, they typically offer the same information to day traders.

Some of the most common day trading charts includes:

1. Line charts

2. Bar charts

3. Candlestick charts

For each of the above charts, you must understand how they work as well as the advantages/ disadvantages involved.

Line Charts

These are very popular in all kinds of stock trading. They do not give the opening price, just the closing price. You are expected to specify the trading period for the chart to display the closing price for that period. The chart creates a line that connects closing prices for different periods using a line.

Most day traders use this chart to establish how the price of a security has performed over different periods. However, you cannot rely on this chart as the only information provider when it comes to making some critical trading decisions. This is because the chart only gives you the closing price. This means that you may not be able to establish other vital factors that have contributed to the current changes in the price.

Bar Charts

These are lines used to indicate price ranges for a particular stock over time. Bar charts comprise vertical and horizontal lines. The horizontal lines often represent the opening and closing costs. When the closing price is higher than the opening price, the horizontal line is always black. When the opening price is higher, the line becomes red.

Bar charts offer more information than line charts. They indicate opening prices, highest and lowest prices as well as the closing prices. They are always easy to read and interpret. Each bar represents rice information. The vertical lines indicate the highest and lowest prices attained by a particular stock. The opening price of a stock is always shown using a small horizontal line on the left of each vertical line. The closing price is a small horizontal line on the right.

Interpreting bar charts is not as easy as interpreting line charts. When the vertical lines are long, it shows that there is a significant difference between the highest price attained by a security and the lowest price. Large vertical lines, therefore, indicate that the commodity is highly volatile while small lines indicate slight price changes. When the closing price is far much higher than the opening price, it means that the buyers were more during the stated period. This indicates likelihood for more purchases in the future. If the closing price is slightly higher than the purchase price, then very little purchasing took place during the period. Bar chart information is always differentiated using color codes. You must, therefore, understand what each color means as this will help you to know whether the price is going up or down.

Advantages of bar charts

- They display a lot of data in a visual format

- They summarize large amounts of data

- They help you to estimate important price information in advance

- They indicate each data category as a different color

- Exhibit high accuracy

- Easy to understand

Disadvantages

- They need adequate interpretation

- Wrong interpretation can lead to false information

- Do not explain changes in the price patterns

Tick charts

Tick charts are not common in day trading. However, some traders use these charts for various purposes. Each bar on the chart represents numerous transactions. For instance, a 415 chart generates a bar for a group of 415 trade positions. One great advantage of tick charts is that they enable traders to enter and exit multiple positions quickly. This is what makes the charts ideal for day traders who transact volumes of stock each day.

These charts work by completing several trades before displaying a new bar. Unlike other charts, these charts work depending on the activity of each transaction, not on time. You can use them if you need to make faster decisions in your trade. Another advantage of tick charts is that you can customize each chart to suit your trading needs. You can apply the chart on diverse transaction sizes. The larger the size, the higher the potential of making a profit from the trade.

When used in day trading, tick hart works alongside the following three indicators:

- RSI indicators – these are used when trading highly volatile securities. They help you establish when a particular security is oversold or overbought since these are the periods when stock prices change significantly.

- Momentum – day traders use this together with tick charts to show how active the stock price is and whether the activity is genuine or fake. If the price rises significantly, yet the momentum is the same, this indicates a warning sign. Stocks with positive momentum are ideal for long trades. You should avoid these if you wish to close your positions within a day.

- Volume indicators – these are used to confirm the correct entry and exit points for each trade. Large trading positions are often indicated using larger volume bars while low positions with little volatility are displayed using small volume bars.

Candlestick Charts

Candlestick charts are used on almost every trading platform. These charts carry a lot of information about the stock market and stock prices. They help you to get information about the opening, closing, highest, and lowest stock prices on the market. The opening price is always indicated as the first bar on the left of the chart, and the closing price is on the far right of the chart. Besides these prices, the candlestick chart also contains the body and wick. These are the features that differentiate the candlestick for other day trading charts.

One great advantage of candlestick charts entails the use of different visual aspects when indicating the closing, opening, highest, and lowest stock prices. These charts compute stock prices across different time frames. Each chart consists of three segments:

- The upper shadow

- The body

- The lower shadow

The body of the chart is often red or green in color. Each candlestick is an illustration of time. The data in the candlestick represents the number of trades completed within the specified time. For instance, a 10-minute candlestick indicates 10 minutes of trading. Each candlestick has four points, and each point represents a price. The high point represents the highest stock price while low stands for the lowest price of a stock. When the closing price is lower than the opening price, the body of the candlestick will be red in color. When the closing price is higher, the body will be colored green.

There are several types of candlesticks that you can use in day trading. One is the Heikin-Ashi chart that helps you to filter any unwanted information from the chart data, ending up with a more accurate indication of the market trend. Novice day traders commonly use this chart because of how clear it displays information.

The Renko chart only displays the changes in time. It does not give you any volume or time information. When the price exceeds the highest or lowest points reached before, the chart displays it as a new brick. The brick is white when the price is going up and black when the price is declining.

Lastly, the Kagi chart is used when you want to follow the direction of the market quickly. When the price goes higher than previous prices, the chart displays a thick line. When the price starts to decline, the line reduces in thickness.

Each of the above charts works using a time frame which is represented using the X-axis. This time frame always indicates the volume of information represented by the chart. Time frames can be in the form of standard time or in the form of the number of trades completed within a specified period as well as the price range.

The software helps you identify the right opportunities by indicating when and how you should start and close positions. They always display the necessary patterns required to estimate future changes in stock prices. Using stock patterns, you can also establish continuations as well as reversals in the stock prices.

Chart software is available in many forms. You may find those that are in the form of mobile apps or others that are web-based. Getting the right software enables you to generate correct charts. This explains why you also need to incorporate technical analysis in your trades.

Most day trading chart tools are available free of charge. Some have a forum where you can learn from experienced traders as you use them. They also come with demo accounts that enable you to master day trading techniques before investing your capital in the business.

How to Choose Day Trading Charts

Before selecting any charts for your day trading engagements, you must consider a number of factors. These include:

Responsiveness - This refers to how quickly the chart can display information about the changing market features. This is the first and most important factor you should always check out for. Any delay in the way a chart displays data means that you will not receive vital information in real-time. You may end up acting on old information to make your decisions, and this can lead to significant losses on your part. Most charts may freeze or crash when your computer runs out of memory. This explains why you need a fast processing machine for your day trading business. You want to ensure that the whole process remains as efficient as possible. When testing a chart for responsiveness, wait for a time when the stock market is busy. For instance, you may try using the chart during a critical financial announcement or news session. If the chart freezes at this point, then you will understand that it is not the best for your needs.

Cost – every trader wants to invest in tools that cost less to acquire and maintain. Years back, trading charts used to cost a fortune. This limited the number of traders that could engage in day trading. For instance, traders could buy market data from stock exchanges, and this would also cost a lot of money.

There are several alternatives available on the market today for you to select from. As you do this, always have the price in mind.

Stability – a good chart is one that remains online and up to date all the time. For you to succeed as a day trader, you must remain on the market most of the time. If your chart keeps disconnecting from the stock market or fails to display market information on time, then it will make you incur more losses. You must, therefore, ensure that you remain connected to the market continuously. If you experience instability as a result of the chart software you are using, feel free to change it. If the instability is resulting from a poor internet connection, you may need to replace it too.

Type of Indicators – if you have ever engaged in day trading before then you understand the importance of technical indicators. Having the right indicators plays a vital role in ensuring you predict the right price movements in the future. Indicators help you to save a lot of capital. They prevent you from making important investment and financial mistakes that may lead to losing your capital. You may create your own indicators, or you may get charting software that has in-built indicators. If you decide to use your own indicators, you must ensure that the charting tools you purchase can be used together with these indicators. If not you might need to stick to those indicators supplied together with your charting software.

Compatibility with your computer – before settling for any charts, check whether it will work well with your current computer resources. This is an important factor as it will determine whether you will continue to use your old machine, or if you will have to purchase a new one. Some charts require a lot of RAM space. If your computer does not have this capability, you will end up adding more RAM. This translates to more yet unnecessary costs. When you are looking around for a chart, ensure that you check how much resources the charts will need. Most chart packages have an indication of the minimum requirements you need for the charts to work well. If this is not clearly stated, make sure you ask your provider about it so that you do not make a blind purchase.

User-friendly - a good chart should be easy to use, read, and interpret. A complicated chart will only make your trading days difficult. Get a chart that simplifies the work of interpreting data. Take your time and research on the available options then choose the best in terms of simplicity and layout. You may consider getting recommendations from other traders, although this does not necessarily mean that the said chart will work for you. Having a complicated chart can make you lose your confidence. You must, therefore, avoid it if you want to have a smooth trading experience

End-user support – once in a while, your chart software may experience a problem that needs technical assistance. As you continue using the software, questions may arise that need the attention of an expert. If the provider is not available to assist or respond to your questions, you may get stuck using the package. Before making a purchase, ensure that you find out the kind of technical support you will receive and how this will be done. Is it via live chat, email, or telephone contact? You can also go through some customer reviews just to understand if the service provider has a history of supporting its clients on technical matters. In case you need a highly responsive system, you may need to avoid those platforms that use the support ticket criteria. Companies that use this criterion to solve customer problems always take a long time to respond to even the most critical issues.

Charts play an essential role, and you can use timed as well as ticked charts for successful day trading. Always remember that different tools are designed for different kinds of trades. You must understand the kind of tools you need as a day trader so that you do not struggle on the market.

Day traders can use technical indicators to provide trading signals and assess the current trade. Keltner Channels, a popular technical indicator, use average prices and volatility to plot lower, middle, and upper lines. These three lines move with the price to create the appearance of a channel.

Chester Keltner introduced these channels in the 1960s, but Linda Bradford Raschke updated them in the 1980s. Today, traders use the later version of the indicator, which is a combination of two different indicators, which are the average true range and the exponential moving average.

Created by J. Welles Wilder Jr. and introduced in 1978, the average true range is a measure of volatility. The moving average, on the other hand, is the average price for specific periods, with the exponential variation giving more weight to recent prices and less weight to less recent prices.

Keltner Channels are useful to day traders because they make trends more visible. When a certain asset or stock is trending higher, its price will frequently come close, touch, or even move past the upper band. In addition, the price will stay above the lower band and middle band, although it might occasionally barely dip below the middle band.

When an asset or stock is trending lower, on the other hand, its price will regularly come close to the lower band or reach it; however, sometimes it will move past the lower band. The price will stay below the upper band and often below the middle band.

Day traders should set up their indicators so that these guidelines hold true, at least most of the time. If the price of a stock is moving constantly higher but not reaching the upper band, the channel may be too wide, and the trader will need to decrease the multiplier. However, an asset that is trending higher but constantly touching the lower band shows that the channel is too tight, requiring an increase of the multiplier.

For their indicator to help them analyze the market, day traders need to adjust it correctly. If they fail to do this, then the guidelines for trading will not hold true, and the indicator will not serve its intended purpose. Once they set up the indicator correctly, day traders should purchase during an uptrend when the price of the asset pulls back to the middle band.

They should place a target price somewhere near the upper band and a stop-loss order halfway between the lower and middle bands. On the other hand, if the price of the asset is hitting the stop-loss too often, and the trader has already made the necessary

adjustments, he/she should move the stop-loss a bit closer to the lower band. This will give the trade more wiggle room and reduce the number of losing trades the trader has. During a downtrend, when the price of the asset rallies to the middle band, day traders should short sell, which means selling the asset with the hope of buying it back at a lower price.

It is also important to place a target near the lower band and a stop-loss order about halfway between the upper and middle bands. This trading strategy leverages the trending tendency and provides trades with a 0.5 risk to reward ratio. This is because the stop-loss point is approximately half the length of that of the target price.

However, traders should not trade all pullbacks to the middle line. If a trend is not present, this strategy will not work effectively. Sometimes, the price of the asset moves back and forth between hitting the lower and upper bands. This method will not be effective in such situations.

Therefore, day traders should ensure the market's pattern is following the trending guidelines. If it is not doing so, they should use a different strategy. The Keltner Channel strategy tries to capture big moves that may evade the trend-pullback strategy. Day traders should use it near the opening of a major market when big movements happen.

The typical trading strategy is to purchase when the price breaks the upper band or sell short when it drops below the lower band within the first 30 minutes of the market opening. The middle band, however, acts as the exit point. This type of trade does not have a profit target. Traders simply exit the trade whenever the price touches the middle band, whether the trade is a winner or a loser.

Introduction to Investing in Stocks, Options, and Forex When most people hear the term Day Trading, they think of the stock market. However, day traders also participate in the forex and futures markets. Some day traders, for example, trade options, but most traders who do so are more likely swing traders who can hold positions for weeks or days, but not fractions of a trading day.

People who want to be successful day traders should initially focus on a single market, such as the stock market. Once they master that market, they can try to learn and practice trading other markets if they choose.

Day Trading Stocks

Those who are thinking of Day Trading stocks should consider a few important factors. These are:

1.   Under U.S. law, the minimum starting capital for Day Trading stocks is $25,000. However, they need to add a buffer above this amount and start with a capital of at least $30,000.

2.   Market hours for Day Trading are from 9:30 am to 4 pm Eastern time. However, traders can still place trades one hour before the market opens.

3.   The ideal periods to day trade stocks are from 8.30 to

10.30 am and 3 to 4 pm ET, when volatility and volume are high.

4.   Day traders can trade a wide variety of stocks. They can also trade the same stock or a small number of stocks every day, or find new stocks to trade each week or even each day.

Based on these factors, prospective day traders will determine whether the stock market is a good option for their Day Trading. If they do not have the initial capital required, for example, they should consider the futures or forex markets, which require less starting capital.

In addition, if they cannot trade during the most ideal trading hours, their efforts will not produce as much fruit as they would have if they were available during those optimal hours.

Day Trading Futures

Some of the important things to consider about Day Trading futures include:

1. There is no legal minimum starting capital required to begin Day Trading futures. Experts, however, recommend starting with $2,500 to $7,000 if one is trading the popular futures contract. The more money one starts with, the more flexible one will be when it comes to making trading decisions.

2. The official market hours for trading the S&P 500 and E- mini are from 9.30 am to 4 pm ET.

3. The optimal time to day trade ES futures is from 6.30 to 1030am and 3 to 4p Eastern time.

4. Commodities futures contracts also provide reliable Day Trading opportunities.

5.   Most day traders who deal with futures often focus on one futures contract; however, others choose futures contracts seeing significant volume or movements on a particular day.

Day Trading Forex

Things to know about Day Trading forex include:

1.   The minimum starting capital required is $500; however, experts recommend starting with $5,000 if one wants a decent monthly income stream.

2.   Forex trades 24 hours a day; however, certain times are ideal for Day Trading than others.

3.   Day traders can trade any different currency pairs, but beginners should stick to the GBP/USD or EUR/USD. These two currency pairs offer more than enough price movement and volume to generate a good income.

Based on these three factors, day traders will likely determine whether this market is appropriate for them to day trade. Those with limited capital should consider Day Trading the forex market, which is more flexible than other markets.

Social Trading

Social trading works somewhat like a social network. However, there is a big difference, which is that instead of sharing pet photos, dinner photos, and selfies, people use social trading networks to share trading ideas. Essentially, traders use this platform to interact, brainstorm and watch the trading results of other professionals in real-time.

Some of the benefits of social trading include:

      1. Access to reliable and helpful trading information

      2. Ability to earn while learning

      3. Quick understanding of the trading market

      4. Ability to build a trading community of investors

Since social trading networks cater for both professionals and beginners, they create a reliable trading community, which allows day traders and other types of market traders to generate an income as they learn.

The allure of this form of financial trading is undeniable. It is more exciting for a trader to earn a living working from the comfort of his/her home, rather than working a regular 9 am to 5 pm gig. However, inexperienced or careless day traders can destroy their portfolios within a few days.

Chapter 2: Risk Management and Account Management

Both account and risk management exercises are activities that coincide as you go through the Day Trading investment cycle. It is very important for you to ensure that you achieve your aims of making significant profits, while at the same time, mitigating losses from the capital in which you invested.

Managing your account and the risks associated with Day Trading involves the responsible handling of the available equity in your brokerage account. You can perform account management through further investment in profitable stocks, ingenious trade maneuverability, or exiting from trade deals that stagnate.

On the other hand, your risk management strategies involve responding appropriately to alleviate prospective losses in an uncertain future and limiting the degree of your exposure to financial risks. The following are some of the primary strategies that you can apply to your Day Trading to ensure active risk and account management:

Hire a Stockbroker

As a beginner or a new investor participating in Day Trading, it could turn challenging if you went at it alone. You need advice on the right stock opportunities in which to invest, guidelines on how to handle probable financial risk exposures, and knowledge of technical analysis to keep track of your capital progress.

A qualified and registered stockbroker typically offers these financial services at a commission or flat fee. You need to seek the assistance of such stockbrokers to tap into their experience and expertise in Day Trading. Besides, the chances of attaining your profitable goals increase when you employ the services of a stockbroker.

Account management and risk management are strategies that are innate to a stockbroker, especially when given access to the account. Therefore, you need to open a brokerage account from which all your Day Trading activities take place. Maintaining liquidity in this account is as essential as making the right trade deals.

Since you may not interact with the stock market all the time, running the trading account becomes the responsibility of your stockbroker. You need to give him or her freedom to make informed choices on long and short trades, however risky they might seem at first. Trust your broker to understand what he or she is doing with the account and hence the need to hire an honest stockbroker, preferably from a well-known brokerage firm.

In addition, it is usual for your stockbroker to have extensive experience with managing financial risks. Most of the strategies meant to combat potential financial threats such as spreads are somewhat complex to understand, let alone apply them effectively. The same levels of complications and fair sophistication apply to the tools used for technical analyses.

You need to follow these analytic tools to make informed choices based on their data. A stockbroker comes in handy at this point to assist in data interpretation. You also get to learn about the various management strategies of which you had no idea previously. Generally, account and risk management in Day Trading is often all about making the correct decisions from technical analysis.

Develop a Trading Plan

This document is a crucial tool for you as a new investor in Day Trading. If you do not possess such a program, then it may be time to develop one that tailors to your specific trading. Creating a trading plan is an activity that you need to perform with the help of your stockbroker. The broker typically has experience in the Day Trading sector, and so he or she can offer you pointers on the trading opportunities that have the potential of being productive. Based on this vital tip, you can create a comprehensive trading plan that contains an overall objective that is set out. Besides, the program should have tactical or short-term goals set at regular intervals during the cycle. The primary purpose of these operational targets is to enable you to keep track of the progress of your Day Trading activities.

Once you complete the creation of a trading plan, you must stick to its guidelines at all times. You and your broker need to have a chance at Day Trading's success. Hence, you both have to adhere to the rules of the trading plan. It sets out instructions on how you should react and what measures to take with your capital under different situations. Since the future of Day Trading is often uncertain, it is essential for your plan to cover emergency financial responses. If you diligently adhere to your trading plan, your likelihood of attaining profitable returns eventually increases significantly. In addition, you will have a policy of intervention to potentially risky financial exposures.

Maintain Simplicity

In Day Trading, you may falsely believe that you need to overextend yourself on high-risk investments to make substantial amounts of return. This belief is a dangerous position for you to adopt when getting into Day Trading. Keep in mind the notion that the underlying stocks are often a more volatile type of security than other investments. Fluctuations in the value of the traded stock are frequent and typically occur over a relatively short period.

You must learn how to make small trade deals on the stock from the low-risk end of the trading spectrum. Beware of succumbing to the desire to stick your neck out for the riskier stocks. Greed and emotional influence are the leading causes of such irresponsible trading practices. In the case of a specific trade deal turning awful, you need to exercise restraint from the urge to make illogical trading decisions to try to cover your previous loss.

Besides, keep an eye out for volatile stocks and avoid trading in them as much as possible. If you can, distance yourself and your portfolio from such stocks. Ask your broker to let go of highly fluctuating stocks entirely due to their corresponding high levels of financial risk. All these missteps are easily avoidable when you stick to the simple trading practices laid out in your trading plan.

As a result, you will evade massive losses associated with complicated, high-risk trading that is subject to a high level of emotional influence. Proper and responsible account management demands that you avoid rash decisions that may lead to prospective losses and missing out on potential profits. Risk management also takes care of itself by minimizing your exposure to the high-risk end of the trading spectrum and keeping clear of volatile stocks.

Establish a Stop-Loss Level

To manage the amount of risk to which you are willing to expose your trading portfolio, you can issue orders that reverse potentially hurtful financial positions. A stop-loss order limits the amount of stock price that you can tolerate without taking a significant financial hit.

This order enables your stockbroker to cease all the Day Trading activities immediately. It allows him or her to instantly stop either buying or selling any further stocks based on the unfavorable prices. The order indicates the specific stock price beyond which you cannot risk either purchasing or offloading, respectively, because doing so would expose you to an apparent financial loss.

Getting into an apparent losing situation is an irresponsible practice on your part. Eventually, you will end up with a depleted brokerage account due to the mismanagement of the available capital that you previously had. Stop-loss orders are especially useful when conducting Day Trading on volatile stocks. It is advisable to set the stop-loss order to an amount that is as close as possible to your trading entry point.

Besides, close monitoring of the fluctuating price of your particular stock is a must to ensure the successful execution of the order when required. As you can realize, when used in this manner on the volatile stocks, such stop-loss orders act as risk management tools that mitigate the financial downside associated with rapidly fluctuating stocks.

Determine Your Position Size

Position sizing involves making decisions on the amount of capital with which you intend to take part in particular day trade. The size of your investment is directly proportional to the level of risk exposure. A high-volume trade will invariably expose you to more financial risks than a small number of trade deals.

Your brokerage account will often get caught in the crosshairs of high-risk transactions and Day Trading practices. Exhaustion of the amount of available capital in your trading account becomes even more likely. Therefore, an early determination of your trading position is essential before engaging in any form of transaction. Your position size divides into an account and trade risk based on the number of shares of stock that you acquire on a particular trade.

For you to minimize any potential financial downfall resulting from the degree of your account risk, you must set a limit on the amount of capital to trade in each deal or transaction. A fixed ratio or small percentage is often the recommended format for this account limit. Maintaining consistency is vital in setting these account restrictions.

Do not keep altering the allocated portion for different trading deals. You should pick one value and apply it to all of your transactions during the Day Trading. A preferable limit should be one percent of your available capital balance or less. Make sure to adhere to the strategy of simplicity by making only small amounts of capital allocations to the low-risk stocks.

In addition to the risks to your trading account, the other financial exposure from position sizing concerns the trade risk. The best strategy to counteract trade risk involves the use of stop- loss orders. The gap between the entry point to your Day Trading and the specific numerical amount set as the limit on the order constitutes your trade risk. As earlier mentioned, this order enables you or your stockbroker to exit from a trade deal upon reaching the set limit of loss. This action results in capping further loss of capital; hence, it contributes to managing financial risk in this manner.

Consequently, you should execute stop-loss orders close to your trading entry point to minimize the likelihood of potential losses spiraling out of control. Be careful not to set it excessively tight to inhibit your ability to carry out any trading. Position sizing is responsible for both account and risk management. The evasive maneuvers described usually contribute towards minimizing risk.

Remember to allow for some flexibility when setting the restriction value on a stop-loss order. You need this leeway to give your stocks a chance to increase in value without encountering an obstacle in the form of the stop-loss order. Such moves enable you to maintain a healthy trading account. As previously mentioned, the number of shares needed for a potentially profitable trade relates to your ideal position size, as shown below.

The ideal number of shares required (Position Size) = Account risk / Trade risk.

Tips for Successful Day Trading and Big Profits

Every trader wants to beat the system; to find the share that shoots up in value and makes them a fortune overnight. Unfortunately, in reality there are very few opportunities like this. Amassing a personal fortune through the stock market is achievable, but it is usually achieved by regularly making small amounts of money and learning from the inevitable losses. Those who stick to a plan and build their funds slowly, using their initial investment and not the profits, can make exceptionally good profits and a comfortable standard of living.

To assist you in achieving the desired results it is essential to apply the following tips to your day trading techniques:

1. Don't Trade Every Day!

This may seem like a surprising piece of advice to give to a day trader; someone who by the very definition of the role trades in a day! However, any type of trading is incredibly stressful. There are days when your trades will go exceptionally well and you will feel like you are on top of the world. On other days the market has gone against you and you will not know which way to turn.

To ensure you stay sane and you have the right attitude when you approach your computer and start trading, you should not commit to trading every day. As a day trader you should have closed all your deals out at the end of the day so, whatever the financial position, you can afford to take a day off. In order to be a good day trader you need to have a healthy life / work balance; this means not being afraid to take a day off, the market will still be there the next day. Even if a great deal happens on your day off there is no guarantee you would have spotted it in the heat of the moment.

<u>2.</u>   <u>*Supply & Demand*</u>

The most effective way of finding the right shares to trade in isto study the market as a whole. You need to locate the places where there is a supply and demand imbalance. This is where more people want the shares than there are sellers, or there are more shares than buyers. These are the shares which are most likely to make you a profit as the market will automatically rebalance itself.

The bigger the imbalance in the availability and requirement for shares the bigger the potential profit. If shares are plentiful and the demand is low then their price will be low. As they get bought they will become rarer and this will force the demand up. The higher the demand is; the higher the price which can be charged.

These imbalances can be created very quickly and will correct themselves quickly. You need to be vigilant when surveying the markets and act quickly when you see the right criteria.

3. _Price Targets_

A price target is an amount that you will sell at, or an amount that you will buy at. Your selling price is often worked out as a percentage of your buying price; this ensures you can allow for any transaction fees and still make a profit.

It is essential to set these prices as soon as you purchase any stock; if you have not already decided the values before. You then need to stick to them. One of the most important elements to becoming a successful day trader is not to be too greedy. If the shares reach your pre-set target then you sell; holding on to make a little extra profit is likely to backfire and cost you a lot of money. You must be content that your calculations are correct and that you are making a profit.

4. _Reward Ratio_

There are many traders who will tell you that the reward ratio is useless. In fact, this means that they do not understand it and how to use it to improve their trading average. Used in conjunction with the other tools and good research it can be an invaluable strategy.

In essence the reward ratio specifies that the reward for every trade deal must be three times the risk associated with the deal. This rule means that for every dollar you invest and risk losing, you should expect to get three dollars back. This is an excellent ratio to adhere to when first starting out; as your experience and knowledge grows you may be comfortable reducing this ratio.

As well as using this simple calculation when deciding whether to purchase stock or not; it can be used to assist with managing your position during stock transactions and whether to sell your stock or not.

5. *Discipline*

It is important to remain emotionally detached from your stock purchases and act in accordance with the right business decision for each scenario. This takes discipline and it an important strategy to ensure successful trading. Failing to stick to your own rules and principles will leave you exposed in a deal for longer than you need to be and can result in huge losses when you could have made a healthy profit. The market can be very volatile and it is important to stick to the plan you have made.

It can be very easy to watch your share prices rise and believe they will keep on doing so, instead of sticking to your business tactics you allow yourself to become emotionally involved and attached to your shares; this can spell disaster! You have spent the time devising the right plan for your situation and must have the discipline to stick to your plan.

6.   *Losses*

Even if you are the best organized and most cautious day trader in the world you will, at times, have losses. This is an inevitable part of any kind of stock market trading. It is essential to accept this and accept any loss when it happens. Assuming you have only invested funds you can afford to lose, it is not the end of the word and you will make money a different day.

Losses only become an issue if you make it one; you must deal with them; learn from the mistake you made and then move on. There is no benefit in going over them again and again.

7.   *Budget*

As already mentioned, day trading is not a get rich quick scheme; it takes hard work and dedication, as well as good planning. Part of your planning stage, before you even start trading, should be to work out your budget. You will need funds available to make your first trade; you will also need to purchase a good computer or desktop; if you do not already have one. Alongside this you will need to download and install the right software. Many brokers will provide software when you set up a brokerage account. You need to ensure you are comfortable with their package and possibly allow funds to add additional packages such as data monitoring or an independent trading software solution.

Your budget will ensure you have enough start up capital to purchase all the equipment you may need and to start trading. There is no minimum amount required to start trading from home, although many online accounts ask for a minimum initial deposit. The more funds you have available the more deals you can try; each one will help you understand which is the right approach for your personality and investment type.

8. *Trading Personality*

Your personality will shape the type of trading you should undertake. If you have the ability to make quick decisions and often do so then you are likely to be good at scalping. Each trade lasts only a few seconds or minutes, before the next one requires a decision.

Alternatively, you may prefer to study all the facts, and then base your decision on these facts and your own personal experience. If you are one of these people then you are more likely to be comfortable and good at long term trading or possibly swing trading. These are trading styles which will give you the opportunity to think through the various angles before reacting.

As well as the ability to make quick decisions there are a variety of other factors which will help you decide which type of trading to undertake:

- **Patience** - the less patient you are the better you are at short term investments.

- **Emotional Vulnerability** – If you are unable to turn off your emotions you may struggle to stick to your own trading rules.

- **Ability to be flexible** – This can be an important trait in some areas of the market

- **Passion** – The more passion you have for the subject the better your inclinations and commitment will be. This trait is essential to being a successful trader.

9.   *The Market*

You need to choose the right market for your personality, time available and even the time of day you would prefer to trade during. There are many different markets and you can choose to day trade in all of these markets. But, when you first start day trading it is advisable to start in one market and work your way up to two, three or even four!

Technology has made it possible to trade in any market around the world, this means that even if your preferred or only available time to trade is between midnight and six in the morning you will be able to trade in one of these markets. This will be one of your deciding factors. The most common markets are the stock exchange and the currency market; but the strategies this book teaches you will apply to any market.

10.   *Demos*

Whether you choose to use the software supplied by your brokerage account or something from an independent firm you are almost certain to be offered the chance to try the software first. It is essential to try out the software; it may be the best product in the world but if you are not comfortable finding your way round it then it will not be the right one for you.

The same applies to the idea of trading on the stock market. The majority of brokers will give you access to a free 'demo' software which will allow you to trade on the stock exchange but without risking any of your money and without making any money. This is an excellent way to build your knowledge of the trading markets and improve your skills.

11. *Trading Plan*

As with any business venture you need a plan. The trading plan will cover your financial abilities and the markets you intend to trade in. It will also cover your risk and how exposed you are prepared to be. A good plan should assess your current skill set to confirm you are ready to start trading; this is a physical and mental state. The plan will also help you to establish your goals and give you something to work for. This may be becoming good enough to make ten successful trades every week; it may even be having a set percentage success rate for your trades.

Whatever goals you choose to set yourself you will need to break them down into achievable smaller goals and then work towards these goals week by week.

Part of your plan should also include making sure you have the time to research your potential investments properly.

<u>12.</u>   <u>*Trading Journal*</u>

Your journal should be filled in daily; it should be a record of your trades, your profits and your losses. Perhaps most importantly you should make notes regarding your thoughts of possible investments and which ones actually performed as expected. This journal will provide you with valuable insights as you continue to trade. It will illustrate to you when you should trust your judgement and can inspire confidence in your operating techniques.

It can also give you some useful information regarding how specific shares reacted in a variety of market conditions. This type of information can be extremely beneficial as you continue and improve your day trading technique.

13. *Flexibility*

Once you have put your own rules into place and become accustomed to working within those rules you will be able to adopt a slightly more flexible attitude. This is not an excuse to say that you can ignore your own rules and chase extra profit! Adopting a flexible approach simple means that you are able to appreciate when a market opportunity outside of your intended scope presents itself to you and that you are not afraid to act on it.

The rules concerning risk and reward still apply but you are not so rigid as to miss an opportunity. The longer you trade and the more experience you gain the more you will see opportunities.

14. *Analysis*

One of the most important things you should do regularly to ensure you become a successful and profitable trader, is to examine your trades and work out when you made the right decision. It may become apparent that there are several occasions when you made the same mistake or even the right decision. You can then study this and work out whether this decision could be applied to other market areas to achieve similar results.

Looking over your performance also helps to keep you grounded as it reminds you that not all your trades work out perfectly. It is one of the best ways of discovering your mistakes and learning from them to ensure you are a better trader in the future.

15.   *Confidence*

Being confident is not the same as being arrogant! However, to be a successful trader it is essential to have confidence in your own abilities. You must believe that you can make the right decision and then follow it through; even if the market conditions change and it turns out to be the wrong decision.

It is only by having confidence in your own abilities that you will be able to make a decision quickly when you need to. If it turns out to be the wrong decision then simply learn from your mistake and move on. Your confidence must go hand in hand with a positive mental attitude.

16.   *Work Place*

Working from home does not mean you should not take your job seriously. You must create time every day to study the markets, review the news and to possibly indulge in your trades. If you do not do your homework and stay in touch with the latest market developments you will have an increased risk of making the wrong decision as you will not be aware of all the facts.

An essential part of working from home and making the time to engage in all the relevant processes is having a separate space to work at; without distractions. No matter what role you perform it is very easy to procrastinate and this can cost you dearly. Create a unique work space that will ensure you are completely focused on the markets and your trades; this will ensure every trade is successful.

17.   *Educate*

There are a variety of options to improve your education and knowledge of the stock market. You should choose the one that suits your personality and needs the best. You may even want to do every method going!

There may be night schools or part time college courses near you that will help you to understand how the stock market works and even provide a variety of tips and techniques to help improve your trading options. You may be able to attend seminars held by professional investors which may improve your knowledge.

But, perhaps the most important way of educating yourself and improving your knowledge of the stock market is to be open to learning every day. Learning can come from contact with other investors or from reviewing your own trading and learning from your mistakes. Provided you are open to improving you knowledge you will continue to learn and develop.

18. *Discussions*

The internet has made it possible for many people to share their experiences and even to provide tips on upcoming stock movements. Whilst you should be cautious about any tips provided by others there is a lot of information which can be absorbed from the online forums.

You can join as many forums as you like and seek advice from others concerning specific trades or simply share experiences. A forum will help you to unwind after a hard day trading with other people who understand the procedures and stresses. It can be an excellent way of learning and de-stressing before you spend time with your family or friends.

19. *Consistent*

Whatever approach you take and whichever markets you trade in it is important to be consistent. This is especially important when you are first starting investing as you will need to know what approach you took in order to adjust and improve on it in future trades.

Consistency is also important as it will help you to both develop an approach which is successful and to stick to that approach. If your techniques are providing consistently good results then you must stick to them and continue trading in the same way. The stock market can provide consistent results if the same approach is taken every time. Find a technique which works for you and stick with it!

20.   *Mobility*

Whatever approach you take to day trading it is essential to remember that it is possible to access information on your phone or tablet. Although the idea conditions may be in your dedicated office space, there will be times when you need to complete other tasks or even attend to family matters. During these times it is still possible to watch your investments and adjust your position as necessary.

Of course, if you are able to finish trading before you have to leave your office then you will be able to enjoy your time away from your work. Being able to trade from anywhere can be a critical component to being a successful trader.

Curb Your Emotions

Emotional influence on Day Trading practices can turn counterproductive very fast if you are not careful. The primary emotions to look out for are self-confidence and fear. Excessive confidence can cause you to have a false sense of self-belief in your trading abilities. As a result, you may end up making illogical trading choices and decisions based on your cockiness.

You should understand that you become more prone to develop a false sense of overconfidence whenever you are on a winning streak. The successive trade deals that end up panning out give you an air of self-belief that could be subject to abuse. You get to trust your super abilities in trading and dare to engage in more risky transactions. It is at this point that you will experience a massive financial catastrophe, especially if you overextend yourself financially. Beware of situations that seem too good to be accurate as well.

The other emotional input of concern is the fear of experiencing losses. Overcoming this fear is possible as long as you trade in amounts of money that you can afford to lose in case the transaction goes wrong. In Day Trading, you are bound to have trouble due to market fluctuations, especially when dealing with volatile stocks.

Losses are part and parcel of Day Trading, and you must learn how to bounce back after a particularly nasty run of successive losses. You may experience crippling fear that could render you unable to continue trading if you do not have a coping mechanism for potential losses. In addition, the fear of further losses may discourage you from taking risks resulting in missing potentially profitable opportunities.

Fear is responsible for holding onto a stock position for too long, as well. Instead of selling your shares at a reasonable profit, you may decide to wait on much higher prices leading to a loss if the trend in stock price undergoes a reversal. Another critical factor to consider in risk and account management is the tendency to chase after quick profits to cover for a recent run of bad trade deals and accompanying losses.

You must adhere to your trading plan guidelines and instructions even during such tough times. Do not modify or alter your response and come up with stupid decisions that you usually would not make. Remember that for you to ensure responsible management of your capital, you need to start making choices based on logic. Emotional corruption can hamper your ability to make significant profits and expose you to unnecessary risks.

Chapter 3: Find Stocks

In Day Trading, you will need to deal in stocks and their fluctuations in prices. Buying and selling stocks depend on the number of shares of a particular stock that you have. When you conduct profitable trade deals, the chances are that you will have a healthy trading account. The available capital in your account is vital to enable you to continue investing in the Day Trading opportunities.

However, if you experience a run of losses and bad transactions, you are likely to run out of capital eventually. A series of successive losses tend to cause an emotional reaction from most traders. Beware of trying to recoup your losses by chasing profits based on rash decisions. It is also essential to trade only with an amount of capital that you can afford to lose. Remember to adhere to your trading plan for guidance and instructions on how to respond to financial losses.

You can also apply the strategies laid out for risk management. Stock markets tend to vary in their trends over time, and hence, you are bound to go through a couple of difficulties. The most crucial aspect of this emotional roller coaster is how you react to both returns and losses. Besides, in case you want to increase your profit margin, you should know how you would acquire more stock for your trade deals.

Since the availability of securities for Day Trading may not be an issue, you should try to focus and narrow down your stock selections. Identification of potentially profitable stocks can be a challenging affair. However, there are tactics, skills, and techniques that you can apply to ensure that you invest in the most productive kind of stock.

Conduct Repeated Day Trading on the Same Stock

This tactic involves carrying out your Day Trading under the same condition's multiple times. You need to identify your most profitable stocks and focus all your trading expertise and time on only these particular stocks. This move ensures that you always get some form of returns from your investment since you already know how it usually performs. Avoid trading in many different types of securities or stocks. The selection of a few stocks whose market trends are easily understandable should be your next step. You can narrow your possibilities to around three or four stocks in which you can become an expert.

Once you have identified the relevant stocks, you must dedicate your full attention and monitoring to their market trends. When choosing your preferred stocks, make sure to select those with sufficient volume in the market. This strategy allows for the adjustment of your calculated position size. When dealing with volatile stock, this flexibility enables you to apply for stop-loss orders with big margins to your corresponding small trading positions.

The opposite move is correct for a calm stock market. You will have the freedom to take an expansive trading position coupled with tight margined stop-loss orders. In addition, using this information, you will get to know the best periods to buy or sell specific stocks that would maximize your returns. The more you trade, the more you will be in a position to acquire more stock at a favorable market price. Eventually, you will end up with a lot of stock held as assets within your Day Trading portfolio.

Conduct Generalized Daily Searches for Favorable Stock

You can decide to perform your Day Trading activities in the old fashion way by looking for the volatile stocks that trend attractively. Volatile stocks are more likely to make significant movements in the course of your Day Trading. This technique requires a high degree of self-discipline to keep searching for productive stocks even during tough periods.

It is different from the repeated trading explained above. This trading exercise does not impose a recommended limit on the number of shares you can seek and does not involve Day Trading on the same stock repeatedly. As a result, you end up actively looking for favorable stocks from the vast online stock market to trade daily.

Ideally, you need to spend your time monitoring the market for the presence of stocks that are big movers and trending well. Consider researching the day before. You need to find out information about the stock availability and potential for returns. This research may include looking into the institution or company. Besides, you can find out how the product performs with market consumers.

For you to maximize your likelihood of acquiring more stock, pay attention to relevant breaking news affecting the stock. Also, be on the lookout for the stocks that earnings are due and any new stocks flooding the market on the following day. All this information should give you an upper hand in your quest to purchase and hold more trading stocks.

Execute A Stock Screener Based on Preferential Criteria

This tool is a computer software program that looks for any available stocks upon its execution. You can search for stocks based on your customizable criteria. Ideally, you should seek a limited number of stock types that show excellent levels of volatility and raw volume. Restrict your search criteria to about three or four stocks as well. Such limitations will enable you to focus all your attention on the effective management of selected stocks and their trading accounts. A weekly stock screener search can occur for you to spend ample time trading on the stocks that meet your search criteria.

Beware of distractions from other commodities that are not on your search results. Succumbing to temptations from a seemingly attractive stock will result in a spiraling fall into your potential financial ruin. Also, note that if a particular stock maintains a regular rate of returns, do not switch stock types.

You have to keep profitable returns, as well. When run correctly with the relevant criteria, a stock screener can supply you with a range of various profitable stocks from which you can choose. Depending on the filtration criteria, the following are some examples of online stock screeners:

1. StockFetcher.com

2. ChartMill.com

3. StockRover.com

4. Finviz.com

To avoid wasting time on endless searches for the biggest movers and the best stocks, try limiting your searches to a handful of stocks. This search should ideally take place once a week, preferably over a weekend. Once you have identified your small group of favorable stocks, spend the rest of the time involved in actual Day Trading. Focus your attention on only these listed stocks for at least the whole week until your next search is due. By following this technique, you will end up accumulating and Day Trading in the kinds of stock that you deeply understand and are customizable to you too.

Chapter 4: Tools and Platforms

People develop and adopt various tools and platforms to enhance a trader's experience while trading. Initially, a beginner may view the whole process of a transaction as being too difficult due to how complex some markets appear to be. However, with the right information, a person can receive proper guidelines that will introduce him or her to the business and gradually propel him or her into expert traders. The knowledge will enable him or her to develop his or her technical and fundamental analysis that will inform his or her successful trading strategies.

Below is information that introduces a person to the tools and platforms that various traders utilize in their businesses. Moreover, there is also an introduction to some trading aspects like Day Trading, technical indicators, chart types, and candlesticks. Read on to learn more.

Day Trading Tools and Services

Day Trading or intraDay Trading takes place when a trader enters a trade and holds a particular market position for a short time before exiting. A day trader opens and closes that position in a single day.

A trader undertakes Day Trading to avoid losses associated with overnight risks and, instead, aims to use volatility to his or her advantage. A trader needs to have some tools and services that are essential to accessing and succeeding in Day Trading. They include:

1.   **Electronics** – A day trader needs a computer and a phone where the laptop or desktop has enough memory to run the trading software without crashing or lagging. Additionally, he or she needs a phone to make relevant communications to appropriate people, such as calling brokers.

2.   **Direct Access Trading Brokerage** – An intraday trader should obtain the services of a suitable broker who fit his or her requirements in Day Trading. He or she needs to hire one who offers a low commission and allows for the use of customized Day Trading software.

3.   **Software** – A trader needs to carry out research and find the Day Trading software that matches his or her needs and strategies well. He or she also should ensure that the computer is compatible with the software and that his or her broker can access it.

4. **Trading Platform** – The intraday trader must learn about various Day Trading platforms and their features and select to use the one that will fulfill his or her trading objectives. Besides, he or she should ensure that the platform matches his or her skills and knowledge concerning trading tools and analysis.

5. **Internet Connection** – A trader must ensure to have an excellent and stable internet connection to help him or her to avoid the errors that take place due to poor accessibility. He or she views old data rather than the current prices on the market since the unstable connectivity results in lagging and misinformation. Additionally, he or she can create backup internet access, such as having different internet providers for his or her mobile phone. In doing so, if one internet provider has issues, the trader can still access the other connection.

6. **Knowledge and Skills** – An intraday trader should continually learn and practice trading to improve his or her skills. He or she can learn individually and practice via online tutorials or use an expert as a guide to perfect his or her trading skills.

7. *Features of the Best Day Trading Platforms*

A Day Trading platform is essential because it helps a trader to transact efficiently and ensure to minimize risks and make profits. The following are some of the best Day Trading platforms and their features:

1. **Charles Schwab** – Provides the best premium features that are critical to a trader's success in the market and is the easiest to learn. It offers competitive rates and has a balance since it provides vital trading and functionality tools while lacking certain customization features.

2. **Tradespoon** – Has flexible rates and suits traders of all levels as it provides professional and widespread trading tools. It has a rich library of studies and historical information that a trader can use to gain further knowledge or customize his or her trading strategies.

3. **TD Ameritrade** – Offers a trader excellent trading tools and guidance to help both beginners and experienced traders to grow in the market. It also provides retirement resources for traders. It has expensive rates, as it is the most resourceful platform that also provides traders with the chance to develop and undertake real-time stock scans and other advanced analysis.

4.**Interactive Brokers** – It provides the best rates and best suits the high-volume traders due to its professional features like programmable order types like algorithmic types. It does not allow for research, but its tools suit the hyperactive and active traders.

5.**E-Option** – Offers the best features for advanced traders as it enables them to access sophisticated and customized tools that they can use to undertake in-depth technical analysis and trade moves.

6.**Fidelity** – Contains several tools that enable a trader to transact efficiently, such as customized profiles, automatic identification of general patterns, chart trading, and drawing tools, among others. It also offers competitive rates due to its practicality.

Day Trading Charts

Day Trading refers to a trader entering and exiting a market position in a single day while charts use historical data to provide a trader with feedback regarding the conditions of a market. A trader using trading charts in his or her trades receives significant additional information that helps him or her to make appropriate decisions in Day Trading. They enable him or her to study the past price movements and patterns that assist him or her to understand the current market and even make some predictions on particular trades.

A day trader needs to understand the various aspects of Day Trading charts, which are technical indicators and the different chart types. Knowledge of these two features enables him or her to possess a comprehension of vital tools that help him or her to make a profit from the trading day's volatility.

Technical Indicators

An intraday trader utilizes technical indicators to carry out technical analysis of the market. They enable him or her to look at and understand the various meanings of chart patterns. The patterns provide him or her with a visual representation of the price movements and trends in the market that allow the trader to make sound and profitable decisions in the trade. Some of the commonly utilized indicators in Day Trading include:

1. *Simple Moving Average (SMA)*

An SMA indicator uses an average that consists of the total amount of the closing prices in a given period and dividing the sum by the number of days in that period. A day trader can make profits if he or she uses a fast-moving average since the slower ones can cause losses if there is a reversal or end of a trend. Many traders frequently use a 10-day moving average because it does not lag and indicates the direction and considerable moves of prices in the market.

2.   *Oscillators*

These refer to indicators such as the Relative Strength Index (RSI) and the Moving Average Convergence Divergent (MACD) that reflect unclear price trends. The signals move between the upper bounds and lower ones, and the subsequent readings provide the day trader with feedback regarding the market conditions.

3. *Volume Indicators*

A volume indicator will signal to a day trader changes concerning the number of trades taking place. The trader will know when there is a considerable amount of transactions and indicate the area in the market where they occur. He or she can then quickly take up an appropriate position and make profitable moves in the Day Trading market.

4.   *Average True Range (ATR)*

These indicators enable a day trader to evaluate the trades before entering it. As a result, he or she makes accurate and well- informed decisions because the ATR indicator utilizes the actual price of securities to provide a precise representation of volatility.

Many traders use different charts to maneuver the Day Trading markets. Each trading chart contains various features that work to provide diverse and useful information to a trader. A trader looks at the graphs and utilizes those that best suit his or her trading aim and strategies. The following are some popular types of charts that a trader can use to interpret and understand the market conditions.

1. *Candlestick Charts*

Candlestick charts are easy to understand and use, and they provide a trader with the most feedback by signaling where a price travels in a given period. They also enable him or her to incorporate information concerning frames of time. In this case, he or she can identify the highest and lowest price points, along with the last closing price that takes place in that particular period.

Candlesticks assist a trader in getting precise visual readings of the market by presenting only relevant information, such as the Heikin-Ashi chart that shows trends and reversals. Different candlestick charts also show various aspects of the market, such as time, volume, and price movements.

Some candlestick charts only use the movements of the price to help a day trader to identify the resistance and support levels. The resistance levels indicate the highest highs of trade, whereas the support levels show the lowest lows. Renko is an example of such a candlestick chart that employs colored bricks to reflect the trends of a trade.

When there is a downward trend, the blocks visible will be black, while white ones will be visible when an upward trend takes place. The bricks also move in terms of the price movement whereby a new white or black block appears in the following column if the price respectively moves above or below the previous one.

Other candlestick charts help a day trader to find points of reversals and sets of swing highs and lows. These charts enable him or her to determine areas and conditions of bias in the market, which assist him or her in making appropriate moves that give him or her gains. An example here is a Kagi chart that uses changes in price directions to signal reversals.

The intraday trader sets a particular reversal amount, and the price direction will shift to the opposite side once it reaches that predetermined percentage. It also indicates swings concerning high and low line signals, in that, the lines become thinner as the market drops below the previous swing. Conversely, the line gets thicker as the stock increases above the prior swing.

2. *Bar Charts*

Bar charts provide a day trader with signals that are easy to read and interpret as they use color, horizontal, and vertical lines to reflect range or price in a given period. The horizontal lines show the closing and opening prices, whereas the vertical lines indicate the price range of a particular duration. Additionally, traders use them along with candlestick charts to reflect the trading actions in the market.

A bar with candlesticks uses the variation between the low and high to show the trading range. The top of the candle or wick represents the high state while the bottom of the candle signals the low one. Moreover, the chart uses different colors on the candlestick to indicate the opening and closing prices within a period of interest. A red candle could represent the closing price at the low end of a candle and have the opening price at the high end. Meanwhile, a green candle reflects its prices in reverse of the red candle.

3. *Line Charts*

Line charts indicate to an intraday trader the history of prices by showing a track of the closing prices in the market. The trader forms the lines when he or she links several closing costs in a given frame of time. He or she uses line charts along with other kinds of trading charts to get essential information for a successful Day Trading experience.

4. *Charts Based on Time Frames*

All the trading charts that a day trader utilizes contain frames of time that he or she set according to his or her aim or trading strategies. The trader can use intraday charts breaking down into 2-minute, 5-minute, 15-minute, and hourly charts. Each time interval indicates the price actions of trade of interest, and he or she can use the information represented to make relevant trading decisions and moves.

5. *Free Charts*

An intraday trader can use free charts that are available online and offer the trader not only with tools for technical analysis but also with advice, demonstrations, and guidelines about chart analysis. Different free charts provide various features such as delayed futures data, real-time data, and selection of frames of time and indicator accessibility. Furthermore, these charts enable a trader to participate in various markets like the forex, futures, stock exchanges, and equity markets. FreeStockCharts and the Technician are examples of free charts that an intraday can access and utilize without spending anything.

Introduction to Candlesticks

The Japanese merchants developed candlesticks to monitor daily momentum and prices in the rice market in the 18th Century. A candlestick is a kind of chart that shows the opening, closing, high, and low prices in a particular period. As a result, it helps a trader to identify the entry or exit points of a market since it signals how the investor's feelings influence the trades.

The broad section of a candlestick is the real body, which a trader uses to determine if the closing price of trade was lower or higher than the opening price. Additionally, they also employ colors to help him or her to identify the state of the closing price more quickly.

The real body of a candlestick is green or white when the stock closes higher and red or black when the stock closes lower. Hence, the colors assist the trader to quickly interpret the market conditions at a glance and make appropriate decisions without wasting time.

The candlesticks' different colors also represent the sentiments of the market by indicating the outlooks of the traders. They signal if the traders have a bearish, bullish, or indecisive approach to the market. A trader then makes a judgment and takes up relevant positions in the market that provide him or her with gains.

Bullish Candlesticks

A bullish sentiment takes place when traders do a lot of purchasing because they expect the price of an asset will increase in a given period. As a result, the bullish outlook will form an intense buying pressure in the market. The bullish candlesticks will have a long green or white real body to show that the stock prices closed at a higher place than the opening price. Furthermore, it helps a trader to determine significant price actions at a particular area and time if a long white candle appears at an appropriate support level of price.

If the price initially moves significantly lower after the open and then shifts to close in the high vicinity, the bullish candlestick forms a reversal pattern called a hammer. The sellers lower the prices in a trading session, and it results in an intense buying pressure, which leads to the trading session ending on a higher close.

Thus, a hammer creates an uptrend, and its real body is short with a lower and longer shadow since sellers are reducing the prices. An inverted hammer indicates a reverse of the hammer candlestick since it develops in a downtrend. Other bullish candlesticks that a trader can utilize in the market include the morning star, the piercing line, bullish engulfing pattern, and the three white soldiers.

Bearish Candlesticks

A bearish outlook refers to the situation where there is an intense pressure of selling in the trading markets. It occurs when traders carry out a lot of selling trades in a particular duration. The bearish candlesticks have a long red or black body that signifies that the stock prices closed at a lower position than the opening price. Therefore, as the day goes on, the stock price falls leading to the opening price is higher than the close of the previous day. It leads to the formation of a long black candlestick that does not have an upper shadow but only possesses a short lower shadow.

Traders also refer to the bearish candlesticks as the hanging man, and they utilize them to try to select a bottom or top in the market. Moreover, the patterns of a bearish candlestick tend to indicate a switch in the attitude of investors. The sentiment changes from bullish to bearish after a length of time. Examples of bearish candlesticks include the bearish harami and bearish engulfing candlesticks.

Indecision Candle

This candlestick differs from the bullish and bearish types in terms of its body shape. While the bullish and bearish candlesticks are long, the indecision candle has a small real body, in that, the open price and the close price are near each other. Additionally, there are long wicks that attach to each side of the body and are equal in their lengths. The candlestick's body also lies between the low and the high, resulting in it being at the center of the entire candle range.

This candle occurs at a trend's top and bottom and can indicate to a trader about price or trend reversals if it develops at significant places on the chart after undergoing long moves. The name of this candlestick comes from the indecisive conduct that it shows since it signals both bullish and bearish activities. The stock closes at around the same place as the opening price because the bears and bulls were both very active in the market.

This double price action leads to there being two long wicks on either side of the candle's body. Their presence and lengths indicate that the price attempted to shift both upwards and downwards in the trading session. Consequently, it signals that no one won in the market and that it failed to maintain higher and lower prices. The Doji candlestick is an example of an indecisive candle.

These features mentioned above provide descriptions and information concerning the various tools and platforms used in trading. A person needs to understand them to allow him or her to gain vital knowledge that will help him or her to trade in the markets successfully.

Chapter 5: Trading Management

Day Trading Risk Management

In all forms of trading, traders have a specific level of risk that they may be willing to take. Since the ultimate aim of participating in any particular trade is to gain profits, your exposure to risk should be as minimal as possible. In Day Trading, the incidence of risk may not be as damaging to small- scale low-risk traders. However, failure to enforce risk management strategies may be financially catastrophic for large investors and companies. The following risk management strategies could be of use to new investors in Day Trading:

a.   Employ stop-loss orders

b.   Take favorable positions

c.   Stick to your trading plan

d.   Make low-risk trades

e.   Seek expert assistance

1. *Stop-Loss Orders*

These orders provide a mechanism for you to minimize the extent of any potential losses. The stop-loss order mandates the trader or your stockbroker to cease a particular type of trade instantly upon meeting specific conditions. Ideally, these orders indicate the range of values beyond which a given trading action begins to become significantly unprofitable. It applies to both short and long trading positions. Falling prices are not ideal for stock sellers, and stock buyers frown on expensive costs.

For instance, you could set a particular limit for the range of losses that you may be willing to tolerate adequately. Beyond this limit, your damages would start affecting your bottom line significantly, hence the need for an immediate halt to the trade deal. For them to act as a risk management tool, you need to have your stop-loss orders in place long before taking part in Day Trading. In this manner, you will be covering a potential loss that is yet to occur as opposed to reacting to real-time unfavorable stock prices.

2. *Position Sizing*

Taking a favorable trading position is the essence of position sizing. Before jumping into any trade opportunity, you should acquire relevant information about that trade. This data should enable you to make the appropriate selection when choosing to take a position. Ideally, rising stock prices with the expectation of a corresponding upward trend in the price chart favor buying stocks. Hence, this Day Trading scenario warrants you to take a long position. Short positions are beneficial when the prices drop or when the trading chart shows a sustained downward trend in the stock price. Position sizing is more of an account management strategy but also applies to risk evasion techniques. If you grow accustomed to taking productive positions, your risk index decreases, and vice versa. Therefore, you should seek assistance with position sizing and how to take up profitable positions if the need arises.

3. _Trading Plan_

You need to keep track of the progress of your Day Trading investments. In this regard, you must stick to the guidelines set out in your trading plan. This plan provides you with instructions on how to react or respond to specific scenarios in the course of your Day Trading. These directives usually offer the best course of action in the event of most adverse financial situations. In addition, if you strictly stick to your plan from the beginning, you will have no risk to manage later. Besides, you could seek the help of your stockbroker when drawing up a new trading plan. Make sure to capture every probable adverse eventuality and how to mitigate the risks associated with it.

Trading plans often discourage you from making decisions based on emotions, which would likely happen in the absence of a trading plan.

Simple Trades

Day Trading often has small margins for either profits or losses. Therefore, you must learn to conduct small but assured trade deals in this strategy. It is advisable to refrain from lusting over the promises of impractically significant returns. The greed resulting from chasing quick profits over short time intervals is counterproductive to your ultimate aim. When you conduct illogical trades using large amounts of money, you are likely to run out of your available capital sooner than you expect. A simple trade has to be low in its risk index, small in amount, and a value that you can afford to lose. Volatility and trade volume are factors that affect your type of trade, but if you stick to logic, your profits will outnumber your losses. Most financial risk exposures are the consequences of rash decisions and poor Day Trading habits. If you have challenges in trying to identify the viable trading opportunities, you could seek the help of other seasoned traders or a stockbroker.

4.   *Expert Assistance*

Whenever you engage in an unfamiliar trading practice, it is advisable to know what you are doing. The same advice applies to investors who are new to Day Trading. Heeding to this counsel will spare you from financial ruin down the line. One way you could make use of available Day Trading expertise is by hiring a stockbroker. Trading blindly without any idea of the expectations is a risky proposition. Stockbrokers are often highly experienced traders in their own right. They know about all the potentially profitable trading opportunities and doomed trades that are bound to go bust.

Therefore, when you have a qualified and registered stockbroker by your side, you are less likely to get yourself into financially risky situations. It is essential that you can predict a wrong trade deal from a mile away, but since you cannot, a stockbroker may be the next best option. In addition to spotting potentially wacky trade deals, your stockbroker is typically responsible for managing your brokerage account. He or she participates in the different trading commitments and takes favorable trading positions on your behalf. As a result, the chances of making a fruitless trade decision are minimal.

Price Action in Day Trading

Price action is one of the strategies used by traders who take part in Day Trading. It relies on the movements in the price of the security under trade. Plotting the raw stock prices against the trading period on a chart is necessary, thereby showing the behavior of your stock value over a specified time. Indicators that are common to other strategies play an insignificant role when using price action.

As a price action trader, you will not bother to find out the conditions affecting particular price movements in either direction. You will take the pattern at its face value because you put more credence to the trends in the stock prices than their contributing factors. As per this reasoning, it could be an excellent time to sell your stock when the prices start rising due to its corresponding increase in value. A downward trend is suggestive of falling prices; hence, buying the stock at favorable prices is possible.

As an investor or trader, your point of entry into Day Trading is dependent on potential profitability and minimal risk exposure. Buying at the least reasonable price and selling at the highest stock price are the two main objectives in price action Day Trading. Besides, technical analysis comes from the price action of a particular stock over a specified period.

Price action mainly deals with the ongoing, real-time

stock price fluctuations. It is an instant form of Day Trading strategy without the lagging period or delays experienced in waiting for the relevant indicators.

You can modify your stock price chart to show distinct price movements in different colors. This color transition alerts you to a trading opportunity due to the obvious and easy to spot a change in price direction. Once again, you will only concentrate on the upward or downward trend in the price and if that particular pattern will hold. The following concepts describe some everyday experiences attributed to price action Day Trading:

a. Price Breakouts

b. Candlestick Charts

c. Optional Indicators

d. Support and Resistance

e. Technical Analysis

1. *Price Breakouts*

A primary concept for you to understand is the Day Trading event of a breakout. It is common in almost all cases of price action trading. A breakout is a sudden jump in stock value in either direction from an extended hovering position. This spike in your stock price is readily visible on a price action chart. A breakout is an indicator that alerts you to a possible trading opportunity. However, it could also be a false breakout, in which case, the prices would soon rebound in the opposite direction.

For instance, if the price of a particular stock keeps fluctuating between $25 and $27 for about a month, you would not think much of the security. Yet, if the stock price goes up to $29 in one day after the month, your curiosity and alertness would peak. This sudden upward spike in the stock price is the breakout. Ideally, you would assume that the price is about to keep rising and continue on this trajectory for the foreseeable future. Therefore, as a price action trader, you would take a long position on the same stock hoping for a significant profit from the increasing value. However, the breakout could turn out to be false, and the spike to $29 was only a one-day occurrence.

In this case, the rebound effect would cause the stock value to start dropping. A possible explanation could be that the upward spike caused many other price action traders to buy the stock, which in turn led to more investors who previously held shares to sell. Based on the mechanism of economies of scale, this influx of stock security into the market causes its price to start falling. The price could decrease by a considerable margin past the initial low of $25 to the horror of the traders who took an initial buy position. If you bought plenty of shares based on the initial upswing in the breakout ($27 to $29), you would experience a massive loss afterward.

This uncertainty is part of the characteristics of price action trading, i.e., you can only know the previous behavior of a particular stock, but you cannot predict its future action. Learn to accept the possibility of losing some capital in such price action trades that do not go according to your expectations. Price action trading is akin to speculative trading. Hence, the best mentality you can have is to try to increase your profit margins on the good days more than your losing margins.

2.   *Candlestick Charts*

Another mechanism that is useful in price action trading is the use of candlestick charts. These charts provide more information about the stock price that may assist you in making a more informed decision. The candlestick chart contains details such as the opening and closing prices of a specific stock; hence, you get to know the range of this value within a day. In addition, the candlestick charts show both the maximum and minimum amount of the stock in a single day of trading. In this case, you can estimate the real value of the stock by averaging these particular values.

Due to this additional data, more accomplished day traders often use a combination of candlestick charts and breakouts in their price action strategies for a detailed source of information. They both eliminate the confusion caused by multiple interpretations of the same price action chart. You may see a downward trend and think that the stock value is decreasing, while another person might conclude that a turnaround or price reversal may be imminent. In the end, you both take contrasting positions on a single trade that are equally justifiable. This need for an overall complete picture enables you as a trader to come up with a trading resolution based on the whole trading status of a given stock price. For instance, a particular stock may show multiple drops in its intraday price while keeping with an overall upward trend on a week over week basis. As a result, such dreaded incidents as the rebounds associated with the stand-alone price action breakouts will not catch you off guard again.

3. *Optional Indicators*

In addition to candlestick charts, you may incorporate a group of specific indicators depending on your objective. However, due to lag delay, trade indicators are not essential to price action trading. In case you need them, trade indicators can easily fit on a price action chart.

Examples of such commonly applied indexes include:

• *Moving average*

This indicator enables you to pick out the mean price movement of your particular stock over a specified time frame. In its purest form, this indicator centers on the average value of your security or commodity under trade based on the most recent behavior of that particular stock.

• *MACD indicator*

The acronym for this indicator stands for Moving Average Convergence Divergence. It depicts momentum by relating the previously mentioned moving average to a specific point on the price chart. This point indicates the price level at which you may decide to purchase stock, thereby making it subjective. Taking a particular position depends on this interaction. A possibly long trading position is considerable if the MACD indicator goes above your level or price point.

• *Stochastic Oscillator*

Just like the MACD, this indicator is descriptive of momentum, as well. First, based on your trading hunch, you decide on an appropriate trend that your stock price will take. This hopeful trend will enable you to estimate the expected value in the stock price at a particular time in the future. Next, sit back and wait for the trading to reach your estimated time. Finally, use the stochastic oscillator to verify whether the current stock price and pattern at this new time match with your earlier speculated expectation.

• RSI indicator

This indicator is suggestive of a market that is either overbought or oversold on a particular security or stock. This description is a measure of the strength of that specific stock within the stock market. Hence, the acronym for this indicator stands for Relative Strength Indicator. It enables you to make an informed judgment on the viability or risks of trading in a certain way and on a particular stock.

• Fibonacci Retracement

This indicator is useful for testing the level of support or resistance when subjected to the trends in the price action chart. You can obtain a detailed perspective of the stock market based on the patterns formed by this indicator. This information guides you on when and how to trade as well as on which particular stocks to trade.

• Bollinger Bands

Whenever you want to find out the usual trading price range of a particular stock, you should use this indicator. Bollinger bands typically show you the stock price limits beyond which breakouts occur. A brief consolidation of the stock price typically occurs within such Bollinger bands. A breached Bollinger band is usually indicative of a breakout, thereby requiring you to alter your taken position.

4. *Support and Resistance*

These terms describe the behavior of the price action trend. Ideally, you often encounter an oscillating pattern in an ordinary stock trading session. Some uptrends typically alternate with their corresponding downtrends. The highest point or level of the stock price that the stock can reach, as depicted by the price action chart, is the resistance. All trends past this point either hold position or reverse their direction downwards. A rise in the price of a particular stock often means that buying securities is the predominant trade activity.

At first, the buyers in the stock market outnumber the available security in circulation, leading to an increase in the price. The price chart, therefore, registers the uptrend. With high stock prices, investors who hold a lot of stock will take up short positions. More stockholders follow suit resulting in a stock market overflowing with that same stock. This time, the particular security outnumbers the buyers, and its price stabilizes, but if this imbalance continues, the stock prices will begin to drop. Therefore, the point at which the stock prices stop their upward trend is the resistance.

Support, on the other hand, is the exact opposite of resistance. It is the lowest price that a given stock reaches beyond which the only further direction becomes upwards. In the above scenario, the high stock prices begin to fall in a saturated market. The fall is due to the concept of economies of scale. More buyers purchase increased amounts of stock at progressively cheaper costs hence the downtrend on the price action chart. This downward direction in the price of commodities would scare any more stockholders away from selling.

Therefore, the market soon runs into a deficiency of available stock. At this stage, once again, the stock buyers outnumber the insufficient stock in circulation. The trend holds steady for a while as per the price action chart. A prolonged state of a low volume of securities in circulation triggers an increase in its price. This outcome is valid because of the more demand from buyers outnumbering the circulating stock supply. This change in the trend of the stock price signals the point of support.

5. *Technical Analysis*

In the case of technical analysis, data from price action trading charts are essential for such indicators as the patterns of ascending triangles. These triangles are useful in predicting an imminent major breakout. This prediction is due to previous attempts at a series of multiple minor breakouts by periods of a rising price trend. The pattern caused by the efforts of these bull trends is typically indicative of a gain of momentum with each attempt. From this informative data analysis, you can expect an overall breakout shortly.

Along with the technical analysis, trend and swing traders use price action as a source of data for their indicators or tools as well. Concurrently, they can obtain information on the levels of resistance and support for the specific trade deals in which they participate. For this data to become productive to them, the swing traders need to have the skills required for price action interpretation. Of more use to such external traders, is the ability to derive relevant predictions of the corresponding breakouts or consolidation from the price action charts. Beware of applying technical analysis to raw price action data. For technical analysis to make sense, you need additional information such as the trading volume, market factors, and investor influence.

In the absence of accompanying technical analysis, the psychological and emotional weight might creep into your decisions. As a result, your mental faculties experience clouded judgment, thereby rendering your incapable of making logical choices. Price action trading is beneficial to small traders looking for low-risk opportunities to invest their small amounts of capital. They are usually in search of a quick profit over a brief period so that a single breakout event may suffice. Complex and in-depth analysis is probably more applicable in large-scale settings, for example, corporations, companies, financial institutions, and wealthy private investors. This category of investors is typically long-term and is often on the hook for massive capital loans over an extended period.

Chapter 6: Beginner's Strategies

Day trading is often characterized by sudden changes in price movements. This is why you need aggressive strategies to survive in the trade. There are strategies that will enable you to generate huge profits while others will only allow you to get some little returns.

As a beginner, you need to understand how the market behaves to succeed in your trading endeavors. The ultimate goal is always to make profit as you reduce the risks involved in each trade. You need a lot of patience and discipline to fully understand and apply some trading principles to your day to day activities. Here are some of the strategies you need to employ before and during the trading sessions to ensure that you succeed in the trade.

1.   Build a watch list

The stock market is made of several day trading opportunities that you can take advantage of. However, most traders miss out on a good number of these opportunities simply because they do not have any watch lists defined. To come up with an effective watch list, you first need to identify the kind of stock that supports the kind of strategies you wish to implement. Before you can achieve this, you must first acquire the necessary skills required for your trade.

It is easy to come up with a great watch list if you understand how the day trading market operates. You, for instance, need to understand how stock prices are determined and how economic cycles impact these prices. Another thing you need to define for you to create an effective watch list is the amount of time you are ready to spend on the trading platform. If you intend to spend only a few hours on the platform each week or month, you can create a list that has very few issues to follow up. If you intend to trade on a daily basis then you need to create a database with hundreds of issues that you need to track. You can always display items in your list on your screens as you trade as these will serve as a guideline for your transactions.

There are various aspects you need to consider if you want to build a strong watch list. Some of these include:

- The account size. With a small account size, you only need a few items on your watch list. The opposite is true for traders with large accounts. When trading, you can always scan through the list and select two or three items that you can execute concurrently. You can sort the items according to priority and choose those that allow you to diversify in terms of stock types and industry sectors. For instance, you may decide to trade in individual stocks as well as ETFs at the same time.

• Time available. You need to understand the amount of time you have available for trading. If you do not have enough time to track hundreds of items then concentrate on a small number that you can execute effectively.

• Expertise in trading options. This will determine whether you should include options in your watch list or leave them out entirely. In case you have the right knowledge to trade options, you can expand your watch list to include other types and strategies of trading instead of confining yourself on stocks. Such items include things like spreads and as well as other call/ put strategies. Since option strategies are always versatile with most market environments, it will be advantageous to you as you may end up making more profit than people who are focusing on stock trading alone.

As you consider these aspects, you must also concentrate on knowing what is on the watch list. You must learn how to track items like the duration of each trade and the volatility level just to understand the kind of risk involved. Master the attributes of each list item as you decide which one to prioritize. Ensure that you note any changes taking place on your list. This is most important when you are engaged in options trading.

2. *Identify the right stocks*

Not all financial instruments are ideal for day trading. You need to come up with a list of stocks you wish to trade in. These should be identified based on your trading needs and goals. Remember, not all stocks are the same, and not all can be traded using your preferred strategies. Therefore it is important that you keenly identify those stocks that can bring you more profit.

To do this, first you need to estimate the amount of capital you want to invest in the business. Once you have done this, you can research the right markets and settle on those that offer the right environment for you to trade. Each day in the time of a day trader brings itself new trading stocks and opportunities. You can always prioritize on the stocks that feature breakouts or those that are highly volatile. Such stocks offer better profit potential. Even stocks with average but consistent volatility are good for trading since you can always get something from them.

As a beginner however, you must confine yourself to a limited number of stocks each day. If you diversify too fast you may risk the little capital you have. There are several factors you need to consider when selecting the kind of stock to trade. Here are some of them:

- **Volume** – stock volume allows you to create positions depending on demand. When a stock features high volumes, it is easier to open and close positions associated to it. If it has low volume then you will struggle to buy or sell stocks and the day may end without you making good profits. The goal of creating orders is to ensure that they get filled at the right prices. Low volume stocks deny you this opportunity since the value of your order may be higher than the available number of stock shares at the time of trade.

- **Volatility** – when selecting stocks to trade in you must consider the volatility level. You therefore need to choose those with higher price movements during the day. Every stock always features a different percentage of volatility. Some stocks experience very small price changes while others always feature significantly large changes.

When checking volatility, have your trading style in mind. You also need to consider the kind of broker you have. For instance, there are traders who find it hard trading stocks that make large price changes. Such traders always concentrate on the stocks that move slightly per day. Stocks whose prices change too fast always need quick action during execution. If as a beginner, you have not mastered this skill, you may wish to avoid such stocks until you are confident enough to carry out such trades. You may need to invest in a stock screener to help reduce the stocks to a number that is manageable. You can specify the percentage of volatility you need and focus on these.

- **Price range** – this is another factor that you need to consider when getting the right stocks for your trade. You can either become a trend trader, range trader or both.

With your stock screener, you can easily identify the kind of stocks that suit your mode of trading. In case you wish to focus on range trading, you should concentrate on those stocks that are likely to range. If you want to trend trade then you should select stocks that a tendency to trend. A good stock screener helps you to separate between trend and range stocks faster. If you decide to sort stocks manually, it may take you a long while and this means that you will miss out on some lucrative opportunities.

These three elements must be considered at the same time. If you fail to consider any of them, you may end up choosing the wrong type of stock to trade. A stock screener allows you to specify those parameters you wish your ideal stocks to have. The screener uses these parameters to list matching opportunities available on the market.

3. *Have entry and exit strategies in place*

As you begin trading, you may keep getting some excellent deals but if you do not understand when to enter or leave the market, day trading may not work for you. The amount of profit you gain from a trade depends on the kind of strategies you lay. Entry and exit strategies are quite numerous on the stock market. If you get the right ones and stick to your trading guidelines, you are most likely to succeed in day trading.

The following are some guidelines that you can use to ensure that your entry and exit strategies remain active throughout the trading session.

- **Focus on the current trend**. The stock market always experiences changes all the time. It is upon you as the trader to adjust your entry and exit strategies accordingly. For instance, when the market assumes an upward trend, you can trade long positions successfully and when it assumes a downward trend you can concentrate on trading short positions. Day trading trends do not last. You need to seize every opportunity as it comes and avoid postponing any opportunities. Identifying certain trends requires a lot of skill and attention. Use trendlines to determine entry and exit points for your positions. You can come up with these lines in real time as the market changes. More trendlines often provide you with more alternatives in terms of the signals available for your transactions.

• **When the market is rising, choose strong stocks.** When it is declining, trade weak stocks. It is often rewarding trading stocks or equities that have a high correlation with indexes. Stocks that are weak when compared with indexes do not offer the best opportunities. Strong stocks always feature higher volatilities than weak ones. This implies that you should seek to purchase stocks whose price is increasing faster than indexes and futures. When the price of the index and future start to decline, the value of stock will not drop that much, giving you a higher potential for profit. When the price of futures and indexes start to decrease, focus on selling stocks whose price is reducing faster than the futures. As the price of the futures changes in the downtrend, the cost of stocks may not change that much,

resulting in higher profits as well.

- **Work with pullbacks**. Trendlines only give you a visual glimpse into the market and how the prices are set to change. It is upon you, therefore, to identify entry and exit points in such circumstances. One way to do this is through the use of pullback points.

The point when the price of a stock starts to move either upwards or downwards then suddenly changes direction is what is called a pullback. You need to start your trades at this point to facilitate maximum returns. The pullback acts as a signal to indicate whether you need to make an entry or exit on the market. You must be quite observant to be able to identify these points.

- **Focus on making profits regularly**. As you start day trading, you want to ensure maximum returns at the end of the day. Due to the dynamics of the market, you will always have some limited opportunities to make profit. Therefore, you do not have to spend a lot of time on trades that are not quite promising. Anytime a trade assumes the wrong direction, you can exit the market when it is still early enough to capture some small profits from the trade. You can do this by: Taking the profits realized from a long position so long as the price is slightly higher than the former high in an uptrend.

1. Taking profits in a short position when the price is lower than the former low price in the present trend. You can always mark entry and exit points on your day trading charts to ensure that you do not bypass them.

- **Avoid trading in stagnant environments**. Sometimes the stock market may stall. Prices do change most of the time, but not always. If the price is moving in small percentages, ensure that the change is large enough to give you more profit than risks before entering a trade. If the price is not trending but moving within a certain range, you may decide to engage in range trading instead of using the trend trading method. During this time, the price may keep moving up and down creating some resistance areas. Take not of these resistance areas to understand when to short sell or long buy positions.

When you are intending to purchase stock in this scenario, locate an exit point at the near top of the price range. If you want to sell, identify an exit point on the lower part of the range that is closer to the bottom. These two points present less risk and high reward. You may decide to create stop loss orders within the range to minimize any kinds of losses you may incur.

It is very easy for you to alternate range trading and trend trading within the same platform. You therefore need to understand how these trading methods work and what time to apply them. Expert traders often begin trading as soon as they get to the market. However, as a beginner, it is important that you take a few minutes each morning to understand how prices are changing and how certain stocks are performing before you start trading. This will help you identify those stocks that are volatile and those that are not. Professional traders always enter and exit positions fast because they have already identified the right trading strategies and discipline required.

2. *Spend quality time on the market.*

You may be wondering the right time frames to engage in day trading. This is a common concern for most beginners and you should not get worried about it. In order to understand the kind of market you are trading in and the patterns involved, you should always spend adequate time on the trading platform. You will be busy monitoring charts, identifying resistance and support levels and checking out price predictions. The kind of chart you decide to use affects the trading time-frame. For instance, you can decide to make use of one-minute trading charts when dealing with positions that need to be opened and closed quickly. However, you must understand that chart periods do not indicate how volatile a particular stock is. For instance, the one minute and five minute charts may both apply to stocks that have the same volatility at the same time.

As a day trader that is just getting started, you must beware of certain timeframes and monitor these closely. Before choosing a timeframe, you must understand that these offer relatively the same information, only the way the information is represented differs. In most cases, short time frames always possess more details than longer ones. Since most transactions take place as soon as the market opens in the morning, you need to use charts to monitor this time specifically. At this point is when most traders make large profits, others losses.

You may identify certain charts and use them the entire day to determine the right time frames to trade. Tick charts are the most used because they always offer traders with more detailed information. They also give you the opportunity to establish whether the market is moving or not. Individuals who focus on one minute and five minute charts are those who wish to monitor every kind of activity taking place on the market.

As hours go by, the chart you would have chosen will keep accumulating some bars especially if you are trading stocks that are largely volatile. Keep monitoring every trend, support and resistance levels as well as the volatility of stocks. Most day traders begin in the morning and by 11:30 they are done transacting. Those who continue with trading always keep of platforms over lunch hour since this period is often characterized by very little activity. Some proceed with the business in the afternoon whole others wait until the day is almost ending to start trading again. In the evening, most charts do not display activity for the entire day but only a few hours.

A good chart will also display price and market trends for prior days. Once you open such a chart, you will easily see this information and a lot more about the pre-market and what took place before the day began. However, you do not need to concentrate on past stock performances as a day trader since your focus should be on what is happening presently. You only need to focus on a stock's and market's history if the strategy you are using depends on it. For a good number of day traders, stock charts always assist them when it comes to placing trades. The charts bear signals that indicate when the market is ideal for trade and when it is not. You must note that the cost of stocks may not be visible on your charts the entire day, yet you need this information to determine the overall performance of the market. You can use more than one chart at the same time to gain a better understanding of different time intervals. Doing this also improves your overall trading experience. The more you trade, the more you can increase your timeframes. Larger timeframes often provide you with a better view of the market. You may increase the number of hours, or customize these sessions to be able to see the price of stocks for the entire day. Once you master some chart patterns, you can comfortably work with shorter time frames and only use longer ones if your strategy requires that you do so.

4. *Reflect on your trading experiences*

Each trading day will always come to an end. This is the time that you need to evaluate how the day has been as a way of identifying what needs to change as you continue trading. You can also decide to step aside from your screens for a few days just to review your plans, strategies and guidelines. This is especially important if day trading has not been working in your favor.

Day to day reflections are very essential for each day trader. It helps you to refresh mentally as you prepare for the next day.

5. *Check your trading frequency*

Most beginners get into the day trading with so much activity that they end up stuck in numerous positions that are not quite promising. It is advisable that as you get started, you trade less frequently until you gain a better understanding of the trading strategy and what it entails. While you are still seeking to adjust to what is happening on the market, it is better to trade less as this is one way of minimizing the risks you get exposed to. When you limit the frequency of your trades, you also get enough time to learn from each transaction that you make. Taking frequent breaks also ensures that you keep your emotions under control depending on the outcome of the previous trades. Here are some of the tips you need to focus on to ensure that you maintain a low trading frequency:

- Do not use scalping strategies

- Concentrate on charts that use larger time frames

- Do not enter or exit trades blindly. Only go for those that are promising in terms of the reward attached to them.

For the few trades that you engage in, ensure that you set stop loss orders for them. If possible, do not adjust these until the day ends. This is because most new day traders tend to make emotional decisions depending on their experience on the market. Often times, these decisions are not always effective and they lead to losses. For instance, you may start comparing the kind of losses and profits made within a day and when you realize that you have incurred losses. You may seek to adjust the current strategies to cover up for these losses. In the process, you may end up risking more of your capital and if the trade ends on the negative, you would have incurred double losses. You thus need to leave this attempt to professional traders who have mastered the use of objective analysis when making day trading decisions.

This also includes avoiding positions you do not have any skill or confidence over. If you know that you cannot control your emotions, it is important that you keep off environments and platforms that will expose you to them. Sometimes you may be required to note some activities down just to ensure that you keep your positions active for a period that is necessary. You can engage in both active and passive management of your positions. Passive management involves the use of day trading orders to set limits for each transaction. Active management is when you are involved in the entire trading process. It entails staying on the trading platform from the start of the trade until the end.

Passive management has one advantage over active management of your day trading transactions. It shields you from changing market parameters unnecessarily.

6. Learn to interpret trading patterns.

As earlier mentioned, day trading strategies operate using two categories of analysis – fundamental as well as technical analysis. When starting your day trading business, it is essential that you learn how to interpret the patterns resulting from these two methods of stock analysis. In case you wish to use technical analysis for your information needs, ensure that you use one that is chart-based. Have a single price pattern that you can apply to all your trades to ensure success. Chart patterns that appear similar over time indicate that a certain stock is likely to assume this same pattern over a longer period in future. You can analyze stocks historical patterns to identify such trends.

When seeking for day trading patterns, always check out for those that outline price actions that are both simple and easy to understand. In case you are unable to determine whether your chart has any patterns, it means that the kind of stock you are trading does not have one. This means that you will need to look for other ways to predict price movements for the said stock.

Getting the right market to trade in is always a plus for every day trade. Before you even get started, you must have already decided on the kind of market you wish to trade on. Every market has its own advantages and disadvantages. Some require more capital to trade than others. Always put this into consideration when thinking on how to get started. For instance, the amount of capital you need to day trade stocks is not the same as what you need to day trade futures. Each market also bears a different profit potential. This only points to one thing – the amount of capital you have when getting started. Once you identify a market, take your time to study its features. You cannot master all the aspects associated with it at once. Therefore you must exercise some level of patience when learning about it. Ensure that it is one you can afford before acquiring the necessary tools and equipment you need for the trade. With the right market and tools in place, you can then establish a time schedule that works for you. Get your strategies and keep practicing how to use them all the time. Choose those strategies that seem more effective over those that aren't. Use a demo account to do this since it just works like a real account. Prepare yourself for any losses, since these will occur once in a while. But ultimately, do not invest cash that you are not ready to lose.

Day Trading is the buying or selling of an asset or security, within the course of a single trading day. A trading day refers to the span of time when a particular forex or stock exchange is open. Trading days are usually seven to eight hours long, from Mondays to Fridays.

Day Trading uses various techniques and strategies to make a profit from price changes for a specific asset. It involves adjusting to events that bring about short-term market fluctuations.

News releases and announcements such as corporate earnings, interest rates, and other economic statistics give information about what the forex or stock market can expect. Day traders can then benefit from the market by attuning to the significant moves the market makes.

Day Trading, therefore, uses several intraday strategies, including breakout trading, scalping, news releases trading, range trading, and high-frequency trading (HFT).

Breakout Trading

A breakout happens when the price of a stock moves beyond the Support or resistance level. The Support or resistance level is the point at which the increase in the price of security stops because of an increase in the number of sellers who want to sell at that price. Day traders use breakout trading to take a position within the early stages of a trend.

A day trader buys an asset when the price of the asset breaks above the resistance level, or the trader sells an asset when the price of the asset goes below the resistance level.

Day Trading uses breakouts because breakout set-ups mark the begging point for significant price trends, significant price swings, and an increase in the unpredictability of the market or volatility. Such breakout set-ups include pullback-consolidation Breakout, reversal-consolidation breakout, reversal at support or resistance level, strong area breakout, and finally, false breakouts or fake-outs.

Pullback-consolidation breakout takes place within the first five to at most twenty minutes as soon as the forex or the stock market opens. The term pullback refers to the price drops that are comparatively short before the prices go back up.

A pullback is usually a few consecutive sessions. Consolidation refers to the case when there is a longer pause before the prices go back up. Pullbacks provide entry points for day traders who want to enter a position when there is a significant upward price movement of a commodity.

Reversal-consolidation breakout happens when a significant move in one direction is followed immediately by a more substantial step in the opposite direction. That is then followed by a long pause or consolidation. After the consolidation, day traders push the price in the reverse direction, assuming that the initial trend was wrong.

Reversal at Support or resistance level is a stage where the stock price has reversed frequently before. When this happens, day traders are not able to push the price of a security in a specific direction.

Strong Breakout happens when a breakout was so strong that it brought about a price gap. Day traders use strong breakouts to buy assets while avoiding selling any commodities in the market. That is to avoid making losses when the price continues to move upwards, following the Breakout. Traders place stop-loss orders when buying assets at this point, to reduce loss.

False Breakouts or fake-outs take place when a price breaks past the Support or resistance level but does not continue moving upward in that direction. When this happens, traders plan their exit by canceling out orders to reduce potential losses. Alternatively, traders avoid taking the first Breakout they see.

Generally, day traders wait until the price moves back to the original breakout level before they trade breakouts. The traders expect to see whether the price will move back to generate either an upward or a downward trend, depending on the direction the traders are trading.

Scalping

Scalping is a Day Trading strategy that day traders use to try to generate small profits on small price changes throughout the day. When scalping, day traders assume that most assets or stocks will complete the initial stage of a movement. However, traders do not know the direction the stock prices will move. That is because, after that first movement, some stocks may stop advancing, while others may continue to develop.

As a result, day traders aim to take as many small profits as they can, while maintaining a higher ratio of winning trades compared to the losing trades. That strategy helps the traders to keep benefits that are equal or somewhat more significant than losses.

Day traders use three types of scalping. The first type is market- making. In market making, the trader attempts to make profits on the gap between the bid and the asking price of a security. The traders achieve this by issuing out a request and an offer for a particular stock. However, a trader makes extremely small profits because he or she must compete with the other market makers for the shares on both bids and offers.

The second type is more traditional, where traders buy large numbers of shares, which they later sell for a profit when there are small price movements. In this case, traders enter into positions for a couple of thousand shares and wait for small price movements measured in cents.

The third type is much closer to the old method of trading. In this type of scalping, a trader puts up a certain number of shares on any set-up from his or her system and exits the position as soon as the first exit signal develops near the 1:1 risk-reward ratio.

News Releases Trading

Day traders trade news events that are worth trading because news events have the capacity to increase volatility in the short- term. Therefore, traders look for financial information that will cause price movements in the currency market. The currency market mostly responds to economic news from the United States (U.S), and to other financial news from around the world.

Traders mostly follow economic news from the eight major currencies. Such currencies include the U.S. dollar (USD), the British pound (GBP), the Euro (EUR), the Swiss franc (CHF), the Japanese yen (JPY), the Australian dollar (AUD), the New Zealand dollar (NZD), and finally the Canadian dollar (CAD).

Generally, the most significant news releases from any country include information on inflation, trade balance, manufacturing industries surveys, interest rate decisions, retail sales, business sentiment surveys, consumer confidence surveys, industrial production, natural disasters, political unrest, and unemployment. Therefore, because the relevance of these releases may change, traders keep an eye on the focus of the market at all times.

Traders trade news releases by looking for consolidation periods ahead of big numbers and trade the breakouts that are on the back of the numbers.

Range Trading

In range trading, day traders employ support and resistant levels to make their trade decisions. In other words, traders take note of overbought (resistance), oversold (support) areas, buy at the oversold area, and sell at the overbought area.

Day traders use this strategy in markets that are constantly fluctuating, with no visible long-term trend. The goal of a trader is to identify points at which stock prices have gone above or below the regular prices but will likely move back to the original value, or points where support or resistance has formed and is expected to hold again.

As such, range trading uses the Support and resistance strategy, and the breakouts and breakdowns strategy. In using the Support and resistance strategy, traders buy when the price is close to the support level, and sell when the price reaches resistance. Traders use technical indicators such as the relative strength index (RSI), the stochastic oscillator, and the commodity channel index (CCI). Traders use the indicators to confirm the oversold and overbought situations when the price oscillates or fluctuates within a trading range.

For example, a trader can buy a stock when the stock price is trading at Support, and the RSI showing an oversold reading below 20, and sell when the RSI gives an overbought reading above 60. To reduce the chances of making losses, a trader can place a stop-loss order outside the trading range.

In using the breakouts and breakdowns strategy, traders enter in the direction of a breakout or a breakdown from a trading range. Traders make use of indicators such as price action and volume, to check whether a price movement is in force.

High-Frequency Trading (HFT)

The high-frequency trading strategy makes use of algorithms to capitalize on short-term market inadequacies.

HFT uses dynamic computer programs to manage a large number of orders within seconds. High-frequency traders achieve this by making use of complex algorithms to analyze various markets and to complete market orders depending on market conditions. Therefore, traders with fast delivery speed profit more than those with slower delivery speeds are.

HFT brings in liquidity to the markets and does away with small bid-ask spreads. The liquidity that HFT produces disappears within seconds, and therefore only traders with quick execution speeds can benefit from it. Additionally, HFT removes small bid- ask spreads, which bring in minimal profits.

Major investment banks, hedge funds, and institutional traders or investors use HFT to handle a significant number of orders at super high speeds. The HFT platforms allow traders to manage millions or orders and evaluate multiple markets and trades within seconds, thus giving the traders a considerable advantage in the open market.

HFT has become popular in the open market following the introduction of incentives that high-frequency trading offers so that institutions can add liquidity to the open market. By giving small incentives, trades acquire more liquidity, and the institutions involved reap benefits from every trade they make, in addition to their high execution speeds.

Day Trading is, therefore, a career that requires traders to understand the basics of the marketplace. Individuals who try to take part in Day Trading without any knowledge and experience often lose their investments. A day trader should, therefore, be skilled in technical analysis and chart reading, to understand the ins and outs of the products or services that he or she trades.

Additionally, day traders should only invest capital, which they can afford to lose. That will help the traders leave out their emotions when trading while protecting them from financial devastation. In addition, a trader needs to have an execution plan in order to have an edge over the rest of the market.

Various strategies that a day trader can capitalize on include swing trading, trading news, and exploiting price differences of identical financial instruments on different forms. These strategies will help the trader to make consistent profits with minimal losses.

However, a profit-making strategy is ineffective without discipline. Lack of discipline can make traders make huge losses because they fail to initiate trades that meet their own standards.

Day traders mostly depend on volatility in the market to make profits. That is to say, a commodity may get the attention of the trader when the price of the commodity continually fluctuates during the day.

In addition, day traders rely on securities that are profoundly liquid because the liquidity gives the traders the opportunity to change their positions without interfering with the price of the security. When the cost of the underlying security moves up, a trader may enter a long position or a buy position, and sell the security when the price moves down so that he or she can profit when the price falls.

Day Trading consequently requires access to some of the most sophisticated financial services and instruments in the open market. Hence, day traders need access to various news sources and competent analytical software. In addition to these instruments, the traders will need to have a competitive edge in the market that will help them to acquire more profits than losses.

A trader can become more competent by taking time to understand how the market works, coming up with an execution strategy, having enough capital to start, and finally, by taking on trading opportunities that are within his or her trading limits. Day Trading requires sound methods that will give a person a statistical edge in every trade he or she makes.

Chapter 7: Technical Analysis

Technical analysis is the study of the price changes and trends of a stock or security. The study involves traders inspecting a stock's trading history through technical indicators and charts in order to determine the future direction of the stock price.

Statistical trends, such as price movement and volume identified from the past, determine future trading opportunities. Technical analysts, therefore, focus on price fluctuations, trading signals, and analytical charting tools to examine the strength or weakness of a specific security.

Technical analysis is more dominant in forex and stock markets where traders limit their attention to short-term price movements. Technical analysts aim to comprehend the market emotion behind the price patterns by looking for trends rather than evaluating the basic qualities of a stock.

Technical analysts assume that markets are resourceful with values representing influences that impact the price of a stock or security. However, the analysts acknowledge that price fluctuations are not entirely haphazard but move in recognizable trends that have a tendency to reoccur in the course of time.

There are two different approaches to technical analysis: the top- down approach and the bottom-up approach. The top-down approach involves evaluating securities that fit into a certain standard. For example, a trader may want securities that moved away from their 50-day moving average as a buying prospect.

The bottom-up approach deals with assessing stocks that appear primarily interesting for potential entry and exit points. For example, a trader may discover undervalued security in a downward trend and use technical analysis to find a particular entry point when the security price stops decreasing.

Different types of traders use different types of technical analysis. While position traders may use analytical charts and technical indicators, day trades may use simple trend lines and volume indicators to arrive at trade decisions. Similarly, traders coming up with computerized algorithms may use a combination of technical and volume indicators in their decision-making processes.

Trendline Analysis

Day traders study trends to forecast the future price changes of stock. Historical trends in the price movement give day traders an idea of what the price movements will be in the future.

Day traders carry out trend analysis on short-term, medium, and long-term time frames. In that way, the traders can determine when the price of a security will rise or fall. Along with that, traders can also predict when the market will rise or fall.

By being able to determine price movements, traders aim to time the market so that the traders can enter long positions or buy when the stock prices are at their lowest and sell when the shares are at their highest buying price.

As such, day traders pay attention to an economic institution's financial information and general economic conditions in order to forecast accurately, the future trend of an investment in the marketplace.

For instance, a trader's trend analysis shows that company X's security is at a low price, and according to past price action, the security's price tends to rise once it hits that low price. Consequently, the trader may take that as an indication that he or she should buy the company's security in order to make a profit when the security price moves up.

However, when the trader miss's information that the company laid off 30 percent of its workforce, in an effort to refinance its debt due to payment problems, then the trader may be setting himself or herself up for a loss.

Therefore, although technical analysts may use large amounts of data to carry out an analysis, there is no guarantee that the analysts' predictions will be accurate.

Volume Analysis

Volume analysis involves the evaluation of the number of shares or contracts that a particular stock or security has traded within a specified period.

Day traders use volume analysis to examine patterns in volumes in relation to price movements. As a result, the traders are able to know the importance of changes in the price of an asset or security.

Like any other technical indicator in the market place, the volume presents buy and sell signals to traders. Traders can know which signal to take by studying the pattern of the price movement. Are the trends strong in one direction? In addition, the traders can look at the moving average at the point of a breakout to determine whether the price movement captures the sentiments of significant investors.

When the demand for an underlying stock is high, it means that many traders have an interest in the underlying stock and are therefore prepared to pay more for it. The volume gives an indication to day traders of how many investors want certain security.

Day traders use two types of volume indicators; the positive volume index (PVI) and the negative volume index (NVI). Both indicators operate based on the previous day's trading volume and the market price of a commodity. Consequently, when the trading volume goes up from the previous day, the traders fine- tune the PVI. When the trading volume goes down from the previous day, the traders adjust the NVI accordingly.

Traders use the PVI and the NVI to evaluate how volume affects price movement. An increase or a decrease in the PVI implies that the volume drives the price movement. Contrariwise, an increase or a reduction in the NVI suggests that the volume has a minimal effect on the price changes.

Candlestick Charting

Day traders use candlestick charting to trace price fluctuations. The traders utilize the candlestick charts to show the price changes during a single time period for any time frame. For instance, each candlestick on a 4-hour chart shows the price movement within four hours.

The peak point of a candlestick displays the highest price a stock traded during the set period, whereas the lowermost position indicates the lowest prices of the stock during that time period. The part in between the highest and the weakest points in the candlestick shows the opening and closing stock prices for that period.

Traders choose the colors to use in the candlestick charts as a way to follow the price movements at a glance. As a result, traders get more visual cues and trends as they carry out technical analysis.

Chapter 8: Trading Mindset

Day Trading, like any other form of investment, is subject to influence from human emotion and psychological impact. Whenever money or capital is in play, people tend to take matters rather personally because of the inevitable consequence of the hope that comes along with the promise of significant returns. People will strive to make money while at the same time, avoid circumstances that may cause them to lose their capital. It is from this zero-sum mentality that the influence of psychology or emotions may creep into a sensible mindset. Such control takes over every aspect of the Day Trading instincts that you learned over time.

Your knowledge goes out of the window when a situation that triggers your psychological response arises. A high degree of counter-productivity thus ensues. It, eventually, leads to the dismissal of logical decisions in favor of hunches as well as the need to chase after fleeting profits and cover your previous losses. For you to manage your Day Trading expertise through challenging scenarios, you need to look out for emotions that alter your reasoning capability adversely. Try to improve and nurture a productive mindset, while at the same time, avoid promoting a mental culture that justifies negativity falsely. The following few behaviors and traits are central to your particular mindset whenever you decide to participate in Day Trading:

Do Not Rationalize Your Trading Errors

This mindset t is one of the leading obstacles to the progress and eventual success of your Day Trading endeavors. You are often prone to justify any trading mistakes that you make to the detriment of moving forward. For instance, you get an entry into a particularly promising trade deal later than necessary in spite of your much earlier knowledge of its potential for profitability. The delay causes you to miss an excellent opportunity at the previous entry point. However, you decide to justify this misstep by convincing yourself of your preference for trading late over missing the same deal entirely.

The downside to such delays is often a faulty sense of size estimation in taking your trading position. Hence, the resulting increased exposure to financial risk you become disadvantaged by. Beware of your procrastination when it comes to productive openings that are currently available in Day Trading. If you possess this tendency, consider getting rid of it as soon as possible before it costs you a lot more capital in the long run. In case you are not prone to the frequent postponement of your responsibilities to a later date, be alert for the development of this mentality with the trading company that you keep. You can quickly become influenced by the kind of traders from whom you seek advice on more complex trading strategies. When present, stockbrokers affect your trading ethos, as well.

Poor trading etiquette from these external sources will rub off on you and vice versa. Try to keep the company of well-known responsible trading partners and stockbrokers when the need arises. Another rationalization scenario involves a run of profitable results. Based on a series of trade deals that made you successive returns, you begin to convince your brain of your seemingly high intelligence. This false belief in your skills may lead you to overestimate your trading expertise. Before long, you may start engaging in Day Trading on a hunch rather than apply logic to your decisions. You stop referring to your trusted trading plan and jump into many trading opportunities haphazardly. After a while, these instances of carelessness and trading arrogance will catch up with you because they always inevitably do. Your chances of plunging into a financial disaster go up.

With your eventual financial ruin come the cases of psychological meltdown leading to a negative feedback loop. A wrong decision from your misplaced sense of conceitedness will invariably lead to high-risk exposure. As a result, you suffer significant losses eventually, and consequently, your emotional health suffers, causing you to spiral into a state of depression. This loop is often self-propagating, meaning that it feeds onto itself. Bad decisions lead to adverse outcomes and a fragile mindset, which, in turn, is prone to make more bad decisions, and the loop goes on and on. Keep in mind that in Day Trading, such a feedback loop is often disastrous. All these adverse effects arise from your initial false sense of justification for a wrong deed.

Beware of Your Trading Decisions

This advice is so apparent that it sounds redundant when mentioned. However, decisions are typically the product of your reasoning and judgment at a particular moment. When it comes to decisions on Day Trading, psychological influence is often a determining factor in the process. Keeping your wits about you is very crucial, especially when everything seems to be out of control. You need to realize that every trade has its ups and downs and how you deal with the challenging times is often more consequential. Try to maintain a logical mindset when making Day Trading choices from a variety of bad options. When it seems that an imminent financial downturn is inevitable, the extent of your loss becomes essential. In this case, you will need to make a sensible decision on the degree of losing margins that you can tolerate adequately.

At this point, you are probably in a state of so many overwhelming emotions that your foggy mental faculties become clouded. An expected human response is to run away from danger, naturally, but in certain situations, fleeing may not be an option. A reflex in a trading scenario often leads to an impulsive decision. Such a choice is, in turn, typically not well thought or deliberative. You should confront your unfavorable circumstances head-on and attempt to fix the situation, however hopeless. This sense of perseverance is usually the essence of most trading excursions, especially when the times become financially rough. Going through the loss of some capital and other Day Trading challenges is often a painful experience that can lead to illogical decisions.

Always remember to uphold vigilance and adhere strictly to the guidelines in your trading plan when confronted with obstacles during your trades. The trading plan usually has instructions on how to handle these seemingly desperate situations. In addition, the prior preparation of any trading guide is generally free of emotional or psychological influence; hence, you can rely on it to maintain neutrality. Also, beware of making trading resolutions when going through a phase with a foul mood. Such conclusions are bound to lead you into a financial catastrophe, especially if you are not careful. Learn to put off the verdict to a time when you can resume logical thinking. When you make any rash decision, it can only result in your further exposure to even more risk.

Keep Your Emotions in Check

Learn to stick to a Day Trading system and method that you trust. Such a strategy may be one that has a history of always making significant returns. Once you master and fully grasp how to apply a specific approach to your trading deals, try to fine-tune it to your preference based on your ultimate objectives. Afterward, stick to this tried, practiced, and tested system in all your searches for valid trade deals. On some days, the stock market may be slow with a low volume of trade. The volatility in such a case is often negligible. However, due to an unchecked emotional influence, you develop a sense of greed or lust for profits.

The desire for benefits on a slow day is common. It leads to the urge to trade on anything to make a small profit. In this situation, you will move from Day Trading into gambling. Trading requires a logical mindset on your part with a lack of psychological attachment whatsoever. Gambling is a consequence of emotional and mental factors running amok in your Day Trading system. If a particular trading style worked on multiple times in the past, teach your brain to consider it. Your trusted trading system will indicate a lack of valid trade opportunities on a specific slow market day. In this case, curb your emotions, desires, and urges to chase a quick profit; however strong they seem.

You should never allow yourself to resort to gambling under any circumstances. Gambling is detrimental to healthy and responsible Day Trading behavior. The risk exposure exponentially rises when you grow accustomed to the desire for profits. If a given day of trading is unfavorable, you should not take part in invalid and unworthy deals. In addition, you should only trade on verifiable opportunities. At certain times, you may experience a series of successive returns in a relatively short period. Learn to know when to stop and how to curb your lust for wanting more returns. Trust your system to trade only on valid deals; however, multiple opportunities are available. An emotion that goes unmonitored in such situations is the greed for more profit.

You convince yourself psychologically that the various deals could be a sign of your lucky day. This mentality in a false belief is wrong, and you need to be aware of it. Your psychology can play deceitful tricks on your logical mind leading to high-risk trading deals. You must realize that in Day Trading, it is almost impossible to get more returns out of a system than what the stock market offers. Emotional corruption also comes into play in a scenario where you bite off more than you can chew.

The greed for substantial amounts of returns may cause you to take high-risk trading positions for a chance at quick profits. However, you must remember that profits and losses are both possible outcomes from a Day Trading session. Therefore, you need to learn to trade in amounts that you can afford to lose. After all, Day Trading involves taking a chance based on a speculative position. You should practice trading in small amounts of money within the confines of low-risk deals. In this case, a potential loss may not be as damaging as the earlier high-risk trading position driven by greed. Eliminate the role of emotions in Day Trading and learn to accept the uncertainty of an unknown future outcome.

Be Patient When Trading

Patience is a crucial trait to have when you take part in Day Trading due to the upswings and downward trends in stock prices. It can become challenging to identify the right entry or exit point for a particular trading opportunity, given the fluctuating nature of a volatile market. However, when you master the art of being patient and studying the trade intently, you can come up with a winning strategy. Having a planned approach is essential, and you should prepare one before engaging in any Day Trading. Often, most seasoned traders include trading strategies for different market conditions in their trading plans. Hence, when making your trading plan, consider incorporating a trading strategy within it.

If unsure of how to proceed, you can always seek the assistance of qualified stockbrokers. They have the experience of encountering various Day Trading scenarios in the real world. If trustworthy, they could provide you with invaluable insights on coming up with a proper strategy. Now it is up to you to stick to the plan in every session in which you participate. Patience demands that you pay attention to the planned strategy and ignore any attractive distractions when trading. For instance, a brief upswing from a potential price action breakout may be misleading. It might cause you to falsely believe that the stock price is about to pick momentum and keep rising on the chart.

However, as attractive as this scenario might be, a sense of diligent patience demands that you ignore it and refer to your strategy. Upon referral to your trading plan strategy, you may encounter the concept of false breakouts. You also learn that these false upswings in trend usually follow a prolonged period of price consolidated. As a result, your patience allows you to evade a potentially wrong entry point to a trading position. You are also able to pick the right exit point from a particular trading session based on strategic patience. The price action chart acts merely as a guide for your trading actions and not the determining factor.

Chapter 9: Day Trading Rules

Day Trading is the ability to buy and sell financial instruments within the same trading day. There is a group of day traders called the pattern day traders (PDT) these are just traders who make more than four trades within five days and who use a margin account to trade. Day Trading has rules, and failure to adhere to certain rules can be costly. Rules also vary depending on location and the volume you trade.

7 Rules of Day Trading

The following rules of Day Trading, if used correctly, can help traders make profits and avoid huge losses.

How to Enter and Exit A Market

Day traders should have a predetermined plan in place of when to enter and exit a market. A trader can quickly find yourself out of the game as soon as you press the enter key if they do not have a plan. As a day trader, you have to accept the fact that you do not control the market. Therefore, one of the key factors to succeeding in Day Trading is usually determined by your ability to enter and exit your trading positions. Knowing the prices at which you wish to enter and exit can help make profits or save you from losing out on more.

When making the plan:

- Use indicators

- Set a target price before you enter the market.

- Know how much stock you plan to trade

- Plan for when to exit the market - when the market is going against your expectations, do you exit your position to avoid bigger losses?

Trading Rush Hours

Another important Day Trading rule is to avoid the first hour after the market opens and the last hour before it closes. It is wise to wait and observe during those times. Do not be eager to jump in as soon as the market opens. The first and last hours are the most volatile times in the market. This is because the stock is likely reacting to some overnight news releases, and this is when the big investors and trading experts compete. In the last hour, traders are also rushing to close out their positions.

Be Cautious of Margin Trading

Another important rule is to trade with the money you have, not borrowed money. It is important to be cautious of margin trading. Trading on margin means that you are borrowing money from a brokerage firm to trade; Money you will have to pay back. A margin account increases your purchasing power and allows you to use borrowed money to increase financial leverage; however, not all trades are profitable. Therefore, you risk losing the small bit of your capital as well as the borrowed money. Margin trading should be used in trades that you are sure will be profitable.

Be Realistic

Another important Day Trading rule is to avoid greed. It is very easy to be carried away by greed when trading, do not lose out on small profits because you think you can make more. It is very important to remain realistic about profits. The market is always changing; sometimes, it is better to settle on a small profit than to make big losses.

Be Knowledgeable

Do not day trade if you do have no sufficient knowledge of what is happening in the markets. Not everyone can trade in the market. Most traders start with paper trading and intense training. You need to be aware of information about the stocks you plan to trade, basic trading procedures, and always be on the lookout for anything that can affect your stocks. You can start by practicing using a demo account; this is a trial and error account, where you do not use real money. This account enables traders to experiment with trading before they can set up a real funded account.

Cut Your Losses

This is the number one rule in trading; cut your losses. Placing a trade is taking a risk; every trader, even the best in the world, has had bad trading days. Losing is part of trading. Traders need to accept their losses when the market starts going against them instead of hoping for a turnaround. This can be a lethal mistake. Have an exit strategy and react accordingly. Accepting your loss reduces the chance of it happening again. By cutting your losses, you learn from it and make the necessary changes to avoid a repetition.

Risk Management Plan

Risk management plans help cut down losses. The idea is to avoid risking more than you can afford to lose. With a risk management plan, even when a trade goes wrong, they still have money to trade tomorrow. Traders follow the 1% rule, which allows them to trade only 1% of their capital on any single trade. This ensures that only 1% of their money is at risk on any single trade.

Other General Day Trading rules

These rules are not binding but can be helpful when making trading decisions:

Keep A Trading Journal

The process of Day Trading can be nerve-wracking, and in most cases, traders do not remember with clarity and context all the moves they made at the end of the day, so as a rule, it is important to journal while you are trading. It does not have to be detailed, and you can write in bullet points and edit later. Journaling gives you the ability to track your trades, gains, and losses. You can also use the information to analyze your overall market performance and tweak your strategies.

Tax Rules

There is no one size fits all when it comes to tax rules. Taxes depend on the country where you are trading. Each country has different tax obligations, and the consequences of not meeting them can be extremely costly. It is important to research on taxes before you start trading.

Manage Number of Trades

A good rule of thumb is to avoid making more than three trades a week. It is more difficult to keep an eye on multiple trades at once, especially if you luck experience. If a trader makes four or more- day trades within five days, the account moves from cash account to a pattern day trade account, also known as a margin account, which has certain limitations like:

• Minimum Account Balance

Day traders who use margin accounts must maintain a minimum balance of $25,000. This does not apply to day traders who use cash brokerage accounts. If the account balance falls below this amount, the owner loses any buying power. This minimum balance can be maintained in the form of cash and securities. Pattern day traders are not allowed to cross guarantee to meet the minimum balance.

• When the minimum capital is not reached

When a pattern day trader account goes below $25,000, they are issued with an equity call. The balance must be restored using cash or other marginal equities. Traders should deposit the funds within five business days, and they are not allowed to make a withdrawal on the amount for at least two working days.

• Increased leverage

Pattern day trade accounts have increased access to margin and, therefore, leverage. They may have access to twice the standard margin amount when trading stocks. The amount is usually decided every morning.

Have A Trading Plan

Another important trading rule is to always have a trading plan and stick to it when trading. One of the worst habits' traders have is trading impulsively without any guidelines. Traders should assess their success or failure on a trade based on how they stuck to their trading plan and not whether they made a profit or a loss. Ensure that your trading plan works for you and stick to it.

Don't Chase Trades

Another rule is to avoid is chasing trades. Sometimes traders decide to chase fast-moving stocks when the market makes large and quick moves in prices instead of focusing on their trading plan. Even though the move can lead to more profits, sometimes trading decisions made in a rash can be costly. Most traders learn the importance of this rule when their poor trading decisions cost them.

Emotions

Another rule of Day Trading is not to let your emotions affect your trading decisions. Emotions have a way of influencing a trader's performance. The two common ones are fear and greed. These emotions can make a trader miss desirable gains or miss opportunities. This is why traders have to follow the rules and stick to the trading plans they made when their mind was rational. Traders should learn to be self-aware of moments when emotions are taking over and counter the response.

A Positive Mindset

A trader should always start his or her trades with a positive mindset. Avoid letting any negative thoughts or situations hinder your judgment abilities. In trading, it is important to focus on your actions, your strategies, and tools to be a success; all this requires a positive mindset.

Be Patient

Day Trading takes years of experience to master. It takes time to develop successful strategies; therefore, patience is key. You might experience losses after losses, which can make you lose hope, but with time, it gets better. Part of being patient is to plan when to buy stock and wait for the best time to sell

Always Use A Stop Loss Order

A stop-loss order is issued when a trader places an order with a broker to buy or sell the stock once it reaches a certain price. Stop- loss orders are ideally used to limit loss. When you have a stop- loss order, you do not have to monitor stock all the time. Sometimes, frequent fluctuations can activate the stop-loss order; therefore, it is advisable to select a stock-loss percentage that allows for such fluctuations.

Embracing Technology

Technology has proven to be very successful in helping day traders view and analyze the market. Technology has made it possible for more and more people to access trading, traders can practice light-speed trading, have a virtual trading platform for
24 hours a day. Traders need to embrace technology while trading, gone are the day one had limited time to trade, now, when one market closes, another opens.

Follow The 80/20 Rule

The 80/20 rules suggest that 80% of your profits should be generated by 20% of your trades. 20% of your work should generate 80% success. This rule can be used to analyze four key areas when trading

• *Trading performance*

This rule can be used to improve trading performance and analyze relationships like which tools, indicators, and strategies are causing the most wins and losses. What day of the month do you make wins and losses?

• *Individual performance*

This rule can also be used to improve efficiency. How much time do you spend on a task, and why? What do you do that reduces or increases your focus on trading? By analyzing such questions, you can know what areas need improvement

• *Market Understanding*

80/20 rule can help one improve their understanding of the market. For example, the market usually does not trend 80% of the time and trends 20% of the time.

• *Strategy performance*

The rule is useful in analyzing the efficiency a trader's strategy is. Are the majority of the wins the result of a specific strategy? Do the tools and indicators influence the strategies positively or negatively?

Use Limit Orders, Not Market Orders

Market orders are used to inform brokers to buy and sell an asset at the best available price at the time of execution. However, the best is not always profitable. Instead, traders should use limit orders. Limited orders have a controlled minimum price and maximum price for buying and selling, and therefore traders can ensure they remain profitable.

Avoid Penny Stocks

Penny stocks are small capital company stocks that are purchased cheaply per share. As the name suggests, these were stocks that traded for less than $1 per share. However, nowadays, penny stock is stocking that trade for $5 per share. So, why should we avoid penny stock?

- They are not traded on public exchanges like regular stocks. Therefore, there is not enough financial information about them to determine if they are good investments. Companies that sell this penny stock are also not subject to certain disclosures, and therefore can mismanage their financials.

- Companies offering the penny stocks are usually new in the market, and therefore it is hard to predict their performance

- Penny stocks are not as liquid as most people would think; people buy and sell them over the counter, and do not trade them on a public exchange. Therefore, it becomes hard to find a buyer if you wish to sell.

- Since penny stocks have low asset value, they have high risk. The company can go bankrupt, making you lose money.

You are better off buying reputable stocks from solid companies.

Number of Stocks

If you are a beginner, as a rule, only buy one or two stocks during a Day Trading session. You can increase the number as you learn the game, but as a newbie, it is advisable to focus on one or two stocks to be able to track and find opportunities. You can easily miss good opportunities if you have too much going on.

Importance of Leverage in Day Trading

Leveraging in trading is the ability to use borrowed funds from brokerage firms to increase one's trading position. It is considered high risk because it increases the amount of profit or loss a trader makes. Leverage is usually given a fixed amount that varies depending on the brokerage firm. Forex trading offers very high leverage ratios. Ratios can be as high a 400:1, and this means a trader with $1,000 in their account can trade up to $400,000 in value. This is because if the accounts are managed properly, the risk becomes manageable.

Leverage is important in Day Trading because:

- It reduces the amount of capital a trader needs to trade, which gives them room to take on other trades

- It allows traders to get greater returns for small up-front investment

- Leverage does not affect any profit or loss that a trader makes.

- Leverage can reduce the risk of certain types of trades.

- Leverage makes the market exciting.

- When you use leverage and make a profit, you can pay back the borrowed amount and still have more money left than if you had just invested your capital

- In some countries, it offers favorable tax treatment.

Generally, a trader should not use their entire available margin. Leverage should only be used when the advantage is on one's side. Most experienced traders usually trade with very low leverage to protect their capital against any trading mistakes they make. Experienced traders should not be afraid of leverage, especially when they learn how to manage it.

How the Securities and Exchange Commission Works

The security and exchange commission (SEC) is a government agency in charge of overseeing the security markets. It also protects investors and facilitates capital formation. The SEC maintains efficient, transparent, and effective markets.

History

Before SEC was formed, the blue-sky laws were enacted and enforced at the state level to protect the public against fraudsters. Although the laws varied across states, all companies offering securities to the public as well as stockbrokers and brokerage firms had to register themselves. These blue-sky laws were found to be ineffective as companies like the Investment Bankers Association ignored them. The congress then created the SEC through the Security Exchange Act of 1934, which was passed after the stock market crashed in 1929. It was created to restore the public's confidence in financial markets.

SEC was to address two notions:

- Companies that sell securities to the public should be honest and release any information to the public that may affect their securities.

- Investors should be treated fairly.

The SEC is made up of three organizational structures:

1. *The Commission Members*

The commission is made up of five commissioners carefully selected by the president, who all belong to different political parties. They retain their seats for five years, and one is designated as chairperson. They may serve for an extended 18 months past their five-year term if there is no immediate replacement.

2. *Divisions*

SEC consists of five divisions:

Trading and Markets - this division monitors how the industry operates, interprets any proposed changes, and oversees self-regulatory organizations like all broker-dealer firms, investment houses, the Financial Industry Regulatory Authority (FINRA). The SEC has delegated the tasks of making rules and enforcing them to FINRA.

Corporation Finance - this division oversees public companies' disclosures and ensures investors get relevant information so that they can make informed investment decisions for the companies.

Enforcement - together with three other divisions, enforcement investigates privately any SEC law violations and takes action on violators. The SEC only prosecutes civil suits; the justice department handles criminal cases.

Investment Management - this division supervises registered investment companies as well as registered investment advisors. The division also administers various federal security laws. Other responsibilities include

- Interpreting laws and regulations for the public

- Responding to no-action requests

- Enforce any matters involving investment firms.

Economic and Risk Analysis - this division integrates economics and data analytics into the core mission of the SEC. The division uses a variety of academic work and market knowledge to help commissions solve complex matters.

When handling civil suits, the SEC can only perform two actions:

- Injunction-this an authoritative warning or order, any violations can lead to fines or imprisonment

- Issue civil money penalties and the disgorgement of illegal profits

3. *Regional Offices*

US SEC has 11 regional offices throughout the country. The regional offices have the following offices:

- The Office of General Counsel-which gives legal advice to the commission as well as represent the agency in court

- The Office of Compliance, Inspection, and Examinations-this office is in charge of inspecting stock exchanges, broker-dealers, mutual funds, and credit rating agencies.

- The Office of the Chief Accountant-ensure any auditing and accounting policies set by the SEC are enforced

- The Office of Information Technology-oversees the IT department

- The Office of internal Affairs-represent the SEC abroad

- The Inspector General

- The SEC Office of the Whistleblower-this office rewards individuals who voluntarily share information that leads to successful law enforcement actions.

Chapter 10: How to be a Successful Trader

Trading can only be productive when traders take the exercise seriously and conduct thorough market research.

A successful trade is one that effectively puts a trading plan into action, among other factors. The trading plan helps to ensure that a trader has a more focused trading strategy and that he or she does not take trades outside of the trading plan. Other factors include trading discipline, technology, and developing a trading style.

Consequently, successful traders take their time to understand how the investment market works and thereby improve their strategy.

Making A Successful Trade Step-By-Step

Executing trades successfully is a process that requires a trader to follow the steps below to have an effective plan.

Making a Watchlist

A watchlist is a record of stocks or securities that a trader looks at to see whether the shares or securities suit his or her trading plan. There are many stocks in the marketplace to keep an eye on, without a watchlist.

Watchlists give the trader an idea of what investments he or she may want to add to his or her collection. A watchlist should be simple and based on current information of the biggest gainers, for example. The best stocks are those whose prices keep moving in a favorable direction.

Therefore, in every single day's watchlist, a trader should try to find the winning stocks from the previous day, especially if the shares have positive news and the right chart breakout. That is because the stocks will continue trading in the market the following day.

Besides, a trader should begin with a wide range of stock selections, and then narrow down stocks according to what he or she is looking for, as he or she observes the trend. When the trader knows what he or she is looking for, he or she will eliminate stocks that do not suit his or her trading strategy.

In addition, it is wise for a trader to list the most popular stocks and to check why the stocks are popular picks for other traders. The factors that make the stock popular will most likely be issues that other traders hold in a high volume. Such considerations should then be the trading standards for the trader.

Moreover, a trader should understand how the fluctuation in stock prices directly affects the way that driving forces react to different commodities in the market. In that way, the trader will develop his or her trading style and have an easy time assessing the patterns of the stocks on his or her watchlist.

There are certain things that a trader should avoid having in his or her watchlist. First, a trader should not have too many stocks on the list. A good number would be anywhere from five to ten stocks. That will help the trader to have a better chance to understand how the trade works.

Secondly, a trader should not focus on big trades. When a trader aims small, he or she misses little, thereby cutting losses quickly. Big trades run the risk of having huge losses. The idea is to win more and get better profit on the wins than the amount one loses because losing is part of the trade.

Choosing and Purchasing Stocks

When buying a company's stock, a trader becomes a stakeholder or a part-owner of that company. The value of the trader's investment, therefore, depends on the general well-being of the business.

Therefore, when buying a stock, a trader should start with a company that he or she knows. In so doing, a trader gets a place to start and avoids buying stocks without understanding how the company intends to make money.

Additionally, a trader should take into account the stock price and valuation. More experienced investors tend to look for securities that are cheap or undervalued to reap benefits when the stock price goes up.

However, a trader should know the kind of stock he or she wants, and he or she should understand that cheap is not always right and expensive is not still bad. A commodity may be cheap because its business is slowing down, and a commodity may be costly because investors expect their earnings to increase rapidly in a few years.

In addition, a trader should evaluate the financial stability of the company before buying the company's stocks. The trader can assess the revenue growth, check the bottom line, check the company's balance sheet to know how much debt the company has, and then finally find a dividend.

After choosing a stock, a trader can buy the stock first by opening a brokerage account. When opening the brokerage account, the trader should find out the brokerage fee.

A broker that charges low or does not charge at all will be an ideal choice. Along with that, a trader should check whether the broker offers educational tools, guidance on trading, stock market research, and easy access to help centers.

Secondly, the trader should identify the stocks that he or she wants to buy by researching companies that he or she already knows from past trading experiences.

Thirdly, the trader should decide how many shares he or she wants to buy. It is advisable to start by purchasing a single stock, to get a feel of what the trade is like and the trader deciding whether he or she would want to continue in the business.

Afterward, the trader can select his or her stock order type. Most investors buy stocks either with market orders or with limit orders. With a market order, the trader is signifying that he or she will buy or sell the security at best available current market prices. A limit order gives the trader more control over the price at which he or she will buy or sell.

Finally, the trader can then improve his or her stock selection to begin the journey of carrying out successful trades officially.

Understanding Entry and Exit

An entry point is the price at which a trader buys or sells a stock. A good entry point marks the beginning of a successful trade. A trader can find a proper entry point by doing market research and maximize profits in each business.

To find valid entry points, a trader should research, study, and learn the relevant parallels and factors that are influencing the market. For example, a trader can study and find an attractive stock but feels that the price of the stock is very high. In that case, the trader will buy if the price reduces to a certain level. That level will be the trader's entry point.

Consequently, the process of finding an entry point requires a trader to practice patience and wait for the appropriate time to buy, to get returns on his or her investment.

After evaluating the market, a trader should then decide whether to enter a long position (buy) or a short position (short). Concerning that, the trader should avoid risking too much. That is, the trader should invest what he or she can afford to lose.

Additionally, a trader should utilize limit orders to buy or sell a currency pair at a particular price or a better price. The use of technical indicators will come in handy when creating trading signals. Technical indicators will give the trader essential information about the market and currency pairs.

Accordingly, a trader should make his or her transactions occasionally, because market conditions can change due to technical influences and financial news releases.

An exit point is the price at which a trader closes the position. A trader may, therefore, sell at an exit point, or buy to close the position if he or she anticipates selling it later at a higher price.

A trader can exit either through take-profit orders or through stop-loss orders. A take-profit order is a limit order that stipulates the exact price of a commodity or the exact profit level in which a trader wants his or her broker to close the trader's position. A stop-loss order, tells the broker to close the trader's position when the stock suffers losses.

When coming up with an entry-exit plan, the trader needs to decide how long he or she intends to be in the trade. In addition, the trader needs to know how much risk he or she is willing to take.

Knowing How to Stop Loss

A broker places a stop-loss order once the stock reaches a particular level. A stop-loss helps to limit a trader's loss on a stock position.

For example, when a trader buys a share at $10 per share, he or she can place a stop-loss order for $8. Therefore, is the security's price falls beyond $8, the broker will sell the trader's shares at the prevailing market price.

A trader can know where to place his or her stop-losses by using the percentage method, the support method, or the moving average method. Many traders use the percentage method.

The percentage method involves calculating the percentage of stock a trader is willing to risk before he or she closes his or her position on the trade.

For instance, if a trader is willing to lose 10 percent of the value of security before he or she exits and the trader owns securities that are trading at $40 per share, the trader would place his or her stop-loss order at $36. That will be 10 percent below the market price of the security.

The support method also allows the trader to tailor his or her stop-loss level to the commodity that he or she is trading. As such, the trader needs to find the most recent level of support and place his or her stop-loss slightly below that level.

For example, if the trader owns a share that is currently trading at $30 per share, and he or she finds $25 as the most recent support level. Therefore, the trader should place his or her stop- loss slightly below $25. Placing the stop-loss slightly below the support level gives the commodity's price space to come down and bounce back up before the trader closes his or her position.

The moving average method requires the trader to apply a moving average to his or her security chart. A moving average is a technical indicator that analyzes the price changes of stocks while

reducing the impact of random price fluctuations.

A trader may want to use a long-term moving average as compared to a short-term moving average to avoid placing his or her stop-loss too close to the stock price and getting closed out of his or her trade too soon.

As soon as the trader puts the moving average, he or she should set his or her stop-loss immediately below the level of the moving average. For instance, if the trader's share is currently trading at
$30 and the moving average is at $26, he or she should place the stop-loss below $26, to allow the stock price space for movement.

Knowing When to Sell

A trader should start selling his or her stock when he or she miscalculated the decision to buy the stock, when the stock price shoots up dramatically, and when the stock has reached an unsustainable amount.

A trader will know whether he or she made a profit or loss the minute he or she sells the stock. While the buying price may help the trader to know how much advantage he or she has gained, the selling price guarantees the profit, if any.

While selling a stock should not be a common occurrence because trading in and out of positions could be detrimental to a trader's investment, postponing the decision to sell the stock when it is the right time to do so may also yield unfavorable outcomes.

For example, a trader may buy a stock at $20 to sell it at $25. The stock price reaches $25, and the trader decides to hold out for a couple of more points. The stock hits $27, and the trader still holds out to maximize on profit should the stock price move further up. Suddenly, the price drops back to $24. The trader waits until the price hits $25 again, but this does not happen. The trader then gives in to frustration and sells the stock at a loss when the stock price hits $18.

Consequently, if a trader sells at the opportune time, he or she will experience the benefits of buying the stock. However, the trader should not try to time the market because timely selling does not necessarily require accurate market timing. The focus should be on buying at one price and selling at a higher price, even when the higher price is not the absolute top.

When a trader discovers that he or she made an analytical error in buying a stock, the trader should sell the stock even if it means that he or she will make a loss.

If a trade does not meet the trader's short-term earnings predictions and the price of the shares takes a fall, he or she should not sell the stock if the business is not losing market shares to competitors. If the company loses market shares to competitors, then that may be a good reason for the trader to sell the stock.

Alternatively, a trader can sell his or her stock when the stock price rises dramatically in a short period for particular reasons. The trader should take his or her gains and move on.

Additionally, a trader could sell when the company's valuation is becoming higher than its competitors are, or when the company's price-to-earnings ratio goes beyond its average price-to-earnings within five or ten years.

However, when a company's earnings decline when the demand is low, and the company starts cutting costs. That would be a chance to exit the position before any further decline in the value of the company's stock.

In addition, a trader could sell his or her stock for financial needs. That may not be a good reason from an analytical point, but securities are assets, and traders have the freedom to cash in their assets when the need arises.

Examples of Day Trades

Trading Breakouts

Given that traders always want to cut losses quickly, trading breakouts is ideal for scanning potential losses because a trader can see when he or she is making a wrong decision.

The trader first needs to identify a price level that represents his or her breakout trading level. Afterward, the trader enters the market once he or she sees that a security price goes beyond the defined range. The trader can then close the stock above the resistance level.

That means, when the price of a stock moves out of a defined price range, a trader can move to a new high or low. For example, a trader can buy when the market price breaks higher, or goes beyond a failed resistance level, and sell when the market breaks lower, or goes below a failed support level.

However, a trader should only buy when the price pulls back to the original breakout point to avoid the likelihood of being trapped in a false breakout.

Trading Ranges

When a trader trades ranges, he or she aims to take advantage of the fraction of the market that is not trending. For example, if the market only trends 40 percent of the time, that leaves the trader with 60 percent to explore.

Trading ranges take into account the support and resistance levels, which develop when the stock price oscillates. The trader first needs to make sure that the stock price does not break above or below any level in between the highs and lows, assuming that two similar highs and lows have already happened in that price fluctuation.

For example, a trader may notice that a particular stock was starting to form a price during a specified period. After the stock price forms the initial peaks, the trader may start placing long or short trades based on the stock's trendlines, along with the resistance and support levels. Trading ranges ends when the stock does not show a breakout from either trendline.

Flag Trading

Flag trading is about a trader identifying flag shapes on a price chart. Flag patterns are easy to spot. The direction in which the flag blows shows the path of the primary trend and indicates that a stock is going through a steady upward trend.

The shape of the flag forms when a stock makes a strong move upward, on high volume, and then consolidates at the top of the pole, on low volume. The trend continues when the stock breaks out of the consolidation pattern on high volume.

Flag patterns can trend either upwards or downwards while following the same volume and breakout patterns. For example, in an upward-trending flag pattern, the price action moves up during the first trend and then declines through the consolidation area. That is an indication that traders have entered the market in a new wave of enthusiasm.

In a downward-trending flag pattern, the price action does not always decline during the consolidation. That is because of fear and anxiety over the falling prices that make traders avoid taking action.

Triangle Trading

Triangle trading has three types of triangle chart formations: symmetrical, ascending, and descending triangles.

The symmetrical triangle forms when the slant of the price's highs and the slant of a price's lows meet at an apex to form the shape of a triangle. What this means is that the market is making lesser highs and lows that are more significant. Neither the buyers nor the sellers are moving the price far enough to create a clear trend.

The ascending triangle forms when there are a resistance level and a slant of higher lows. That is an indication that there is a certain level that the buyers cannot seem to go beyond. However, the traders put pressure on the resistance level for a breakout to happen. While the breakout may not occur quickly, the traders are at least able to push the price up by a margin.

The descending triangle is just like the ascending triangle only that it is inverted, and traders consider it a breakout pattern. The breakout happens when the stock price falls through the bottom horizontal trendline support while a downtrend begins again. The bottom trendline or the support, in this case, becomes resistance.

Chapter 11: Tips for Beginners

Traders undertake Day Trading because it offers them the chance to take advantage of small movements of the price while avoiding the losses linked with overnight risks. An intraday day trader uses various trading strategies and analytical skills to make appropriate decisions that give him or her money. The more experienced a trader is, the more prepared the trader is to succeed in the market.

On the other hand, a beginner in Day Trading does not have the training and experience that will add additional protection against losses. Thus, he or she uses caution, technical and psychological strategies, and strict discipline to allow him or her to make money and manage the associated risks. Here is information concerning advice for profit achievement, and the dos and don'ts that provide tips for success in Day Trading for a beginner.

Advice and Methods for Beginners

A beginner starts Day Trading with the hope and belief of achieving success in the market. The trader feels that he or she is ready to undertake the trade with the knowledge and skills that he or she possesses. Nonetheless, there are some tips that he or she can follow that will enhance his or her trading experience and increase the chances of success. Some of the advice and methods that can assist a beginner in Day Trading are:

Carry out Research Continuously – Continually researching enriches a trader's knowledge and skills, which help him or her to create and apply better and profitable strategies and decisions.

Prepare and Follow a Trading Strategy – Always have a trading plan before undertaking trade and adhere to its guidelines. It helps a trader to know which position to take and the entry and exit strategy.

Control of Emotions – A trader is a human who experiences emotions as he or she trades. Day Trading is a fast-moving market with high risks involved. A trader may be in a profitable position at a time, but swings in the market can change quickly, and he or she starts experiencing losses. The fear of losing in the market can make a trader think and react to trade emotionally, which can lead to further losses. He or she should manage his or her feelings and use only the factual data to make decisions in the market.

Reserve Time for Trading – Day Trading needs a trader to commit time to the business, as he or she needs to track price movements, make trading strategies, and make appropriate judgments of the trade. It is a full-time job, and the trader needs to take it seriously by fully concentrating on the trading tasks.

Prepare Funds for the Investment – A trader must set aside some amount of money specifically for trading. Moreover, within that amount, he or she should decide on a trading formula that will determine the money to risk for each trade. In so doing, he or she will manage risks whereby he or she will still have money in the first account even if a deal fails. He or she will only lose that small percentage in that particular investment.

Having a Risk Management Strategy – Day Trading requires risk management strategies that will help a trader to avoid or minimize any losses in a trade. Besides money management, a trader also needs to prepare exit strategies in case of unfavorable changes in the market, such as developing a stop loss.

Properly Time the Trades – Day Trading involves fast movements of prices and sudden changes in market conditions. A trader needs to get his or her timing right to ensure the entry and exit of trade results in success. It also helps him or her not to miss trading opportunities.

Know When to Quit – A trader should know when to exit a trade and abandon a particular trading strategy. If a plan or deal is not working, he or she should know when to stop to prevent further losses.

Stop Focusing on the Money – The trader should concentrate on the trading strategies to ensure that they will help him or her trade successfully. Focusing on the money will make the trader become anxious or impatient with the market and end up making rash decisions that are detrimental to the business.

Realistic Expectations about Profits – Being realistic about Day Trading will help a person to trade better and eventually succeed in the business. He or she will know the realistic chances of success and will work within those realities. He or she will not make rash decisions in an attempt to make impossible profits.

Use Appropriate Type of Orders – Day Trading incorporates the use of orders to manage risks and minimize the losses in the market. A trader should utilize the right order according to his or her trading condition. He or she can choose to use limit orders or market orders to enable precise trading and making profits.

Avoid the Penny Stocks – They say cheap is expensive, and the same applies in Day Trading. A trader should avoid penny stocks because they have low chances of success and are mostly illiquid.

Begin with Small Trades – A trader should take small steps as he or she starts in Day Trading. He or she begins with few trades and uses them to enhance his or her skills and experience before slowly advancing and using more share in the trade.

Take Full Advantage of the Technology – Technological advancement provides a trader with access to various education, tools, and software that can help him or her to succeed in Day Trading. He or she should take advantage of these features to continually learn and practice, which will build his or her expertise and confidence in the trades. They will also help him or her to enhance his or her technical, analytical skills.

Keep a Record of the Trades – A trader needs to take notes about all the trades that he or she undertakes. He or she writes about the trading experience where he or she includes details about the planning, entry, and exit of the trade. These records will help him or her to keep track of historical data regarding a particular market. They will also provide him or her with a reference that he or she can use to make predictions about specific trades.

Learning from Losses – The trader should learn from the trading experiences that he or she goes through in the market. He or she needs to take the losses as lessons that guide him or her on how to avoid failure.

Take Responsibility of the Trade – A trader should bear the responsibility for all outcomes in his or her trade because he or she made the decisions concerned. He or she should not blame the market for any losses or failures that he or she experiences.

Maintain discipline in the Trade – The trader should always maintain control in all aspects of Day Trading. He or she should strictly follow the guidelines of the trading strategies to ensure successful trade.

Day Trading requires a trader to spend a lot of time and effort to achieve success. An expert trader knows to follow specific trading rules and procedures to ensure that he or she will make profits and avoid experiencing losses. However, beginners lack the experience and end up making mistakes that make their trades unsuccessful. Below are some of the errors that lead to failed trading:

Timing Poorly in Trade – Day Trading is all about timing, and failure in getting it right can lead to considerable losses. The trader uses his or her timing wrong and loses trading opportunities since the price already moved to an unfavorable direction.

Trading Without a Plan – A trader starts trading without any plan or strategy regarding the trade. Hence, he or she does not know how to deal with a crisis or a sudden change in price action. It leads to an overall failure of the trade.

Changing the Trading Strategy Frequently – A trader should use a strategy that he or she understands and suits the trade. However, he or she may change the plan so much that none of them works successfully. A strategy that suits one deal may not suit another, and likewise, the trader cannot use too many plans on the same trade.

Chasing Trades – A trader becomes impatient and anxious about market conditions and decides to pursue the market in an attempt to make profits quickly. However, the market is a shadow, and he or she will not succeed in catching and controlling it. Rather than waiting for the trade to present an opportunity, his or her impatience leads to failure since he or she exposes himself or herself to more risks.

Averaging Down – A trader continues to hold on and add to a losing position in the market in the hope that the price trend will reverse and start giving him or her gains. He or she loses a lot more when the reversal does not take place.

Taking a Position before the news is out – A trader decides to take a particular trade in the market in an attempt to anticipate the news release. The unknown risk here can lead to considerable losses since the price may move against his or her expectations after the announcement of the report.

Trading immediately after the News – A trader can place himself or herself in a losing position when he or she starts trading soon after the release of the news. The price initially moves quickly and sharply after the announcement but may change direction once the volatility reduces. It can result in a trader experiencing loses as the price moves in the opposite direction.

Trading Without a Stop Loss – Trading without a stop loss exposes a trader to experience potentially unlimited losses. A stop-loss helps him or her to manage the risks by moderating losses since the trader can exit the trade when the price shifts against him or her.

Risking Excessive Capital – A trader who does not have proper money management risks the amount of money for investment. He or she uses all or a significant percentage of his or her capital on one trade instead of utilizing a smaller portion and breaking it down. Thus, he or she ends up losing his or her entire budget if the business fails to lead to reckless utilization of funds. The trader risks more money that causes him or her to lose sleep.

Psychological Weaknesses – The trader here lets his emotions decide the actions that he or she takes when Day Trading. The fear, greed, and impatience lead to him or her making rash judgments and exposing himself or herself to higher risks in the market. He or she also underestimates the market and makes hasty decisions that lead to failed trades.

Trading Correlated Pairs – A trader increases the risks when he or she transacts using correlated pairs in the market. He or she loses the double if they move against him or her since they link to each other. Hence, he or she doubles his or her

losses when trading correlated pairs.

Going All In – The trader risks everything and takes a more significant trade than usual due to the temptations of doubling profits. However, he or she loses significantly if the business fails.

Following the Crowd – A trader follows the decisions and actions of other traders in the market. Rather than thinking and making his or her judgments, the trader follows the crowd. He or she does not stick to the guidelines of his or her trading strategy and instead makes moves that might ultimately lead to a losing position in the market.

Having Unrealistic Expectations – The trader has an impractical view of the market and has high expectations of profits. He or she makes highly risky decisions to try to obtain that gain. Nonetheless, the risks he or she faces leads to foreseen and unexpected losses from the trades of interest. Additionally, he or she does not accept losses since he or she sees profits as the only results in the market.

Leaving Out the Margins – A trader forgets about margins and ends up trading with money that he borrowed from a broker. Margin can help a trader to increase gains when he or she applies it appropriately. Hence, a trader leaving it out leads to the collapse and failure of a trade.

Utilizing the Wrong Brokers – A trader can use a broker who manages his or her trades poorly. The broker may lack knowledge or access to specific essential trading software and may have poor communication skills. These features cause the trader to have a wrong broker who will create financial trouble that can escalate to trading failures.

Lack of Knowledge and Training – A trader rushes into Day Trading without having the necessary skills and experience for ensuring success. He or she ends up taking more on his or her plate and ends up failing miserably in the markets.

Lack of Post Trade Analysis – Trading without recording the trade and its aftermath can lead to a trader repeating mistakes that previously caused losses. The post-trade analysis provides him or her with an account of the trade's history, which can inform future trading strategies. However, the absence of such a report can make a trader lose the chance of identifying critical decisions and learning from them.

Trading Using Fundamental Data – A trader using fundamental data to undertake Day Trading fails because intraDay Trading uses technical analysis to make trades. Day Trading involves price movements in the short-term and a trader gambles when he or she ignores the trading strategies and starts utilizing economic data.

Poor Discipline while Trading – A trader fails to stick to his or her trading plan and becomes messy in the market. Disorganization leads to him or her, making unclear decisions that can cause losses. He or she may want to undertake different positions at a sensitive time since the lack of discipline causes panic and confusion.

Why and How Most Traders Fail

Trading in the stock market requires a combination of skills and experience to ensure that a trader can make profits. An intraday trader also applies them to enable him or her to gain in a single day while simultaneously try to avoid losses in the market. However, many traders seem to experience more losses than gains while trading in the short amount of time of intraday markets. These traders fail because they have weaknesses regarding their knowledge, skills, mindset, and expectations of a trade. Here are how these factors affect a trader and lead to his or her failure in the market.

1.   *Inadequate Knowledge*

Knowledge is an essential tool to possess in any aspect of life. It is especially vital to a trader as it provides him or her with the expertise that develops and improves his or her trading skills. Thus, when a trader does not have adequate and proper education concerning trading, he or she sets himself or herself up for a disastrous trading experience. He or she does not understand the trading tools and lacks analytical thinking that forms the essence of trade. Consequently, he or she cannot make trading strategies nor implement risk management rules, leading to losses and failure in the stock market.

2. *Poor Skills*

Some traders fail in the markets because they know but not the skills needed to achieve success. A trader who does not continually practice his or her trading will result in having poor skills. Day Trading is a business that requires a person to learn and train continuously for several years before he or she can identify as a proper trader. However, many traders have little training, experience in the markets, and view themselves as qualified. It leads to the traders taking on more than they can handle, which ultimately leads to failure.

3. *Mindset*

The psychology of a trader can determine whether he or she succeeds in the trade. Most traders may fail in trading despite having adequate skills and experience due to psychological weaknesses. They approach the trades with the wrong emotions and attitudes that lead to unsuccessful ventures.

a)   **Emotions** – A trader lets his or her feelings influence his or her decisions and actions in the market. He or she allows his or her fear of losing money to control him or her. The trader ends up panicking and rushing into risky decisions that cause losses.

b)   **Attitude** – A trader has a flawed approach where he or she lets greed and overconfidence dictate his or her judgments. The trader thinks he or she is invincible and views the market as a playground. He or she takes risky positions that eventually lead to failure.

4.   *Unrealistic Expectations*

Most traders think that they will succeed and leave no room for losses. Such a trader believes that his or her trading strategies are perfect, and he or she takes trades with higher risks. He or she trades assuming in luck rather than the actual conditions of the market. As a result, he or she risks too much and applies poor trading strategies that backfire and lead to significant losses. Additionally, a trader's unrealistic expectation of profits leads to him or her being impatient and enters a trade with little training and planning. These factors combine to ensure the failure of a trader in the market.

Day Trading involves certain risks, especially since it takes place in a short amount of time. A person needs to know the conduct and attitude to have, and the mistakes to avoid when trading. Learning and understanding these tips for Day Trading will help a beginner to start and continue the trade successfully.

Chapter 12: Taking Profits

The primary objective for you to engage in Day Trading is to attain significant returns on your capital. For this aim to be attainable, you must apply productive strategies to your Day Trading involvement. In Day Trading, patterns in the stock price are bound to recur, and if you are keen, you can spot these trend repetitions. You can have a particular trend that matches a similar one that you encountered previously. The recurrence may not match the actual price values, but the overall uptrends and downtrends may be identical. The time frame between the similar trends may vary between days and weeks, but the resemblance is noticeable when you sharpen your focus.

Based on these recurrences, you can take advantage of this knowledge to make profits from Day Trading. If you know how the stock price behaved last time, you can accurately predict its future movement. This assumption is valid as long as the circumstances and price patterns match. Using a price action chart, you can put your newfound strategy into action. A majority of these approaches involve looking out for an event called a breakout. The following scenarios describe various setups in which the breakouts favor entry into a particular trading position:

1. _IPC Breakout_

This breakout acronym stands for Impulse, Pullback, and Consolidation. This phrase describes the behavior of the stock price on the price action chart. You need to look for a pattern characterized by these movements in the value of its stock. Usually, within the first few minutes, a cycle in Day Trading will start with a significant move in a specific direction in the form of an impulse wave. A pullback reaction typically follows this impulse wave.

A pullback is akin to applying instant brakes on the sharp initial impulse movement. From the pullback section, you will notice that the price hovers over a small range for a while. This period is the consolidation phase, where the stock price experiences a sideways movement. Note that the consolidation phase confines itself within the margins of the first impulse wave.

In the case of a fall in stock price beyond the open end, a different outcome may ensue. In this scenario, you will have both hovering and pullback happening at a value much lower than the opening stock price. At this point, your patience comes into play. You need to stand by for a potential breakout in the direction of the earlier impulse wave. Pay attention not to perform any trade in the event of a breakout in the reverse direction. The activation of a buying position is dependent on the stock price, breaking at a value that is greater than the consolidation level. For instance, in case the earlier scenario ensued, and the stock price pulled back after an initial drop, trading is valid only when the breakout occurs over the consolidation.

When buying, it is advisable to take a long position on a small bid above the highest point of the consolidation phase. Taking a long trading position allows you to make a profit from a later increase in the price of the stock. In case you become interested in taking a short trading position, you can make an equally tiny bid below the lowest point of the consolidation.

A short trading position enables you to make a profit from a later drop in price. In both trading positions, you will determine your entry point based on a potentially favorable future outcome. This particular pattern setup is typical of the beginning of a trading session. Movements that take place close to the opening time are usually significant and potentially profitable. Always remember to discern the price action trends carefully before trading since any setup that lacks the distinctive sections is probably wrong.

2. *RC Breakout*

A Reversal and Consolidation breakout lacks the smaller pullback section found in, the earlier setup. In this case, you will have the usual significant impulse section, followed by a much higher reversal. Note that the reversal occurs in a direction that is opposite to the impulse wave. The reversal section is immediate to the impulse without any signs of a previous pullback. Due to the slight difference between RC and IPC breakouts, you need to pay special attention to the reversal trend. You should ignore any movement that occurs before the reversal. Wait for an imminent pullback from the reversal spike that ought to be smaller than your first or preceding impulse. The reversal wave now acts as your point of reference with which comparisons of the pullback and later consolidation take place.

Once you achieve a level of price consolidation, follow the guidelines as before in the earlier setup. If the breakout occurs either above or beneath the extreme points of consolation, you can take a relevant trading position. Always bid small amounts of your capital in Day Trading since the margins are rather low, as well. An example of an RC setup involves an initial drop in the stock price of about 50 cents followed instantly by a reversal of, say 70 cents.

In this case, you need to concentrate your focus on the reversal rally of 70 cents that puts you back in the money anyway. The initial fall in price is the impulse wave, and it causes a distraction of which you should be wary. The more significant reversal should be your reference point, especially since you currently have an overall net trend of going upward. A pullback and consolidation phase should come after the reversal phase and finally accompanied by the awaited breakout.

3. *Check for Reversal at Support and Resistance points*

These two points signify the general pricing regions of a price action chart as opposed to real stock values. Support occurs when the falling trend of a particular stock price reaches its minimum point for that same trading cycle. The stock price cannot continue dropping beyond the support level. At support, the trend undergoes a period of consolidation before a reversal takes place. Upon reversing its direction, the price trend keeps rising to a point beyond which any further price increase becomes impossible.

This maximum level of the stock price is the resistance. Both support and resistance are typically indicative of how the various trading positions affect the movements of the stock market price. The economies of scale with the supply and demand forces are applicable here as well. In the context of Day Trading, excessive buyers lead to resistance, while support is the result of too many sellers. Once you identify the support and resistance regions, look out for the presence of consolidations at these levels.

A positive trading signal occurs in case of a breakout over the consolidation section at a support point. The same is valid for a breakout that happens beneath the consolidation at the resistance level. Beware of the market behaving unexpectedly. In rare circumstances, the stock price may breakout above the consolidation phase at the resistance level. In addition, the same might happen at the support region, and you encounter a breakout below the price consolidation. Although highly unlikely, these kinds of unusual breakouts are still possible. In such cases, you need to exit from your trading position immediately. You could use the breakout as your exit point. Therefore, your level of concentration has to be sharp to stay alert to such improbable eventualities.

4.   *Strong Area Breakout*

This strategy enables you to participate in Day Trading above and below the resistance and support levels, respectively. These trending patterns are rare but still possible; hence, you need to develop and have a proper approach in place in case they arise. These regions located beyond the support and resistance points are the so-called Strong Areas. It is within these areas that you need to search for the relevant breakouts for you to conduct your trading.

First, you should take note of a trend that reached up to identical values at the resistance or support level multiple times. This pattern shows that the restrictive level is about to break. Based on the volume of trade in the stock market, such a trend is predictable. It is bound to break either its resistance or support. Trading on such values is often challenging because the margin beyond which the pattern exceeds the limit is usually small. You can decide to take a long position on a breakout trend that breaches the resistance.

However, beware of the lack of a sustaining rally beyond that level. Therefore, you should continue bidding only smaller amounts of capital on any breakout above the resistance level. The same reasoning applies to traders taking short positions on those breakouts that breach the support level. The amount of profit from such Strong Area breakouts is often insignificant compared to the larger margins experienced with the standard price action trading.

5. *False Breakout*

This type of breakout is useful as a confirmatory tool for other trading strategies. A false breakout is indicative of a price that attempts a particular movement, but fails and eventually goes in the opposite direction. For instance, consider an RC breakout setup where the reversal was higher than the initial impulse. After the reversal section, you would experience a brief pullback followed by a consolidation. Your expectation from the consolidation phase would likely be that the price takes an upward trend. This assumption is per the direction of the much higher reversal pattern.

However, due to the market forces, there is usually a small breakout downward for a brief moment straight after the consolidation phase. This breakout is false since the price would once again reverse and continue on its new upward trajectory. Knowing how to interpret and utilize false breakouts is essential in confirming the validity of your taken trading position. Using false breakouts in this manner is akin to proving a negative.

ROI

When you take part in Day Trading, you should expect a return on investment that corresponds to your input capital. Large amounts of capital outlay are typically disadvantageous due to the low rate of return. Investing in small amounts of money regularly usually results in a more productive rate of returns. Success at Day Trading is often a prerequisite for you to attain a significant return on your investment. The following factors affect your capital's margins of profits directly:

1. *Risk on Each Trade*

This risk refers to the amount of your capital that is in danger of losing its value whenever you trade. It also refers to the trading position that you take every time you participate in Day Trading. For you to maximize your returns, you should have this risk under control. Risk management is achievable by setting a maximum limit on the amount of capital with which you can trade. For instance, you can set a limit of one percent of your available equity for commitment to a particular trade.

Also, use stop-loss orders to enforce this resolution. You need to adhere to these conditions strictly, every time you engage in any Day Trading transaction. It often becomes more comfortable to estimate your position size once you have both the stop-loss and entry point values. You need to realize that risk is a potential loss, and therefore, your aim must be to gain more money than you lose. You should learn to risk as little as possible while maintaining a higher margin for any probable profits.

2. *Reward to Risk Ratio*

As mentioned earlier, you should strive to be in a position where your profit surpasses the amount of capital that you lose. This ratio shows you this relative association between the two outcomes. For you to get on the right track towards gaining profits, your reward to risk ratio has to be higher than one. Whenever you minimize your risk to one percent of your capital, you are in an excellent position to gain from any particular trade. This position is reinforce-able by the fact that your denominator in the ratio would become the one percent. For maximum returns, the preferable reward to risk ratio is 1.5 to 1. A reversal in the price trend or your premature exit from the trade is the only limitation to your returns. Beware of your stop-loss level whenever you seek a higher reward to risk ratio.

3. Win Rate

As the name implies, this rate describes the percentage of your trade deals that turned out profitable. This rate has a close relation to the reward to risk ratio and is often in use simultaneously. To maintain an excellent ratio that is acceptable for your level of returns, you need a win rate above fifty percent. For instance, with a rate of 1.5 to 1 and a win rate of fifty percent, you will gain an overall return of twenty-five percent on the trade. Your profits are calculated as follows: (50% of 1.5) minus (50% of 1). As you can see, win rates below the recommended fifty percent would result in a loss of your capital.

4. Number of Trades

Since your specific aims concern the win rate, and the reward to risk ratio, the number of trades in which you can trade is limitless. You can take part in trading as many times as it takes you to maintain your statistics at the recommended values. The more trades you take part in, the more your overall margin of returns. However, the trick is to keep to the fifty percent profitability rate. As a result, if you want to engage in more trades, make sure not to lose a significant number of them. With all these factors in place, you can now control your returns on investment.

Every trader wants to beat the system; to find the share that shoots up in value and makes them a fortune overnight. Unfortunately, in reality there are very few opportunities like this. Amassing a personal fortune through the stock market is achievable, but it is usually achieved by regularly making small amounts of money and learning from the inevitable losses. Those who stick to a plan and build their funds slowly, using their initial investment and not the profits, can make exceptionally good profits and a comfortable standard of living.

To assist you in achieving the desired results it is essential to apply the following tips to your day trading techniques:

1. Don't Trade Every Day!

This may seem like a surprising piece of advice to give to a day trader; someone who by the very definition of the role trades in a day! However, any type of trading is incredibly stressful. There are days when your trades will go exceptionally well and you will feel like you are on top of the world. On other days the market has gone against you and you will not know which way to turn.

To ensure you stay sane and you have the right attitude when you approach your computer and start trading, you should not commit to trading every day. As a day trader you should have closed all your deals out at the end of the day so, whatever the financial position, you can afford to take a day off. In order to be a good day trader you need to have a healthy life / work balance; this means not being afraid to take a day off, the market will still be there the next day. Even if a great deal happens on your day off there is no guarantee you would have spotted it in the heat of the moment.

2. Supply & Demand

The most effective way of finding the right shares to trade in is to study the market as a whole. You need to locate the places where there is a supply and demand imbalance. This is where more people want the shares than there are sellers, or there are more shares than buyers. These are the shares which are most likely to make you a profit as the market will automatically rebalance itself.

The bigger the imbalance in the availability and requirement for shares the bigger the potential profit. If shares are plentiful and the demand is low then their price will be low. As they get bought they will become rarer and this will force the demand up. The higher the demand is; the higher the price which can be charged.

These imbalances can be created very quickly and will correct themselves quickly. You need to be vigilant when surveying the markets and act quickly when you see the right criteria.

3. *Price Targets*

A price target is an amount that you will sell at, or an amount that you will buy at. Your selling price is often worked out as a percentage of your buying price; this ensures you can allow for any transaction fees and still make a profit.

It is essential to set these prices as soon as you purchase any stock; if you have not already decided the values before. You then need to stick to them. One of the most important elements to becoming a successful day trader is not to be too greedy. If the shares reach your pre-set target then you sell; holding on to make a little extra profit is likely to backfire and cost you a lot of money. You must be content that your calculations are correct and that you are making a profit.

4. *Reward Ratio*

There are many traders who will tell you that the reward ratio is useless. In fact, this means that they do not understand it and how to use it to improve their trading average. Used in conjunction with the other tools and good research it can be an invaluable strategy.

In essence the reward ratio specifies that the reward for every trade deal must be three times the risk associated with the deal. This rule means that for every dollar you invest and risk losing, you should expect to get three dollars back. This is an excellent ratio to adhere to when first starting out; as your experience and knowledge grows you may be comfortable reducing this ratio.

As well as using this simple calculation when deciding whether to purchase stock or not; it can be used to assist with managing your position during stock transactions and whether to sell your stock or not.

5. *Discipline*

It is important to remain emotionally detached from your stock purchases and act in accordance with the right business decision for each scenario. This takes discipline and it an important strategy to ensure successful trading. Failing to stick to your own rules and principles will leave you exposed in a deal for longer than you need to be and can result in huge losses when you could have made a healthy profit. The market can be very volatile and it is important to stick to the plan you have made.

It can be very easy to watch your share prices rise and believe they will keep on doing so, instead of sticking to your business tactics you allow yourself to become emotionally involved and attached to your shares; this can spell disaster! You have spent the time devising the right plan for your situation and must have the discipline to stick to your plan.

6.   _Losses_

Even if you are the best organised and most cautious day trader in the world you will, at times, have losses. This is an inevitable part of any kind of stock market trading. It is essential to accept this and accept any loss when it happens. Assuming you have only invested funds you can afford to lose, it is not the end of the word and you will make money a different day.

Losses only become an issue if you make it one; you must deal with them; learn from the mistake you made and then move on. There is no benefit in going over them again and again.

7.   _Budget_

As already mentioned, day trading is not a get rich quick scheme; it takes hard work and dedication, as well as good planning. Part of your planning stage, before you even start trading, should be to work out your budget. You will need funds available to make your first trade; you will also need to purchase a good computer or desktop; if you do not already have one. Alongside this you will need to download and install the right software. Many brokers will provide software when you set up a brokerage account. You need to ensure you are comfortable with their package and possibly allow funds to add additional packages such as data monitoring or an independent trading software solution.

Your budget will ensure you have enough start up capital to purchase all the equipment you may need and to start trading. There is no minimum amount required to start trading from home, although many online accounts ask for a minimum initial deposit. The more funds you have available the more deals you can try; each one will help you understand which is the right approach for your personality and investment type.

8.   *Trading Personality*

Your personality will shape the type of trading you should undertake. If you have the ability to make quick decisions and often do so then you are likely to be good at scalping. Each trade lasts only a few seconds or minutes, before the next one requires a decision.

Alternatively, you may prefer to study all the facts, and then base your decision on these facts and your own personal experience. If you are one of these people then you are more likely to be comfortable and good at long term trading or possibly swing trading. These are trading styles which will give you the opportunity to think through the various angles before reacting.

As well as the ability to make quick decisions there are a variety of other factors which will help you decide which type of trading to undertake:

- Patience - the less patient you are the better you are at short term investments.

- Emotional Vulnerability – If you are unable to turn off your emotions you may struggle to stick to your own trading rules.

- Ability to be flexible – This can be an important trait in some areas of the market

- Passion – The more passion you have for the subject the better your inclinations and commitment will be. This trait is essential to being a successful trader.

9. *The Market*

You need to choose the right market for your personality, time available and even the time of day you would prefer to trade during. There are many different markets and you can choose to day trade in all of these markets. But, when you first start day trading it is advisable to start in one market and work your way up to two, three or even four!

Technology has made it possible to trade in any market around the world, this means that even if your preferred or only available time to trade is between midnight and six in the morning you will be able to trade in one of these markets. This will be one of your deciding factors. The most common markets are the stock exchange and the currency market; but the strategies this book teaches you will apply to any market.

10. _Demos_

Whether you choose to use the software supplied by your brokerage account or something from an independent firm you are almost certain to be offered the chance to try the software first. It is essential to try out the software; it may be the best product in the world but if you are not comfortable finding your way round it then it will not be the right one for you.

The same applies to the idea of trading on the stock market. The majority of brokers will give you access to a free 'demo' software which will allow you to trade on the stock exchange but without risking any of your money and without making any money. This is an excellent way to build your knowledge of the trading markets and improve your skills.

11.   _Trading Plan_

As with any business venture you need a plan. The trading plan will cover your financial abilities and the markets you intend to trade in. It will also cover your risk and how exposed you are prepared to be. A good plan should assess your current skill set to confirm you are ready to start trading; this is a physical and mental state. The plan will also help you to establish your goals and give you something to work for. This may be becoming good enough to make ten successful trades every week; it may even be having a set percentage success rate for your trades.

Whatever goals you choose to set yourself you will need to break them down into achievable smaller goals and then work towards these goals week by week.

Part of your plan should also include making sure you have the time to research your potential investments properly.

12.   *Trading Journal*

Your journal should be filled in daily; it should be a record of your trades, your profits and your losses. Perhaps most importantly you should make notes regarding your thoughts of possible investments and which ones actually performed as expected. This journal will provide you with valuable insights as you continue to trade. It will illustrate to you when you should trust your judgement and can inspire confidence in your operating techniques.

It can also give you some useful information regarding how specific shares reacted in a variety of market conditions. This type of information can be extremely beneficial as you continue and improve your day trading technique.

13. *Flexibility*

Once you have put your own rules into place and become accustomed to working within those rules you will be able to adopt a slightly more flexible attitude. This is not an excuse to say that you can ignore your own rules and chase extra profit! Adopting a flexible approach simple means that you are able to appreciate when a market opportunity outside of your intended scope presents itself to you and that you are not afraid to act on it.

The rules concerning risk and reward still apply but you are not so rigid as to miss an opportunity. The longer you trade and the more experience you gain the more you will see opportunities.

14. *Analysis*

One of the most important things you should do regularly to ensure you become a successful and profitable trader, is to examine your trades and work out when you made the right decision. It may become apparent that there are several occasions when you made the same mistake or even the right decision. You can then study this and work out whether this decision could be applied to other market areas to achieve similar results.

Looking over your performance also helps to keep you grounded as it reminds you that not all your trades work out perfectly. It is one of the best ways of discovering your mistakes and learning from them to ensure you are a better trader in the future.

15. *Confidence*

Being confident is not the same as being arrogant! However, to be a successful trader it is essential to have confidence in your own abilities. You must believe that you can make the right decision and then follow it through; even if the market conditions change and it turns out to be the wrong decision.

It is only by having confidence in your own abilities that you will be able to make a decision quickly when you need to. If it turns out to be the wrong decision then simply learn from your mistake and move on. Your confidence must go hand in hand with a positive mental attitude.

16. *Work Place*

Working from home does not mean you should not take your job seriously. You must create time every day to study the markets, review the news and to possibly indulge in your trades. If you do not do your homework and stay in touch with the latest market developments you will have an increased risk of making the wrong decision as you will not be aware of all the facts.

An essential part of working from home and making the time to engage in all the relevant processes is having a separate space to work at; without distractions. No matter what role you perform it is very easy to procrastinate and this can cost you dearly. Create a unique work space that will ensure you are completely focused on the markets and your trades; this will ensure every trade is successful.

17. *Educate*

There are a variety of options to improve your education and knowledge of the stock market. You should choose the one that suits your personality and needs the best. You may even want to do every method going!

There may be night schools or part time college courses near you that will help you to understand how the stock market works and even provide a variety of tips and techniques to help improve your trading options. You may be able to attend seminars held by professional investors which may improve your knowledge.

But, perhaps the most important way of educating yourself and improving your knowledge of the stock market is to be open to learning every day. Learning can come from contact with other investors or from reviewing your own trading and learning from your mistakes. Provided you are open to improving you knowledge you will continue to learn and develop.

18. Discussions

The internet has made it possible for many people to share their experiences and even to provide tips on upcoming stock movements. Whilst you should be cautious about any tips provided by others there is a lot of information which can be absorbed from the online forums.

You can join as many forums as you like and seek advice from others concerning specific trades or simply share experiences. A forum will help you to unwind after a hard day trading with other people who understand the procedures and stresses. It can be an excellent way of learning and de-stressing before you spend time with your family or friends.

19.   Consistent

Whatever approach you take and whichever markets you trade in it is important to be consistent. This is especially important when you are first starting investing as you will need to know what approach you took in order to adjust and improve on it in future trades.

Consistency is also important as it will help you to both develop an approach which is successful and to stick to that approach. If your techniques are providing consistently good results then you must stick to them and continue trading in the same way. The stock market can provide consistent results if the same approach is taken every time. Find a technique which works for you and stick with it!

20. *Mobility*

Whatever approach you take to day trading it is essential to remember that it is possible to access information on your phone or tablet. Although the idea conditions may be in your dedicated office space, there will be times when you need to complete other tasks or even attend to family matters. During these times it is still possible to watch your investments and adjust your position as necessary.

Of course, if you are able to finish trading before you have to leave your office then you will be able to enjoy your time away from your work. Being able to trade from anywhere can be a critical component to being a successful trader.

Conclusion

Thank you for making it through to the end of Day Trading for Beginners: How to Day Trade for a Living, Proven Strategies, Tactics, and Psychology to Create a Passive Income from Home with Trading Investing in Stocks, Options and Forex. Let us hope it was informative and able to provide you with all of the tools you need to achieve your goals, whatever they may be.

Now you are aware that Day Trading is the process of purchasing and selling assets within the same day, often using borrowed funds to take advantage of small price shifts in highly liquid indexes or stocks.

Day traders use short-term trading strategies and a high level of leverage to take advantage of small price movements in highly liquid currencies or stocks. Experienced day traders have their finger on events that lead to short-term price movements, such as the news, corporate earnings, economic statistics, and interest rates, which are subject to market psychology and market expectations.

Day traders can use technical indicators to provide trading signals and assess the current trade. Keltner Channels, a popular technical indicator, use average prices and volatility to plot lower, middle, and upper lines. These three lines move with the price to create the appearance of a channel. Chester Keltner introduced these channels in the 1960s, but Linda Bradford Raschke updated them in the 1980s. Today, traders use the later version of the indicator, which is a combination of two different indicators, which are the average true range and the exponential moving average.

Created by J. Welles Wilder Jr. and introduced in 1978, the average true range is a measure of volatility. The moving average, on the other hand, is the average price for specific periods, with the exponential variation giving more weight to recent prices and less weight to less recent prices. A trader using trading charts in his or her trades receives significant additional information that helps him or her to make appropriate decisions in Day Trading.

Managing your account and the risks associated with Day Trading involves the responsible handling of the available equity in your brokerage account. You can perform account management through further investment in profitable stocks, ingenious trade maneuverability, or exiting from trade deals that stagnate.

On the other hand, your risk management strategies

involve responding appropriately to alleviate prospective losses in an uncertain future and limiting the degree of your exposure to financial risks.

Technical analysis is the study of the price changes and trends of a stock or security. The study involves traders inspecting a stock's trading history through technical indicators and charts in order to determine the future direction of the stock price.

Statistical trends, such as price movement and volume identified from the past, determine future trading opportunities. Technical analysts, therefore, focus on price fluctuations, trading signals, and analytical charting tools to examine the strength or weakness of a specific security.

Day Trading, like any other form of investment, is subject to influence from human emotion and psychological impact. Whenever money or capital is in play, people tend to take matters rather personally because of the inevitable consequence of the hope that comes along with the promise of significant returns.

After reading this book, your next step should be to practice what you have learned by signing up and becoming a Day trader. When you apply these tips, you will become an expert day trader much faster.

Finally, if you found this book useful in any way, a review on Amazon is always appreciated!

Stock Market Investing, Forex and Swing Trading for Beginners

Discover the STRATEGIES to MAXIMIZE PROFITS in the Stock and Forex Market, Build your PASSIVE INCOME with Dividends & Swing Trading

Matthew Douglas

Table Of Contents

Introduction

Welcome to the world of Stock Market Investing. In this informative guide, we will give you the knowledge that will empower you to take control of your own financial future!

Stock market investing provides an unprecedented way to grow your income and wealth. In this book, we will introduce you to the stock market and show you how to invest efficiently and effectively, using time-tested strategies that will help to minimize your risk. Most people set up a 401k or IRA and don't give any further thought to their retirement plans. In this book, we will dive into managing your portfolio yourself so that you – and not some paid advisor – can direct where your portfolio goes, apply your own investment strategies, and pick investments that you believe will grow your income and wealth.

In this book, we will cover everything you need to know in order to get started. We will explain what to look for when buying stocks and show you how to trade online, using some exciting commission free opportunities with mobile apps. We will also explore different ways you can get into stocks, including buying individual stocks, exchange-traded funds and mutual funds. Then we'll enter the world of bond investing and not only see how you can invest in bonds, but we'll look at ways to leverage the stock market to do it.

We'll also discuss more advanced techniques such as options trading, day trading, and swing trading. Finally, we'll review some common beginners' mistakes to help you mitigate your own risks.

This book is written to take a beginning investor, someone who is starting to invest in the stock market or has dabbled in the stock market without much success and introduce them to a complete trading system that many professional traders use!

This book covers all aspects of investing/trading and will cut years of wasteful time and misleading learning.

In the past, there wasn't access to good information, you had to go to library or you had to subscribe to newspaper just to read stock table in the back of business section of the newspaper. Then had to get on the telephone (not cell phone) with your broker just to buy a stock. The problem today is just the opposite. One there is abundance of information to sort through, second there is way too much conflicting, misleading and salesy information. I call this "feel good" information. It will promise you the world, make general theoretical pitches, about becoming a millionaire and retiring on the beach, all for low price of $19.99 without teaching you anything!

We'll leave it up to you to decipher the good information from the bad. Your aim should be to learn, apply and get results. Whether this information comes in form of flashy salesy new website or crumbled up piece of paper! FOCUS ON THE CONTENT!

This book lays the foundation you can build on, simplifies the process and takes the noise out. You will see things differently even after the 1st chapter.

You see, most professional traders use a trading/investing system, they don't haphazardly go in and out of trades. They trust their system and they don't buy or sell just because someone tells them to, they do their research. They see the numbers companies are producing, make sense of them and apply them to their trading system. They understand the price of the stock and value of the stocks are different. In addition to numbers they also use technical analysis and indicators to get in and out at the right time.

The following chapters will discuss different aspects of the stock market. The stock market is a broad field where you can explore different elements before becoming a successful stock market investor. Before throwing your money into a business, you have no idea how it works, and the book will highlight some of the guidelines to follow. Also, some critical tips and begin making money within a short time in the stock market. Besides, there are different platforms where you can start with investments and earn big.

That said, you will also learn about why the stock market is an excellent choice for you, primarily as an individual with interest in engaging in stock market investing. There are several benefits other than making money and creating wealth. In most cases, becoming a pro in stock market investing provides you with a piece of extensive knowledge in engaging in risky investment businesses with significant possibilities of creating profits. More so, you become readily suited to predict the success of a company before putting your money in it.

There are plenty of books on this subject on the market, thanks again for choosing this one! Every effort was made to ensure it is full of as much useful information as possible; please enjoy!

Chapter 1: Stock Market Investing Explained

The stock market refers to the collection of markets and exchanges where regular activities of buying, selling, and issuance of shares of publicly-held companies take place. Such financial activities are conducted through institutionalized formal exchanges or over-the-counter (OTC) marketplaces which operate under a defined set of regulations. There can be multiple stock trading venues in a country or a region which allow transactions in stocks and other forms of securities.

While both terms - stock market and stock exchange - are used interchangeably, the latter term is generally a subset of the former. If one says that she trades in the stock market, it means that she buys and sells shares/equities on one (or more) of the stock exchange(s) that are part of the overall stock market. The leading stock exchanges in the U.S. include the New York Stock Exchange (NYSE), Nasdaq, the Better Alternative Trading System (BATS). and the Chicago Board Options Exchange (CBOE). These leading national exchanges, along with several other exchanges operating in the country, form the stock market of the U.S.

Though it is called a stock market or equity market and is primarily known for trading stocks/equities, other financial securities - like exchange traded funds (ETF), corporate bonds and derivatives based on stocks, commodities, currencies, and bonds - are also traded in the stock markets.

Understand the Stock Market

While today it is possible to purchase almost everything online, there is usually a designated market for every commodity. For instance, people drive to city outskirts and farmlands to purchase Christmas trees, visit the local timber market to buy wood and other necessary material for home furniture and renovations, and go to stores like Walmart for their regular grocery supplies.

405

Such dedicated markets serve as a platform where numerous buyers and sellers meet, interact and transact. Since the number of market participants is huge, one is assured of a fair price.

For example, if there is only one seller of Christmas trees in the entire city, he will have the liberty to charge any price he pleases as the buyers won't have anywhere else to go. If the number of tree sellers is large in a common marketplace, they will have to compete against each other to attract buyers. The buyers will be spoiled for choice with low- or optimum-pricing making it a fair market with price transparency. Even while shopping online, buyers compare prices offered by different sellers on the same shopping portal or across different portals to get the best deals, forcing the various online sellers to offer the best price.

A stock market is a similar designated market for trading various kinds of securities in a controlled, secure and managed the environment. Since the stock market brings together hundreds of thousands of market participants who wish to buy and sell shares, it ensures fair pricing practices and transparency in transactions. While earlier stock markets used to issue and deal in paper-based physical share certificates, the modern day computer-aided stock markets operate electronically.

How the Stock Market Works

In a nutshell, stock markets provide a secure and regulated environment where market participants can transact in shares and other eligible financial instruments with confidence with zero- to low-operational risk. Operating under the defined rules as stated by the regulator, the stock markets act as primary markets and as secondary markets.

As a primary market, the stock market allows companies to issue and sell their shares to the common public for the first

406

time through the process of initial public offerings (IPO). This activity helps companies raise necessary capital from investors. It essentially means that a company divides itself into a number of shares (say, 20 million shares) and sells a part of those shares (say, 5 million shares) to common public at a price (say, $10 per share).

To facilitate this process, a company needs a marketplace where these shares can be sold. This marketplace is provided by the stock market. If everything goes as per the plans, the company will successfully sell the 5 million shares at a price of $10 per share and collect $50 million worth of funds. Investors will get the company shares which they can expect to hold for their preferred duration, in anticipation of rising in share price and any potential income in the form of dividend payments. The stock exchange acts as a facilitator for this capital raising process and receives a fee for its services from the company and its financial partners.

Following the first-time share issuance IPO exercise called the listing process, the stock exchange also serves as the trading platform that facilitates regular buying and selling of the listed shares. This constitutes the secondary market. The stock exchange earns a fee for every trade that occurs on its platform during the secondary market activity.

The stock exchange shoulders the responsibility of ensuring price transparency, liquidity, price discovery and fair dealings in such trading activities. As almost all major stock markets across the globe now operate electronically, the exchange maintains trading systems that efficiently manage the buy and sell orders from various market participants. They perform the price matching function to facilitate trade execution at a price fair to both buyers and sellers.

A listed company may also offer new, additional shares through other offerings at a later stage, like through rights issue or through follow-on offers. They may even buyback or delist their shares. The stock exchange facilitates such transactions. The stock exchange often creates and maintains various market-level and sector-specific indicators, like the S&P 500 index or Nasdaq 100 index, which provide a measure to track the movement of the overall market.

The stock exchanges also maintain all company news, announcements, and financial reporting, which can be usually accessed on their official websites. A stock exchange also supports various other corporate-level, transaction-related activities. For instance, profitable companies may reward investors by paying dividends which usually comes from a part of the company's earnings. The exchange maintains all such information and may support its processing to a certain extent.

Functions of a Stock Market

A stock market primarily serves the following functions:

Fair Dealing in Securities Transactions: Depending on the standard rules of demand and supply, the stock exchange needs to ensure that all interested market participants have instant access to data for all buy and sell orders thereby helping in the fair and transparent pricing of securities. Additionally, it should also perform efficient matching of appropriate buy and sell orders.

For example, there may be three buyers who have placed orders for buying Microsoft shares at $100, $105 and $110, and there may be four sellers who are willing to sell Microsoft shares at $110, $112, $115 and $120. The exchange (through their computer operated automated trading systems) needs to ensure that the best buy and best sell are matched, which in this case is at $110 for the given quantity of trade.

Efficient Price Discovery: Stock markets need to support an efficient mechanism for price discovery, which refers to the act of deciding the proper price of a security and is usually performed by assessing market supply and demand and other factors associated with the transactions.

Say, a U.S.-based software company is trading at a price of $100 and has a market capitalization of $5 billion. A news item comes in that the EU regulator has imposed a fine of $2 billion on the company which essentially means that 40 percent of the company's value may be wiped out. While the stock market may have imposed a trading price range of $90 and $110 on the company's share price, it should efficiently change the permissible trading price limit to accommodate for the possible changes in the share price, else shareholders may struggle to trade at a fair price.

Liquidity Maintenance: While getting the number of buyers and sellers for a particular financial security are out of control for the stock market, it needs to ensure that whosoever is qualified and willing to trade gets instant access to place orders which should get executed at the fair price.

Security and Validity of Transactions: While more participants are important for efficient working of a market, the same market needs to ensure that all participants are verified and remain compliant with the necessary rules and regulations, leaving no room for default by any of the parties. Additionally, it should ensure that all associated entities operating in the market must also adhere to the rules, and work within the legal framework given by the regulator.

Support All Eligible Types of Participants: A marketplace is made by a variety of participants, which include market makers, investors, traders, speculators, and hedgers. All these participants operate in the stock market with different roles and functions. For instance, an investor may buy stocks and hold them for long term spanning many years, while a trader may enter and exit a position within seconds. A market maker provides necessary liquidity in the market, while a hedger may like to trade in derivatives for mitigating the risk involved in investments. The stock market should ensure that all such participants are able to operate seamlessly fulfilling their desired roles to ensure the market continues to operate efficiently.

Investor Protection: Along with wealthy and institutional investors, a very large number of small investors are also served by the stock market for their small amount of investments. These investors may have limited financial knowledge, and may not be fully aware of the pitfalls of investing in stocks and other listed instruments. The stock exchange must implement necessary measures to offer the necessary protection to such investors to shield them from financial loss and ensure customer trust.

For instance, a stock exchange may categorize stocks in various segments depending on their risk profiles and allow limited or no trading by common investors in high-risk stocks. Derivatives, which have been described by Warren Buffett as financial weapons of mass destruction, are not for everyone as one may lose much more than they bet for. Exchanges often impose restrictions to prevent individuals with limited income and knowledge from getting into risky bets of derivatives.

Balanced Regulation: Listed companies are largely regulated and their dealings are monitored by market regulators, like the Securities and Exchange Commission (SEC) of the U.S. Additionally, exchanges also mandate certain requirements – like, timely filing of quarterly financial reports and instant reporting of any relevant developments - to ensure all market participants become aware of corporate happenings. Failure to adhere to the regulations can lead to suspension of trading by the exchanges and other disciplinary measures.

Regulating the Stock Market

A local financial regulator or competent monetary authority or institute is assigned the task of regulating the stock market of a country. The Securities and Exchange Commission (SEC) is the regulatory body charged with overseeing the U.S. stock markets.

The SEC is a federal agency that works independently of the government and political pressure. The mission of the SEC is stated as: "to protect investors, maintain fair, orderly, and efficient markets, and facilitate capital formation."

Stock Market Participants

As a beginner, it is vital to learn about those who you will trade within the stock market, especially when in need of making significant profits. There are three categories of market participants, private retail, public corporations, and institutional investors. Private retail investors entail individuals who buy shares from companies and sell them privately without including the company. That is, they buy these shares at a given price and sell them to other buyers at a profit. On the other hand, institutional investors involved organizations such as banks, hedge funds, as well as insurance companies. While public traded companies include companies, who sell their shares to buyers.

Initially, the stock market was full of individual wealthy businesspeople who traded their shares in specific corporations. However, the trend changed with the stock market dominated by institutions such as exchange-traded funds, pension funds, mutual funds, investor groups, and other financial corporations.

As such, institutional investment, mainly in the stock market, has revolutionized the industry more so in the introduction of standard and exorbitant fees to all investors. As mentioned, the participation of stock market trading may occur in three forms; private, institutional, and foreign trading. In this case, investors can trade in the way of direct or indirect buying and selling of stocks.

When engaging in direct trading, you are buying and selling your shares directly with the company without any interaction with private investors in the stock market. That is, you buy shares from institutions and public companies and selling than when the shares are at a profit. On the contrary, indirect trading involves interacting with an individual seller or buyer who acts as a broker. These traders usually buy shares from institutions and big companies and sell them to other buyers or buy them from them and sell them to companies. As a beginner in the stock market, it is crucial to buy and sell these shares to private retail investors as understand how the stocks operate to avoid significant losses.

Along with long-term investors and short term traders, there are many different types of players associated with the stock market. Each has a unique role, but many of the roles are intertwined and depend on each other to make the market run effectively.

• Stockbrokers, also known as registered representatives in the U.S., are the licensed professionals who buy and sell securities on behalf of investors. The brokers act as intermediaries between the stock exchanges and the investors by buying and selling stocks on the investors' behalf. An account with a retail broker is needed to gain access to the markets.

• Portfolio managers are professionals who invest portfolios, or collections of securities, for clients. These managers get recommendations from analysts and make the buy or sell decisions for the portfolio. Mutual fund companies, hedge funds, and pension plans use portfolio managers to make decisions and set the investment strategies for the money they hold.

• Investment bankers represent companies in various capacities, such as private companies that want to go public via an IPO or companies that are involved in pending mergers and acquisitions. They take care of the listing process in compliance with the regulatory requirements of the stock market.

• Custodian and depot service providers, which are institution holding customers' securities for safekeeping so as to minimize the risk of their theft or loss, also operate in sync with the exchange to transfer shares to/from the respective accounts of transacting parties based on trading on the stock market.

• Market maker: A market maker is a broker-dealer who facilitates the trading of shares by posting bid and ask prices along with maintaining an inventory of shares. He ensures sufficient liquidity in the market for a particular (set of) share(s), and profits from the difference between the bid and the ask price he quotes.

Also referred to as the equity market and share market, the stock market is the combination of both buyers and sellers engaging in an economic transaction, though not physical, of stocks or shares representing claim ownership of businesses. In other words, the stock market is where the company or a private individual sells part of the company to potential owners through private or public stock exchange. For example, the selling of private company shares sold through equity crowdfunding to investors to create capital to expand these businesses. The most common stock market is the public stock exchange, where different buyers and sellers engage in trading of stocks.

Stock market investing dates back in the 12th century when farmers in France used to trade with debts before setting to buy and sell their goods and services using government securities. In the mid-13th century, bankers joined trading using securities, and later Italy began introducing shares in the 14th century. Over time, different countries in Europe adopted the system, and various companies engaged in selling through shares leading to the creation of shareholders. The formal birth of the stock market occurred in the 17th and 18th centuries, where several Dutch financial innovators created the model of the stock market used today.

Since the introduction of stock market investing, the size of the market has significantly developed with the United States, Japan, and the United Kingdom are the leading in market capitalization. In 2017, the total market capitalization globally reached about $79.225 trillion, with the number increasing in 2013. The stock exchanges also rose to 16 worldwide, with different companies listing their stocks in the stock exchange trading like stocks, bonds, and other forms of securities. In some cases, stock market investors may trade using 'over the counter' method through dealers where they can readily buy or sell their shares.

The stock market, like other businesses, has its ups and downs depending on the operations of how investors alter their financial prices concerning the market equilibrium. Prices of stocks typically shift and may affect the stock market either positively or negatively. When talking about the market equilibrium, investors may become optimists, therefore driving prices to become quite high benefiting traders. Similarly, they may become pessimists, eventually driving prices too low, resulting in losses and a decline of stock value. This has led economists to debate and determine if stock markets are essential and useful.

According to the interpretation of different economists, there are multiple factors that contribute to these trends in the stock market. Some of the common elements have been linked to political and financial news originating from different sources. Irrationality in the market is another aspect but also depends significantly on economic news and other relevant market events. Crashes in the stock market are mostly a negative outcome when the stock market value deteriorates, leading to the loss of billions in companies and among investors. Crashes are primarily attributed to panics, and loss of confidence with the most known crashes include the Wall Street Crash of 1929, Stock Market Crash of 2008, and Black Monday of 1987.

Over the years and the crashes witnessed before, different market analysts have come up with means of predicting how the stock market operates. Using trading strategies, the technique identifies online precursors based on Google trends searched data regarding shares. When the search volume is too high, it hence suggests that there are possibilities of losses in the future. Similarly, the decline in search volumes indicates that the stock market will become stable in the coming few months. The prices of stocks usually captured in the form of stock market indices, therefore, vary depending on the search data volume. Some of the indexes include the FTSE, Euronext, and S&P.

Set Your Goals

When considering stock market investing, it is essential to find long-term goals as it is a venture which takes some time before you start gaining profits. That is, understanding the purpose of your investment in the stock market and what you need the funds for in the future. In this case, avoid creating short-term goals as the market does have a guarantee of offering return due to its volatility. Therefore, calculate your input or capital and the desired output you wish to have and benefit from stock market investing. There are multiple calculators online you can use to determine your wealth and the potential outcome.

Learn About Risks

When venturing into stock market investing, you should understand that this is a risky investment with no guarantee of achieving your goals, especially when you begin trading blindly. As such, you should develop risk tolerance abilities enabling you to build your psychology when selling. Risk tolerance is affected by factors such as age, wealth, and education. Risk tolerance varies between individuals, more so on perception about the stock market. When you learn more about the stock market, you are likely to view it as a low risky venture when compared to those with a limited idea about the stock market. Learning about the risks, therefore, allows you to avoid activities that may drive you to losses while capitalizing on less anxious investments.

Understand the Basics

Engaging in the stock market with limited knowledge about how they operate is usually a direct ticket to lose your money. Prior to investing, take time to familiarize yourself with what the stock market entails, the risks, and the accompanying benefits. Learn about the securities, both individual and public, among other vital areas. Having a general knowledge about the stock market provides a higher probability of investing in the most profitable and top-yielding shares with limited loss chances. However, if you fail to understand the basics, then you are on the verge of throwing your money without any success in the stock market.

Investment Diversification

This a technique used by several successful investors such as Buffet eschews who understand how to avoid losing everything in case the stock market collapses. Besides, they can quickly learn about the perils with higher chances of creating losses in the market and prevent them. As a beginner, when you choose to build your stock diversification techniques while focusing on the less risky stocks, then you are likely to generate profits with your first investment. Cautious investors typically own and continually buy shares from different companies as well as internationally. As such, this keeps your assets safe in situations where one or more of your investments are affected.

Avoid Loans

Stock market investing is a risky business, especially for beginners, as it allows for a limited guarantee of payouts. Besides, it does not allow for short-term profits when in need of cash to pay out your loan and broker. For instance, when you are less in money and opt to borrow to boost your returns, there are two possibilities. You may either gain from the loan with 100% of your investment or fail leading debts from both the lender and your broker. Consider the situation where you use your own money, and the chances are that you will earn up to 300% of your investment and make payments only to your broker. In this case, you will have double benefits when compared to acquiring leverage. Loans can become beneficial or detrimental when it comes to investing in the stock market.

Steps of Investing in the Stock Market Successfully

Make a Plan

The stock market offers different ways where you can approach it by using different methods of your investment and become successful. The crucial initial step to consider in developing your plan, which will detail how you wish to invest and how vulnerable you will be when choosing your stocks. You may choose the do-it-yourself method where you will select stock and stock funds yourself without any alterations from other individuals such as investors. Similarly, you may decide to seek help from brokers or other experienced individuals in the stock market to help you in selecting the stocks suitable for your investment.

Open an Account

For someone to engage in stock market investing, he or she has to open an account, usually a brokerage account. Most beginners are recommended to use a Robo-advisor to guide through the process of account opening. There are two primary options you can use when opening an account. The first is through a do-it-yourself alternative to open a brokerage account. Brokerage accounts are usually quick and inexpensive when buying stocks and other relevant activities with a platform of choosing from different accounts of your choice. Another is a passive option where you use a Robo-advisor to open an account.

Learn the Variation of Individual Stocks and Stock Mutual Funds

This step is usually for those who choose a do-it-yourself method as you have limited guidance on what the stock

418

market entails. Therefore, you can choose between individual stocks or stock mutual funds. Individual stocks mean that you buy one or more shares from a company and capitalize on it while stock mutual funds refer to purchasing small stocks from different companies under one transaction. A stock mutual fund is quite beneficial as you diversify your shares; therefore, lessening risks while individual stocks have the potential of generating more income at once.

Set Your Budget

Many new investors in the stock market usually are troubled by the amount they are to invest to venture and gain profits. However, the answer to this question depends on the cost of the share you are buying, ranging from a few dollars to a few thousand. For instance, EFTs usually have stocks that cost less than $100, while mutual funds have a minimum of $1,000. Others may depend on the duration of your investment in the stock market, with longer investments yielding more returns.

Invest

Becoming more successful in the stock market begins with establishing less risky approaches as well as taking paths with higher profits. In today's world, different successful stock market investors have explored the basics with limited knowledge about intricate strategies, which might create more wealth. After successfully underlying the above steps in place, now you are ready to invest but ensuring that you don't get greedy and end up engaging in more risky investments. Ensure you remain in contact with your broker and avoiding instances that may drain your wallet without the probability of generating profits.

Benefits of Investing in Stocks

Getting Started at Low Costs

It is no secret that many people in the United States and around the world wish to get rich quickly with minimal struggle. When you choose to engage in stock investing, you only need to set aside some few dollars by purchasing shares from one or more companies. This technique has been used by many people globally who have been considered to be among the wealthiest. For beginners, you can use a few dollars to put in an index fund or dividend reinvestment plan. Once you buy and own a fraction of shares, you can begin earning and creating more capital to expand and therefore maximizing your profits.

Growing Wealth

Majority of those venturing in stock market investing focus on increasing their wealth despite the accompanying risks it comes with. Besides, buying and selling shares may become essential aspects when you wish to develop from scratch though you have to be patient. Since 1926, the stock market has an average annual return of 10 percent, as reported by the S&P 500. However, the market behavior tends to change rapidly with more rise, fall, and crash or stock value experienced frequently. In this case, when you decide to invest with the aim of growing your wealth, always be aware that it is a guarantee but a risky business.

Long-Term Earnings

Stock market investing accompanies a continuous earning process, especially when you buy shares with minimal chances of creating risks. When you focus on the right stocks and choose wisely, the chances are that you are going to earn continually over a long period of time. However, the truth is that there can never be big profits without engaging in risks. No matter how vulnerable you are to losing your money, the positive outcome behind it will ensure you earn substantial amounts within a given time. As an investor, a stable and reliable investment usually pays off, especially when well-planned and analyzed.

Easy to Trade

The stock market provides a flexible and straightforward benefit where you can quickly sell or buy shares at any time. Similarly, the term "liquid" used in stocks suggests that you can buy, sell, and turn your shares into cash immediately at meager costs. Your best interest is to ensure that you trade with ease at any time while quickly accessing your funds, especially when you are in a hurry. As mentioned, the benefits may out way the risks for cautious investors, therefore, building your investments in the stock market.

Two Way Investment Plan

As a beginner, depending on your choice of the investment plan, you have two options for earning money through buying and selling of shares. As to become more successful, you primarily have to buy shares at low costs and then sell them at a considerable price. Others invest in fast-growing companies that appreciate fast in their initial presence in the market. You may choose to take advantage of short-term investment and earn quick shares or focus on company earnings or stock prices and create a long-term investment plan. Both options of investing in the stock market are crucial for investors as they solely focus on obtaining profits. However, choosing a desirable option remains determined by capital, goals, and plan of a given investor.

Essential in Diversifying Investments

When you invest in more than one business, the chances are that you will remain in a stable state despite the failure or crash of the market. The same is possible when it comes to the stock market, as you can readily trade several shares without the need to focus on one. For example, if you are investing in more than five markets, and two of them fail or collapse, you will remain safe as the other three would sustain you. However, if you invest in one and it collapses, then you will probably end up losing all your investments at a glance. Therefore, the stock market enables you to diversify your investments by acquiring different shares from different companies, and the remaining is a stable financial situation in case of failure.

Not everyone who buys and sells stocks is a stock trader, at least in the nuanced language of investing terms. Most investors fall into one of two camps. Depending on the frequency in which they transact and the strategy driving their actions, they're either "traders" (think Gordon Gekko in the movie "Wall Street") or "investors" (as in Warren Buffett).

What is stock trading?

The term stock trader typically refers to someone who frequently buys and sells stocks to capitalize on daily price fluctuations. These short-term traders are betting that they can make a few bucks in the next minute, hour, days or month, rather than buying shares in a blue-chip company to pass along to their grandkids someday.

Stock trading can be further refined based on certain criteria:

Active trading is what an investor who places 10 or more trades per month does. Typically, they use a strategy that relies heavily on timing the market, trying to take advantage of short-term events (at the company level or based on market fluctuations) to turn a profit in the coming weeks or months.

Day trading is the strategy employed by investors who play hot potato with stocks — buying, selling and closing their positions of the same stock in a single trading day, caring little about the inner workings of the underlying businesses. (Position refers to the amount of a particular stock or fund you own.) The aim of the day trader is to make a few bucks in the next few minutes, hours or days based on daily price fluctuations.

Devote no more than 10% of your portfolio to trading

Even if you find a talent for investing in stocks, allocating more than 10% of your portfolio to individual stocks can expose your savings to too much volatility. Other ground rules to manage risk: Invest only the amount of money you can afford to lose, don't use money that's earmarked for near-term, must-pay expenses (like a down payment on a house or car, or tuition money) and ratchet down that 10% if you don't yet have a healthy emergency fund and at least 10% of your income funneled into a retirement savings account.

Practice, practice, practice. But not with real money

There's nothing better than hands-on, low-pressure experience, which investors can get via the virtual trading tools offered by many online stock brokers. Paper trading lets customers test their trading acumen and build up a track record before putting real dollars on the line. (Several of the brokers we review offer virtual trading, including TD Ameritrade and Interactive Brokers.)

Lower risk by building positions gradually.

There's no need to cannonball into the deep end with any position. Taking your time to buy (via dollar-cost averaging or buying in thirds) helps reduce investor exposure to price volatility.

Measure your returns against an appropriate benchmark

This is essential advice for all types of investors — not just active ones. The bottom-line goal for picking stocks is to be ahead of a benchmark index. That could be the Standard & Poor's 500 index (often used as a proxy for "the market"), the Nasdaq composite index (for those investing primarily in technology stocks) or other smaller indexes that are composed of companies based on size, industry and geography. Measuring results is key, and if a serious investor is unable to outperform the benchmark (something even pro investors struggle to do), then it makes financial sense to invest in a low-cost index mutual fund or ETF — essentially a basket of stocks whose performance closely aligns with that of one of the benchmark indexes.

Ignore "hot tips"

In many cases, they are part of a pump-and-dump racket where shady folks purchase buckets of shares in a little-known, thinly traded company (often a penny stock) and hit the internet to hype it up. As unwitting investors load up on shares and drive the price up, the crooks take their profits, dump their shares and send the stock careening back to earth. Don't help them line their pockets. If you're looking for a guru, bookmark Warren Buffett's annual letters to shareholders for commonsense advice and observations on sane, long-term investing.

Keep good records for the IRS

If you're not using an account that enjoys tax-favored status — such as a 401(k) or other workplace accounts, or a Roth or traditional IRA — taxes on investment gains and losses can get complicated. The IRS applies different rules and tax rates, and requires the filing of different forms for different types of traders. (Here's an overview of the IRS rules for stock traders.) Another benefit of keeping good records is that loser investments can be used to offset the taxes paid on income through a neat strategy called tax-loss harvesting.

Keep your perspective

Being a successful investor doesn't require finding the next great breakout stock before everyone else. By the time you

424

hear that XYZ stock is poised for a pop, so have thousands of professional traders and the potential likely has already been priced into the stock. It may be too late to make a quick turnaround profit, but that doesn't mean you're too late to the party. Truly great investments continue to deliver shareholder value for years, which is a good argument for treating active investing as a hobby and not a Hail Mary for quick riches.

Choose your trading partner wisely

To trade stocks you need a broker, but don't just fall for any broker. Pick one with the terms and tools that best align with your investing style and experience. A higher priority for active traders will be low commissions and fast order execution for time-sensitive trades (like our picks for best online platforms for active traders/day traders). Investors who are new to trading should look for a broker that can teach them the tools of the trade via educational articles, online tutorials and in-person seminars (see NerdWallet's round-ups for the best brokers for beginners). Other features to consider are the quality and availability of screening and stock analysis tools, on-the-go alerts, easy order entry and customer service.

No matter what, the time spent in learning the fundamentals of how to research stocks and experiencing the ups and downs of stock trading — even if there are more of the latter — is time well spent, as long as you're enjoying the ride and not putting any money you can't afford to lose on the line.

Stock Market Basics

The stock market is made up of exchanges, like the New York Stock Exchange and the Nasdaq. Stocks are listed on a specific exchange, which brings buyers and sellers together and acts as a market for the shares of those stocks. The exchange tracks the supply and demand — and directly related, the price — of each stock. (Need to back up a bit? Read our explainer about stocks.)

When people refer to the stock market being up or down, they're generally referring to one of the major market indexes.

Stock trading information

Most investors would be well-advised to build a diversified portfolio of stocks or stock index funds and hold on to it through good times and bad. But investors who like a little more action engage in stock trading. Stock trading involves buying and selling stocks frequently in an attempt to time the market.

The goal of stock traders is to capitalize on short-term market events to sell stocks for a profit, or buy stocks at a low. Some stock traders are day traders, which means they buy and sell several times throughout the day. Others are simply active traders, placing a dozen or more trades per month.

Investors who trade stocks do extensive research, often devoting hours a day to following the market. They rely on technical analysis, using tools to chart a stock's movements in an attempt to find trading opportunities and trends. Many online brokers offer stock trading information, including analyst reports, stock research and charting tools.

Bull markets vs. bear markets

Neither is an animal you'd want to run into on a hike, but the market has picked the bear as the true symbol of fear: A bear market means stock prices are falling — thresholds vary, but generally to the tune of 20% or more — across several of the indexes referenced earlier.

Younger investors may be familiar with the term bear market but unfamiliar with the experience: We've been in a bull market — with rising prices, the opposite of a bear market — since March 2009. That makes it the longest bull run in history.

426

It came out of the Great Recession, however, and that's how bulls and bears tend to go: Bull markets are followed by bear markets, and vice versa, with both often signaling the start of larger economic patterns. In other words, a bull market typically means investors are confident, which indicates economic growth. A bear market shows investors are pulling back, indicating the economy may do so as well.

The good news is that the average bull market far outlasts the average bear market, which is why over the long term you can grow your money by investing in stocks. The S&P 500, which holds around 500 of the largest stocks in the U.S., has historically returned an average of around 7% annually, when you factor in reinvested dividends and adjust for inflation. That means if you invested $1,000 30 years ago, you could have around $7,600 today.

Stock market crash vs. correction

A stock market correction happens when the stock market drops by 10% or more. A stock market crash is a sudden, very sharp drop in stock prices, like in October 1987 when stocks plunged 23% in a single day.
While crashes can herald a bear market, remember what we mentioned above: Most bull markets last longer than bear markets — which means stock markets tend to rise in value over time.

The importance of diversification

You can't avoid bear markets as an investor. What you can avoid is the risk that comes from an undiversified portfolio.
Diversification helps protect your portfolio from inevitable market setbacks. If you throw all of your money into one company, you're banking on success that can quickly be halted by regulatory issues, poor leadership or an E. coli outbreak.

To smooth out that company-specific risk, investors diversify by pooling multiple types of stocks together, balancing out the inevitable losers and eliminating the risk that one company's contaminated beef will wipe out your entire portfolio.

But building a diversified portfolio of individual stocks takes a lot of time, patience and research. The alternative is a mutual fund, the aforementioned ETF or an index fund. These hold a basket of investments, so you're automatically diversified. An S&P 500 ETF, for example, would aim to mirror the performance of the S&P 500 by investing in the 500 companies in that index.

The good news is you can combine individual stocks and funds in a single portfolio. One suggestion: Dedicate 10% or less of your portfolio to selecting a few stocks you believe in, and put the rest into index funds.

Chapter 2: Stock Market Explained in an Easy Way

There are many ways for beginning investors to buy stocks, each with advantages and disadvantages. If you want low fees, you have to put more time managing your investments. If you wish to outperform the market, you'll pay higher fees. If you want a lot of advice, you'll have to pay more as well. If you don't have much time or interest, you might have to settle for lower results.

Perhaps the most risk is from the emotional aspect of investing. Most stock buyers get greedy when the market is doing well. Unfortunately, this makes them buy stocks when they are the most expensive. On the other hand, a poorly performing market triggers fear. That makes most investors sell when the prices are low.

Selecting which way to invest is a personal decision. It depends on your comfort with risk. It also depends on your ability and willingness to spend time learning about the stock market.

Buy Stocks Online

Buying stocks online costs the least, but provides little advice. You are only charged a flat fee, or a percent of your purchase, for each transaction. It can be the riskiest. You obviously get little or no advice. It requires you to educate yourself thoroughly on how to invest. For this reason, it also takes the most time. It's a good idea to review the top online trading sites before you get started.

Investment Clubs

Joining an investment club gives you more information at a reasonable cost. But it takes a lot of time to meet with the other club members. They all have various levels of expertise. You may be required to pool some of your funds into a club account before investing. Again, it's a good idea to research the better investing clubs before you get started.

Full-Service Brokers

A full-service broker is expensive because you'll pay higher fees. However, you get more information and recommendations. That protects you from greed and fear. You must shop around to select a good financial professional that you can trust. The Securities and Exchange Commission offers helpful tips on how to select a broker.

Money Manager

Money managers select and buy the stocks for you. You pay them a hefty fee, usually 1-2 percent of your total portfolio. If the manager does well, it takes the least amount of time. That's because you can just meet with them once or twice a year. Make sure you know how to select a good financial advisor.

Index Fund

Also known as exchange-traded funds, index funds can be an inexpensive and safe way to profit from stocks. They simply track the stocks in an index. Examples include the MSCI emerging market index. The fund rises and falls along with the index. There is no annual fee. But it's impossible to outperform the market this way because index funds only track the market. Even so, there are a lot of good reasons why you should invest in an index fund.

Mutual Funds

Mutual funds are a relatively safer way to profit from stocks. The fund manager will buy a group of stocks for you. You don't own the stock, but a share of the fund. Most funds have an annual fee, between 0.5 percent to 3 percent. They promise to outperform the S&P 500, or other comparable index funds. For more, see 16 Best Tips on Mutual Fund Basics and Before You Buy a Mutual Fund.

Hedge Funds

Hedge funds are like mutual funds. They both pool all their investors' dollars into one actively managed fund. However, hedge funds invest in complicated financial instruments known as derivatives. They promise to outperform the mutual funds with these highly-leveraged investments.

Hedge funds are privately-held companies, not public corporations. That means they aren't regulated by the SEC. They are very risky, but many investors believe this higher risk leads to a higher return.

Selling Your Stocks

As important as buying stocks is knowing when to sell them. Most investors buy when the stock market is rising and sell when it's falling. But a wise investor follows a strategy based on his or her financial needs.

431

You should always keep an eye on the major market indices. The three largest U.S. indices are the Dow Jones Industrial Average, the S&P 500, and the Nasdaq. But don't panic if they enter a correction or a crash. Those events don't last long.

If you don't have a lot of time to manage your stocks, you should consider a diversified portfolio. That means holding a balanced mix of stocks, bonds, and commodities. The stocks will make sure you profit from market upswings. The bonds and commodities protect you from downswings.

The specific mix is your asset allocation. It depends on your financial goals. If you don't need the money for years, then a higher mix of stocks will provide a greater return in the long run. If you require the money next year, you'll want more bonds.

Rebalance your portfolio once or twice a year. It will automatically make sure you buy low and sell high. For example, if commodities do well and stocks do poorly, your portfolio will have too high a percentage of commodities. To rebalance, you'll sell some commodities and buy some stocks. That forces you to sell the commodities when prices are high and buy the stocks when prices are low.

Common Mistakes to Avoid

You've probably heard that investing money in the stock market is the best way to grow your wealth over the long-term. But that's only true if you avoid mistakes—and unfortunately, many of your natural tendencies can seriously handicap your ability to get rich on the stock market. For instance, we're set up to listen to the news, follow the crowd, and run for safety when danger is afoot—but those tendencies can turn the stock market into a losing proposition. Here are some of the little investment mistakes you need to learn to sidestep if you want to make money from your investments.

1.   Trading Too Much

The more you buy and sell your investments, the greater your chance of losing money. If you invested $10,000 in the S&P 500 in 1995 and stayed invested through 2014, you would've earned 9.85 percent annually or $59,593. Yet, if you missed the best ten days during that 19-year period your return would have fallen to 6.1 percent. Nineteen years later, your initial $10,000 would be worth $30,803. Timing the market is a losing proposition, and even the best rarely win.

2.   Ignoring Fees

Before turning over one-dollar to a financial advisor or investment fund, understand the fees. Yes, every fund has an investment management fee, which ranges from 0.03 percent to over 1.0 percent.

The SEC.gov website explains the impact of higher fees on your investments, but here's an example: Assume that you're a conservative investor and invest your $100,000 inheritance for 20 years in funds that returns an average of 4 percent annually. At the end of the 20 years, the investment that charged a 1.0 percent fee would be worth $180,000. The investment that charged 0.25 percent would be worth $210,000. That's a $30,000 difference between the high and low fee funds.

Don't make the mistake of paying high fees. You can get wide diversification from Schwab's S&P 500 Index Fund (SWPPX) for a rock-bottom 0.03 percent annual management fee.

3.   Not Investing Enough in Your 401(k) to Snare the Employer Match

If your employer matches a percent of your contribution into your 401(k) or 403(b), then you're throwing away free money if you don't contribute. Many employers match your own retirement plan contribution dollar-for-dollar up to 5 percent. If you're earning $70,000 per year, not investing $3,500 in your own retirement account is not only depriving yourself of the chance to build up a robust retirement account but you're telling your employer, "I don't need your $3,500, why don't you keep it!"

4.   Putting Investments in the Wrong Accounts

Taxes play into most financial decisions, and it'll cost you to place your financial assets in the wrong accounts.

Once you've maxed out your 401(k) match, it pays to be smart about which investments go where, as different investments get taxed differently. If you're looking for investments to put in a taxable account, you should look to stocks, low-turnover stock mutual funds, and municipal bonds that you expect to hold for the long term. That's because your stock gains are taxed at the capital gains rates, generally lower than the ordinary income tax rates. In most cases, you're best off placing bonds, taxed as ordinary income, in tax-advantaged retirement accounts.

5.   Trying to Beat the Market

Don't try to beat the market, because chances are that you won't. Chasing glamorous momentum investment strategies aren't likely to pay off. In 2015, 66 percent of active money managers failed to beat the market returns. If you like those odds, consider that between 2005 and 2015, 82 percent of active fund managers failed to beat the returns of the S&P 500 market index.

Great investors from Warren Buffett to John Bogle champion investing in low-fee, market matching index funds. And the historical stock market data backs up the recommendation to invest for the long haul in index funds.

To get rich in the market, choose a sensible asset allocation, invest in low fee index funds, and avoid these investment mistakes. You won't become an overnight millionaire, but over the long term, you'll be set up for financial success.

6.   No Trading Plan

Experienced traders get into a trade with a well-defined plan. They know their exact entry and exit points, the amount of capital to invest in the trade and the maximum loss they are willing to take.

Beginner traders may not have a trading plan in place before they commence trading. Even if they have a plan, they may be more prone to stray from the defined plan than would seasoned traders. Novice traders may reverse course altogether. For example, going short after initially buying securities because the share price is declining—only to end up getting whipsawed.

7.   Chasing After Performance

Many investors or traders will select asset classes, strategies, managers, and fundsbased on a current strong performance. The feeling that "I'm missing out on great returns" has probably led to more bad investment decisions than any other single factor.

If a particular asset class, strategy, or fund has done extremely well for three or four years, we know one thing with certainty: We should have invested three or four years ago. Now, however, the particular cycle that led to this great performance may be nearing its end. The smart money is moving out, and the dumb money is pouring in.

8.   Not Regaining Balance

Rebalancing is the process of returning your portfolio to its target asset allocation as outlined in your investment plan. Rebalancing is difficult because it may force you to sell the asset class that is performing well and buy more of your worst-performing asset class. This contrarian action is very difficult for many novice investors.

435

However, a portfolio allowed to drift with market returns guarantees that asset classes will be overweighted at market peaks and underweighted at market lows—a formula for poor performance. Rebalance religiously and reap the long-term rewards.

9.   Ignoring Risk Aversion

Do not lose sight of your risk tolerance, or your capacity to take on risk. Some investors can't stomach volatility and the ups and downs associated with the stock market or more speculative trades. Other investors may need secure, regular interest income. These low-risk tolerance investors would be better off investing in the blue-chip stocks of established firms and should stay away from more volatile growth and startup companies shares.

Remember that any investment return comes with a risk. The lowest risk investment available is U.S. Treasury bonds, bills, and notes. From there, various types of investments move up in the risk ladder, and will also offer larger returns to compensate for the higher risk undertaken. If an investment offers very attractive returns, also look at its risk profile and see how much money you could lose if things go wrong. Never invest more than you can afford to lose.

10.   Forgetting Your Time Horizon

Don't invest without a time horizon in mind. Think about if you will need the funds you are locking up into an investment before entering the trade. Also, determine how long—the time horizon—you have to save up for your retirement, a downpayment on a home, or a college education for your child.

If you are planning to accumulate money to buy a house, that could be more of a medium-term time frame. However, if you are investing to finance a young child's college education, that is more of a long-term investment. If you are saving for retirement 30 years hence, what the stock market does this year or next shouldn't be the biggest concern.

Once you understand your horizon, you can find investments that match that profile.

11. Not Using Stop-Loss Orders

A big sign that you don't have a trading plan is not using stop-loss orders. Stop orders come in several varieties and can limit losses due to adverse movement in a stock or the market as a whole. These orders will execute automatically once perimeters you set are met.

Tight stop losses generally mean that losses are capped before they become sizable. However, there is a risk that a stop order on long positions may be implemented at levels below those specified should the security suddenly gap lower—as happened to many investors during the Flash Crash. Even with that thought in mind, the benefits of stop orders far outweigh the risk of stopping out at an unplanned price.

A corollary to this common trading mistake is when a trader cancels a stop order on a losing trade just before it can be triggered because they believe that the price trend will reverse.

12. Letting Losses Grow

One of the defining characteristics of successful investors and traders is their ability to take a small loss quickly if a trade is not working out and move on to the next trade idea. Unsuccessful traders, on the other hand, can become paralyzed if a trade goes against them. Rather than taking quick action to cap a loss, they may hold on to a losing position in the hope that the trade will eventually work out. A losing trade can tie up trading capital for a long time and may result in mounting losses and severe depletion of capital.

437

Conflicting Stock Investing Advice That's Preventing You From Making Money

You know that when you sell your stock, someone is buying it from you. When you buy your stock, someone is selling it to you. This means there are investors out there that are thinking completely contrary to you. Are they misguided, or are you? Someone has to be wrong......right?

This is because there is too much information, too many methods, too many opinions out there! I didn't know where to start! I realized whatever method I just learned, there is a method that is 100% contradicting to what I just learned, so which is the right one? I would learn a method only for that method to be debunked short after. I found myself all over the place trying different things.

There were sleazy salesy/workshop selling me garbage (green arrow I buy/red arrow I sell, with no explanation as to what they meant). Then there were honest people who swear by their system, but they are in direct contradiction by other honest people who swear by their system! Finally, there were sites/blogs that have way too much data, they look impressive, but I have no idea how to make any sense of the information they provided. As a novice investor I didn't know where to start. Imagine you have two friends who have each made billions from the stock market, both are sincere in teaching you how to invest/trade. You are learning from both, the only problem is, anytime there is a shift in the market one of them tells you to buy and the other tells you to sell! You want to trust them both, so sometimes you follow one's advice and other time you follow the others, but you aren't making any money!

I would advices you not to follow someone's advice blindly, follow a certain principal or create a trading system, without understanding it! You will be all over the place, and when their system fails you won't be able to modify it since you didn't learn how the system worked in the first place! This is why I'm against someone touting stock picks or have this one strategy that has made them millions. If they have totally convinced you, you can try their system on the side, but focus on learning for the long term, and stock piling blocks of knowledge...you will be better off in long run! Let me attempt to cut out 10 years of noise in next 3 pages!

Growth Stocks Are Traded Differently Than Value Stocks

There is a very popular saying in the stock market "Don't try to catch a falling knife". This means never buy a stock that is falling! As you can imagine the stock may continue to fall and can possibly bankrupt you! I once bought a stock that I didn't sell as it was coming down. It went all the way down and then became worthless! The commission to sell the stock cost me more than what the stock was worth! I couldn't sell the stock and it was a bitter reminder every time I logged in and saw my investment had turned into $.000012! I had to call my broker to remove security from showing up in my portfolio.

In 1999 there were many dot com companies that never made it back. When the stock market was crashing, if you continued buying into investment that was falling you may have dumped good money after bad and lost it all! NASDAQ ETF QQQ was $120 in early 2000 then it tanked for 2 years, all the way down to around $20 in 2002. It did not rise over $120 until 2016! If you held on to that ETF in 1999 and continued buying on its way down, at some point you may have run out of money. On top of that you didn't breakeven for up to 17 years! That means for 17 years you made 0% on your investment! Now could that money be invested elsewhere for better returns?

In 2008, same thing happened again to lesser effect. I'm not singling out a stock, I'm talking about general market (many stocks)! It holds true even if you stuck to your ETFs, mutual funds and indices index.

In 2000 and in 2008, some of my stock investment became worthless and I lost money. I learned I will never hold on to a stock that is falling, or just teeter tottering again! I will only invest in stocks that are rising day after day and will sell & get out if the stock is not moving up or turns down. Why would I ever invest in a security that is or has fallen so much when I can get out and wait for the market to start going up again (Growth investing)?

Then I learned that's exactly what Warren Buffet and other millionaire investors do! Warren Buffet looks at these stocks as a good bargain, he buys them when they have fallen and everyone else is selling, below what they are worth (value investing). One of his famous quotes "Price is what you pay. Value is what you get"!

At this time, you should be asking yourself:

DO I BUY WHEN THE STOCK PRICE COMES DOWN OR DO I SELL?

There are books written arguing growth vs. value investing. I don't want to make a case which is better but want you to understand this concept. Otherwise you will hear different guru's (Warren Buffet vs. William O'Neil) and may hear conflicting buy/sell zones and you will be all over the place!

Fundamental Analysis Entry Points

Fundamental analyst will tell you the best way to invest in a company is to figure out how the company is doing (by its performance) by studying its cash flow, earnings, expenses, assets and liabilities; all of which can be found in its 10k to give you better understanding of the overall status of the company. If the stock value is right, then buy and hold! Then as the company grows, so will your shares. They are not concern about short term trending up or down.

Technical analyst focuses on the stock chart's pattern, trendlines, moving averages, support and resistance and many

440

other indicators, all of which gives you clue into when to buy and sell stocks. Technical analysts usually aren't concerned with who is running the company, what their annual report or 10k states.

These two methods could trigger different buy/sell points contradicting each other on when to enter and exit a trade. I will show you how to find great companies, run the numbers, do the fundamental analysis then apply technical analysis on them. We will learn both and then incorporate them into one system.

Investing Concept is Different Than Trading Concept

There is a difference between short-term trading and long-term investing. When you invest in a company, you are hoping to reap the profits as that company builds wealth over a longer period. You are hoping the company will be worth a lot more in the future through ups and downs. The theory is that as company grows so will its overall value and in turn your investment in it. This requires some forecasting and usually a buy and hold strategy, as it will take some time for the company to grow.

Trading involves short term buying and selling of a security. You are hoping to take advantage of the short-term gain or a trend and get in & out of positions relatively quickly. You are hoping to beat "buy and hold" strategy which is usually implemented with longer term investing. You are less concerned of the long-term prognosis of the company.

You can see how a great short-term trading opportunity maybe triggering different buy/sell signals than long-term buy and hold strategy.
In this book I will use investing and trading interchangeably but understand that trading is usually short-term, and investing is usually long-term.

Prevent Loss vs. Buy On Dips

441

Should you buy on dips or place a stop loss to avoid bigger loss? These two methods can also trigger different buy/sell signals. While one analyst buys every time there is a dip, because they see the dip as a buying opportunity to buy a stock for less. Another analyst is afraid that it could be on its way down and wants to prevent further loss and gets out. If the market comes up after the dip the first analyst will have bragging right for buying at a lower price. However, if the market dip turns into bear market, the second analyst will argue that getting out early was the right decision. Who is right? I don't know a lot more goes into their call, but you can again see different buy/sell signals here.

Chapter 3: Mutual Funds

Mutual Funds Vs ETF

Both mutual funds and ETF are concepts of pooled fund investing created to provide a diversified investment for investors. Besides, mutual funds and ETF are both regulated by the Securities Act of 1933, the Securities and Exchange Act of 1934 and the Investment Company Act of 1940. They two also comprise of between 100 and 3,000 varying individual securities as well as appealed by individual investors. However, mutual funds and ETF have multiple variations depending on the operations and how investors readily capitalize on the market. More so, ETF is quite cheap, liquid and accessed quickly by an investor than when compared to mutual funds which are typically expensive and comprises of limited assets.

Index Funds Vs ETF

An ETF is among the most flexible and efficient investment strategies for investors when compared to mutual funds. Index funds are a representation of theoretical segments of the market across all businesses, including large and small companies as well as those under different industries among others. Unlike an ETF, index funds are responsible for settings rules of investing in stocks and keeping tracks but are not investable. On the other hand, Exchange-Traded Funds are essential for investment and assets traded platforms such as securities. As mentioned, they operate similar to the stock market where they can sell or buy in a public stock market.

Types of ETFs

When in need of making money in the ETF business, it is crucial to learn the different types available to ensure you capitalize on the preferable option. There are multiple types of ETF markets out there that operate almost similar but with slight differences. As ETF entails a vast area of trading of assets, it, therefore, allows for institutions and individual investors to benefit differently. Each type of ETF on the same note possesses benefits essential to suit the needs of a particular investor.

Stock EFT

Stock EFT is a type of asset tracking that focuses on equities trading usually like shares but varies to how mutual funds operate. Prices typically change throughout the day despite market closure and can track specific industries such as real estate or an entire index of equities in the market. As such, it provides an opportunity for investors to gain exposure to a handful of stakes, therefore, limiting risks associated with single trading stocks. Some of the benefits of stock ETFs are flexibility, low costs of trading, accessibility, and tax efficiency. Besides, stock ETFs accompanies minimal management fees which are usually high, especially when considering brokerages who charge more online.

Sector ETF

This is a type of Exchange-Traded Fund which focuses on stocks and securities investments for a particular industry. Sector ETF is mostly utilized for hedging and speculating, therefore, becoming among the most popular for investors. These ETFs primarily are designed for US-based stocks with some operating globally to track performances of the sector at hand. In this case, the Global Industry Classification Standard is one of the subcategories of sector ETF crucial for tracking financial industry standards. Under the Global Industry Classification Standard, there exist other sectors which are utilities, consumer staples, energy, telecommunication services, and real estate, among others.

Commodity ETF

Commodities are typically basic goods which are also essential areas for investors to input money and gain income. Commodity ETFs, therefore, enables investors to have exposure to individual commodities while providing them in a simple, cost-effective, and reduced risk. This type of ETF also may focus on one or more specialties and may also include futures contracts. It primarily tract the trend of commodity indexes offered in different types. Commodity ETFs can, therefore, be provided in the form of equity, exchange-traded notes, future-based funds, or physical-backed funds. Every kind of commodity accompanies both its advantages and disadvantages depending on the individual investment goals, risks, and cost tolerance.

Bond ETF

This is an ETF that solely tracks the performance of bonds and works similarly to mutual funds bonds. Bond ETFs are managed passively, therefore, promoting market stability due to its liquidity and transparency. The bonds trade throughout the day through centralized exchange markets as well as helping investors to gain exposure due to their structure of trading on significant indexes. In its operations, a bond ETF works like individual bonds and investors can readily receive payments that are fixed at a scheduled period usually every six months. However, bond ETFs accompany some disadvantages which may offer limitations for investors. Some of them include putting of an investor's assets at more risk when compared to individual bonds.

Currency ETF

Currency is another type of Exchange-Traded Fund primarily used to track the performance of one or more currencies against the US dollar in the foreign exchange market. It also includes cash deposits, swap contracts, and short-term debt currencies. Specific investors initially accessed the trading of these types of assets, but the rise of ETFs has created more room for different people to trade currencies. Like the most type of ETFs, currency ETF allows investors to be exposed to the foreign exchange market, especially for those who hope to transact in futures or forex market. One problem, however, associated with this type of Exchange-Traded Fund is that the currencies in the market are usually affected by the changing microeconomic activities, therefore, creating risks for investors.

International ETFs

International EFTs entail investments made solely in foreign securities and may include a specific country, regionals or global. It may also include equities and fixed return securities usually invested internationally. The index may sometimes vary between fund managers with others having substantial and diversified value in the market of different countries. International ETFs have become more common in the United States with globalization and financial policies opening up more room for investors to interact with the global market. In most cases, there has been an increase in emerging ETF markets which have played a significant role in ensuring that there are more asset markets accessed globally by investors.

How to Pick the Best ETF

Exchange-Traded Funds have been considered by different investors who have dedicated to making money using different types of ETF. For beginners, choosing the right or desired type of ETF may become a challenge, therefore, causing a complicated situation. In most cases, investors may end up landing on unnecessary or rather EFT types which may impact their investment strategies. Other than the varieties available, you may face a challenge when determining the inversing style or market capitalization for a successful investment plan. When venturing into ETF business, your goals, risk, and capital tolerance drive your portfolio on what exactly you wish to engage in.

The first step to making good money in ETF is to narrow down to the desired type of investment which would drive your income. That is when you have clearly highlighted your goals, learn about the different types and requirements of your long-term plan of increasing wealth. There are a lot of ways to do this, but it is essential to use a screener as it is a broad topic to cover. Even after selecting the right type of ETF, you will then have multiple considerations for a successful strategy. Other techniques to use to build your best ETF are to learn about the competition as ETF business has the most competitive environment.

Issuers have developed different products that are specific and straightforward differentiating themselves from the competition. As the market becomes more specific to attract beginners and other investors readily, ETF has developed techniques to help in selecting desirable and effective strategies of becoming among the best learning performance of the market. As such, you should consider factors such as level of assets which should considerably be at minimal, trading activities in the market, underlying assets and indexes and the position of the market. Another great benefit that helps you to choose the right EFT is that you are frequently notified by the issuers about liquidations, especially when the market is expected to drop in trades.

How Investors Earn From Investing In ETFs

Like mutual funds, investing in ETFs also accompanies buying and selling of assets and operate almost identical. The profits generated also depend on the type of investment an investor chooses to put their money and gain their desired income. ETFs also are like trust funds making investors invest any kind including stocks, commodities and bonds, and indexes. In other words, when you buy ETF stocks and hope to make money, your initial capital gain and dividends would significantly determine the profits to generate. The same is applied to other types of ETFs, for instance, if you have bond fund EFT, then you are to make interest income. Real estate ETF is primarily to ensure you make profits from rents and property sales, among others.

Increasing Your Earnings in ETFs

Invest On What You Know

Investing in ETFs may accompany significant challenges as well as losses, mainly when you invest in unknown exciting companies. When engaging or selecting your desired type and investment plan, avoid placing your assets on specific on the attractive market, which has a higher probability of failure. That is, there are numerous ETFs out there that utilize different concepts of investments. When you decide on choosing a given ETF to generate profits, begin with having extensive knowledge about it. Besides, check how such a market operates and learn more about the probability of gaining big rather than spending years generating pennies.

Maintain Your ETF Expenses

This is usually not problematic when it comes to ETFs as this type of investment is affordable essential for those without access to managed accounts. In some cases, ETFs are vital for those with minimal capital to begin investing in different sectors and grow their assets. However, it is indispensable to keep your expenses at a reasonable level to avoid overspending or losing what you never budgeted for. You can do this by consulting with your financial planner, advisor or use do-it-yourself plan to budget yourself. Ensure that you maintain your expenses while keeping at optimal, not letting them increase or decrease.

Avoid Short-Term Expectations

This is a problem that arises mostly from beginners as they may go for making quick money which is usually not the case when it comes to ETFs. When investing in ETF, especially in these securities, you should focus on the long-term goals. For instance, periods between 2007 and 2009 saw a decrease in holdings in which you are to persevere as an investor to ensure you adhere to what this business comes with. As such, more so beginners, you should ensure that you develop long-term strategies and goals as well as being tolerated to challenges the market may come with. Avoid short term expectations which are usually disappointing when the market fails to meet your expectations.

Learn Continually

It is said that experience is the best teacher. The same is also applied in ETF business as having adequate general, and specific knowledge enables you to build your accomplishments in this industry readily. As a beginner, it does not imply that you have to invest in ETF in order to gain experience previously, you can begin by learning about this industry by readily accessing articles created by successful investors. You can as well build your learning by checking different resources that develop your knowledge while keeping you on the forefront to achieve the best. Similarly, ensure you continually learn more about ETFs even when you begin investing. The market is continually changing, as to keep track, you need to learn new things each day to familiarize yourself entirely with what to expect in the future.

Interact Well With Issuer

It is possible to launch and develop your ETF without seeking external help, especially when you are venturing into the business for the first time. Despite so, it is crucial to maintain your interaction with an issuer who provides additional assistance when it comes to putting your money on specific assets. ETFs demand for adequate time and expenses to yield the best while offering multiple means of creating final products. As most assets are available at low costs, having a well-established relationship with issuers develops your communication which promotes possibilities of gaining more income over time.

Common Mistakes to Avoid When Investing in ETFs
Loss of Focus

Investments are usually long term and demand the need to readily remain on point despite the challenges experienced frequently. Many successful investors always advise beginners to understand that for any investment scheme to succeed, you need to maintain your focus without limiting yourself due to problems associated with variation in market prices. This is one of the significant issues which affect generating a substantial amount of money at the end. When you develop your plan that you would buy assets and maintain them for years, then you should stick by it. However, some may end up selling or buying other shares due to loss of focus on what they planned initially. In this case, you put yourself on the risk of losing big or extending the period in which you would begin enjoying your benefits.

Lack of Investment Strategy

Though most investors recommend that you invest while focusing on the market value, it is crucial to learn that the ETF business changes regularly, especially when the day closes. Though rare, this is a mistake that originates if you fail to change how you invest your money. By developing your plan, you should be able to create a technique where you keep track of the market performance and avoiding those with failing values. In this case, ensure that you maintain your initial strategy while focusing on how your money grows or changes over time. However, you should avoid frequent selling and buying as it attracts significant commission fees, especially when dealing with online brokerages.

Lack of Adequate ETF Diversification Researches

As mentioned, there are always the most minimal chances of benefiting in Exchange-Traded Funds, especially when you have no idea what you are getting yourself into. The same applies when you fail to choose your desired type of ETF to capitalize on and generate more income. This is a problem attributed to the lack of courses which makes you understand how ETF is a significant contributor in diversifying your investments in the sector. This way, you will have faced the problem of redundancy and the risk of not specializing in essential liquidity options. As an investor, you are therefore more vulnerable to fail and lose your money within a short time.

Making Unnecessary Conclusions

As an investor, you are venturing into the investment industry with the aim of making profits despite the risks associated. The same is also applicable to ETFs as it consists of challenges but with significant benefits. Unlike other investments, ETFs are flexible and have different strategies used to make it among the most unique in the market. This is one of the best options, therefore for investors who assume that the prices will go down despite trading at low costs. However, this is not the right track to go if you have an online brokerage which also charges some fee from your trade. It is then vital to avoid making conclusions about a given stock, bond, index, and other securities but instead leans about then and makes conclusive results.

A mutual fund is a pooled fund of money from multiple investors that is used to purchase assets on their behalf. Mutual funds invest in many different areas, such as stock market indexes, different sectors, large cap, small cap, etc. You can also find mutual funds that are structured for growth or value and to meet the many different investment goals that people have, such as investing in bonds. In some ways, mutual funds are like exchange-traded funds. One important difference is that

451

mutual funds don't trade on the stock market. Mutual funds are only traded once at the close of each business day.

Benefits of Mutual Funds

Like exchange-traded funds, one of the benefits of mutual funds is that they provide a ready-made way to have diversified investments. This will help to mitigate your investment risk. Mutual funds can be very highly diversified; some may hold hundreds if not thousands of investments in underlying assets. So, you get huge diversity when you invest in a mutual fund, however, remember that you will get the same diversity when you invest in an exchange-traded fund, and there are several advantages to taking that route.

Another advantage of mutual funds is you can find funds that are set up for your investment goals ahead of time. So, for investors that don't want to think about what they are doing, using mutual funds is a conservative approach to investing that is basically a set it and forget it approach.

Minimum Investments

If you are going to invest in an exchange-traded fund, you can buy as little as a single share to get started. This isn't the case with mutual funds. They are going to require a minimum investment. The required minimum investment isn't going to be very large, but will be at least $1,000 and can range as high as $5,000.

Fees

The fees for mutual funds can be relatively high, and besides the way that they are traded, this is one of the biggest arguments against them. A "load fee" is charged every time you buy or "redeem" shares of the fund. You don't sell shares of a mutual fund, you redeem them, that gives them back to the company that manages the mutual fund. Load fees can be quite large, going as high as 8%. That is huge when you consider the practically nonexistent fees of exchange-traded funds. Moreover, load fees can be complicated.

There are front-end load fees charged when you buy the shares, and back-end load fees charged when you redeem shares. Back-end load fees can be variable, depending on how long you held the shares. The longer you hold the shares, the lower the fee. So, they are encouraging you to stay in the fund.
There are also "level-load" fees that are charged once per year.

Actively Managed vs. Passively Managed Funds

Funds can be actively or passively managed. A passively managed fund is typically one that tracks a stock market index like the S&P 500. Passively managed funds, as you might guess, charge lower fees than actively managed funds. The goal of a passively managed fund is to match the return of the index that the fund tracks.

Actively managed funds mean exactly what the name says; they have an active manager or managers that run the investment portfolio. As you might imagine, that costs money. The fund managers will buy and sell assets in the fund in an attempt to beat the average return of the stock market. So, they are doing what you would be doing yourself if you manage your own stock portfolio.

Generally speaking, beating the average return of the stock market is not an easy task. However, some research exists showing that actively managed funds often beat the market. That said, they don't beat it by huge amounts, and the massive fees that mutual funds require can wipe out any gains from having the fund actively managed. Long term studies that have been done actually show that passively managed funds return nearly three times as much as actively managed funds.

Exchange Traded Funds vs. Mutual Funds

If you enjoy dressing up in a suit and going to an office to hand over your money to pay fees, and then let the professional manage your investment account for the next 30 years, then mutual funds might just be right up your alley. All joking aside, mutual funds are suitable for some people and not suitable for others. If you are the kind of person who has an interest in actively managing your stock investments, then you are probably not going to be someone who is interested in mutual funds.

The bottom line is that in reality, exchange-traded funds basically offer the advantages of mutual funds but without the constraints and extra fees. Mutual funds are a bit of hassle when compared to exchange-traded funds. As we mentioned above, long term studies at best (from the perspective of mutual funds) don't beat passively managed funds, and in fact, 30-year studies have shown much better returns from passively managed funds. Even if we accept that many mutual funds can beat the market, you have to ask yourself if it's worth paying all those extra fees in order to get active management.

With exchange traded funds, you're in complete control. You can trade day to day if you want to, and you don't have to pay any "back end" fees if you want to sell your shares. So, exchange-traded funds offer the diversity, convenience, and ability to invest in many different sectors and types of investments in one package, but they are far more flexible. When you are investing in exchange-traded funds, you are in complete control and don't have to worry about some mutual fund company.

But most importantly, you don't have to pay for all the high fees. There are fees associated with exchange-traded funds, but they are trivial. There used to be less difference when commissions were more of an issue, and so you'd be looking at paying the broker a commission for trading an ETF. But for example, you can trade commission free on Robinhood. And outside

Robinhood, many brokers are offering commission-free trades on ETFs. So that negates that old argument.

Problems Buying and Selling

Since mutual funds only trade once per day after market close, this can cause issues if you want to buy and sell shares. Suppose it's in the middle of the day and the S&P 500 is really moving. So, you want to buy shares in SPY. It trades like a stock, so you just pull out your smartphone and buy the shares. You see the price right there when you place your order.
In the same scenario with a mutual fund, if you decide in the middle of the day that you want to buy shares of an S&P 500 mutual fund, you will know what the price was the previous day. However, you can't know what price you're going to pay for the shares if you placed an order at that moment because the fund is not going to trade until after market close. That is a huge disadvantage.

Investing In Index Funds

Many financial advisers you will meet will gush over the need to invest in index funds, and they have a point. Index funds are popular for many reasons—they are a low cost, diversified, easy and hands-off way to invest in the stock market.

All the same, many of us have heard the phrase "index funds" or read a piece of writing that mentioned it, but it floated away without our understanding of what it actually meant. Well, this chapter dives into the mire of financial facts and knowledge to enlighten you on this incredible form of investment to get you making the elusive passive income you have always desired. You could even become an expert and teach others.

Like most people, it is likely that you have never heard of John Bogle. He came up with the index funds concept and is also the Vanguard Group founder. The investment world does not give him as much recognition and credit as he deserves, especially now that he went on forced retirement and left his company under management. However, this man was a fierce voice in the mutual funds' sphere. He has long talked about the high fees that companies charge and their lack of accountability to the shareholders, excessive taxation, and other constraints within the fund.

Bogle is not only vocal about the lack of or inadequate professionalism in the industry but also has some advice for investors concerning about picking the right index funds to invest in. Bogle believes that it is impossible to know how to choose the right individual stocks as well as to buy each just at the right time. In fact, if each person tries to beat and outsmart each other in the market, then the society will be trying to trick itself, which is unwise. Instead, Bogle came up with the index fund as a way of getting rid of all investment constraints. He believed that index funds would take out all the risks brought by individual stocks, the market, and the management, leaving the investors to juggle stock market risks.

The Index Funds

Index fund by definition is an exchange-traded fund or a mutual fund that is designed in a way that matches the returns the investors would acquire from the ownership of all securities that are in a stock market index like the Standard & Poor's 500 (S&P 500) and the FTSE 100 Index. The performance of the securities themselves in the stock market reflects the performance of the index funds.

The index fund follows a number of pre-determined rules to ensure that it keeps track of the specified underlying investments. One of the rules is that an index should track dominant indexes such as the S&P 500, the Dow Jones Industrial Average, or the FTSE 100. There are also other rules that govern areas related to tracking error minimization, tax management, and the kind of trading strategies that traders take up in their quest to increase their profits and reduce the costs of trading. Some index funds even have CSR rules based on social and sustainability concerns.

When you invest in index funds, just as the name suggests, you purchase an index. The cost of buying the index is equal to the value of the stocks therein. Each index contains a varied selection of stocks packaged together, taking out the need to purchase individual stocks. Because of this, an index performs in tandem with the stocks it is tracking, except for the small deficit called a tracking error.

Index funds track the performance of an index passively unlike other actively-managed funds. At all points, index funds do not outperform the market; they merely follow in the steps of the performance of the index. In addition, since their portfolios are not managed actively, in the buy and sell fashion meant to generate profit, it is cheaper to maintain and manage them compared to those that are actively managed.

Sometimes, some schemes are not able to match the performance of the index, which means that the index funds are not of equal value to the index. This is the tracking error mentioned earlier, and it is vital for an investor to keep a close eye on this figure when making index fund investment decisions. The tracking error shows the extent of deviation of the index fund's returns from the index it is tracking. A low tracking error indicates good performance and vice versa.

Each index fund has unique rules for all the stocks included in it. These rules are called the rules of construction, and they set the standards for the companies that wish to be included in that particular index. For example, S&P 500 Index Fund, which is the most common index fund in the U.S., follows the rules set by the S&P Dow Jones Indices to govern the S&P Index. The FTSE 100 index tracks large company stocks from 100 of the largest companies traded in the London Stock Exchange. An equity index fund would include stocks that share characteristics like profitability, value, size, and the companies' geographical locations. It may also only include companies from the United Kingdom, the United States, the emerging markets, Non-US, or from companies in the Frontier Market.

Index funds drawn from the same geographical location may be divided further to include the indexes of companies based on factors like the companies being small, medium-sized, large, large value, small value, real estate, investment capital, small growth, large growth, fixed income or gross profitability, among other like factors. Company stock is purchased and placed in the specified index fund after meeting the parameters or rules. Those that move out of the parameters are sold. The primary advantage of an index fund is that an investor does not need to take much time to manage the index or spend time analyzing different stocks and their portfolios. In fact, many investors lack the knowledge, skills, and experience needed to make decisions like this.

How to Invest in Index Funds

As you begin to dip your toes into the investment waters, it can be challenging to know where to go. You must have a ton of questions too, many of which lack a definite answer. If you intend to invest to cover future expenses or to secure your retirement, you are probably seeking out the best long-term investment method. Ideally, you want a method that will embrace diversity, one that will not distract you from your daily activities and one does not attract burdensome trading costs. In many ways, investing in index funds with the help of low-cost brokers will solve all these problems in one swoop! So, how do you go about it?
Here are the five critical steps that will guide you in this endeavor:

•   Learn all there is to do with index funds and how they work

- Conduct an in-depth comparison of all the online brokerage companies available in terms of the fees charged and the functionality
- Consider adding ETFs to your index fund investment
- Only when you feel ready, open a trading account
- Buy index funds consistently and reinvest the dividends so that the funds grow and multiply themselves continually.

Index funds offer a fantastic stress-free strategy for building wealth that will get you started in your quest to venture deeper into the financial market. The learning curve is not as steep as most people imagine it to be because it is easy to open your own online brokerage account and to start investing immediately.

To start today, look up an online brokerage that offers a selection of index funds that you could be interested in. This is ideal for investors who want to cut out the middleman altogether. A Vanguard account, for example, would be ideal and easy to open. The company only asks for information on your checking account, but once you create the account, you can go ahead and start the business. Everything is managed electronically.

Almost all Vanguard accounts require an initial $3,000 to get to the fund directly or $1,000 as a Vanguard target date fund. The initial buy-in will surely have you saving all dimes and nickels you can find; you need to get your foot in. Vanguard offers invaluable tools that will allow you to make successive investments automatically such as allowing you to make investments each week or each month direct from your checking account, rolling up your dividends back to the index fund and others.

Taking the direct investment route is quite advantageous. For starters, the fees charged when investing directly are quite low, 0.1% to 0.2% of the principal investment fund, which is insignificant in comparison to the returns you expect from your investment.

Other people like to avoid the process themselves and instead, opt to use the services of a broker. There are a number of brokers in the market such as Schwab, TD Ameritrade, Ally Invest, and E*TRADE. The process of investing with them is similar to taking up the challenge yourself. You are asked to sign up with them online, provide details of your checking account and then start buying. Almost all brokerages charge a transaction fee for every buy or sell. Therefore, if by chance you sign up with TD Ameritrade and buy a Vanguard fund, you will be asked to pay Ameritrade's transaction fee for each sale or purchase, in addition to Vanguard's management fees.

In a situation like this, the solution is to purchase ETFs. The fees charged for ETFs are always lower than the amount that would be charged for an index fund of the same amount. For example, the Vanguard 500 index fund charges a 0.14% expense ratio or the management fees, while the SPDR 500 that tracks similar stock as an ETF only attracts a 0.0975% expense ratio.
Indeed, the key to making any investment is to move and get started immediately before life gets in the way; it tends to do that. The sooner you get your money growing and multiplying, the more time you give it for growth.

Below is a summary of the steps you should take when you want to go about investing in index funds.

1.   *Ensure that you can meet the minimum investment for your intended index funds.*

Many index funds will require you to make an initial investment of between $2,000 and $3,000. This is the primary charge you pay to get the index funds, and once you have cleared it, you are free to start earning, although in small amounts. Each index fund will have a unique investment minimum, high or low. You only need to look through the market to identify one that is in your budget.

1.   First, if you do not have a lot of starting capital, opt for an ETF index fund first.

Not having enough money ought not to stop you on your journey to securing your financial future; you can begin with an ETF fund. An ETF fund tracks the indexes of major companies like Google, Microsoft, and Apple on the S&P 500. These funds are a good bet because the companies are stable, and it is likely that you will get a good return from them. In addition, the investment minimum for these companies is very low.

Going by this option is similar to index funds because you will not have to choose individual stocks; they are already classified and grouped.

If you can afford the investment minimum for index funds, go right ahead and buy, by yourself through either your account or a broker.

2.   For a good return on investment, lean towards small-cap and mid-sized index funds.

Index funds from these companies have more significant returns in the long run because the company itself is growing. However, spread out the risk by putting more of your funds on the mid-size index and less on the small-cap indexes.

3.   Ensure that you create a diversified portfolio.

An index funds investment can also be a portion of your larger investment portfolio. They help to strengthen your overall finances. In addition, ensure that the index funds themselves are diverse as discussed in chapter one above. Your broker, financial adviser, or the mutual fund company can offer you advice on how to add your new investment into the current portfolio, or how you can create a new diverse portfolio using index funds.

4.   Ensure that the index on the funds is equal to or is close to the returns expected.

Companies trading index funds will have a quote page that shows the expected returns for the investment you make. There are also multiple quote pages online. Your broker could also provide you with one. Ensure that the index funds you intend to purchase on average have returns higher than the fees you will be paying. You should only invest in index funds whose returns completely cover the costs that will be charged. Also, make sure to avoid those that do not do well typically and those that offer the investors a constant return.

5.   Opt for a brokerage company that has a variety of index funds.

Companies like Vanguard, State Street Global, and BlackRock are considered leaders in the index funds market, and they offer a wide range of index funds from which you can choose. Ensure that the company you are eyeing has the kind of index funds you are looking for before you commit to it. If you intend to make your investments in small amounts once you pay the minimum investment, opt for a mutual fund company because it does not impose any transaction fees for deposits.

6.   One-time investments are best made through a broker.

Some brokers charge a transaction fee every time you input some money into your fund. If your choice broker does this, seek to make your investment as a lump sum, and if you have to add to it, only do so on rare occasions. This is also suitable for persons who operate using a personal brokerage account or for investors dealing with individual brokers instead of dealing with an established large mutual fund company.

Kindly also take note of the fact that some brokers also charge an additional processing fee for each transaction, while others will offer free trades for loyal clients.

7.   Your banking information is required.

As you open an account or sign up with a mutual fund company, bank details, and a routing number are critical, and you will always be asked to provide them. Primary, these details are meant to provide a place where you will collect your returns from your investment. The broker or the mutual funds' company you select will also access your minimum investment from there.

In this, you are cautioned to only provide this sensitive information to brokers and companies you trust. If you are required to submit the information using the Internet, ensure that you are using a secure site and that the right protections have been installed.

8.   Ensure that you pay all the fees linked to your index funds.

Typically, index funds attract fees but are often cheaper than stocks and other funds. Before you purchase any of them, look at the expense ratio for each. Most brokers and mutual fund companies often have broken down this cost into different kinds of fees. These fees should only be 0.1 percent or 0.2 percent of the principal amount to be invested. Compared to what you will make at the end of the investment period, this amount is negligible.

9.   Pay up all the costs upfront.

It is necessary that you pay up the entire initial investment, the commissions, and any other associated fees upfront. Once you have done that, relax and watch as your returns flow back in.

10.   It is essential to monitor the progress.

Just like any other investment, merely making a deposit is not enough; you need to keep an eye on what you have planted. Again, it is advisable not to do this too often, to avoid being stressed and discouraged when the index funds are not performing as expected. Typically, index funds are stable and will not change too radically, which takes out the need to monitor them all the time. It is okay to check on them at least one in a year to take note of the progress, so that you may be assured that your investment is still secure and doing well.

Some people compare the progress of their index funds to that of others. The comparison helps you identify index funds that are doing much better than yours is. If you find that this is the case, you may switch to the one that is performing well after some years, increasing the returns.

1. **Do not stop at the initial deposit.**

Develop the habit of adding small amounts of money into your fund, possibly once every month, or several times in a year, to increase the principal amount and consequently your returns. In the event of a windfall or you find yourself with extra money after paying your bills, or you receive dividends from other investments, deposit the extra money into your fund. If your broker charges a transaction fee, reduce the number of times you make the deposits, opting for more substantial sums deposited few times instead of depositing small amounts every time you get them.

2.   Trade non-performing index funds.

In the event, an index fund is consistently not performing as you were expecting, sell it through your broker or the mutual fund company. Beware that these dealers will charge a small fee, typically $10 per trade, but the non-performing index funds will be out of your hands in the end.

In the event, you need the money you invested or would like to shift your investment, cash out! If you need the investment income to pay some bills or that you want to try out an alternative mutual fund or stocks, you may also cash out. Your broker or the company will aid in this process but will charge a small fee.

Trading Index Funds

The process of buying an index fund is done in three simple steps. They are:
•   Making the decision on where to buy—this involves going through a list of brokers and their fund selection, factoring in the cost of the trade and seeing if there are options that do not require you to pay a commission.
•   Choosing a preferred index—choose a company to buy from based on the index it follows, whether the S&P or any other.
•   Looking at the investment income and other costs charged—this allows you to select the index fund and the brokerage company that suits your pocket.
The steps listed above are further discussed in this section below.
Step 1: Deciding Where You Want to Buy Your Index Funds
You have the choice of buying your index funds from a mutual fund company or seeking the services of a broker. This is also the case for persons purchasing ETFs although they are traded throughout the day, unlike index funds.

When you are choosing between these options, ensure that you consider the following factors:

•   Convenience: get a funds provider who has the capacity to meet all your investment needs. For example, if you have decided to invest in mutual funds, and perhaps to add some stocks to it, the mutual fund company or the broker you choose should be able to provide you with both. They should act like a hub or a one-stop shop such that everything you may need is already available. For example, if you require screening tools and additional stock research, a discount broker who also offers index funds will provide you with personalized service delivery.

• A selection of index funds: If you desire to purchase your index funds from different funds categories and families, a big mutual fund company should be able to provide you with a wide array of funds from which you can choose. However, although these companies are large, a discount broker will likely have a larger selection.

• Is it Free? See if the providers you are eyeing for offer commission-free ETFs or free transactions for mutual funds. This criterion is used to rate brokers.

• The costs of trading: Some brokers and mutual fund companies have scrapped off all transaction and commission fees, in a bid to please their current customers and attract new ones. However, others will still impose these fees. If you happen to lean towards one that imposes a fee, ensure that the fee is fair. Typically, you will be asked to pay $20 as a mutual fund commission or $10 if you are trading in ETFs and stocks.

Step 2: The Choice of an Index
Index funds are designed to track indexes, which makes it worthwhile to check out the indexes first before purchasing the funds. One of the very known indexes is the S&P 500 Index. It tracks 500 companies. Its portfolio is composed of popular, large, U.S.-based and other variations of companies. You can be sure that it represents a diverse industry spectrum. There are also other indexes, and they have attached index funds.

Each index has assets and stocks that are chosen based on certain basic criteria. Some of the factors considered when placing the companies in various indexes include:

• Geography: stocks placed together based on geography are those that trade in the stock exchange market and other international exchanges.

• Company's capitalization and size: Stock is differentiated based on the size of the company from which it is produced. It may include small, medium, or large companies.

• The type of assets traded: Some funds track cash, others commodities, others domestic bonds while others concentrate on international bonds.

• The size and the opportunities of the market they are from: The stocks could be from an established market, an emerging market or any other definition of a market.

• The Industry or the business sector: Stock is drawn from companies that primarily focus on technology, consumer goods, fashion, healthcare services, hospitality, electronics, and other utility items.

Although the fund provider will provide you with an assortment and a variety of choices, you only need to invest in one. Buffet says that you only need to choose a broad stock and you will have sufficiently diversified.

You should also note that the index funds themselves are not rigid and you can come up with a customized allocation in case you want a selection that provides additional exposure in the market. For example, you may include more stock from emerging markets or increase the proportion given to small companies.

Step 3: Take Note of the Minimum Investment Requested, Among Other Costs

One of the highest selling points for any products, including index funds, is the cost of acquiring it. Low cost of purchasing and maintenance is particularly attractive to consumers, as opposed to high costs. Low-cost index funds are easier to run particularly because they are designed in such a way that they automatically follow in the steps of an index. This, however, does not mean that all index funds are cheap.

Although index funds do not need active management, they carry administrative costs that are subtracted from the returns of an investment. Two funds could carry the same investment goal, such as the need to track the S&P 500 index but their management costs could vary greatly. They may even differ by a fraction of a percentage point, and the difference may seem insignificant for now. However, in the long run, the small fee could take a toll on returns from the investment. Normally, a large fund attracts smaller fees.

Therefore, as you evaluate index funds, consider the following major costs:

• The expense ratio: The expense ratio is one of the major costs that are taken out of the returns an investor is supposed to receive, often calculated as a percentage of the total amount invested. You should find the expense ratio in the prospectus or look it up in a financial site. Quoting some figures, the Investment Company Institute released in 2016 for context, stock index funds attract a 0.09% average annual expense ratio while bond index funds attract a 0.07% ratio. The expense ratio for an actively-managed stock is 0.82% while that of actively-managed bond funds stands at 0.58%.

• Investment Minimum: This is the principal minimum amount a potential investor should have in his person when going out to purchase index funds. It is the minimum investment requirement, and as stated earlier on, it can rise to

$3,000. Once the investor has met that threshold, he is allowed to continue investing, even in smaller amounts.

• Tax-cost Ratio: Ownership of index funds attracts taxes that are imposed on all capital gains that are kept in checking accounts but for the IRA and the 401(k) accounts.

Just like the expense ratio, the tax-cost ratio has a significant effect on investment returns. For many years, the tax-cost ratio has stood at 0.3% of all returns, although the rate can change.

• Account Minimum: The account minimum is an entirely different concept from the investment minimum. While the minimum amount of money that can be in a brokerage account is $0, it does not mean that the investor is free to take out the investment minimum required for the specific index fund.

Other Important Considerations

Investors are increasingly taking up index funds as the choice method of investment for reasons like the ease of use, acquiring immediate diversity, and for their returns, which beat those of active funds with time. Therefore, as you put the final touches in your choice of index fund, here are a few other considerations to make and questions you can ask yourself.

Are you new to investing? If indeed you are new, get to learn the ropes of index funds investments. This book will comprehensively and adequately teach you all you need to know regarding this kind of investment

What type of investment do you intend to make? You need to make a decision on the type of investment which you would like to include in your portfolio. If you are seeking long-term growth, choose stocks and if you are looking for stability, pick bonds. If you already own either of the two, seek to balance the two. In addition, besides choosing between the bonds and the stocks, you need to decide on the level of diversification you intend to bring.

What are your financial goals? In answering this question, you ought to state what your main investment drive is. Some people save for retirement, others for a vacation in the future, while others invest in having available funds when their children join colleges. Whatever your goals are, ensure you invest in a fund that will make your money available at the time when you need it.

Are the index funds working as it should? The index funds you choose should replicate the index's performance. To ensure that this is the case, check its returns on the quote page. You should see the returns it has given in the past periods and compare this performance with that of the benchmark index. If the returns are close but not identical, do not panic because it is likely that they have also factored in the costs of managing the funds and the taxes. However, if the returns are lagging far behind by a margin bigger than the expense ratio, you ought to be alarmed.

Is the index fund you are targeting too expensive? If you are working with a tight budget, invest in ETFs instead, because they also track the index. Instead of just buying a small slice of the major mutual funds, start out with the ETFs, and you can purchase index funds later on.

Are there promotions running that you could take up? Sometimes brokerage firms offer promotions such as a cash bonus, or more. Although this should not be the predominant factor influencing your investment decision, it would be nice if you got to enjoy it.

Balancing and Rebalancing Index Investments

If you are yet to balance or rebalance your investment portfolio, it is possible that you have taken on too much risk that dissolves your diversification or you have leaned too heavily on a particular kind of investment type. It is also possible that your stocks are falling as your bonds rise, foreign stocks could be doing better than the domestic stocks, or small-cap stocks could be outperforming large-cap stocks.

Resetting the balance in cases like these requires you to ignore your emotions and preferences, sell off the most recent overachievers, and use that money to add onto the stock of the underachievers. Over time, you will see that it is ideal to sell your holdings when high and to buy when low. This process of selling and buying depending on the position of the stock is sometimes called the rebalancing bonus. Doing this may even add an entire percentage point to your annual average returns in the case of a long-term investment.

Rebalancing Methods

There are two principal methods of rebalancing a portfolio. Neither is more effective than the other, investors can choose either based on their preference. Each is easy to carry out especially if the stock in the portfolio had been chosen widely so that it represents clear asset classes.

The As-Needed Method

In this method, you keep checking on your portfolio regularly and work to reestablish a balance when things are out of hand, even if it has only been a year, a month, a week, or a day since you rebalanced the portfolio. Carefully take note of the changes in your stock and take note of instances that require you to buy or sell some stock. The As-Needed approach provides a large rebalancing bonus, but the associated high costs and the inevitable taxation eat up this bonus. It is also likely that an investor will lose on the momentum that sometimes allows securities to go higher than they should go.

The Calendar Approach

This method is quite common, and it involves changing the allocations in your portfolio going by the calendar. Many financial experts say that the ideal timing is at least after a year or 18 months, and many people prefer doing it after 18 months. However, if you are making money and living off your portfolio, you may want to make the changes more often so that it can continue making regular cash, perhaps every six months.

The calendar approach is of an advantage primarily because it gives you the discipline of sticking to a regular schedule. It also leads to lesser trading, which means that the fees and taxes that the transactions attract are low. This method also ensures that you are not there rebalancing all the time, which allows your portfolio to take a momentum that could drive your investment towards much profitability over time.

If you choose to take up this rebalancing approach, consider trading any part of your portfolio that has either grown by more than 10% away from the intended position or one that has shrunk by the same measure. This is to say that if your portfolio plan has a 20% to large-cap growth, you should sell or buy the portfolio if it falls short and gets to 18% or exceeds the limit and to get to 22%.

For someone who owns an ETF or a smaller portfolio rather than a mutual fund portfolio, try to stick to 15% instead of the common 10%. This is because the smaller a portfolio is, the smaller the positions, which means that your trading costs will be very high too. Certainly, you do not want to have to pay a whopping $10 just for trading a single index ETF worth $100.

The Best Time to Purchase Index Funds

Most seasoned index fund investors feel that there is not an appropriate time to invest in index funds; you just do it when you do it. However, it is important to take precaution by realizing that some market conditions will give index funds an upper hand over their counterparts, the actively-managed funds.

As you may have realized, the long-term investors are indifferent about timing because they do not have to worry about a thing. Once they have made their investment and bought index funds, they just have to wait for them to perform in the market and fetch them some returns. They do not have to worry about costs and other factors because index funds are inexpensive and easy to maintain by nature, the investors are assured that they will get decent returns. This is not the case for short-term investors.

Short-term investors who choose to invest in index funds have to employ short-term strategies such as looking out for the market conditions, and other factors that make the environment favorable for this kind of investment.
If you wish to trade in stocks, do it when the Bull Market is strong. The ideal time for selling stock is when prices are going up for all sectors, including the prices of different mutual fund types. At this time, it is easy to miss the trading window to major markets and active fund managers must move fast to match or even beat them.

For example, in 2006, the market was in the final calendar year run of the current Bull Run, and the Vanguard 500 Index was able to beat more than three-quarters of the larger blend funds. The same happened in the years 2010 and 2011 when the stocks had fully recovered from the 2008 financial crisis, and the Vanguard 500 Index beat 70% and 80% of its peers yet again.
When the economic conditions are weak, it is time to trade bonds. Navigating a bond market may prove difficult, and fund managers who deal with actively-managed funds especially find it rough because they lose to index funds such as the Vanguard Total Bond Market Index (VBMFX).
For example, this happened in 2011 when the economy slipped a bit during recovery. Bond funds had a positive year, and stock funds were also quite lucky because they were able to evade the negative returns. In fact, the VBMFX rose higher than 85% of all other intermediate-term bond funds.

It is also quite important for you to note that index funds are more likely to lose to actively-managed fund when the markets are volatile. They are less likely to do well in this environment, but an active fund manager will sift through the bonds or the stocks and end up outperforming even the major market indices. A market with such an environment is often called a stock-picker's market.

Kindly also note that just like any other markets, there will be some stocks or bonds that will perform better than others, even in   a   volatile   market   will.

Chapter 4: Exchange Funds

Exchange traded funds, or ETFs as they are often called, are a very exciting way to invest in the stock market. There are many advantages to an ETF as opposed to buying individual stocks. You can use exchange-traded funds to track major stock indexes, such as the Dow Jones Industrial Average, the S&P 500, small-cap stocks, mid-cap stocks, large-cap stocks, growth funds, value funds, real estate, gold, stocks in developing markets – you name it, it can be tracked with an ETF.

Essentially exchange-traded funds are like mutual funds, but they trade like stocks. So, you can just buy and sell shares the same way you'd buy and sell shares of Apple or Facebook. Unlike mutual funds, they are not actively managed by a financial guru so the fees are much lower. Also, while mutual funds only trade once a day, exchange-traded funds trade throughout the day like stocks because they are stocks.

ETFs Offer Automatic Diversity

When you invest in ETFs, you can choose between different indexes and sectors, among other things. So, you get automatic diversity because the fund is investing across a wide array of companies on your behalf. One of the most popular ETFs that are out there is SPY, which is a fund that has invested in the companies that make up the S&P 500.

Imagine the difficulty you would have investing in all 500 companies, and then having to adjust the portfolio looking to weight the fund to get more money invested into companies that performed better, and then taking companies in and out of your investments as the makeup of the S&P 500 changed. Of course, this would be a complete nightmare.

So why not let someone else handle all of that for you? You can just invest in that fund and then let the market do the rest.

There are exchange-traded funds for many different sectors and investment goals. Finding the right ones for your situation will require a bit of research.

The Main Companies offering ETFs

There are many investment firms that offer exchange-traded funds, but the main ones that you should spend your time looking at include:
- State Street SPDR
- iShares
- Vanguard

While you are going to find that these companies offer funds that cover many of the same sectors and indexes of the markets, you are going to want to go head to head comparisons. Two funds that invest in the Dow Jones Industrial Average are not going to give you the same returns, for example. The reason is that while they are invested in the same companies, the weightings of the investments may be different. So, fund A may invest in companies 1,2,3, & 4 by putting 25% of the fund in each company, but fund B might put 30% in company1, 40% in company 2, 15% in company 3, and 15% in company 4. Why would they do that? They might believe that companies 1 & 2 have much better growth potential.

So how are you going to find out which fund is better? By studying their past performance. Compare returns for different funds against each other and pick the one that you feel is best. Many times, the differences won't be stark. You will also want to have a look at fees associated with each fund, but for those coming from mutual funds you will be pleasantly surprised, the fees associated with exchange-traded funds are negligible.

Use Exchange Traded Funds to invest in ... everything

One of the things about exchange-traded funds is that you can put money into virtually anything. This makes them exciting and can offer an opportunity to build a real diversified portfolio but only by using stocks. For example, you can buy shares of VGIT, an exchange-traded fund offered by Vanguard. This fund invests in intermediate-term Treasuries – U.S. government issued bonds. So rather than buying the bonds themselves, you can buy shares in this fund.

GLD is a fund offered by SPDR that invests in gold. So, you can invest in gold, but do it by owning shares of GLD, rather than going out and buying gold itself.
Let's take a look at funds that can help you build a diversified portfolio that suits your investment goals.

Remember – these are stocks

Although we are mentioning funds offered by different companies, you don't have to go to that company to invest. So, while you could open a Vanguard account, you don't have to. These funds all have stock tickers, you can just log into your brokerage account and simply buy shares in whatever fund you like.

A look at some example funds

For examples of large-cap funds, we'll have a look at offerings from Vanguard. Stock ticker VIG is a dividend appreciation fund. It tracks the "Dividend Achievers Select Index" on NASDAQ.

VUG, on the other hand, is a large-cap fund that tracks growth stocks. The ten largest holdings in this fund include Microsoft, Apple, Amazon, Alphabet (Google), Facebook, VISA, Mastercard, Home Depot, Boeing, and Comcast. Notice that by investing in this fund, you're automatically exposed to these ten companies while only having to make one investment.
When you look at each fund, you can also look at the weighting the fund has by sector. For example, this Vanguard fund has

34.9% invested in technology, 20% in consumer services, and 13.9% in industrials.

Different funds that cover the same general goal will have different weightings by sector and different companies in their portfolios, although there may be a lot of overlap. These differences will impact the performance of each fund.

VTV is another large-cap offering by Vanguard. It is listed as a large-cap value fund. The holdings in this fund are quite different, reflecting the different goals of the fund. This time the top 10 holdings are: Berkshire Hathaway, JP Morgan Chase, Johnson & Johnson, Exxon Mobile, Proctor & Gamble, Bank of America, Cisco Systems, Pfizer, and Intel.

VOT is a mid-cap growth fund managed by Vanguard. The holdings on this fund include Roper Technologies, Red Hat, and Twitter, among others. Vanguard considers it to be in their highest risk category, but if you are looking to add more aggressive growth to your portfolio, it's an option to consider as opposed to making the investments yourself. Vanguard also has a few small cap funds. You can also invest in microcap ETFs, IWC is a microcap fund offered by iShares.

Tracking index funds is one of the best ways to use ETFs. We've already mentioned SPY, but there are many other stock indexes that you can track to invest in different areas. Some of the other index funds and sectors you can track with ETFs are:

- NASDAQ Composite Index: Mostly technology stocks traded on NASDAQ
- Wilshire 5000: Designed to track the entire stock market. Not as popular as SPY
- S&P Mid-cap 400, Russell Mid-cap, Wilshire US Mid-cap: Track mid-cap companies
- Russell 2000: Tracks small cap companies
- Sector funds: Track energy, healthcare, finance, utilities, etc.

478

- Emerging markets
- Real estate
- Corporate bonds, including junk bonds
- Precious metals, including gold and silver

ETFS and Dividends

One question many people have does ETFs pay dividends. The answer is yes, they do. So, if you are looking for a way to build an income investment portfolio based on dividends, exchange-traded funds can be part of that process. Dividends are paid out quarterly. The proportion of dividends you receive will depend on what percentage of the fund you own. So, if you own 0.1% of the fund, you will receive 0.1% of the dividends.

ETFs and Bonds

We will discuss this in the next chapter, but we are going to mention here that you can use ETFs to invest in bonds, but more importantly, you do receive any interest payments from the bonds.

ETFs Make it Easy

One of the nice things about using ETFs to build a diversified portfolio hitting different market capitalizations, sectors and so forth, is that you can diversify your portfolio without having to study the details on dozens of stocks and companies. Of course, different things appeal to different people; some people actually want to put the time in studying companies and their performance, while others will prefer the hands-off nature of ETFs.

What I like to do is mix it up, so I will invest 50% in individual stocks, and the other 50% of my stock market investing goes to ETFs. There is no reason to be exclusive one way or another unless you really want to.

Chapter 5: Dividend Stocks Passive Income

Dividend investing is one of the most accurate ways to generate a passive income stream. With dividend stocks, you only invest once and earn forever! Passive income refers to the type of income that you create even when sleeping: it is something desired by many. This income generation method can build your wealth either by helping cover your monthly expenses or reinvesting. Dividends are the best fit as a passive income source. This is because the income is sustainable, requires little maintenance, grows faster than inflation and can also be tax-advantaged. It might take you time to get a reasonable amount of dividend income, but time is always on your side in this case.

What Are Dividends?

Dividends, just like many other financial subjects, are simple at on the surface but very complicated underneath. From a surface point of view, dividends are paid to give out a company's earnings to its shareholders. You must be aware that being a shareholder in a company that pays dividends `entitles you a share of its profits. A perfect dividend policy is beneficial to both the company and the shareholder. Many investors chose to invest in great dividend-paying companies as the basis of their portfolio. This technique is referred to as dividend growth investing. In this case, growth refers to the growth of dividend payments over some time. Since the 1990s, the average annual dividend increase is always around 6%. This, however, is not a fixed rate; it isn't unheard of for companies to have a yearly dividend of 10% or more!

Dividend Investing

If you are not sure about dividend investing is, this topic is for you. As mentioned earlier, dividends refer to a way companies share success with its shareholders. It is like a portion of the total earnings paid out you as the shareholder. You can choose to get your dividends in the form of cash or more shares. You might want to know what dividend dates are? For instance, a company can declare a dividend of y dollars. The day this information was relayed is known as the declaration date, the time is, however not that important. When looking at a dividend, there are two significant dates you should know. Ex-Dividend Date- you must own a stock before this date so that you can receive the bonus. Payment Date- This is the day money is paid to shareholders. The Record Date is technically the date you need to be recorded as a shareholder to be entitled to dividends. This date is always two business days after the ex-dividend date: this is solely because trades take two days to settle. It has lesser importance to an investor than the ex-dividend date. It is, however, good to know what the record date is. Additionally, pay more attention to the ex-dividend date!

How to Compare Stocks for Dividend Investing

There are two ways you can look at dividends and determine how good they are. Both of them are pure math. The dividend yield is a certain percentage showing the amount of money the profit is compared to the share price. The higher the amount, the better: this means you earn more passive income out of your investment. For example, if the average dividend amount of the company is 3.46%, it means you earned $3.45 in dividends for every $100 you invested. The second you can use to determine whether the dividend id proper is the dividend payout ratio: this refers to the paid dividends and divided by the company's total earnings. You should ask yourself if the company make sufficient profit to the cover for the dividends they promised you.

Lastly, look at the dividend growth rate. Most companies tend to increase their dividends over time, and this metric establishes the rate at which they do so. The higher your dividend payment grows, the more your passive income grows. If you remember, we said earlier that the average dividend growth rate for most companies is around 6%. Put in mind that you are building a 6-figure portfolio that may contain individual

481

stocks or various funds. And, don't just look at the dividend! It is only a smaller part of the bigger picture in this case. Instead, look at the stocks and the company growth rate as a whole

When to Reinvest or Not to Reinvest

Remember, when we discussed the two options when it comes to when acquiring your dividend? You should consider that in this situation. It can be easier two chose to base on that because you will know what your investment objectives are. Here, the simple thing you ought to do is taking the dividend in cash form. You now have the cash you can do whatever you want with. If you prefer passive income to withdraw the money from your trading account, this is the option you should go with.

Considering your age, this could be the best decision as you will take advantage of the compounding magic. On the other hand, reinvesting your dividends enables your shares to compound into more shares. Companies make it easy to do this through a feature called The Dividend Re-Investment Plan (DRIP). DRIP automatically converts all your dividends paid into the shares without charging you a commission, and in some cases, you will get a 2-3% discount. To enroll in the DRIP program, simply consult your stockbroker. For your information, not even stock has a DRIP; its existence depends on the company's management decision.

Dividend Growth Investing: Case Study

In this case, we make up a situation to show you just how great dividend growth investing can be. Let us assume you bought $10,000 worth of Toyota shares on the New York Stock Exchange in early 1999. Below is how much you will have at the moment. 243 share of Toyota worth $41.02 each $4296.34 in passive income in the next 12 months ($1.22 per share annually) 2.96% dividend yield ($296.45/$10,000). You should note that the example had to be set in the USA Stock Exchange because all these financial calculators online-only support American tickers. Fast forward to 2019; you made five times your initial investment mainly due to capital gains. Interestingly, your passive income grew even more, multiplying itself more than seven times the initial amount. The outcome (passive income growth) was due to two factors: dividend reinvestments and dividend pay raise.

How to Start Chasing Dividend Income

Below are the three steps you can take to start chasing your dividend income.

1.   Pick a Type of Account

The first thing you need to do is pick a type of account you prefer to work with. Dividends are taxable in some countries, meaning you could benefit from keeping them legally registered accounts like RRSP or TFSA. Deciding where to place your investments can be a very confusing thing. Below is what you need to take away from this subtopic. TFSA: applies Canadian, American, and other international stocks and ETFs RRSP: Refers to Canadian, American, and other foreign stocks and ETFs. Unregistered Accounts: Canadian, American, and other International stocks and any margin trading engagements (paying maximum taxes on dividends and handle riskier investments to get capital investments just in case an investment goes wrong). Generally, the fee charged on profits is lower than that charged on a regular income. There are, however, many rules and exceptions, especially regarding US Stocks. It is hard to find a one-fits-all answer, and I would recommend you to consult a professional, especially when your portfolio grows bigger.

2.   Choose a Stockbroker

As you might know, the broker needs to provide the type of account you required in Step 1. You will also want a broker that offers a DRIP when chasing dividends. You should, therefore, be careful with the kind of broker you are opting for. Preferably, go for brokers that support registered accounts like RRSPs and TFSAs.

3. Decide between ETFs and Stocks

The essential dividend growth investing pertains to picking individual stocks using the metrics we discussed earlier in this article. There are plenty of ETFs in different countries that mainly focus on dividend income and have little management expenses. While ETFs charge a fee that digs into the returns, it is a shallow maintenance strategy. You don't need to look at individual companies and their payout ratios. Instead, what you need to focus on is the distribution you earn and the yield it provides you.

4. Keep on Contributing and Investing

This is a continuous process that does not stop once you purchase your first stocks. The case study we used above focused only on a one-time investment tracked over 20 years later. You should, therefore, be making regular deposits and slowly be picking up even more ETFs and dividend stocks. This will result in your passive income stream growing even at a faster rate. Ideally, you can use a DRIP where possible for most of your investment life to accelerate growth.

Creating Passive Income with Dividend Stocks

Dividends are passive income. You get the benefits of dividend income after investing some upfront time to make your decision. Additionally, you are a minority owner in the business and have no control in the decision-making process. Neither, do you have to spend much of your time managing your investments: just a few efficient readings and you are good to go. You can, therefore, carve out a little amount of time to keep an eye on your investments. With the increase in the speed of information and different mobile apps, the dividend has been made very easy in today's word. Historically, dividend investing has been regarded as a risk-averse method for investors to invest in the stock market.

Dividend investing is one of the best ways to increase income through passive income. Living off the bonuses is not a sprint but a marathon. You should not, however, take the marathon lightly. You should have the urge to increase both your income and your retirements. Plant your precious dividend seed by investing in the dividend growth stocks. What will it need? Well, an average dividend yield of around 3% in your portfolio, you will need approximately a $3.33 Million portfolio to earn $100,000 annually in dividend income.

The annual dividend yield refers to the calculation of the general percentage of a dividend per share in received in relation to the stock price. It is a good barometer of the annual income earned from investing in a stock. For example, if you invest in a $100 stock, and it pays $2 per share in dividends. This is equal to a 4% dividend yield a year.

It is not possible to start living off your dividends right away after investing, but it can happen over some time. But with a good plan and strategy, you can achieve the goal of passive income and living off dividends sooner than you imagine. The key to living off dividends is focusing on dividend growth stocks. The dividend growth stocks increase annually, which increases your income without you doing a single thing! Remember when I talked about planting a seed? Well, if you invest the right way, your seed will grow into a huge redwood tree!

How to Generate a Passive Income Annually from Dividend Stocks

So, how do you generate a passive income each year from dividend stocks? When you are building a dividend portfolio, start scaling smaller positions that you will continue to develop over sometime. First, use a brokerage that gives the lowest commission fee on trading. They are brokers that allow you to trade utterly commission-free on all the stocks and options. This is a very lucrative deal because options are usually essential to purchase. When properly used, options are an excellent way to mitigate risk in your account or portfolio. These are the best stocks when it comes to covered call writing.

As I have said many times before, investing in dividend stocks is the best way of generating passive income in the long run. However, choosing which stocks to involve in a dividend portfolio can be a challenging task for some investors. With the availability of a wide range of options, it could be very beneficial if you become selective and go beyond a company's dividend yield in search of the best opportunities. By so doing, it could lead to a more sustainable and higher passive income in the long run. Below are some of the aspects you should consider when it comes to investing in dividends.

Track Record

While the past performances might not be the best guide to the future, companies that have the unquestionable capability of delivering profits over a long period may be economic moats. For instance, they may have a stronger brand and lower costs. This suggests that their future dividend growth will be robust and resilient. This can be better if that company has a history of rewarding its shareholders by paying out dividends with profit gains.

Management Focus

Through reading and analyzing a company's annual report, you can be able to ascertain management standpoints in the future dividend growth. For instance, several management teams will pay attention to the reinvestment of excess capital to enhance future sales and the profitability of the business. As much as this can be a good move in some situations, it may not offer the most appealing outlook for investors seeking a passive income. Company management may apply a higher risk approach that looks to expand the business into new territories markets at a fast rate. This could imply that reduced dividend growth is just ahead. It could, therefore, be a good idea ensuring that the focus of company management from a risk/reward point of view, are aligned to those of the investor.

Company Type

While different industries like technology might offer more earnings growth ratio, they are doubtful to give generous dividend growth due to massive investments of capital. Similarly, a less mature business may need more significant investments and might be unable to pay out dividends to the shareholders. Therefore, it can be prudent for an investor to carefully assess the maturity of the business as well as its sector stability before purchasing. For the investors seeking more than just a passive income, mature stocks working in more established industries could be the right place to start when choosing the best income opportunities.

Diversification

As much as a lot of investors prefer to majorly focus on the potential return from investing their funds in the stock market, learning how to reduce the risk could be the most sensible starting point. After all, you can gain from getting a passive income in a short period, only for the dividend income to be hit by huge losses further down the line. Therefore, looking to reduce a company risk could be a worthy move. This is the danger posed by difficulties encountered by businesses that can lead to a decline in the stock price. In portfolios that have a small number of stocks, the company-specific risk will be extremely high due to a single stock's decline resulting in major loses for the general collection.

However, a well-diversified portfolio may not be impacted too severely even when one of its members experiences financial difficulties. While the general stock market provides the potential to make high levels of capital growth in the long run, it also allows creating a high rising passive income. As you might be aware, investing in any stock means you are risking. There will always be loopholes or chances of losing money should a business establishment fail to deliver as expected. You can, however, reduce the risk through diversification. Obtaining high yields may also help make the reward/risk ratio from the buying dividend stocks very appealing.

Additionally, holding income shares over a long period may keep costs to a minimum while earning an increasing passive income. In portfolios that have a small number of stocks, the company-specific risk will be extremely high due to a single stock's decline resulting in major loses for the general collection.

High Yields

As much as it might sound obvious that buying high-yield stocks is an excellent means of making a monthly passive income, it is nevertheless the quickest method of achieving that goal. When determining which stocks the investor might be interested in, it could be worth working in reverse. What this means is, first find out how much income you need in a single month. Secondly, consider the average yield you need from your portfolio to hit the target. This way, you will be in a better position to exclude those stocks that give dividend returns way too low to provide your preferred level of monthly income.

Long-Term hold

With the increasing number of stocks available to investors in different sectors and countries, it is very tempting to keep switching from one capital to the other depending on the current state of things in the economy. In terms of being the best way to use your funds, this may seem like the best idea at the time, but the harsh truth is that buying and selling regularly can result in inflated dealing costs. Similarly, it may also mean that stocks kept in a portfolio are not given the time they need to be profitable. Therefore, holding dividend stocks over a prolonged period of time could be the best method of generating a passive income. This means the investor will only use little effort and stand a good chance of potentially higher returns.

Assessing a company's record of growth and the way it pays its dividends, as well as its strategy, can lead to an increased growth rate in an investor's passive income. Similarly, assessing a company's maturity and the industry it's operating in may lead to more clear income outlook. Diversifying among a wide range of stocks can help cut risks while opting for stocks that match with the investor's risk/reward goals can lead to a better shareholder experience.

Chapter 5: Bond Investing

Bonds are an interesting financial instrument that has been around for centuries. As we mentioned earlier, they were originally used by local Italian governments to raise funds. In those days, they were perpetual, so you would give your principle to the government and then receive interest payments for life. Maybe they could be thought of as the oldest annuities instead.

Later, bonds were issued with maturity dates as they are today. That is the date when the bond expires and you're supposed to get your money back, and the interest payments stop. A bond that doesn't mature is irredeemable. A bond is redeemed when you turn it in to get your principal back.

Bonds have traditionally been a "safe" investment used by investors to protect their capital. You can also trade bonds on the bond markets, and profit from changes in bond prices that happen when interest rates go up and down. We will be discussing how all this works below.

Bond Basics

Let's get started by talking about the basic concepts behind a bond and the basic characteristics that all bonds have regardless of who or what is issuing the bond. The first thing to know about a bond is that it's a loan that you make to the organization in question that issues the bond. In return for the money (the principal) that you provide to the bond issuer, they will make regular interest payments to you for the life of the bond, although as we will see, there are other ways to make this arrangement. Therefore, when you buy a bond, you are a creditor the same way that a bank is a creditor when they loan someone money to buy a car or to do home improvements.

Since a bond is a loan, it is formally known as debt security. Since bonds can be bought and sold on secondary markets, we

490

say that they are negotiable. Bond prices fluctuate up and down inversely with interest rates. We'll see why below, and we'll also look at some examples of changing bond prices and try to understand why the prices change the way that they do.

Even though you can buy bonds from and hence issue debt to a company, a bond does not entitle you to an ownership stake in the company. It's only a loan to the company, but you have no rights regarding the company unless it goes bankrupt, in which case you'd have a claim on its assets. If a company does go bankrupt, by common law bondholders have priority over those who own stock in being repaid.

Who Issues Bonds

Bonds are issued by many different types of institutions. Corporations issue bonds. The United States government (and other governments) issue bonds. State, country, and city governments also issue bonds. Indeed, some of the most popular bands in the 20th century were municipal bonds, or "munis," which offer a tax shelter. They were often used by the wealthy to park money during eras of high tax rates so that they could avoid paying them.

Definitions

Now, let's familiarize ourselves with some of the important definitions that are associated with bonds. These definitions will help you understand how bond trading operates and help you to buy bonds if you decide you want to do that as a part of your investing strategy.

Par Value/Principal

The par value is the same as the principal. This is also called the nominal value. A bond is issued as a sheet of paper that has a value printed on it, which is the par value. It's also called the face value. So, when a bond sells for the first time, if the par value is $10,000, then you have to pay $10,000 to get the bond. However, it called the nominal value or face value because, on the markets, bond values change.

So, if you decide to sell the bond on the secondary market, you might get more than $10,000 for the bond, or you might get less than $10,000 for the bond depending on what conditions dictate. When the term of the bond comes to an end, you will be paid back the face value. As we will see when we discuss U.S. Treasuries, some bonds work a little bit differently.

Coupon

The word coupon is used because of its historical legacy. The coupon is the interest rate for the bond. In the old days, bonds were actually issued with coupons that you could tear off and take in to receive your interest payment. Interest payments can be made with different frequencies depending on the issuer of the bond, however, the interest payments for most bonds are either paid twice a year or annually.

Clean Price and Dirty Price

The clean price is the price of the bond minus accrued interest. The dirty price of a bond is the price of the bond, including the accrued interest.

Yield

Yield is the return an investor can expect from owning the bond. If you simply buy the bond from the issuer and hold it, then the yield will be just the interest rate or coupon of the bond. Current yield is given by the annual interest payment/price of the bond x 100. Bond prices and yields move opposite one another. So, the higher the yield, the lower the bond price. The higher the bond price, the lower the yield. This will make more sense later.

A more complex calculation that is often considered is yield to maturity. That calculation takes into account the difference in the price that you paid for the bond as compared to its par value, the number of years until maturity, and the interest rate of the bond.

Redeem a Bond

This means to turn it in to receive your principal back, and interest payments cease.

Maturity Date

The date the bond expires, so the date is redeemed.

Callable Bonds

A bond can be called. That means that when the issuing entity calls the bond, it has to be redeemed and essentially the bonds life has come to an end at a date of the issuing entities choosing, prior to the maturity date. That means you get your principal back and interest payments stop.

The Health of Issuing Entity

While the interest rates paid by bonds are influenced by the overall interest rates, they are also influenced by the financial health of the entity that issues the bond. This is the same principle at work that you find when an individual goes for a loan. A person with good credit can get a loan with low interest rates. A person with bad credit has to accept a loan with high interest rates.

The same thing happens in the case of bonds. If a company with a checkered history is raising capital by selling bonds, then it must offer high-interest rates. The lowest quality bonds are known as "junk bonds." Like a loan to a person with a bad credit history, they carry more risk, and there is some risk that you could lose your principal. However, some investors are willing to assume that risk for the high-interest payments.

Zero Coupon Bonds

This is a different kind of bond that pays no interest. Instead of paying regular interest payments, the bond will be sold at a price that is lower than the face value. However, when you redeem the bond, you are paid the face value of the bond. So, for example, suppose you buy a $100 zero coupon bond with a 6% interest rate. You will actually pay $94 for the bond. Then in 12 months when you redeem the bond, you get paid $100.

How Bond Prices Vary

The basic rule for bond trading is that when interest rates rise, bond prices drop. They do so because the higher interest rates will be available by purchasing new bonds, so the old bonds have less appeal. On the other hand, if interest rates drop, bond prices rise. In that case, the older bonds that paid higher interest are more valuable than the new bonds.

So, let's say that you purchase a $10,000 bond, and the interest rate is 6%. If the interest rate drops to 4%, what is the price of the bond if you try and sell it on the secondary market? In that case, the interest rate dropped, so the bond price is going to rise. The interest payment is $600. To estimate the new bond price, we take the price that would be paying $600 at 4% interest.

That would be:

$600/0.04 = $15,000

Now consider an alternative scenario. If the interest rate rises to 7%, then the bond price will drop. It will drop in such a way that the price paid to buy the bond on the secondary market would work out so that $600 is 7% interest. So, the new bond price is:

$$\$600/0.07 = \$8,571.43$$

When the bond reaches maturity, the face value of the bond is returned. So, if you bought the bond on the secondary market for $8,571.43, and you got the $600 interest payments, you'd make a little profit when the bond reached maturity, and you get the $10,000 principal.

Municipal Bonds

Municipal bonds are issued by state and local governments to help fund operations, like building new streets or libraries. Short term municipal bonds have maturity dates 1-3 years from the date of issue, but most municipal bonds are long term, expiring in a decade or more. They have been attractive to wealthy investors because they provide a way to earn long term interest payments.

The interest is usually not subject to Federal income tax, so historically they have provided a ready-made tax shelter. When top tax rates were 90%, you could avoid paying them by investing in municipal bonds. There are two types of municipal bonds. General obligation bonds are used for day-to-day operations. They are "backed" by the taxing authority of the government entity that issues the bonds.

Revenue bonds are not backed by the taxing authority of the government, but rather from revenue that might be generated from a given project. For example, if the government in question issues the bonds to help build a new highway, they can collect revenue using tolls.

495

You can invest in bonds online by checking out brokers that specialize in bond trading. You can also invest in corporate bonds issued by large companies like Apple and IBM.

United States Treasuries

Perhaps the most famous bands of all are those issued by the federal government. At least until now, these have been considered the safest investments in the world. The debt of the U.S. government keeps rising, and at this point, investors don't seem to be bothered, but at some point, bonds issued by the U.S. government may be less appealing, which would lead to a rise in interest rates paid by the government.

You may have heard about U.S. Savings Bonds. Interest from US savings bonds is tax-free for local and state taxes. They are non-negotiable, meaning that they cannot be traded on secondary markets. Since they are not tradable, the value of the savings bond does not change with time as interest rates change, the way regular bond prices can.

Savings bonds are a type of zero-coupon bond, so they do not pay interest payments, and the maturity is 15-30 years. However, you can redeem the bond if you've held it at least 12 months. When you redeem the bond, you are paid the face value plus interest. However, you are penalized if you redeem the bond early, and the final three months of interest will be withheld.

Savings bonds are priced from $25 up to $10,000. To either buy or redeem a US Savings Bond, you go to the Treasury Direct website run by the federal government. If you are looking for a short-term investment via the United States government, then you can consider Treasury bills. These have terms lasting from a few weeks up to one year. Just like savings bonds, they are zero coupon bonds so you will not receive interest payments. In the case of treasury bills, they are sold at a discount. Then when you redeem the bond, you get paid the full-face value. The difference between the discounted price you bought the bond for and the face value payment is the interest.

A Treasury note is an intermediate-term bond. They have maturity dates that range from 2 years up to 10 years. Unlike savings bonds and Treasury bills, Treasury Notes pay interest. The interest payments are paid every six months until the maturity date. At that point, you can redeem the bond and receive your principal back.

Finally, there are Treasury bonds. These are long term investments with a maturity date that can be 30 years. They also pay interest every six months. If you live long enough to redeem the bond, you can receive your principal back.

Corporate Bonds

Investors can also look at corporate bonds. They will pay higher interest rates than government issued bonds because they are higher risk. You can buy corporate bonds from a broker, the way you can stocks. The issues at hand in choosing which bonds to buy are similar even though the investments themselves are quite different. So, you will want to take time to review the company's fundamentals before investing in their bond offerings.

There may be additional information to consider, such as how good the company is at handling credit. Just like you have a credit rating, bonds are rated as to their quality, which in a nutshell can mean how much risk there is that you'll lose your principal. As we noted earlier, the riskier the debtor, the higher the interest rate. High-risk corporate bonds can pay handsome interest rates and are known as junk bonds.

Buying Bonds Through Funds

You can buy bonds directly, but one of the easiest ways to get in the bond market is to invest using exchange-traded funds or mutual funds. As with stocks, diversification with bonds is just as important. If some company is issuing bonds that have a junk rating, you might fantasize about putting all your money in to get the 9% interest rates they are paying so you can have a nice income without having to work, but if the company goes bankrupt or simply doesn't pay the principal back, well then you've lost some money.

You can protect yourself with diversification and buying into a fund that invests in bonds on your behalf is the best and safest way to do that. A bond ETF holds investments in bonds, but they trade like a stock on the stock exchange. Maturity dates won't be your concern, because the managers of the fund take care of the underlying assets on your behalf.

One interesting feature of a bond ETF is that you still receive the interest payments. But even more to the point, you get interested payments each and every single month. Remember that bonds typically pay interest either once every six months or once a year. The good thing is bonds all have their own date when the interest is paid, so when you invest in a fund that contains a large number of bonds, they are distributed throughout the year, so you will get monthly interest payments. This can make investing in bonds via a fund more attractive.

You can use bond ETFs and mutual funds to invest in every type of bond, from municipal bonds to corporate bonds and also US government bonds. If you go through an ETF or mutual fund, you can save yourself the headache of having to trade on the bond markets. Your fees will also be much lower.

Chapter 6: Strategies & Risk Management

There are a number of different ways to approach stock investing, but nearly all of them fall under one of three basic styles: value investing, growth investing, or index investing. These stock investment strategies follow the mindset of an investor and the strategy they utilize to invest is affected by a number of factors, such as the investor's financial situation, investing goals, and risk tolerance.

Below, we're going to address the three basic styles or stock investment strategies that investors commonly use to approach investing in stocks.

Value Investing Basics

The strategy of value investing, in simple terms, means buying stocks of companies that the marketplace has undervalued. The goal is not to invest in no-name companies that haven't been recognized for their potential – that falls more in the venue of speculative or penny stock investing. Value investors typically buy into strong companies that are trading at low prices that an investor believes don't reflect the company's true value.

Value investing is all about getting the best deal, similar to getting a great discount on a designer brand.

When we say that a stock is undervalued, we mean that an analysis of their financial statements indicates that the price the stock is trading at is lower than it should be, based on the company's intrinsic value. This might be indicated by things such as a low price-to-book ratio (a financial ratio favored by value investors) and a high dividend yield, which represents the amount in dividends a company pays out each year relative to the price of each share.

The marketplace is not always correct in its valuations and thus stocks often simply trade for less than their true worth, at least for a period of time. If you pursue a value investing strategy, the goal is to seek out these undervalued stocks and scoop them up at a favorable price.

Value Investing Long-Term

The value investing strategy is pretty straightforward, but practicing this method is more involved than you might think, especially when you're using it as a long-term strategy. It's important to avoid the temptation to try to make fast cash based on flighty market trends. A value investing strategy is based on buying into strong companies that will maintain their success and that will eventually have their intrinsic worth recognized by the markets.

Warren Buffet, one of the greatest and most prolific value investors of the century, famously said, "In the short term, the market is a popularity contest. In the long term, the market is a weighing machine." Buffet bases his stock choices on the true potential and stability of a company, looking at the whole of each company instead of simply looking at an undervalued price tag that the market has assigned individual shares of the company's stock. However, he does still prefer to buy stocks he perceives as "on sale".

The Basics of Growth Stock Investment Strategies

For decades, growth investing has been held as the yin to value investing's yang. While growth investing is, in the most basic terms, the so-called "opposite" of value investing, many value investors also employ a growth investing mindset when settling on stocks. Growth investing is very similar, in the long-term, to value stock investing strategies. Basically, if you're investing in stocks based on the intrinsic value of a company and its potential to grow in the future, you're using a growth investing strategy.

Growth investors are distinguished from strictly value investors by their focus on young companies that have shown their potential for significant, above average growth. Growth investors look at companies that have repeatedly shown indications of growth and substantial or rapid increases in business and profit.

The general theory behind growth investing is that the growth in earnings or revenue a company generates will then be reflected by an increase in share prices. Differing from value investors, growth investors may often buy stocks priced at or higher than a company's current intrinsic worth, based on the belief that a continued high growth rate will eventually boost the company's intrinsic value to a substantially higher level, well above the current share price of the stock.

Favorite financial metrics used by growth investors include earnings per share (EPS), profit margin, and return on equity (ROE).

A Fusion of Value and Growth

In truth, if you're considering a long-term approach to investing, a fusion of value and growth investing, as Buffet so effectively employs, may be worth your consideration. There are good reasons to back up taking these stock investment strategies.

Historically speaking, value stocks are usually the stocks of companies in cyclical industries, which are largely made up of businesses producing goods and services that people use their discretionary income on. The airline industry is a good example; people fly more when the business cycle is on an uptrend and fly less when it swings downward because they have more and less discretionary income, respectively. Because of seasonality, value stocks typically perform well in the market during times of economic recovery and prosperity, but they are likely to fall behind when a bull market is sustained for a long period of time.

Growth stocks typically perform better when interest rates drop and companies' earnings take off. They are also typically the stocks that continue to rise even in the late stages of a long-term bull market. On the other hand, these are usually the first stocks to take a beating when the economy slows down.

A fusion of growth and value investing offers you the opportunity to enjoy higher returns on your investment while reducing a substantial amount of your risk. Theoretically, if you employ both a value investing strategy for buying some stocks while using a growth investing strategy for buying other stocks, you can generate optimal earnings during virtually any economic cycle, and any fluctuations in returns will be more likely to balance out in your favor over time.

Passive Index Investing

Index investing is a much more passive form of investing when compared to that of either value or growth investing. Consequently, it involves far less work and strategizing on the part of the investor. Index investing diversifies an investor's money widely among various types of equities, hoping to mirror the same returns as the overall stock market. One of the main attractions of index investing is that many studies have shown that few strategies of picking individual stocks outperform index investing over the long term.

An index investing strategy is usually followed by investing in mutual funds or exchange-traded funds that are designed to reflect the performance of a major stock index such as the S&P 500 or the FTSE 100.

Some stock trading rules include the following:

- Buy rising stocks and sell falling stocks

- Trade only when the market is clearly bullish or bearish; then trade in its general direction

- Never average losses by buying more of a stock that has fallen

- Never meet a margin call – get out of the trade

- Go long when stocks reach a new high; sell short when they reach a new low

The Bottom Line – Finding Your Own Way

Each investor has to discover their own personal stock investment strategies that best suit their individual wants or needs, as well as their investment "personality". You may find that combining the three approaches discussed here is what works best for you.

The investing strategy or strategies you employ will often change during the course of your life as your financial situation and goals shift. Don't be afraid to shake things up a bit and diversify the ways in which you invest, but strive to always maintain a firm grasp on what your investment approach entails and how it will likely affect your portfolio and your finances.

Narrowing Down The Best Stocks

This may sound a little too virtuous, but I personally don't like to invest in companies that don't align with what I want in this world! When I was new to investing, I once owned a tobacco stock that was making me real good money. It was hard for me to sell that stock, but ultimately, I did. I just didn't want to contribute to something I fundamentally disagreed with. What you agree or disagree is up to you, but remember when you buy a stock, you are investing your money into that business/industry/sector and hoping they grow and in turn you will share in their profit. You are contributing to their growth. If you don't want more of what that company represents in the world, why invest in them? When you are making good money, it's hard to be morally grounded, but when you have over 4,000 other companies, you can afford to be picky. In all honestly, my shares in that company is like a drop in the ocean, it didn't have any impact on them! This is just my fundamental belief. As Mohandas Gandhi said, "Be the change that you wish to see in the world." Great now that our conscious is clear, let's move on.

Investing in the Long Term

When you have a list of stocks either from a screener, recommendation from other people, blogs and other trustful sources. Make sure you are clear on your trading plan. I.e. Is this a trading opportunity or a long-term investment? We will discuss trading strategies later, and you may not necessarily look for these criteria for trading opportunity.

Let's assume this is a long-term investment. In that case, you want to make sure the company is large enough, meaning it can't go under that quickly! You can get this information by simply looking at its market cap. I like to see that company that is at least 100 million or greater. Is this company reputable? Will they be going strong in 20 years? Are their products/service in demand; will they be in demand in long term? Who are their competitors and how are they doing? Do you see another company taking them over? Are they iconic? Ask all the questions that prove to you that the company has been around, will be around, faces little competition to be taken over (all companies have competition, you need to see if the threat of competition would dwarf your pick). Are they leader in their industry, how long do you see them in this role?

Upper Management/Insider Trading:

Once you weed these companies out, find out who is at the helm? Where is the captain? Is there a leader with passion or just an upper level employee collecting a big fat paycheck? Who is the CEO, what does he/she believe in? Is this just a job or do they really want to grow the company? First and foremost, do you find them to be honest and ethical? If they are not honest with you, then it really doesn't matter how smart they or how hard working they are! Then you want to know if they are up for the job, how are they investing your money in the company? All this matter when you want to invest in a company. The problem here is reading through the fine line. No CEO comes out and says they want to tank their company. This is where you may want to see "insider trading", does upper management own shares in that company? Are they buying/selling those shares? What price did they buy? What price did they sell? Why are they selling? Insider trading can be found at many sites like: www.nasdaq.com & www.gurufocus.com

Chapter 7: Valuing Your Stock

You have picked few companies that you think might be a good investment, but you aren't sure! If you were to think like a professional investor, you would probably want to know how much a company is worth before you bought it! Once you know how much a company is worth, you can then determine if it's a good or a bad buy. If you went to dealership to shop for a car, it would be nice to know what the mark-up is before you started to negotiate. SEC (Security Exchange Commission) requires a company makes their financial data available to publicly traded companies! They are showing you the numbers, it's your job to make sense of them! Now, even though so much goes into what the value of a stock (potential of a company-as discussed earlier), we will attempt to find the raw value of a company based on what they have reported!

Once I'm done with screening for few good companies. I like to see the profile of that stock (www.finance.yahoo.com), type in the stock symbol and click on profile. Read what the company does. Other sites like www.morningstar.com are very effective once you need to dive into deep data-paid subscription (which provides you 10 yrs. of data as opposed to 5 yrs.) as well. You can use their free version until you feel comfortable.

When I'm investing (not trading) in a company and I have read their profiles, I want to connect with that company! I want to know that company inside-out, I want to believe in their upper management, I want to share their passion, understand that company and maybe that industry. Once I do this, then I can better start to understand their financials, understand how to value that company, and to understand if it makes sense to invest in that company. This is all part of fundamental analysis, that will help you evaluate and see if the company is worth investing in.

Once I've done the above research, I can then get up to date information about the company by reading their newly published quarterly/annual reports. This is where I get up to date information about the company's numbers. The idea of "I think that company is great because of ... [add your own theoretical reasons]" ends here. This is also how some professional fund managers research prior to investing in a company!

What we will do next is to find out EXACTLY how much a stock is worth, using real numbers from 10k.

Just a note, if you are trading (short-term) and not investing (long-term) this may not be as important, you may get by with technical analysis and strategies (discussed later).

Value Of Your Stock vs. Current Price (Is It A Good Buy?)

Value investors believe that a stock is worth a certain price and they go through method of valuing that stock. Valuing a stock is to find out how much that stock is worth. Not in theory but in numbers! If you are able to know how much a stock is actually worth and you know how much a stock is trading at; you can easily see if it's undervalued (stock is trading below the market price-in that case it may be a good buy) or overvalued (stock is trading higher than market price-it's overpriced and not a good buy).

Keep in mind, there are many different valuation formulas, techniques, and methods, but ultimately this is where the rubber meets the road! Frustrating part in running various valuation formulas is that they can show great disparity. It's still important that you run various valuation and then use other means to forecast its true value. This way you get a base point and a good range.

If this sounds foreign to you, don't worry I will walk you through the entire valuation, step by step.
The information and data to value a company can be found on many sites, start with your broker's site. These sites derive their

values from annual & quarterly reports that are reported by the companies. If the sites don't provide the data you need, you can usually find these reports (10k or 10Q) on company you are investing website --> investor relations --> see the filings (usually at the bottom of the page).

In nutshell, you would want to find if the company is making profit after all expenses are paid. If you can keep good profits year after year, the company is growing, a profitable company is going to be able to take that money and reinvest in itself so it can grow or pay the shareholder in form of dividend.

This is where you need clear mind, get your thinking cap on! THIS IS THE TIME YOU NEED BE MOST ALERT, AND MAYBE SIT WITH PAPER AND PENCIL-Here we go, let's start with our first valuation.

Valuation Calculation Formula 1:

Earning of the Owner

This valuation method was first introduced by Buffet in 1986 Berkshire letter. The overarching principal is to find out how much free cash flow did the business earn. If we know the amount of "extra cash", positive cash flow (cash in our pocket after all other bills are paid), we can use that money to grow. This is the principal behind owner's earnings. Buffet calculated the owner's earning by opening financials on the company. This is how owner's earnings are calculated.

Reported Earning (net income from cash flow statement) + Depreciation (depreciation, depletion and amortization in cash flow statement) +/- Noncash charges (receivable/payable or employee stock compensation) - Maint. Capex (cash flow statement)

In this example, I'm using "FB" data derived from www.marketwatch.com. We will be using 12/31/2017 data.

508

Step 1:

Go to www.marketwatch.com and on right side, type in ticker symbol: FB.

We will be first finding the market cap or market capitalization. This refers to the total dollar market value of a company.

On this site you can see this under overview tab (this information is available on many other sites, including your broker's site under research tab). We will be noting the following:
1.   Market Cap-550.27B
2.   Shares Outstanding -2.965B (all shares owned by shareholders, that's "B" for billions, you see why your and my 100 shares doesn't move the stock price)
Note: Number you see here is the current market cap, which is probably different from what the market cap was on 12/31/2017.

Now just to make sure your math is right. You can divide the Market cap by shares outstanding, should = Price of the stock. (This may be a little off since some sites round this number off, since value may be in millions or even billions).

So, in our above example, we can take 550.27b/2.965b=$185.59 should be roughly the price of the stock at this time and it is!

Step 2:

Next, we will click on financials and go to --> Cash flow statement and note the following:

1.   Net income = 15.93B
2.   Depreciation, Depletion & Amortization (they are basically a write off over the years) = 3.03B
3.   Deferred Income Tax = (-377M or -.377B)

4. Account payable (money that the business owes but have not yet paid) = (138M or .138B)
5. Account Receivable = (money the business needs to collect but have not received) (1.61B)
6. Capital Expenditure - Under investing activities (money spent on acquisition for upgrade and maintenance of assets) = (-6.73B)

Now we are going to add all the above numbers

$$15.93B$$
$$3.03B$$
$$-.377B$$
$$.138B$$
$$-6.73B$$

Total =11.99B this is the owner's earning
Step 3:

Next let's see what kind of return we feel FB can potentially have. For that we will usually look at last 10 years return and average them out to give us some sort of starting point. FB has only been around 5yrs as of 2017. FB has had return of 33.92% for the last 5yrs/annually. Do we expect this company to continue to continue to produce 33.92% annually year after year? I don't, but for lots of technology company it's not unusual. Now you can calculate this based on different percentage. You shouldn't really go less than 10% (this is the minimum you should expect in the stock market). If you are not able to make at least 10%, then it may not be worth the risk you are taking. Let's do some calculations based on different percentages:

if we are going to base it on minimum amount, we are willing to expect (10%):

Owner's earning 11.99b x 10 = 119.9b and divide it by shares outstanding (2.965b) =

119.9/2.965b=$40.44.

At 33.92%:

11.99b x 33.92 = 33.92 406.70b/2.965b = $137.17 is the value of the stock according to our valuation 1.

Currently (as of 12/31/17), FB price is at $186.15, will it ever come to $137.17, I don't know.

According our first valuation scenario FB is over-priced at $185.15 as of 12/31/17! Now FB may never come down to $137.17, let alone $40.44. There are lots of reason for this. As I mentioned a lot of money is poured into hope and potential. Investors are buying on potential worth of the company in the future. People are willing to pay more now for potential! Potential is sometimes caked into the price.

In this case FB is overpriced ($185) based on value investing calculation ($137). I can put FB on my alert list and once FB moves under $137.17, I will be alerted. If FB is on downward trend at that time, I won't jump in and buy but rely on my technical analysis to find a good entry point (discussed in next chapter). Until I see the turnaround/reversal I won't jump in since I really don't know how drastic the fall may be! We will cover when to get in, in next section.

Valuation Calculation Formula 2

Discounted Cash Flow Method

Valuation 2 is based on Discounted Cash Flow. If you know the rate the company is growing, you can expect the stock price to grow in similar fashion. Growth can be measured in many ways. For example, we can look at company's revenue, dividends,

GDP, sales, cash flow, price to earnings ratio, and equity. Since you are measuring the rate the company is growing you will need series of data. This can be every quarter or every year. You can get data for any of the above growth rate and compare/contrast them to give you a better gauge.

We will revisit www.marketwatch.com to obtain this data and calculate the growth rate for "Free Cash Flow". As I mentioned earlier, if you have free cash to grow your business, it triumphs other numbers. Cash is king! You can do many things with cash, which you can't do with tied up assets.

Step 1

Let's go back to marketwatch.com.
Ticker is FB --> Go to financial statements --> Cash Flow statement --> Click on "View Ratios" --> At the bottom of the sheet you will see "Free Cash Flow":

These are the data for FB:
2013 - 2.86B
2014 - 3.63B 26.78%
2015 - 6.08B 67.57%
2016 - 11.62B 91.19%
2017 - 17.48B 50.49%

These figures are provided for you, and may vary little bit, since the number above are rounded to two digits and on excel calculation, they are rounded to 9 digits (based on it being in billions). If you get raw data and wanted to calculate your own growth rate. Use the following formula:

(2014 Free cash flow - 2013 Free Cash Flow)/2013 Free Cash Flow
(3.63B - 2.86B) / 2.86B = 26.92% (Growth rate from 2013 to 2014).

Step 2

Now, let's identify some terms, so you know what we are calculating here.

Year: We are going to use data for last 5 years, if you can get 10years they may give you better indication. You most likely will have to pay for this data. Check with your broker If they are providing this information to you.

Cash Flow: This is how much cash is left over for the company to reinvest in itself, we have series of data to give us a rate.

WACC Formula: Weighted Average Cost of Capital, this is minimum return I expect to earn from this company. Your calculation of how much a stock is worth in the future, depends on how much return you are expecting from this stock. As a default I like to use between 7-15% minimum return. This obviously depends on the risk for that stock. For example, if the stock is risky, I would like to earn higher return, since I'm putting higher risk on the table. FB is also a technology stock, they rise fast, and they fall faster. FB has earned great returns as of 2017. Those returns are usually not sustainable. When the company does fall, it will also fall hard, as most growth/tech companies do. Now let's say through the fall and rise, I still expect 8%-10% return here.

Discount Rate: How do you find the present value of investment that may be worth $1,000 a year from now, 2 years from now or 10 years from now? You will have to work backwards. In other words, you will have to discount this amount by a particular interest rate (WACC). Assuming WACC is at 8%, we will be discounting this by 8%.

Discount Rate Formula: $(1 + WACC)$Number of years discounted $(1 + .08)1 = 1.08$, $(1 + .08)2 = 1.17$, $(1 + .08)3 = 1.26$, etc.

Present Value: Now that we know the rate and we know the future cash flow stream that we have forecasted, we can work backwards and figure out the what the current value or discount value should be. This would make sense since $1,000 now is worth more than $1,000 in 5 years, as long as WACC is greater than 0.

Present Value of Future Cash Flow: Future Value/ (1 + WACC)Number of years discounted

Cash Flow of 2.86B at 8% a year out would be worth 2.65B.
Cash Flow of 3.63B at 8% 2 years out would be worth 3.11B.
Cash Flow of 17.48B at 8% 5 years out would be worth 11.90B.
Perpetual Growth Rate: Rate at which company will continue to grow after the foreseen horizon that we have calculated for. The perpetuity growth rate is typically between the historical inflation rate of 2-3% and the historical GDP growth rate of 4-5%. The number to use here would be 2-5%, based on what your assumption on how well this company will continue to grow. Facebook is growth stock, it hasn't reached a point where its growth has been capped. It may be more than 5 years before the stock reaches its full potential. Therefore, I'm going to use 5% here. This also depends on your horizon. How long are you planning on keeping this security? If you are going to get out before this security reaches its full potential, you can potentially raise the 5% as company is still growing.

Terminal Value: In this case, we are doing calculation on 5 series of data, however what would be the value on 10 series of data, 100 series of data or even infinite amount? Are we expecting FB to continue to grow at 8% forever? Probably not, at some point in time the company will grow as much as its going to grow, and from that point it will grow at a stable rate, using perpetual growth we will figure out its terminal value. Terminal value is sum of all cash flows from an investment after forecasted period at perpetual growth rate.

Chapter 8: How to Get Started

Best Demo/Paper Trading Sites

If you are brand new to investing, this chapter is for you. If you have never traded a security, you may want to start by paper trading. This will mimic live trading, but it will be with fake money! It's like a trial run before the race.

You can create this account on many sites. You will be simulating live trading, with no real money. You can see how well you do. This also allows you to trade based on different strategies without having to risk anything. The simulated website will keep track of all your earnings, profit and losses as if you invested real money. You can create different portfolio and try different strategies (discussed in later chapter) and see which you feel comfortable with and are profitable.

Paper trading will ease you into real trading, you can build your confidence on how trading works, build your style and implement your strategies; because there is also no risk and allows you to practice and be bold in your trades. I would recommend you practice for six months on various sites prior to investing real money.

Here are best sites you can paper trade with at time of printing this book:

1. Avatrade
2. Tradingsim
3. Stockfuse
4. Investfly

You can also opt to do paper trading with broker sites (sites where you can do actual trading). The advantage to these sites is if you like the layout and the look and feel of it, you can then invest real money and begin real trading without learning the look and feel of a new broker.

516

Best broker sites that offer paper trading are:

1. Think or Swim
2. Tradestation
3. InvestorJunkie
4. Ninjatrader

Best Brokerage Accounts-What To Look For

Before you can start investing and trading your money, you will need to open a brokerage account. Once you place a trade order the broker will execute that trade for you. There are many sites that will be competing for your business, so do your research. Some of the factors to consider are the following:

• Are there any promotional deals that are being offered?

• What is the minimum investment-$500? 2,500?

• Does it provide premier tools (not only the research tools you find on free sites)?

• What other features do the brokers provide? Brokers are constantly updating features to the latest technology. For example, some provide alerts on SMS and other only provide alerts on email.

• What are the commission fees? (typically range from $5-$10 per trade). Commission fees do add up but focus on what you are getting with each broker. Among many features, some less reputable brokers have higher slippage. For example, when you put a market order (order at current price), some broker will buy a security at $47.20 others may buy at $47.24, this $.04 difference (slippage) times the amount of shares you are purchasing could wash away $5 you are saving on brokerage fees.

- Some brokerage accounts are geared towards advance traders, that provide little hand holding, little support but their commission fees are reasonable and vice versa.

- APP functionality (download their app and play with it).

Below are few notable brokers who had earned the highest marks at the time of the book writing. However new ones make the list all the time so do you own research as well.

- Merrill Lynch
- Ally
- E-trade
- Ameritrade
- Tradestation
- Interactive brokers
- Charles Schwab
- Fidelity

Funding your Brokerage Account

Once you have picked a brokerage, you can go their website and click on "open a new account" or "sign up" link. This will walk you through applying for new account application, where they will ask you for your social security #, driver license, employment status, etc. Make sure you are using a secure server here as you will be entering all your private information. At the end of your application you will create your username/password. Mostly all the brokerage firms' websites should walk you through this process very easily. Once this is done you will have to fund that account by linking your checking account bank to your brokerage bank and transferring money electronically or writing a check to them. Since each firm maybe slightly different, it's best to contact the brokerage firm if you have any questions with this process. It will take few days before you see the money appear in your brokerage account, so allow some time for this.

If You Never Traded, Here Are the Basics on Placing A Trade

If you have had a demo account, you should be somewhat familiar with trading and the sites functionality.

Once you fund the account:

You will see several tabs, most common are below:

Account --> Summary, Balance, Account holdings/position, Activity, etc.
Trade--> Stocks/options, order status, etc.
Research --> Charts, Screener, Ratings, etc.

Once you play with these options, they should be self-explanatory.

Four most common trade orders you will be placing:

Market Order: An order to buy or sell a security at once at current market price. This type of order guarantees that the order will be executed but does not guarantee the execution price. A market order generally will execute between the current bid (for a sell order) or ask (for a buy order) price. This maybe different than last traded price you see, however, it should be close to that. If you like the stock at current price and want to own it without penny pinching this is the order you want to place.

Limit Order: An order to buy or sell a security at a specific price. If you submit a limit order to buy a stock for $50, this trade will get activated and then becomes a market order and gets executed. Since market is moving very rapidly, even though your order at $50 is activated, it may not get executed exactly at $50. Some orders may be bought for a little less or for more than $50 (i.e. $50.02 or $49.94, etc.). This is ideal trade when you are not in front of your computer or when you only want to buy/sell at a particular price point. You can place limit order and forget about it, if the order gets executed your broker will most likely email you.

Stop Loss Order: This type of order is usually placed to avoid further loss. It's the price you want to get out at. For example, currently you own a stock at $113, however you want to get out if the price starts to fall below $100. You would place the order to sell at $100, when the stock reaches $100 the stock becomes market order and is executed (the actual price you sell maybe few cents above/below due to market fluctuation). As the name implies, you are stopping further loss.

Stop Buy Order: An order that is placed at a stop price above the current market price. This order is placed generally when the stock is fluctuating at a certain price level but has not had a breakthrough. However, once you know there is a breakthrough, you anticipate the stock going much higher. For example, if the stock is fluctuating between $40-$50, however if there is a breakthrough you anticipate an uptrend to go on for a while. Therefore, you will put a stop buy at $52, if the stock starts to cross at $52, your order will get executed.

A stock account is an account opened by an investor at a brokerage firm for stock trading. As a new investor, before entering the stock market for securities trading, you must first open a stock account. With this "passport", you can trade securities. Opening a stock account is a prerequisite for investors to enter the stock market.

Understanding the process of stock trading in the market

As the saying goes: "Do not arbitrarily buy stocks at random, you must do some homework before investing to be successful." After understanding the basic knowledge of stocks, investors must also specify how to conduct stock trading and specific matters needing attention. As well as various trading operations, etc., only when you are prepared, you can move forward steadily.

Basic Process of Stock Trading

Investors who have small and medium level capital have few disadvantages like less knowledge on how the stock market and trading work for example. While starting it feels too overwhelming to spend time reading market theory and market. This usual disadvantage of less knowledge may be prone to a great risk when trading and investing in stocks.

Therefore, the stock market must first understand the various stocks in a comprehensive and detailed manner, understand the listed companies, master the stock market, look at the six roads, listen to the eight parties, and carefully trade. Among them, the most important point is to be familiar with the stock trading process.

The first thing a new investor has to do is to open a stock account (i.e. shareholder card) for themselves. A stock account is equivalent to a "bank account", and investors can only buy and sell securities if they open a stock account.

In short, success requires the right approach, and stock trading is a profound knowledge. If you think that you can make money by buying and selling stocks casually, and you rush into the market, you will lose a lot. We suggest that investors must keep in mind the trading process of stock trading and accumulate certain stock knowledge and operational experience in order to obtain investment success.

Basic Process of Opening an Account

Opening an account is also known as opening an account, and investors can apply at the brokerage counter or online. There are many brokers in USA which can open an account for you. Just do a quick research in google about best brokers in your region. Investors can choose one which they like to open an account.

At present, if you want to buy and sell stocks listed in NYSE, investors need to open the New York Stock Exchange stock account respectively.

You can also join by using the company or its authorized account opening agent. For example, Google Securities Registration Co., Ltd. is the only statutory body for investors in New York.

Choosing the Right Transaction Type

It is the investors' responsibility to choose their own trading methods, as well as access methods to use in the future. They need to sign the appropriate opening dealings with the securities business department that includes bank transfer, telephone entrustment, mobile phone stock trading, and online trading, to name some.

Nowadays, transactions are basically online transactions. Investors should consider whether there are online consultation services, stock mobile phone trading software, telephone voice report, and other services, in addition to online transactions so that the transaction is convenient and smooth.

Choosing a Securities Company That Suits You

Many investors who have just come into contact with the stock market may have such doubts. It is important to research which securities company is feasible and good for your trading.

What kind of securities the company should be chosen?
Choosing a securities company that suits you is still very important for a newcomer. After all, in the case of a fast pace of life in modern society, it is necessary to prepare for work before opening an account, and to avoid the trouble of switching customers in the future.

Stock Selection Practice Based on Multiple Elements

When the market is booming, why do you actively choose stocks, but still do not make money?

When the market is in a downturn, how to accurately choose growth stocks and firmly hold them?

Investors can only continue to stabilize their profits if they choose the growth stock based on the correct factors. This section not only allows you to completely abandon the law of inertia but also teaches you to be an investor who always thinks independently.

As the saying goes: "No matter what A shares and B shares are, making money is the only good stock." How to choose a good stock is the most urgent thing investors want to know. The stock market is broad and fluctuating, and there is no fixed good stock. It is very important for different investors to find stocks that suit their investment style. Regardless of whether the broader market falls or rises, stock-picking is the most important thing. It is difficult for you to make money if you choose stocks that are bad.

Investors have surpluses, losses, and different levels of profit and loss. In fact, they are mainly caused by different stock-picking. The idea and method of stock selection are varied and varied, but the most suitable stock selection method for retail investors should be the K-line chart.

There are very few investors who succeed in choosing the best stock and enjoy the huge return of investment when they sell those stocks back. It is a known fact after hundreds of interviews with the famous investors that they look at K-line chart of different stocks at every point of their trading time.

In the process of selecting stocks, the first choice is the shape of the stock. It is usually selected from the daily chart of the stock, and sometimes it is also selected by the weekly chart. This is completely reflected in the investor's personal preferences, and there is no regulation.

In short, the K-line study of stock opening, washing, and pulling up, some principled things will never be outdated. For example, the amount of open positions can determine the breakthrough height whereas the moving average system determines the breakthrough time. The control intention of line is simple and undisturbed whereas the price fluctuations do not leave space for short-term customers, and the volume must not be scattered.

Element 1: Stock Selection Based on Fundamentals

The stock price often changes according to the fluctuations of fundamental factors such as certain economic indicators, economic policies, global economic situation, and domestic and foreign emergencies. The analysis of these factors is the main basis for judging the current market conditions and selecting stocks.

Fundamentals include as described below in detail.
a) Diplomacy and politics
b) Finance and economics
c) Exchange rates and interest rates
d) National conditions and popularity
e) Social needs and market supply
f) Economic cycles and stock market trends
g) Regulatory agencies and listed companies
h) Industry prospects and product mix, chairman and management
i) Corporate growth and market share
j) Debt ratio and profit margin
k) Resource structure and market capacity.

It is no easy task to fully understand and be familiar with it. Only by learning while operating normally, while learning and operating, capital and knowledge and experience grow simultaneously.

Analysis of the market outlook:

We can understand a k-line chart of a company as explained below.

From the analysis of K-line chart, the company's performance is improving, and the future may continue to grow. The stock market is expected to continue to strengthen. As the country's economic situation continues to evolve and change, the country's economic policies will naturally make corresponding adjustments. The main impact of national economic policies on stock prices is always should be researched.

Therefore, investors must have a deep understanding of the country's major economic policies and conscientiously implement the entire stock trading process in order for investment to be successful. If investors can choose stocks according to policies, and at the same time spend time to understand the fundamentals of listed companies through market research, and then learn them to use technical analysis to select good buy points it will be easy to earn big money in the stock market.

In the period of inflation, if the price increase is too large, the actual assets of the residents will shrink, causing market instability. In order to control inflation, the state will push interest rates up, and liquidity in the market will decrease, thus causing stock prices to fall.

Use of industry Development Prospects

When choosing stocks, we attach great importance to two conditions: First, the industry's development trend is good, and it can have a sustained upward trend in the foreseeable time. The Second reason is, it is easy to miss the bull stocks in the current period, so the industry turning point needs to be on the industry.

Use the development prospects of the industry to analyze the basic situation of the proposed investment company including the company's operation, management, financial status and future development prospects. The intrinsic value of the research company is used to determine the reasonable price of the company's stock.

And then by comparing the difference between the market price and the reasonable price one should determine whether to buy the company's stock. Usually when people choose stocks, they must consider the influence of industry factors and try to choose stocks in high-growth industries, and avoid choosing stocks in the sunset industry. For example, USA's communications industry is a typical sunrise industry. The listed companies in the communications category are favored in the stock market. Their market positioning is usually high, and they often become "high-priced aristocrats" in the stock market.

Use Value Investment Stock Selection

The intrinsic value of a stock determines the price. To stabilize the profit and avoid the risk in time, the intrinsic value of the stock must be analyzed.

Value-for-money stock selection refers to the research of further sub-sectors in the industry with the best trend in the large sector. Followed by selecting the sub-sector with the strongest trend, and then selecting the fundamentals in the sub-industry according to the concept of value investment.

Element 2: Selecting Stocks Based on Psychological Aspects

The stock-picking psychology is an activity in which investors make psychological expectations about the stock value when they choose the target. To Cultivate a good stock-picking psychology investor should pay attention to the following aspects:

First, take advantage of the trend and follow the bull market trend to select stocks, in order to get big profits or sometimes lose money.

second, make a portfolio investment by choosing different types of stocks. The target stocks are combined to invest in market opportunities and correct a bad stock-picking mentality.

Prepare for stock selection

Some people say that the stock market is like a battlefield, and a battlefield without smoke can make investors become heroes of the world, and it can also make investors scared. For investors who want to enter the stock market, they must first be psychologically prepared.

Using the stock price effect to select stocks

The Price Comparison effect refers to the direct comparison of the stock price in the secondary market with the direct comparison between the same type of company, such as operating results, tradable equity, and funds raised. Specifically, there are the following aspects.

a) For stocks between the same geographical sector, choose stocks with lower stock prices.

b) Compared with individual stocks in the same industry, choose stocks with lower stock prices.

c) Compared with the stocks of the same speculative stocks, choose stocks with lower stock prices.

d) For stocks of the same size as the tradable shares, choose stocks with lower stock prices.

The "price comparison effect" is one of the most important market drivers driving the ever-changing securities market. For example, the Tesla Electronics Group, which was listed in 2009, has a total initial share capital of 256 million dollars and a circulation of 70 million shares. The forecasted performance in 2009 was 0.17 dollar per share. The company is mainly engaged in the production of cars belonging to the Automobile industry from 2009.

Panasonic and other home appliance companies have fallen into the "dead aristocracy" in the market. Therefore, for such a company that is mainly based on home appliance production and has no future development prospects and poor business performance, investors generally adopt a scornful attitude. The stock price on the first day of listing showed a downward trend. The decline in the two days was nearly 30%.

However, market investors have also overlooked one of the most critical factors - the "price effect." In 2009, the stock price of home appliance stocks was still basically positioned at 10 dollar or more. At that time, Panasonic had a minimum of 12 dollar, Phillips had a minimum of 15 dollar, and Samsung had a minimum of 11 dollar. The average price reached more than 10 dollars, so the price of the Electronics Group, which was only 5 dollars at the time, was obviously undervalued. In the future, its share price would have doubled by 10 dollars in two months. The successful speculation of the stock can be said to be the best example of the opposite price effect.

Bull Market and Bear Market Picking Skills

The stock market can change at any time. Investors should learn to buy stocks at different times, use the characteristics of each period, and comprehensively analyze and practice.

1. Bullish market
In the concept of rational investors, "it's not much of what you earn today in the stock market, but who is living in the stock market for a long time".

If you are thinking make more money than you are investing then there are too many cases of great joy and great sadness in the stock market. Many people who have been in the stock market a few years ago have already disappeared, and they fell before the bull market. Whoever survives for a long time means that the market gives more opportunities. New investors can pay attention to the "three highs" theory of short-term stock-picking.

2. Bearish market
In the bear market, the difficulty of stock-picking is far greater than the bull market, and the market is constantly going down. The decline, the trend of most stocks is also downgraded and only a very small number of stocks go against the trend. Although it is very difficult to select stocks in a bear market, there are certain ways to follow them, as follows.

Select stocks whose fundamentals have undergone major changes and whose performance is expected to surge.
Whether in the bull market or in a bear market, such stocks are sought after. As the fundamentals have improved, they must be reflected in the stock market sooner or later. Of course, you need to pay attention to the timing when choosing, and don't wait until the stock price has risen to a high point.

Select stocks with long-term good development prospects.

A company with good development prospects is the target pursued by most people when they choose stocks. These companies have bright prospects for development, stable operations, and are favored by many people.

It may be high and the performance is measured in advance. However, in the bear market, it may fall sharply with the market, and even plummet, which provides investors with a good buying opportunity can get a good stock at a very low price. At the same time, it should be noted that the selection of such stocks should be based on the medium and long-term, and cannot be expected to obtain high profits in the short term.

Select individual stocks involved by the main agency.
The main institutions in the stock market are powerful that the average small and medium-sized investors can compare with some inflexible weaknesses. Once they are involved in a single stock, they have to hold a long time, especially in a bear market unless they recognize the export bureau.

Otherwise, we must use every opportunity to rebound and wait for opportunities to raise stocks. Small and medium-sized retail investors should have a relatively large profit opportunity if they have the right time to intervene, the cost price is below the banker's level, and they should not be greedy for excessive profits.
Select stocks that have fallen in the late bear market.

In the late bear market or the bear market has been going on for a long time, some stocks have fallen overall. By using comprehensive basic analysis and technical analysis the downside has been limited and can no longer fall. Even if the broader market continues to fall, these stocks will stop falling early and take the lead in rebounding.

The summary shows that the important thing in the bear market is to pay attention to the market trend and understand the hot spots in the market and the policy changes. Investors should choose not to buy instead, they should prepare for the future by preparing to select individual stocks, considering it would have a chance for bull market.

Element 3: Stock-picking Based on Price Changes

Stock prices are highly unpredictable, and this is one of the reasons that stocks have higher returns. From the rise and fall of market stocks, you can find strong stocks and weak stocks on the disk. In general, the stock price is the leading indicator of market fundamentals that is, the stock price may have begun to react before the news has not reached the market. So, observing the fluctuations in stock prices helps to guess the actual changes in the market.

Therefore, stock investors must learn to understand market behavior and be a "smart lamb." Stock investors should not have individual fear effects and must have the strength to be the ruin of the boat by learning to choose stocks according to the market.

Using market speculation to pick stocks

The subject matter is an excuse for speculating stocks and is a tool used to stimulate market sentiment. Some subjects do have substantive content, while others are purely rumoring where some are even deliberately spread rumors. In addition, most of the subject matter of the listed company itself cannot be determined casually, and many specific situations require specific analysis. But the market is characterized by the fact that as long as there is subject matter, the market is willing to dig and accept, and the real role of the subject is neglected.

The theme of the stock market has both positive and negative effects. When using the theme to find the best investment opportunities and stock selection, the operation should pay attention to the problems.

For long-term value investment stock selection, it is generally necessary to choose stocks whose price is lower than the value, that is, the stock that usually costs 4 cents to buy one dollar. Any such stock must be a stock that is generally not favored by the market, so there will be low prices. The price is in the top shipping phase or at the bottom of the pull-up phase.

Using market hotspot stock-picking

In a popular saying: Hotspots are the sectors or stocks that are popular in a given period of time. These stocks that are popular in a certain period of time are often referred to by investors as "hot stocks" at the time. If investors look at the stock's rise and fall, they will find that they are mostly in the forefront of the rise.

It should be noted that there is no constant hot spot in the stock market. Similarly, there are no constant strong stocks and weak stocks. As the saying goes, "the wind and water turn", the strong stocks and strong sectors in a certain period may become weak stocks and weak sectors in another period, and vice versa.

Therefore, investors should always keep their heads clear and be good at adjusting their investment strategies in time according to the changes in market strength, so as to seize the new hot spots in the market in time.

For small and medium-sized retail investors, they can choose the corresponding stocks close to the market hotspots. People use Hot stock-picking, trend timing, small profits into profits, and then evolve into a stable profit model.

Use of shareholder changes in stock selection

Changes in shareholder status are also an important reference factor for investors to choose stocks. For example, the number of shareholders is the number of all shareholders of a single stock. The smaller the number of people, the more concentrated the chips. In a more general way, the main force has already sucked up the goods, so the stock price will rise. On the contrary, if the number of shareholders increase it means that the main force is being distributed, and many of the chips are picked up by the retail investors. The stock price will naturally come down, and the profit will naturally fall.

In general, the change in the number of shareholders tends to complete a cycle from "a large number of people → gradually decreasing → the lowest value (inflection point) → gradually increasing → a large number of people". In these four stages, investors are more profitable when they intervene in the second stage, especially in the middle and late stages of this stage, the probability of success is quite high.

Investors need to conduct a statistical analysis of the changes in the number of shareholders to better grasp the trend of the market and individual stocks. Pay special attention to the several points shown in during the specific analysis.

Using K-line stock-picking

The K-line chart is the basic means of stock analysis, allowing investors to fully and thoroughly observe the real changes in the market. From the K-line chart, you can see the overall trend of the market, as well as understand the fluctuations of the daily stock market. It is the most popular stock technical analysis method.

In the big bull market, it is often seen that the varieties that are continuously pulled up are exceptionally outstanding in short-term performance, and the returns are considerable. In the near-term market, such stocks are constantly emerging, and the opportunities are worthy of attention. As shown, it is the trend of Amazon Group from May 2014 to the beginning of 2014. In general, these short-term opportunities are all chasing operations, so it is necessary to find a strong and continuous rising variety to ensure that the participating stocks have sufficient short-term profit opportunities, and this can be found from the K-line. trace.

The stock selection focuses on the timing of the stock-picking, which is subject to an important principle - not to bottom out on the way down (because I don't know when it is the bottom). Only stocks with the trend established are selected. Among the stocks with established trends, the stocks with the strongest trend and the best gains are found to operate.

From the K-line analysis, those stocks that continue to rise generally have two situations:

•   First, far from the historical high, the current price is far lower than the average market cost of the stock and the rising resistance is very small.

•   Second, the stock is in the record is high, and the technical consolidation is relatively full. The chips have been mastered by large funds, and they are quickly separated from the cost area after rushing.

The general rule of operation of the market is: If a stock hits a new high (or recent high), then the probability of a new high in the future will be high; on the contrary, if a stock hits a new low (or recent low), then the possibility of a new low in a period of time is also great. Investors need to remember that stocks in the downtrend channel will only make you lose money or lose profit.

Using the moving average stock-picking

The Moving Average (MA) originally means the moving average that is indeed calculated using different prerequisites. Since we make it into a line, it is generally called the moving average, or the moving average. It is the sum of the closing prices of a certain period of time.

The moving average line has indicators of 5 days, 10 days, 30 days, 60 days, 120 days, and 240 days. Among them, the 5-day and 10-day short-term moving averages are the reference indicators for short-term operations, called the daily average index; 30-day and 60-day are the medium-term moving average indicators, called the average moving average indicator; 120 days, 240 days is The long-term moving average indicator is called the annual average indicator.

Investors can use the moving average as a reference when selecting stocks.

Indicators that are present in the moving average can reflect the trend of the price trend. The so-called moving average is to average the stock price for a certain period of time, and then make an average line image based on this average. Investors can analyze the daily K-line chart and the average line in the same picture, which is very straightforward.

The most common method of moving averages is to compare the relationship between the moving average of the securities price and the price of the securities themselves. When the price of the security rises above its moving average, a purchase signal is generated. When the price of a security falls below its moving average, a sell signal is generated.

This signal is generated because it is believed that the "line" in the moving average is a strong criterion for supporting or blocking prices. Prices should rebound from the moving average. If it does not rebound and breaks through, then it should continue to develop in that direction until it finds a new level that can be maintained.

Using morphological analysis to select stocks

Morphological analysis is a relatively concise and practical analysis method in the field of technical analysis. It summarizes and classifies some typical forms of stock price movements. Morphological analysis is a combination of a few days of K-line expansion to a period of tens of days or even a period. These numerous K-lines constitute a number of different trajectory patterns, and the long and short sides are analyzed by studying the trajectories that the stock price has passed. The contrast of power changes will make corresponding judgments to guide the actual operation.

Using trend line stock-picking

The trend line is a graphical way to display the predicted trend of the data and can be used for predictive analysis which is also known as regression analysis. Use the trend line to extend the trend line in the chart to predict future data based on actual data.

An important principle of stock trading is that it is "following the trend" and cannot "move against the trend." Among them, "potential" is the direction and trend that is, the direction of stock price movement. Usually, there are three directions for the trend: an upward trend, a downward trend, and a horizontal trend (no trend).

In the stock market, investors can only make money by buying low and selling high, so it is especially important to select stocks with an upward trend. That is to say, in the stock selection, it is necessary to select stocks in the K-line graph where each of the subsequent peaks and valleys are higher than the previous peaks and valleys (i.e., one bottom is higher than the bottom).

The two connected lows with uptrend stocks are connected in turn to arrive at an uptrend line. Usually, the uptrend line plays a supporting role in the stock price. Once the uptrend line is formed, the stock price will run above the trend line for a while. Based on this principle, investors can select stocks above the uptrend line.

Chapter 9: Technical Analysis

It's easier and faster to evaluate and see the security snapshot on a chart than to read their annual report. That's not to say charting is more important, it just gives me a faster snapshot of how securities are behaving. i.e. some charts move in a pattern, which makes them more predictable, and this is seen very quickly in a chart than a financial document. Growth company that is making new high, year after year can be reflected in a chart quickly, than digging through 10 years of financial documents.

I also may not want to invest in a company for a long term, I may just want to trade a stock. Understanding technical analysis is key for traders, who are looking for short-term in/out in hopes of make a profit.

Even after you find a company you love, find the right valuation, you still just don't buy it! You now need to have a good entry point. I've seen companies that have great numbers, continue to tank (I have no idea why), maybe public doesn't know about them, maybe rumors, maybe they are hidden gems, maybe I don't have my numbers right and maybe I'm missing something, I really don't know why. What this tells me is I can't just a buy the right company at the wrong time and wait forever for them to turnaround. Once I've done the fundamental analysis and found a company to be great, then I need to get in at the right time! This is where I use the technical analysis (charting & indicators), along with several strategies.

Technical analysis can involve many complex techniques with 100's of different indicators. I want to cut to the chase and introduce you to most widely use indicators and strategies that are most commonly used by professional investors and traders.

538

Charts

Line Chart

Line chart are simply connected with close of the day. Line charts are important when you want to take the noise out of the chart, they usually get the close of one day and the close of the next day and connect them through dotted line.

Bar Chart

These charts plots open, high, low and closing price.

Candlestick Chart

They are my favorite, since they provide the most information. Up candle is clear or blue and down candle is red or black. Up candle means that the chart is on bull or upward trend, meaning it closed higher than it opened. Down cancel means that the chart is on bear or downward trend, meaning it closed lower than it opened. The lines extending up and the lines extending down are the high and low of the day.

Indicators
Moving Averages (MAVG):

Moving averages are very popular and many, many investors and fund managers pay attention to them. Moving averages takes the price over "X" period and averages them out. This could be over 10, 20, 50, 100, 200 days. These averages help you identify the trend of stocks. In an upward trend moving averages follow the stock (are under the stock price). In downward trend these moving averages are above the stock. Thus, crossing of price and MAVG are crucial trigger point, especially to most technical traders. There are two main type of moving averages. Exponential, which will have current periods weighted more heavily and simple where all price points have equal weight. Main point to keep in mind here is if the moving average is below the stock price the stock is bullish and if the moving average is above the stock price than the stock is bearish.

In this ARLP chart you will see that when moving average is mostly under the stock the stock is on upward trend, when the moving average makes its way above the stock the stock is falling or on downward trend. Thus, the crucial point is when the moving average is crossing the stock price. This is when buying and selling happens.

Volume

Volume shows how many trades are being made over specified period (usually day). If the volume is higher you are probably going to be able to trade in/out faster as more people are buying/selling. Volume tells us number of shares that are being traded, it does not tell us if those traded are being bought or sold. We don't know exactly how many shares are being bought or sold but if you look at the stock price move substantially with high volume, you can guess if there are more sellers or buyers. If the stock price is moving up and the volume is higher you know there are more buyers putting money into that security. If the stock price is moving down and the volume is higher you can guess there are more sellers taking their money out of that security. Remember huge moves are usually fund managers who are deciding to take their money in or out. If you start to see stock price continue to rise but the volume is "drying out" getting less, you can assume that interest in that stock is getting less and thus maybe warning of a reversal. If the stock starts to decline with higher volume, you know that sellers are starting to sell. If you are having hard time figuring out if the volume is high or low, you can also have MAVG on volume and see if volume is higher or lower than the MAVG.

540

Some of the indicators relating to volume you may want to learn are: On-Balance Volume Indicator, Chaikin Money Flow and Klinger Volume Oscillator.

Support

Is a floor or base. It's historical price level at which stock no longer falls but either moves sideways or reverses up. Crossing of support level is a key alert for technical traders. Chart below shows "HALL" chart with support at $10.

Resistance

Resistance is the ceiling which stock prices can't break above. A price at which the security has hard time breaking through. Once this price is reached stocks usually move sideways or start to reverse direction and move down. Chart below shows "HALL" chart with resistance at $11.75.

Trendlines

There is no stock that moves continuously straight up or straight down. In an upward trend (bull trend) stocks usually rise, consolidate (move sideways) and then move back up in staircase. In a downward trend (bear trend) stocks move down, consolidate and move down again. They may do this again and again to form a trend. In a rising stock, you can connect/draw a line at the lows of the stock price (as seen below) to form a rising trendline. Same can be done on dropping stock to form a declining trendline. If you can figure out this pattern, you can better understand your entry points and understand if this a bull or bear market/stock.

RSI: Relative Strength Index:

The relative strength index (RSI) is a technical indicator developed by J. Welles Wilder. RSI can be used as a momentum indicator, but it is graphed as an oscillator. Most importantly it is used to show you overbought (too many investors have bought this security and soon investors will start to take the profit and thus stock should decline) and oversold (too many investors have sold this security and soon investors will start to buy the stock, since it's a bargain and the price should rise) condition. Traditionally the RSI is considered overbought when above 70 and oversold when below 30, however you can modify these settings to fit your chart, some also use the setting 80/20.

The below chart is "T" AT&T from 2013-2018. The top part is RSI and the bottom part is the price of the stock. RSI has two horizontal lines at 30 (bottom) and 70 (top). The vertical lines are drawn anytime RSI is >70 or <30. This chart illustrates that when RSI <30, the stock price is oversold and thus should be bought and will rise and when RSI>70, it is overbought and thus should be sold as price will drop. Again, bear in mind no one indicator will be right all the time as in this case, however it does illustrated how RSI could possibly be used to show overbought/oversold condition.

MACD

Moving Average Convergence Divergence is a momentum indicator that shows the relationship between two moving averages of prices. At first this may seem over complicated, but let's break it down.

1.   The MACD is usually calculated by subtracting the 26-day exponential moving average (EMA) from the 12-day EMA, this would be your MACD line.
2.   A 9-day EMA of the MACD Line is plotted with the indicator, it's called the signal line. It is primarily used to see the trend.
3.   The MACD-Histogram measures the difference between MACD and its 9-day EMA.

Chapter 10: Buy & Sell with Confidence

Many beginners get confused by the different roles that traders can play in the market. Most investors involved in options are simply trading. This means that you buy an options contract to open your position. You can choose to buy a call option, a put option, or a combination of call and put options. When you buy an option contract you have no obligations under the option, and you are free to sell them to others. In the same way, on the stock market, you don't actually make a deal with someone to sell your option, you simply place an order through your broker, and they handle it for you.

Traders buy and sell options hoping to make profits from the transactions as the share price moves up and down. If you get stuck with an option that is out of the money and close to expiration, you are out of luck at that point and it will probably expire worthless.

You can also sell to open. For example, you will be obligated to if the option is exercised by the buyer. Using industry jargon, we say that you have been assigned. They say you are a "writer", but you don't actually write a contract as an individual investor. You simply get on your brokerage contract, and you find existing options for a given stock. When you find one you like, you place an order to sell it through your broker. People sell options because they can earn a monthly income by doing so, even though selling comes with some risks.

Maximum Financial Risk

If you buy options, the maximum risk to you is the money you paid to buy the option. So, if you buy an option for $100 your risk is $100.

If you sell call options, the risk is that you will have to sell the 100 shares of stock. If you own the stock the risk is that you will lose the shares. If you don't already own the stock, then you face financial risk. The risk per share is the difference in price between the market price and the share price.

If you sell put options, the risk is that you will have to buy the shares at the strike price. So, your total risk is the strike price x 100 shares. That is the absolute financial risk, of course you might be stuck with shares of stock that are worthless. As we will see, there are ways to protect yourself from having to buy the stock.

Chapter 11: Avoid Beginner's Mistakes

If you can avoid these mistakes when you are just getting started, you will be way ahead of the pack and will also save yourself a lot of losses and misery. Write down these "Commandments" on a sticky note and put it on your computer screen:

Don't buy stocks that are hitting 52-week lows

We have already discussed this point, but it bears repeating, simply because so many new traders lose a lot of money trying to catch the proverbial "falling knife." In spite of what everyone will tell you, you are almost always much better off buying a stock that is hitting 52-week highs than one hitting 52-week lows.

Has a company that you own just reported some really bad news? If so, remember that there is never just one cockroach. Bad news comes in clusters. Many investors recently learned this the hard way with General Electric, which just kept reporting one bad thing after another, causing the stock to crash from 30 to 7. There is no such thing as a "safe stock." Even a blue-chip stock can go down a lot if it loses its competitive advantage or the company makes bad decisions.

A cascade of bad news can often cause a stock to trend down or gap down repeatedly. If you own a stock that does this, it is often better to get out and wait a few months (or years) to reenter. Again, there is never just one cockroach.

Never buy a stock after you have seen the first cockroach. When a stock goes down a lot, it can affect the company's fundamentals as well. Employee and management morale will deteriorate, the best employees may leave the company, and it may become more difficult for the company to raise money by selling shares or issuing debt.

Conversely, when a stock goes up a lot, it can improve the company's fundamentals. Employee and management morale will be high, everyone at the company will want to work harder, it will be easier to recruit new talent, and it will become easier for the company to raise money by issuing stock or debt.

If you stick to stocks that are trading above their 200-day moving averages, or that are hitting 52-week highs, you will do much better than trying to catch falling knives.

Don't trade penny stocks

A penny stock is any stock that trades under $5. Unless you are an advanced trader, you should avoid all penny stocks.

I would extend this by encouraging you to also avoid all stocks priced under $10.

Even if you have a small trading account ($5,000) or less, you are better off buying fewer shares of a higher-priced stock than a lot of shares of a penny stock.

That is because low-priced stocks are most often associated with lower quality companies. As a result, they are not usually allowed to trade on the NYSE or the Nasdaq. Instead, they trade on the OTCBB ("over the counter bulletin board") or Pink Sheets, both of which have much less stringent financial reporting requirements than the major exchanges do.

Many of these companies have never made a profit. They may be frauds or shell companies that are designed solely to enrich management and other insiders. They may also include former "blue chips" that have fallen on hard times like Eastman Kodak or Lehman Brothers.

In addition, penny stocks are inherently more volatile than higher-priced stocks. Think of it this way: if a $100 stock moves $1, that is a 1% move. If a $5 stock moves $1, that is a 20% move. Many new traders underestimate the kind of emotional and financial damage that this kind of volatility can cause.

In my experience, penny stocks do not trend nearly as well as higher-priced stocks. They tend to be more mean-reverting (Mean reversion occurs when a stock moves up sharply from its average trading price, only to fall right back down again to its average trading price).

Many of them are eventually headed to zero, but they are still not good short candidates. Most brokers will not let you short them. And even if you do find a broker who will let you short a penny stock; how would you like to wake up to see your penny stock trading at $10 when you just shorted it at $2 a few days before? I learned that lesson the hard way. It turned out that I was risking $8 to make $2, which is not a good way to make money over the long term.

To add injury to insult, a penny stock might appear to be liquid one day, and the next day, the liquidity dries up and you are confronted by a $2 bid/ask spread. Or the bid might completely disappear. Imagine owning a stock for which there are now no buyers.

Stay away from all stocks under $10. Also stay away from trading newsletters that hawk penny stocks. The owners of these newsletters are often paid by the companies themselves to hype their stocks. Or they may take a position in a penny stock, send out an email telling everyone to buy it, and then sell their stock at a much higher price to these amateur buyers.

Watch the movie "The Wolf of Wall Street" if you'd like to see a famous example of the decadent lifestyle and fraud that often surround penny stocks. Viewer discretion is advised.

Don't short stocks

If you are an advanced trader, feel free to ignore this rule. If you are not, I would seriously encourage you not to ignore this rule.

In order to short a stock, you must first borrow shares of the stock from your broker. You then sell those shares on the open market. If the stock falls in price, you will be able to buy back those shares at a lower price for a profit. If, however, the stock goes up a lot, you may be forced to buy back the shares at a much higher price, and end up losing more money than you ever had in your trading account to begin with.

In November 2015, Joe Campbell broke 2 of the 5 commandments. He first decided to trade a penny stock called KaloBios Pharmaceuticals. To make things worse, he decided to short it.

When he went to bed that evening, his trading account was worth roughly $37,000. When he woke up the next morning, the stock had skyrocketed. As a result, not only had he lost all of the $37,000, but he now owed his broker an additional $106,000.

And there was no way out. If you owe your broker money, they can haul you into court and go after your house and savings.

Sometimes even the wealthiest investors can be wiped out by shorting a stock. During the great Northern Pacific Corner of 1901, shares of that railroad stock went from $170 to $1,000 in a single day. That move bankrupted some of the wealthiest Americans of the day, who had shorted the stock and were then forced to cover at higher prices.

If you do end up shorting a stock, remember that your broker will charge you a fee (usually expressed as an annual interest rate) to borrow the stock. In addition, if you are short a stock, you are responsible for paying any dividends on that stock (your broker will automatically take the money out of your account quarterly).

For all of these reasons, shorting stocks is clearly an advanced and risky trading strategy. Don't try it until you've been trading for at least 5 years, and you have the financial stability to withstand a freakish upwards move in a stock. And never short a penny stock. It's just not worth it.

Don't trade on margin
In order to short a stock, you will need to open up a margin account with your broker, as Joe Campbell did. You'll also need a margin account in order to trade stocks using margin.

When you buy a stock on margin, it means that you are borrowing money from your broker, in order to purchase more shares of stock than you would normally be able to buy with just the cash sitting in your brokerage account.

Let's say that I have $10,000 in my margin account. Most brokers in the U.S. will allow me to go on margin to purchase $20,000 worth of stock in that account. What this means is that they are lending me an additional $10,000 (usually at some outrageous annual interest rate like 11%, which is what E*Trade currently charges) to buy more shares of stock.

If I buy $10,000 worth of stock and the stock goes up 10%, I've just made $1,000. But if I can increase the amount of stock that I'm buying to $20,000 using a margin loan, I will have made $2,000 on the same 10% move. That will mean that my trading account has just gone up by 20% ($2,000/$10,000).
Of course, if the stock goes down 10% and I'm on full margin, I will have lost 20% of my account value. Trading on margin is thus a form of leverage: it amplifies the performance of your portfolio both on the upside and the downside.

When you buy a stock using margin, the stock and cash in your trading account is held as collateral for the margin loan. If the stock falls enough, you may be required to add more cash to your account immediately (this is called "getting a margin call"), or risk having the broker force you to immediately sell your stock to raise cash. Often this will lead to your selling the stock at the worst possible time.

When you open up a new brokerage account and you are given the choice of a "cash account" or a "margin account," it's OK to pick "margin account." A margin account has certain advantages, such as being able to use the proceeds from selling a stock to immediately buy another stock without having to wait a few days for the trade to settle. If you never exceed your cash buying power in a margin account, you will never be charged fees or interest. In that way, it's quite possible to have a margin account, but never to go on margin.

If, however, you don't trust yourself, open up a "cash account." That way, you will never be allowed to trade on margin.

Don't trade other people's ideas

There are two main reason for this. The first reason never to trade someone else's ideas is that they probably don't know what they are doing. If you get a hot stock tip from your neighbor or at the gym, it's best to ignore it. They probably have no idea what they are talking about.

Second, even if you get a really good and legitimate trading or investing idea from someone else, you will probably not have the conviction to hold on to it when the going gets tough. That conviction can only come from developing a trade idea yourself. When you have designed a trade, or researched an investment for yourself, you will have the conviction to hold on. You will also know where your stop loss is, in case the stock goes south. Have you noticed how hot stock tips never come with a recommended stop loss level?

Also, never place a trade based on something that you have just read in Barron's, Forbes, The Wall Street Journal, or have just seen on CNBC. Never buy a stock based on an analyst upgrade, or sell a stock based on an analyst downgrade.

I've seen analysts finally downgrade a stock only once it has fallen 50%. Analysts are lagging indicators. They tend to upgrade stocks that have already moved up, and downgrade stocks that have already moved down. There is also a strong selection bias among analysts. The best analysts get hired by hedge funds, and you never hear from them again. The worst analysts stay at the banks or brokerage houses, and continue to dispense their mediocre advice. Huge amounts of money have been lost by following their advice.

Should you even follow Warren Buffett's advice, as I suggested in a previous chapter? Yes, and no. His advice is definitely much better than a hot stock tip from your neighbor. On the other hand, if you listened to him religiously, you missed out on all of the great tech stocks of the last 20 years. He waited until Apple and Amazon were up many thousands of percentage points before finally purchasing them.

Anyone can learn to think for themselves in the stock market, and come up with their own trading and investing ideas. That is the goal behind all of my books and trading courses.

Rather than giving you a fish, I would much rather teach you how to fish for yourself. That is the path to true financial freedom.

Getting anxious to receive a dividend

The way this works out is you see a stock with a good dividend payment, and so, you try and buy it as close as possible to the ex-dividend date to get paid right away. Doing this is creating a situation where you can get yourself into trouble by letting emotion start to take over. Normally, emotion isn't as much of a problem for dividend investors, but once it gets it foot in the door, you can start running into financial problems. The key to avoiding this problem is to take a long-term investing viewpoint and buy shares on a fixed and regular basis.

Only paying attention to yield

It's true that yield can be an important indicator, but you shouldn't be entirely focused on it. Remember that if you are investing in dividends, it's the dividend payment that is the most important metric. Going back to AbbVie (yet again), the forward dividend is $4.28 per share, with a yield of 5.39%. Now, remember the BDC we mentioned a couple of chapters back, Apollo Investment Corp? That BDC had an incredible yield. Checking it today, the yield is 11.52%. But the dividend is only $1.80.

Let me ask you, would you rather make $4.28 per share from AbbVie or only make $1.80 per share? That $4.28 is an extra $2.48 in your pocket, per share. So, an investment in AbbVie might be more prudent if making money from the dividend income is your goal.

Another reason to not get too hyped up by yields is they can be inflated by a declining stock price. One of the first companies we looked at was Consolidated Communications, which has a shockingly high yield of 38%. And guess why? Because their $1.55 dividend payment is for a stock that is only selling for around $4 a share. A high yield on something that has, unfortunately, become a penny stock may not be something that fits your investment goals.

Whether or not yield is important will depend on a wide variety of factors that you are using to evaluate potential investments. But don't just focus on yield alone, look at the entire picture.

Failing to look for growth

On average, dividend investors tend to be more conservative than other types of players in the stock market. Maybe not as conservative as people who will only buy mutual funds, but certainly more conservative than your average growth investor. The goal with dividends is to seek out stable companies that are mature, but you should also get growth-oriented companies that are paying dividends into your portfolio as well. While they may be paying a lower dividend right now, over time, a growth-oriented company may end up paying a higher dividend than an old stalwart like Wells Fargo or Johnson & Johnson.

You will want to look at the company's history of paying dividends and see if you spot a trend, and that trend would be increasing dividend payments. Don't look at absolute amounts, look at percentages, and choose companies that raise their dividends by a significant percentage at least once a year.

Not investing in dividend ETFs

Individual stocks are fun to invest in, and people love the excitement of doing the research and being able to track all the different companies. That's great and you can get some great buys in your portfolio. However, you should also invest some of your money into ETFs so that you can take advantage of the massive diversification. This will also act as a hedge to help keep a part of your portfolio stable and secure. I would recommend putting between 25-40% of your dividend investments into 2-3 different ETFs, probably one that tracks dividend aristocrats, and also include a REIT to diversify your exposure.

Not Diversifying Enough

We've covered a wide range of investments in this book, and you should be investing in all of them. How you allocate your investments are up to you, but strictly buying stocks might be leaving opportunities on the table. For example, there is no reason not to invest in REITs, either individually or through an ETF. You should also invest in at least five MLPs so that you can take advantage of the high distributions and enjoy the tax advantages as well.

Only investing in stocks

Well, okay, we are repeating ourselves ... but there are other good investment possibilities out there for income investors. We included one in this book, that was the possibility of selling covered call options. You can use that to generate income now or to magnify the impact of compound interest by reinvesting the money you get from premiums. Another investment that people oriented toward dividends should consider is investing in bonds, which can help generate more monthly income. It's not as lucrative as it once was, due to the lower interest rates we've had over the past 20 years, but it can still add to your income and provide some level of protection for your money. ETFs are a great way to invest in bonds and diversify beyond just investing in dividend stocks.

Buying stocks because they are cheap

Remember that sometimes you get what you pay for. That doesn't mean you have to buy the most expensive stocks on the market in order to build wealth using dividend investing but remember, some stocks might have a low price – because they are not a good investment. As we've noted before, a declining stock might try to use a high dividend payment or yield in order to try and attract investors, who otherwise aren't all that thrilled about investing in the company.

Now, sometimes, a company that is set for better days in the future might have a low share price. Remember, to figure out where the company stands, you need to look at the company's fundamentals. Look to see how things are changing over time and research the company to see what new products are coming out and so forth. Sometimes, a cheap stock really is a bargain, but you can't go on price alone.

Being Afraid to let go

One of the downsides of dividend investors who by nature are going to be more conservative is that they sometimes can't let go of a stock that isn't worth holding anymore. It can feel like you're betraying your plans when you are investing with the hope of generating a lifelong passive income from dividend payments, and the stock starts performing so badly, it's clear to the mind but not the heart, that you need to get out.

Use the same muscles in your brain that you would use to evaluate a cheap stock you were thinking of buying and analyze the company. Read what the experts are saying about the company.

A good rule of thumb is to use three stock services to see what they are saying, so you could use Zacks and Morningstar plus one other as we discussed in parts of this book. If 2 out of 3 agree that something is a sell or a strong sell, then sell your shares and move on. You can use the proceeds from the sale to invest in a new stock or put it into an existing stock already in your portfolio that is already performing better.

Not taking your taxes into account

Remember, investing in the stock market isn't free, and any cash you take out is going to be taxed. You may not like it but that's the way things go. So, it's important to be familiar with the tax laws that apply to dividend stocks so you have an idea of what you're going to have to pay from the various profits you are making in this enterprise. You don't have to have the expertise of an accountant, but don't take money out and say you're going to worry about the taxes later. Have some idea of what the taxes might be and be sure to pay estimated taxes so that you don't find yourself falling behind later and then having a massive tax bill.

Another concern and this are the one I was really getting to when it comes to failing to take into account taxes, is that you overestimate your profits. When you figure taxes into your transactions, you might find out that your gains are not as great as you thought they were. If you are going to be building an income from dividends, it's a good idea to have an accountant rather than trying to fly alone using tax software.

Not Doing Due Diligence

The final mistake that we'll look at in our list is taking a cavalier attitude toward your investments. Many people don't put the time into studying the market and the companies they are investing in or want to invest in, and as a result, they don't invest nearly as well as they could. Rather than keeping abreast of what's going on, they just invest in what they feel like investing in. That could make the difference between making $26,000 a year or $75,000 a year from your investments. When you are going to buy a stock, you should be able to clearly explain to someone else the exact reasons that you would buy the stock and what you're expecting to get out of it, as far as both the dividend payments and capital appreciation of the shares.

Tax Implication

This part of the book is the least enjoyable. But let's face it; most of us don't know much of anything about how our complex tax code is going to be applied when it comes to the stock market and to dividends. If you're a beginning investor, that is definitely true. The first advice that should be given is that if you build up a large portfolio of stocks, you're going to need to use a professional accountant. But having some understanding of the general rules will help as well. Remember in the last chapter, one thing we mentioned is you don't want to get into a situation where taxes end up cutting into your profits.

Ordinary versus Qualified Dividends

The first thing to be aware of is the difference between ordinary and qualified dividends. The kinds of dividends that we've been talking about in this book are ordinary dividends. That means that the income from them is, well, ordinary. In other words, the proceeds are taxed as ordinary income.

A qualified dividend comes from a capital gain. Following the kind of investments that we have described in this book; you're probably not going to be getting qualified dividends.

Example: Suppose you're in the top tax bracket. You get $100,000 in qualified dividends. That is taxed at the capital gains rate, so you'd owe $20,000 in tax.

Example: You get $100,000 in ordinary dividend payments from your investment in IBM. Since they are more than $1,500, you have to fill out a schedule B and then report them with your 1040.

Tax Forms

The dividends that you get from an investment in dividend stock will be reported on a form 1099-DIV. If you are getting dividend payments from an s-corporation or trust, they will be reported on a form K-1. Note that investments in vehicles like an MLP will generate a K-1.

Dividends that you reinvest

Unfortunately, the geniuses in Congress didn't see that it was fit to prevent this in the interest of promoting investment, but dividends that you reinvest are still subject to tax, so you have to report any dividends that you receive on your tax return and pay taxes for ordinary income on them.

Example: You earned $25,000 in dividends, but you reinvested them buying more shares. You still have to pay the tax on them. Like the example above, they are more than $1,500, and so, you need to report them on schedule B of your 1040.

Some tricks to lower your tax burden

If you have an individual retirement account, your money in the account is allowed to grow tax-free. One downside is that the wise old men of Congress limit how much you can invest in an individual retirement account to around $5,500 -6,500 per year depending on age. However, there is a nice trick you can use with dividends inside the individual retirement account. You can use the account to buy dividend earning stocks.

Then, when the dividends are paid, they are paid inside your IRA. That means that they are tax-free, and you can reinvest them inside the IRA. Keep in mind that when the money is taken out of your IRA after you retire, if you have a traditional IRA, you're going to have to pay taxes on it at that time (a Roth IRA means you pay taxes on the money now, but the money is tax-free later when you withdraw it).

So, the procedure to avoid paying taxes on dividends is:
• Open an IRA or use an employer retirement account like a 401k
• Buy dividend stocks inside the retirement account
• Reinvest the dividends inside the retirement account
• That way you won't face taxes on the dividends
The same trick can be used to massively grow your retirement accounts using covered calls. So, you buy shares inside the IRA, and then sell covered calls with the IRA account.

Odds are good that most of the time the options aren't going to be exercised. So, you make, say, $2,500 profit a month selling covered calls, and it's inside your IRA, and it's going to be tax-free since the account is allowed to grow tax-free.

Then you use the funds from your covered calls to keep buying more shares. So, although you're only limited to putting in a relatively small amount each year after you've built up a few hundred shares, you can start earning money from selling covered calls and reinvesting the dividends. Then, when you start pulling money out of the IRA when you've retired, you will pay taxes on the money at that time.

Chapter 12: Introduction to Forex Trading

People trade currencies all the time but most do not trade for profit. If you have ever traveled to another country you probably weren't able to use your own currency from home. Whenever you went out to eat, took in a show, or bought a souvenir you had to use the local currency. So, you had to go to an exchange house to make an exchange. Conversely, when you returned home and you had extra money from the country you visited, you had to make another exchange. If you held onto the currency for an extended period of time you probably noticed a discrepancy in what you paid for it and what you got back over the length of time. This is the basic concept of trading on the Forex Market but on a much grander scale.

It is the foundation that Forex trading was based on. Of course, when you're trading on the foreign exchange things can definitely be a bit more complicated. Not only are there more things to keep your eye on when trading but you'll more than likely be dealing with huge sums of money at a single time. The Forex Market is a $5.3 trillion dollar a day industry and it is growing every minute. To put that into perspective, the New York Stock Exchange traditionally trades about $169 billion every day. Yes, big banks, corporations, insurance companies, and individual investors like you are trading many of the currencies used around the world on this very same market. Millions of dollars in profits and losses are happening every second and it is such a volatile market that its make-up is changing by the second.

No doubt, it is a whole new world of excitement and adventure if you can stand the pressure. Now, with the Internet feeding into nearly every house on the planet, you can easily enter this market, make these trades, and garner yourself a tidy profit all from the comfort of your own home.

561

By now, you've probably had a little practice in trading on the Forex Market and hopefully having enough success so that you want to kick it up a notch. Perhaps up until this point you've been simply dabbing in the market possibly playing a little on the Mini-Forex. Whatever it is that brought you here you have a lot to look forward to. The Forex Market can be a real gold mine for the right investor; the one who is sharp enough to see the brass ring and reach for it.

Here in this book we will include a list of proven strategies you can use to propel your trading skills forward so that you can make even more consistent gains and be astute enough to avoid many of the losses you are bound to incur. After reading these pages you will be able to:

•   Match the type of trading you do with your personal style of investment.
•   Know important indicators and identify them in chart patterns.
•   Select specific strategies to navigate the market and identify trends.
•   Avoid many of the mistakes that other traders make.

Consider this book an easy source of reference material that covers many of the concepts practiced when trading Forex. Here you will get an even better understanding of analysis and how it applies to Forex and build your confidence when it comes to maximizing your profits.

If you're ready to change your foreign exchange strategy and try something new and exciting then great profits await you in the following pages. Let's get started!

Chapter 13: What is Forex

Forex is without a doubt, the largest trading platform in the world. Its volume in daily trade is larger than most countries' total assets. At a daily trading rate of $1.3 trillion dollars the potential for huge profits is off the charts. People will tell you that they trade for the excitement, for the challenge, and for the rush but we know the truth. It all comes down to the money. Without the temptation of cash, you can get all of that other stuff on a Six Flags Roller Coaster.

The Forex Market, foreign exchange market, or the FX is the most liquid investment market in the entire world. Liquid investment simply means that one can take those assets and turn them into cash at a moment's notice. Yes, your profits earned on the foreign exchange are just as solid as those sitting in your savings account but with the potential to make you a whole lot more cash.

Before we delve right into the huge strategies that can make that happen, let's just have a quick review of the fundamentals involved with trading in foreign currency. Here are a few things that you need to remember:

- **Exchange Rate**: The exchange rate is the amount of money you have to pay to purchase foreign currency. This is a number that is in a constant state of flux depending on the supply and demand.

- **Currency Pairs:** Currency Pairs are the two currencies you are exchanging. The Forex Market is generally quoted in pairs. For example, the pair AUD/CAN simply represents the exchange of Australian dollars for Canadian dollars.

- **Base Currency:** When looking at a currency pair, the base currency is usually the first one listed in the pair. It is sometimes referred to as the commodity.

- **Counter Currency**: When looking at a currency pair, the counter currency is usually the second one listed in the pair. It is sometimes simply referred to as the money.

- **Major Currency Pairs:** The most commonly traded currency pairs around the globe are considered major currency pairs. These usually have a very high market liquidity and can maintain the tightest spreads. All Major Currency Pairs have USD as part of the pair. They include...

EUR/USD
GBP/USD
USD/CHF
USD/JPY
USD/CAD
AUD/USD
NZD/USD

- **PIPS:** This stands for Price Interest Point and is primarily used to determine the value of a currency pair. You might sometimes hear it referred to as a tick. It represents the smallest possible change in the value of the exchange rate of a specific currency pair.

- **A Lot:** A lot is the size of the trade you make. A nano lot is 100 units, micro lot represents 1000 units of currency. A mini lot is 10,000 units and a standard lot is 100,000 units. When you trade you will buy in one of these lot sizes.

- **Leverages:** It can be frightening to trade at such large amounts and it would be completely out of reach for the small investor. This is where leverage comes in. Leverage is the ability to borrow money to affect the trade. If a currency has a leverage of 50:1 for example, it means that you can trade a thousand dollars of currency for a mere $20 deposit. This is to hold the position open and is often referred to as the margin requirement.

It is important to understand though that leverage could be a dangerous tool in the hands of someone unprepared. While using leverage does make it easy to trade in quantities otherwise well out of your league one must also be prepared for the possibility of encountering losses as a result of the trade. In the case of the loss, the investor will have to find that money from somewhere to cover the difference.

Now that you've completed a basic review of the terminology, let's take a look at a few other bits and pieces that Forex traders need to be aware of.

Trading Sessions

You already know that the Forex Market is open 24/7, which mean that you can trade currency at any time of the day or night. Still, that does not mean that you can trade every currency at any time. Unless it is one of the major currencies, you'll have to make the trade at the time that country's exchange office is open. Let's take a look at the market hours for many of these major currencies.

City	Open (EST)	Close (EST)
London	3:00AM	12:00 Noon
Frankfurt	2:00AM	11:00AM
New York	8:00AM	5:00PM
Chicago	9:00AM	6:00PM
Tokyo	7:00PM	4:00AM
Hong Kong	8:00PM	5:00AM
Sydney	5:00PM	2:00AM
Wellington	5:00PM	1:00AM

As you can see, there are times when some markets are trading do not overlap with other countries. However, if you are trading one of the major currencies you should have no problem making a trade. But, if you're trading a minor, less popular currency, you'll have to find the best trading time and make sure you're available for it. As a final note on this point, the market is most active from the moment the London market opens until the New York market closes.

The peak trading time is when those two sessions are overlapped, which is primarily from 8:00AM to 12:00 Noon EST. Because this is the busiest time of the market, it is the perfect time to maximize your profits.

It is not hard to see why trading on the Forex Market is becoming increasingly popular. With the Internet now reaching nearly every corner of the earth, even the small-time investor has a chance to capitalize on the trillions of dollars that pass through their market on a daily basis. Not only is the market available to investors 24/7 there are a host of other advantages that make this type of trade so appealing.

• It is extremely liquid and investors can go long or short at any point.
• There is no bear market in that the potential to earn or lose is always present.

- Leverage also opens more doors for the small investor to trade currency.
- Forex trades come with very low commissions and a tight spread.
- International trade is easier than it ever has been.

No matter what you set out to do on the Forex Market, the potential for huge profits is high. Still, you definitely need a plan of action in order to make those profits happen and it starts with determining exactly what kind of trader you are.

Chapter 14: Understand your Trading Style

There are all kinds of people who trade on the foreign exchange. From business executives to housewives, from government officials to students, anyone who has the wherewithal to take on the fast-paced movement of activity, the risks, and the unpredictability, this is the market of all markets.

While there are a lot of people who are trading on the foreign exchange, they can be classified into three separate groups. As you read through the next few pages, try to find out which class best fits your goals as a trader. Each class of trader has their own goals and expectations from the market and while there is no clear-cut list of requirements, where you fall on this list will depend largely on your risk assessment, the amount of time you want to prepare, and a long list of other factors.

The Scalper

Scalpers are fast movers. They enter the market quickly and just as quickly move out. They tend to hold their trades for extremely short periods of times, sometimes only for a few seconds before they try to sell again. The scalper uses the market's volatility to their advantage. Get in, get out, repeat.

This pattern is likely to be repeated many times throughout a single day.

Interestingly enough, they make considerably smaller trades in comparison to other traders. Their means of profits however is primarily due to their frequency of trading rather than from holding investments for a longer period of time. To be an effective scalper there are certain characteristics that you must embrace.

• You must be able to make decisions at a moment's notice.
• You must have a strong emotional constitution to keep you from getting attached to the trade.
• You must function more like a machine when you're in trading mode.
• You must be able to accept losses quickly and move on to the next trade and not dwell on the negative.

Strategies That Scalpers Use When Trading
Scalpers know how to make quick profits and move on. In order to do this, they may mix and match several systems to get the job done. It is not unusual to see them scoping out 1-5-minute time frames on a chart in search of that quick buck.

The term 'scalping' is often used to refer to the regularly 'skimming' of small profits. They do this by entering and exiting positions repeatedly throughout the day in effect rarely holding a position for more than a few minutes at a time.

Their approach to trade seems very chaotic as they are in a constant search for the next quick profit turnover. They often refer to tick charts, 5-minute, or 1-minute charts to get the indicators they need. Some seek out high-velocity moves in the socio-economic arenas that can have an impact on the movement of prices. For example, releases of the nation's employment statistics or GDP numbers trigger a huge reaction on the market and the scalper is usually poised to take advantage of such announcements.

Why Scalp?

The scalper's strategy is to glean 5 to 10 PIPs from every trade. By repeating this process throughout the day, using high leverages, the profits can really mount up. Think about it, with a standard lot, the average PIP is valued at around $10. That means that if they are successful in skimming of 5 PIPs per trade and they do this 10 times a day, they are earning at least $500/day, a very profitable return for a part-time trader.

Who Scalps?

Scalping is not a skill that anyone can develop. You need to have very distinct characteristics to be a good scalper.

•   You must love sitting in front of the computer. You will have to sit there for hours on end.
•   You must be able to hold your concentration for long periods of time so you don't miss even the slightest opportunity. The opening may only be available for a few seconds before it disappears.
•   You must be able to react quickly and not overthink every move. Scalpers do everything fast; analyzing every move could slow you down and you'd lose many opportunities to trade and turn a profit.

Scalping Strategy

Like all Forex trades, research is at the very core of your career. While Forex is an international market it is still unregulated so it is up to you to know how much margin is required and what your options are in case of a loss.

While you can trade on your own through a trading platform it is highly recommended that you use a broker to facilitate the trades for you. Many offer special extras that can assure you get on the right path to success. Still, the platforms that one broker uses can be very different from other platforms so learn all you can about them, even missing one detail could turn out to be very costly.

Liquidity

Scalpers look for the most liquid markets, which are usually found in the major currency pairs. Even among the primary currency pairs, some currencies tend to be more liquid than others. The best time to trade these markets is when they overlap. This is the time when you find the potential for higher profits.

Insurance

Scalpers always make sure they have more than one escape route. Most work online and they need to react fast. What is your alternate plan for exiting a trade if you lose Internet connectivity? This is why working with a broker is beneficial. If something goes wrong your broker can step in and close the transaction. They also have on hand other plans that can get them out of a trade quickly.

One of the main rules for scalpers is to look for trends in the charts. They usually use 5-minute and 1-minute charts to find the best times to enter and exit a trade. They are always looking for the trends.

•   They first study the 5-minute chart to find the current trend. There is a saying among traders on the Forex Market. A

Trend is Your Friend, and there is no place where this truth exists than on the Forex Market. Keep in mind that there is psychology involved in market movement and it is psychology that determines much of the activity that leads to these trends. It is important to know how to identify these trends if you want to be effective at technical analysis. As a general rule, if an investor has found an uptrend, they will stick it out while they look for any sign that it's going to reverse. When that sign appears, they quickly exit the trade and walk away with their profit. The primary trends they are looking for are bullish and bearish but there are at least three possible trends that they need to know about.

• The Bullish Trend: To find the bullish trend using the 5-minute charts...
• Look for candles that are making higher highs and higher lows.

• Check the price – If it is more than 5-EMA (Exponential Moving Average) then it is a bullish trend.

Once you've found the bullish trend look for the same trend on the 1-minute chart.
• Search for a reversal candle (this may be formed after a correction in price. If you find the reversal candle (it could also be called a hammer, doji, morning star) on the 1-minute chart, they enter the trade above the closing price for that candle.
• Make sure the stop-loss is only a few PIPs down from the reversal candle.
• Finally, exit the trade after the 1-minute candle closes below the 15-EMA.
• The Bearish Trend: To find the bearish trend follow the same steps as listed above but instead check for the lower lows first on the 5-minute chart and then again on the 1-minute chart. If the lower highs are below the 5-EMA mark then it is bearish.

571

• Another option is to look at the current price. If it is below the 5-EMA on the 5-minute chart, then you can conclude it is bearish.

Once you've determined that the short-term trends are bearish do a search for similar entries based on the 1-minute chart.

• Find the bearish reversal candle on the 1-minute chart. It should be located after a pullback or a price reversal. Enter the trade just underneath the closing price of the reversal candle.

• Place the stop-loss only a few PIPs above the high of the reversal candle.

• Exit the trade when the 1-minute candle closes above the 15-EMA.

• The Neutral Trend: The only trend a scalper wants to avoid is the neutral trend. These trends are neither bullish nor bearish.

The Intraday Traders

The Intraday Trader doesn't work as fast as the Scalper. They usually hold their trades for a little longer. While they may make some trades that last only a few minutes it is not uncommon for them to hold onto them for a few hours. Because of this they make fewer trades per day but the flip side is that they can turn higher profits or losses with every trade.

Basically, Intraday trading happens when there is a position that can be opened and liquidated within a typical trading day. It is considered to be one of the most difficult kinds of trade you can do yet it is very popular for a number of reasons.

1.   The small size of the investment

2.   The ability to gain huge advantages from margin trading and leverage

3. The ability to take on several positions throughout the day

4. It has the potential to be more profitable than long-term trading

The Intraday Trader has a very difficult challenge in that the results of his market are often influenced by numerous market noises and daily fluctuations. Therefore, all traders need to be sharp enough to catch the small fluctuations that can range from as little as a few PIPs to as many as a few hundred.

Just like other traders in the market, the sole purpose of the Intraday Trader is to earn profits. Their ultimate goal is to take advantage of the fluctuations in the prices to make more money.

The Intraday Personality

• Independent: Most traders work from home without someone telling them what to do or when to do it. To be successful you have to be self-motivated and thrive in a controlled setting.

• Decisive: This type of trader needs to make decisions fast. Since the market can change quickly a good trader must be able to process information quickly and come to a decision. They rely a lot on their own experience but also from having a good understanding of research and preparation before coming up with a strategy.

• Disciplined: They need to stay on task even when there are distractions around them. They are determined enough to come up with a plan and stick with it until it no longer works to their benefit.

• Open-Minded: Traders need to follow profitable strategies to their conclusion even if they don't see immediate results. They are willing to try several strategies one right after another, continually improving their technique until they find what works best for their situation.

• Technically Savvy: This does not mean you have to be an expert at computer programming but you should be able to know how to navigate a trading software program effectively and be willing to try new programs as they become available. Bottom line, you need to stay well ahead of the curve.

• Financially Secure: While they don't have to be independently wealthy, they do have to have enough liquidity to be able to trade and cover their losses. They should always keep some reserve cash on hand just in case.

Intraday Strategies

The basic idea behind Intraday Trading is very similar to that of Scalping. They first determine if the trend is bullish or bearish but using a higher time frame (up to 30-minutes). Once the trend is determined, they enter the market following the trend but at a lower time frame.

Ideally, the best time frame for Intraday Trading is a combination set up consisting of 3-minutes and 15-minutes. While this may not be a hard and fast rule, it seems to work best for most traders.

There are several different strategies that can be used for Intraday Trading. As we mentioned earlier, Intraday Trading responds to what are called "noise movements," in the market. Basically, these are price movements without any explanation. They don't follow any particular trend and are often very confusing. It is usually after the fact that the trader fully understands these movements and what triggered them.

There is one other key difference between an Intraday Trader and a Scalper. An Intraday trader can be done with a neutral trend so they can utilize even more strategies to navigate the market than the scalper.

The Swing Trader

The Swing Trader is willing to hold their trades for an even longer period of time. While they could hold onto their trades for as little as a few hours, it is not uncommon to see them held for several days. It is the perfect middle ground for the trader. Unlike the Scalper, who has to spend most of his time buried deep in charts, analyzing even the slightest movement of the market, the Swing Trader is not so involved. The time he invests, while short, is not so committed but still opens the door to many investment opportunities that can bring in profits.

How long they hold onto their trades will depend largely on the timing of each trend. Swing Traders usually exit the trade as soon as their exit conditions are met or they realize their prediction was wrong.
With this type of trend, the profit potential is usually much higher than with Scalpers and Intraday Traders simply because they hold the trades for a longer period of time. Unfortunately, this is also the reason they need to have wider stop-losses in place. It is the only way to avoid taking on a negative hit during market volatility, the same is true for losses as well.

Swing Traders also face more risks because of the longer holds on trades. Since the Forex Market is open around the clock there is the possibility that losses can accumulate even after the exchange house closes for the day in the country where that currency is used.

Why Swing Trade?

There are two main reasons why someone would consider swing trading. First, unlike the Scalper or the Intraday Trader, swing traders do not need to check their charts so frequently. Because their plan is to hold the trade until their conditions are met, watching for the frequent fluctuations in the market is not necessary. If they have established a good stop-loss threshold there is no need for such close monitoring. For this reason, they tend to have a much more relaxed schedule, which is perfect for those who have busy lives, full-time jobs, or are otherwise committed.

This type of trading (also called position trading) is also not as stressful. Swing Traders are not looking for a gain every day. They are perfectly content to sit back and wait for the perfect time to harvest their earnings. Since they are in it for the long haul the amount of stress and anxiety is considerably less.

This is not to say that swing trading is a piece of cake. It still requires careful research and technical analysis to choose the right currency to invest in. However, those that are willing to dedicate the time to doing the proper research before the investment have a very good chance to make a go of it in swing trading.

Who Does Swing Trading?

The ideal person for Swing Trading has to be:

• Patient: because they must hold onto their trades for extended periods of time not knowing if their strategy will work.

• Has limited time to monitor their charts: It is better suited for those who already have full-time commitments like work or school but still have a lot of free time to keep abreast of the global scene.

• Calm: It can be difficult to withstand the pressure of watching trades going against you while you're trying to wait it out. Because there are numerous fluctuations during the shorter time frames it can look pretty scary until it is time to exit. If you've done your research well then you can trust your technical analysis and ride it out.

Who is Not the Best Person to be a Swing Trader?

Swing Trading is not for everyone. If you're a person who enjoys the faster pace of life, it is probably not for you. People who are often impatient and want fast results will probably be frustrated with this type of trading. If you tend to get emotional when you lose at something or you need to spend long hours watching your results you may find that you miss out on so much.

Whether you have a full-time job or you just have a little sense of adventure, make sure that your ability to manage this type of trade will be a very positive one.

The Goal of the Swing Trader

The Swing Trader's goal is to identify the "swings" in a medium length trend. They are careful not to enter a trade until they are confident they have a probability of profit.
There are a number of strategies that can be very effective for Swing Trading. We will begin to discuss many of these strategies in the following chapters but for now here are just two simple ones to start with.

Keep in mind that the amount of time determines the type of strategy Swing Traders use. While, the strategies listed here are used by Swing Traders they are predominantly technical strategies, which can be used by any type of trader. The key component and common ingredient are the support and resistance lines. A common thread in these are to:

1. Follow the trend.

2. Trade in a counter position to the trend.

Regardless of the approach you take, it can be an immense help to be able to see and recognize the price action. Remember that market movement does not move in a straight line. Even in conditions where the movement is in one direction, there is a constant push-and-pull happening as the trend performs. This creates a more step-like pattern rather than a direct line in one direction. In an uptrend, the market creates higher highs and in a downtrend the market creates lower lows.

Follow the Trend

When following the trend, the Swing Trader is looking to tap into and follow a short trend. They generally look for periods on the chart when the support and resistance levels are weak. This can be seen on a chart in a number of different ways. A trend could last for a few hours or it could last for a week or more. At some point during the trend, it is interrupted by short periods pulling it in the opposite direction. Afterwards, it will continue moving in the direction of the trend creating a sort of zig-zag pattern on the chart that is steadily moving upward or downward in the direction of the trend.

If it is an upward trend, you will see short bursts of downward movement before continuing its upward climb. However, you will also see that even those short bursts of downward movement are steadily rising as well. While the overall trend is steadily moving upward there is definitely a pullback that continues to interrupt the straight line.

On an uptrend, the Swing Trader is looking for the bullish swing. Once he has determined that the trend is going to continue before he invests. There is no sure-fire way to know how long the trend will last or at what point the pullbacks will start to strengthen and pull the direction back the other way but there are a few steps the Swing Trader makes to decide when to enter the game.

1.   Find the trend.

2.   Wait for the countertrend or the pullback.

3.   Enter the trade after the countertrend is exhausted.

The sign to look for is evidence that the market has begun to set higher lows once again. This is an indication that the pullback is over and the trend is moving again. Let's see how this works.

Let's say we're buying the currency pair USD/AUD at around 4:00PM in the afternoon. As we look at the chart we see there is an uptrend showing steadily rising highs but we also see the lows are also increasing. So, we decide to enter the market at 1.1082.

One of the first things you will do is put your stop-loss in place. Let's say we place it at the lowest point of the counter-trend that just occurred. Assuming the level was hit at 10:00PM two days earlier, we'll set the stop-loss at 1.1042. This means that we could lose as much as 40 PIPs before we can exit the trade.

This is a very basic and easy to follow strategy that could yield a risk-reward ratio of 1:2. There are 40 PIPs at risk so we'll place our limit 80 PIPs higher at 1.1162.

Assuming that the currency price reaches that point. At that point, you sell and you have earned a profit of 80 PIPs.

Another version of this strategy allows you to extend the profits even further. In that case, you would not set a limit and instead run the profit for a long as possible. There is no telling how long the trend will go or how high the market will rise so we avoid trying to determine a price target.

What we should always keep in mind is that the trend never goes in a straight line so we should fully expect the push and pull as the trend continues. That means that we have to be flexible enough to accept some negative pull along the way. It also means that once the trend breaks and the opposite trend takes over you will accept some losses before you actually realize what has happened and exit the trade.

To protect against this, traders place a stop at the lowest point of the past 20-hour low. This allows you to follow the trend and ride the wave but to get out when the trend reverses and moves in the other direction.

If we exited the trade at 1.1097, there is a profit of 15 PIPs. It would be considerably less than the profit in the previous strategy but it has the potential to bring a lot more profits if the trend continues. While investing this way can bring losses, usually the profits will outweigh such losses that may occur when the trend actually does reverse itself.

The Counter-Trend Strategy

The next strategy is to trade counter to the way the currency is trending so you can expect the opposite result. However, we will still use the same principle of searching out the short-term trends developing. The difference is with the Counter-Trend Strategy, the profits will come from the frequency of their breakdown. The same rules apply as in the first two strategies.

1.   Steadily increasing highs indicates an uptrend

2.   Steadily increasing lows indicates a downtrend.

3.   There will be a series of pullbacks before the trend resumes its direction.

With that information, a counter-trend trader will look to enter the trade when it is self-correcting its direction. Here's how to do this:

•   Identify and follow the uptrend.

•   When a new high follows a series of lows that break the highs, enter a short sale. (you are expecting a reversal)

•   If the market continues its trend you need to exit the trade.

This is a tricky strategy because of the unpredictability of the market. When the market reverses, it doesn't necessarily mean that the trend is broken. As we stated before, trade moves in an erratic pattern and is not consistently moving in just one direction. There is always a constant push and pull against the direction of the trend. So, when the market reverses, it could be only a small pull in the opposite direction or it could be the beginning of a new trend. The only way to be sure is to ride the wave and see where it takes you.

However, if it seems that the trend will continue, you must be humble enough to realize your prediction was wrong and take your losses.

All of the strategies we've discussed here are very simple and easy to follow. Still, for them to be successful you must be able to identify and understand the price action before you can be successful in Forex Marketing. The more you understand the ins and outs of price action the more likely you'll want to develop your own strategies to make sure that you trade in a way that will not only bring you confidence but reap huge rewards in the process.

Chapter 15 : Advanced Forex Concepts

Now that you have mastered all the fundamentals of Forex trading, it's time to delve a little deeper into the subject. In this chapter, you will learn the concepts and ideas that sit at the very core of the foreign exchange.

Average Directional Index

This is one of the more important indicators you'll find on your price action charts. It is used to determine whether or not a currency price is trending or if it is in a range. The term Average Directional Index (ADX) is a way to let the trader know how strong a trend is or if it is even a trend at all. In many instances, the ADX is the most important indicator of all you can use.

As a rule, when you trade in the direction of a strong trend it lowers the potential risk but boosts up the potential profit. But unless you have a way to measure the strength of a trend you still don't know where you stand. With just the basic strategies we've learned so far, all you can determine is whether or not it is a trend. The ADX can help to fill in the blanks. But before we can use it there are a few new terms we have to learn.

Moving Average: The moving average indicator is used to filter out the "noise" picked up by random price movements. It follows a trend or lags behind because it is based on the price history. There are two different types of moving averages.

1.   The Simple Moving Average (SMA) - an average determined over a defined number of time periods.

2.   Exponential Moving Average (EMA) - focuses on a range of more recent prices.

Moving averages are more commonly used in defining the trend direction, support and resistance levels.

The calculations of the ADX are based on the moving averages of currency prices over a set period of time. In most cases the time period is 14 bars however you can adjust this default setting to your specific needs.

Directional Movement (DI): An indicator used to identify if a definable trend is trending or not. It is very useful in determining what direction a price is moving. The DI can tell you when it is best to go long or short.

• When the +DMI is on top the trend is up
• When the -DMI is on top the trend is down.

The ADX is used to measure how strong the trend is regardless of which direction it is moving.

Many traders watch the ADX indicator carefully waiting for it to reach a value of 25 or higher. More aggressive traders will enter the market when it reaches 20 to get ahead of the game. Each is represented by a straight line across the chart. The line on top is referred to as the dominant DMI, which is stronger and more likely to show the actual direction the price is moving.

A plus Directional Movement (+DI) shows how strongly the price moves upward and a negative Directional Movement shows how strongly a price is moving downward. They will buy only when the+DMI line is higher than the -DMI line. You can find the DMI indicators on the price action chart by the where its line is located on the chart and whether it is thick or thin. A thick line represents the +DMI and a thin line represents a -DMI. When the trend reverses itself, the position of the two lines will cross. When the trend starts to decline the -DMI will be positioned on the top.

How it Measures Trend Strength

ADX values are used to distinguish stronger trends from the weaker and less stable ones. A low ADX is usually an indication of an accumulation of distribution. If the price remains below 25 for more than 30 bars, it is considered to be in a variety of conditions and the price patterns are pretty easy to pick-out. These prices will move upward or downward fluctuating between resistance and support levels. With a low ADX value, a trader knows that eventually the price will break its barrier and start a new trend and the opposite is true with a high ADX value.

While the ADX is an excellent tool for determining the strength of a trend, what it cannot do is determine when a trend is reversing. This is because as the ADX line continues to move upward past the 25-value mark, it can also move against the direction of the trend even when the price bars are still moving with the trend. If this happens, it can be difficult to determine if the trend is trying to reverse itself, is starting to slow down, or is consolidating in some way. For that reason, it is not recommended that you use the ADX to determine if a trend is ending or not.

It is important to understand that the ADX does not identify a trend or its direction, that is what the DI is for. So, the assumption that a declining ADX means the trend is ending is not accurate. What it does mean is that the trend is beginning to weaken and the price is entering a period of consolidation or retracement. This is a temporary reversal in the price of the currency; something that is pulling against the current trend.

Strategy for Using the ADX

There are several ways a trader can use the ADX value in trading. Since price is probably the most important sign you will read in a chart, every trader needs to first know the price and its history. Then they will read the ADX value to understand what is happening to the price. The information you gather together should give you a better picture than what the price alone can reveal. This is often the case with breakouts, which usually occur when the currency price is in consolidation. While some breakouts are the result of a disagreement between buyer and seller over price or some other matter, it can indicate a change in the balance of supply and demand.

The ADX value can tell you if this breakout is one that is going to last or if it is a dead end when it comes to trade. The ADX 25 threshold means that anything over that has a price that is strong enough to continue the breakout over a period of time. Using ADX as a Range Finder

The same rule applies in converse. It can be difficult to pick-up when a price moves into a range. The ADX value can tell you if a trend has weakened and is moving into a range situation. This happens when the ADX moves below the 25-value threshold.

When a price is in a range, its general movement is usually in a sideways direction and indication that the set price is agreed upon between the buyers and the sellers. You will see this by the ADX value also moving sideways under 25 where it will remain until the balance of supply and demand has another shift.

There will be signs to help you to identify when a price has fallen into a range.

1.   Use the ADX to find out if the price is trending or not.

2.   When trending, make your entry on the pullback and in the direction of the trend.

3.   When ranging, when there are reversals and support, trade long. When there is resistance, trade short.

Finally, here are a few tips to help you know when to do what:

When to Buy: If the +DA is higher than the -DI and the ADX and +DI are above the -DI and rising it is a good time to buy. The exit point is the point where the +DI falls below the -DI.

When to Sell: If the -DI is higher than the +DI and the ADX and the -DI is above the +DI. The exit point for this trade is when the -DI falls below the +DI.

Bottom Line: Trade on reversals at support (long) and trade on resistance (short).

Using ADX With Chart Patterns

When learning the basics of price movements, we learned that the price of a currency is really moved by the will of the people. It would be so much easier if we were able to just count the nuts and bolts of each transaction but there is often a psychological element to the price movement that we also have to factor in. The good news is that there are certain chart patterns that can help you to identify crowd behavior and trade accordingly. Understanding these chart patterns is essential to your success as a trader. There are quite a few of these chart patterns, which I am sure you will learn over time but for now, we'll only discuss the three most common patterns.

1. Bullish
2. Bearish
3. Continuation

Bullish Patterns

Once the currency price has declined for a period of time, you will notice some external behaviors affecting the price. These will create a bullish chart pattern. Some of these have been given names including:

- The Inverted Head and Shoulders
- Rounding Bottoms
- Double Bottom
- Triple Bottom

The Inverted Head and Shoulders: This pattern appears after a long drop in currency price. You will usually see this when a trend reverses from an already existing downtrend and starts back upwards. It usually happens in this order.

- The currency first goes through a downtrend then it rises again. This will appear like a trough on the chart. It becomes the first shoulder.
- The price then falls again and appears as a deeper trough, which appears like a head on the chart.
- The price falls and rises again but not as far as the second. This becomes the second shoulder.

The Rounding Bottom Pattern

Another very reliable pattern to know is the Rounding Bottom Pattern. Sometimes referred to as the Saucer Bottom, it is made from a long chain of price consolidations followed by a change to a bullish pattern.

It is formed from the following steps:

1. Starts with a long downtrend that creates a whole new low level. This makes up the rounding bottom and could take several weeks to form.

2. The prices then start a slow rise. This forms the right half of the pattern.

3. As the pattern climbs back up to the level where it started, a bullish confirmation is reached.

4.   The breakout begins and the prices begin a rapid climb.

Volumes: This pattern is an indication that there is a large volume of currency being traded. The volume starts on the high end, then declines to its lowest point, and then advances again as it steadily increases.

The Rounding Bottom does not need to follow a smooth line as it falls and then rises but instead can appear jagged with lots of highs and lows. It also doesn't need to be symmetrical but the general flow of the pattern should still be clear.

Traders using the Rounding Bottom pattern can:

• Buy long
• Exit short positions
• Plan target prices
• Choose their stop loss

And they can do this all with relative assurances that the pattern will play through. It is an ideal method for choosing the long-term movement of currency.

The Double Bottom Pattern

The Double Bottom Pattern shows a prominent bullish reversal pattern, which is made up of two almost completely identical troughs one right after the other. This pattern can be used as an indicator of a currency reversing from bearish to bullish.

Identifying a Double Bottom

The Double Bottom pattern can be identified by a major downtrend starting a few months before. The price will then drop into a trough where it will fall to a point lower than the current downtrend. This is the first bottom.

The price will then begin to rise again until it forms a peak, which is where it meets the resistance point where the price can advance no further.

The price will then start another decline where it will form a second trough.

Then it will rise again in price until it reaches the previous resistance level.

Once both bottoms are completed, the price will break out and start a new bullish trend.

Volumes: As the bottoms are formed the volume levels are very low with only a slight increase as it moves up to form the peak. The volume then falls again to form the second low. But as it advances from the second trough it begins to increase again until it ends up higher than when the price was first formed before the first trough.

Traders who use the Double Bottom can effectively select entry points for long positions, strategically plan their exit points on short positions, and know where to place their target price and stop-loss positions.

The Triple Bottom Pattern

The Triple Bottom Pattern is very similar to the Double Bottom with one additional trough before it takes a bullish reversal and rises in price. This pattern is not always easy to identify but once it is fully formed, it is a great way to identify when a trend is about to turn from a bearish downturn to a bullish uptrend.

Identifying the Triple Bottom Pattern

This pattern starts with a downtrend but there will be three attempts to push the price down through a support area. Each attempt will result in a trough at the bottom but it will eventually push through and turn into a bullish trend.

The Triple Bottom Pattern is very effective in showing a struggle between the buyers and the sellers. In the end, the buyers succeed in reversing the trend and pushing their way into a bull market.

The first trough is formed with a downtrend, then the price will climb to form a peak before dropping again to create the second trough. Once again, the price climbs again forming another peak before taking another dive downwards forming the third trough creating the third bottom. When the third bottom is formed, the price breaks through the neckline and the trend becomes bullish. Below is a picture of a Triple Bottom pattern.

Volumes: As you can see, the volume levels are very low when each of the bottoms are formed. A small increase in volume occurs during each of the peaks with the final rise through the neckline after the third bottom.

Traders can use the Triple Bottom pattern selecting the right long and short positions, identifying the target price and planning for stop-loss levels.

Bearish Patterns

With the Bearish Chart patterns, the price of the currency can increase for an extended period of time. This can trigger external factors that can cause the price to reverse. Some Bearish patterns you should know are the Head and Shoulders, Double Top, Triple Top, and the Rounding Top.

Head and Shoulders

591

The Head and Shoulders pattern predicts the reversal of a trend from bullish to bearish.

Identifying the Head and Shoulder Pattern

When the currency price happens in the following order it forms a Head and Shoulders pattern:

1.   An extended bullish trend

2.   The price begins to rise and form a peak

3.   Then it quickly turns downward creating a trough. This is the left shoulder.

4.   The price will begin another climb forming a peak that is higher than the highest price of the left shoulder.

5.   The price begins another decline to create an even deeper trough. This is the head.

6.   The price rises again to form a third peak but no higher than the first.

7.   Finally, the price falls again until it reaches the level of the first trough creating the second shoulder.

Think of an imaginary line running through the first and second trough. Consider this as the neckline. When you are sure you are looking at a Head and Shoulder pattern, it means the bullish trend is taken over by the bearish trend.

Notice that there is a definite uptrend in the currency price but as soon as the pattern is completely formed, the price breaks through the neckline on a downward spiral creating a bearish trend.

Volume: As the first shoulder is formed, the volume level is at a high point. The same is true when forming the head but when the second shoulder is completed, the volume drops even lower.

The Head and Shoulders pattern is considered to be one of the most dependable reversal patterns a trader can rely on. Using this pattern, a trader can confidently identify the ideal place to set their stop-loss level for their long positions and be able to choose short positions, and plan their target prices when taking their short positions.

The Rounding Top Pattern

Sometimes referred to as the "Inverse Saucer" the Rounding Top Pattern can be spotted at the end of a currency uptrend. A trader can detect a currency reverse from bullish to bearish with this pattern.

Identifying a Rounding Top Pattern

The Rounding Top pattern evolves in the following manner:

1. There is an uptrend that lasts for an extended period of time.

2. The price will rise even further until it creates a new high. This will be the highest point of the Rounding Top.

3. Once the high develops, the prices will begin to slowly drop forming the right half of the pattern.

4. When the pattern returns down to the reaction low, it creates a bearish trend and the prices will begin a quick spiral downward.

Volumes: With this type of pattern the volume levels tend to run high at the beginning of the price increase but will drop just as quickly after it peaks. As the price drops, the volume will see a gradual increase until it is the highest as the price breaks down.

With this pattern, traders will know when to exit their trades, how to choose new short positions, set their stop-losses, and plan their target prices.

The Double Top Pattern

Another bearish reversal pattern is the Double Top. A trader will usually observe this pattern at the end of a bullish run.

Identifying the Double Pattern

The Double Pattern unveils in the following order.

1.   A few months before the pattern begins there is a significant uptrend in price until a new peak price is form. This is the first top.

2.   The price begins to drop until it forms a trough. This creates a support area where the price cannot drop any further (the neckline).

3.   It pushes its way up again until it forms the second peak at the same level as the first top.

4.   The price will then experience another decline falling back down to the neckline once again completing the second top.

5.   After the two tops are completely formed, the price breaks down and the trend turns bearish.

Traders can use the Double Top pattern to choose the most favorable entry points when taking short positions, they can plan their exit points when it comes to long positions, choose target prices, and set up stop-losses.

Triple Top Pattern

The Triple Top pattern is a rare one. It appears as a bearish reversal signaling the end of a bull run.

Identifying a Triple Top Pattern

The Triple Top pattern unfolds in the following order.

1.   The currency starts as an uptrend before setting a new high in price. This is the first top.

2.   The price then begins a decline forming a trough. This makes the support area that prevents the price from falling any further (neckline).

3.   The price then pushes upward to create the second peak formed at the same point as the first one.

4.   The price begins another decline and turns back down towards the neckline, completing the second top.

5.   The same pattern repeats itself for a third time.

6.   When all three tops are formed, the price begins to breakdown and remains in the decline until it becomes bearish.

Traders can use this pattern to help them choose their entry points for short positions, exit points for long positions, and select a target price or a stop-loss.

Continuation Chart Patterns

There are other types of chart patterns that a good currency trader should know about. These can be:

1. Flag Patterns
2. Bullish Rectangle
3. Bullish Pennant

These often develop during an uptrend and are an indication that the trend will continue on for some time. However, whenever the patterns fall they indicate a downtrend, thus they are named:

1. Flags
2. Bearish Rectangle
3. Bearish Pennant

These tell us that the current downward cycle is expected to continue.

The Rectangular Pattern

When your chart shows a flag pattern has developed during an uptrend it is an indication that the price will continue on moving upward in a bullish trend for an extended period of time.

The Triangle Pattern

With an Ascending Triangle, it is an indication that the price will move in an upward direction. When it is a Descending

Triangle, it is an indication that the price will continue on a downward trend.

The Fibonacci Retracement

A very useful indicator for traders is the Fibonacci Retracement, which is used to locate areas where the currency price receives support or resistance.

If there is a lot of price movement either upward or downward, there is evidence of support or resistance in what is call the Fibonacci retracement levels. These levels remain consistent and will not change.
These levels are created first by drawing a trend line from the high to the low prices. The idea is to take two extreme points (the highest high and the lowest low) and then divide the vertical distance by the key Fibonacci ratios (23.6%, 38.2%, 50%, 61.8%, and 100%).

This indicator is one of the most popular among traders. Once the levels are identified, they draw horizontal lines at these points and use them to identify where support and resistance levels may be. But before we can fully grasp these ratios and how they are used we need to take a closer look at the Fibonacci sequence in general.

The Fibonacci sequence is a series of numbers as follows:
0, 1, 1, 2, 3, 5, 8, 13, 21, 35, 55, 89, 144 .....

Every number in the sequence is simply the result of the two preceding numbers. The sequence can continue indefinitely. The interesting point about this is that each number is valued at exactly 1.618 times greater than the number before it. It is this relationship that exists between every number in the sequence that becomes the very foundation that determines the rations used in retracement.

Let's take the key Fibonacci ratio of 61.8% - sometimes called "the golden ratio" is found simply when you divide one number in the sequence by the following number. This formula looks like this:

8/3 = 0.6153, and 55/89 = 0.6157

The same general rule applies when you use the 38.2% ratio. By dividing one number in the sequence by the number that is located two places to the right as follows:

55/144 =0.3819

You can do this again with the 23.6% ratio by taking any number in the sequence and dividing that number by the number three places to the right.

8/34 + 0.2352

No one fully understands why but these ratios seem to have an important role to play in a wide range of things that happen in our lives. Consistently they have been used to determine crucial points in the market that can have a major impact on the way currency prices move as well. It seems that the direction of the trend before is expected to continue once the currency price has retraced itself back to one of the ratios listed above.

From these ratios, a trader can locate the levels up to where the currency price could correct. These levels can be labeled as supports or resistance depending on the movement of the currency.

Using the Fibonacci levels, traders can take on new trades, be pretty sure where to place their stop-loss levels, set target prices, and know when to exit a trade.

Chapter 16: Advanced Forex Strategies

For the advanced trader, it is not enough to know the strategies to use when you're trading currency. All of the ones listed so far have proven to be effective in the past and have led many a trader to a successful trade. The question that remains is whether or not you want to use a ready-made strategy and apply some methodology recommended from your broker or if you want to trust your hand with taking one of the many free strategies offered online.

While a free strategy may be an exciting way to get your foot in the market door, you have no way of knowing its track records, how effective it worked and what kind of traders found success with them. Many of them are just new, untested ideas, and there is no way to know what that strategy will do for you.

The strategies offered here have already been tested and proved worthy of being a part of your arsenal.

The Bladerunner Trade

This strategy is one of the most popular price action strategies among traders. It uses pure price action to find the perfect entry points. The tools you use for the Bladerunner are candlesticks, pivot points, round numbers, and support and resistance levels.

What you don't need are chart indicators unless you really want them for additional assurance. If you choose to use an indicator, many traders use the Fibonacci retracement or the 20 Exponential Moving Average (EMA) discussed earlier in this book.

You can use the Bladerunner with any currency pair and it can be used in any time frame but with this exercise we'll keep it down to the 5-minute charts. While it can be used at any time of the day, it will probably work best when you use it during one of the busier trading sessions.

This strategy has been aptly named the Bladerunner because it works like a knife to divide the price.

Trading Signals

Trading signals with this strategy are usually sent when the currency prices are trading below the EMA, they may test the EMA several times before sending out the signals. This can happen both in the bullish direction and the bearish direction in reverse.

When the price exceeds the 0-EMA threshold, the bias is on the bullish side. Naturally, we would expect that at some point the price would attempt to move down, hit the 20-EMA, and then begin another ascent continuing its upward movement. The same theory is true if the price is below the 20-EMA. You can anticipate an upward movement until it touches the 20-EMA and then reverses itself and continues on its downward movement.

But what happens if the price doesn't follow these expectations and a few candlesticks are able to close above or below the EMA in the opposite direction? One can assume that at some point very soon the price will begin to move in a whole new direction, but only after it has retested the 20-EMA several times.

Bladerunner Strategy

There are two requirements a trader must look for in order to apply the Bladerunner strategy.

1.   The price must first break out of its range and is unable to consolidate. It must be trending at the time.

2.   It must attempt to retest the 20-EMA several times.

1.   Use candlestick formation to predict when the price will hit the 20-EMA.

2.   Place a short-term trade at the point when the price starts to retest the 20-EMA.

3.   Place a separate trade when the price has rebounded in the direction of the original trend.

4.   At the point where the candlestick rebounds to the 20-EMA, look for it to close in the same direction it came from, to avoid getting caught in a fake out.

The Daily Fibonacci Pivot Trade

This strategy combines the Fibonacci retracements with daily, weekly, monthly, and yearly pivots. The strategy is also based on the Fibonacci sequence and uses the same critical points we see on the charts that show the price having strong support or resistance. If you are looking to enter a new trade you need to know when the prices are approaching these Fibonacci pivot points.

The Fibonacci Pivot Trade utilizes three reference points. If your position is bullish then you want to factor in the range from the last low to the most recent high and then back to the most recent low. This will give you a top side extension.

On the other hand, if your position is bearish, you need a range that takes the most recent high, the last low, and then back to the most recent high. This will give you a downside extension. No one is entirely sure why but the market seems to be attracted to the 100% Fibonacci extension level (equal legs that extend from the highs and lows) but this strategy has a very strong track record.

Using the Fibonacci extension levels will give you a better ability to predict the direction the market is going. But with this strategy, we are not going to use this by itself but in conjunction with the pivot points on the chart. The point where the market pivots and turns in another direction starting a whole new trend.

Guidelines for Buying

1.   Wait for the 100% Fibonacci extension to be reached.

2.   Wait for the daily close.

3.   Only enter the trade in conjunction with a pivot point (make sure you stay above the pivot point to keep it valid.

4.   Set the stop-loss at 10 PIPs below the pivot point.

5.   Exit at 50% retracement.

Guidelines for Selling

1.   Wait for the 100% Fibonacci extension to be reached.

2.   Wait for the daily close.

602

3. Only sell when in conjunction with a pivot point (make sure that you stay below the pivot point).

4. Set your stop-loss at 10 PIPs above the pivot point.

5. Exit at 50% retracement.

The Bolly Band Bounce Trade

This is a well-known strategy used by all kinds of traders, which relies on the principle of reversion to the mean. It happens when prices are found at the extreme ends of the outer bands. When this happens, prices tend to pull back to the mean. In the beginning, the Bolly Band Bounce was traded when prices fell to the lower Bollinger Band and sold when the prices had climbed to the upper Bollinger Band. Now, if you apply this methodology it can be difficult to avoid losses. This is primarily because prices tend to hover at the edge of the band, especially when it is at the extreme outer bands.

So, the question remains. How do you effectively use the Bolly Band Bounce and avoid incurring losses? There are three different ways to do it.

Use Candlesticks for Confirmation

You can always use candlestick patterns as a back-up strategy to make sure that the prices will actually bounce off the outer bands and reverse back towards the mean. Consider the candlestick patterns when the price is approaching the outer bands, this can help to make the trade more effective.

Use Divergence

When prices trade near the outer bands, compare the highs/lows to the oscillator to find the divergence. This is one of the easiest ways to find trend changes that are about to happen.

Support/Resistance

You can also look for support or resistance levels in both the horizontal direction as well as with trend lines. Each time prices begin to approach the outer bands, traders can enter a trade using either a long or short position by simply booking prices to the mean Bollinger band or they could target the next support or resistance level.

It is easy to see why so many like using the Bolly Band Bounce. It is a very flexible strategy that can be adapted to several different types of technical analysis. It is this flexibility that allows it to be incorporated into other existing strategies that can be used as a complement for price action trading.

The Forex Dual Stochastic Trade

Stochastic oscillators can be a very useful tool for forex traders. You might want to use these oscillators in conjunction with other market indicators but your results may not be as stellar as you hope. Even one stochastic oscillator alone may not be enough to yield the kind of results you want.

However, when you use a Dual Stochastic Trading system, it can make a huge difference in the quality of the opportunities you find. If used with the right parameters they can let you know when a currency pair is trending but is still overextended during a short-term retracement.

The strategy concentrates on trading when two indicators are showing completely opposite values. By using both the fast and the slow stochastics when they are about to reach their limits, it opens up a trading opportunity.

Understanding the Single Stochastic Strategy First

With the single stochastic strategy, it compares a currency pair's closing price with its overall price range over a given period of time. The line you see marked %K shows the current market price and the line marked %D is there to "soften" the %K line and shows the price as a moving average.

There are three types of stochastic oscillator indicators: fast, slow, and full. The one marked fast is based on the original equation %K and %D. When looking at the fast version, the %K will appear to be rather choppy and inconsistent, and %D shows a three-day moving average for %K.

In previous stochastic strategies, reliance on %D to find buy and sell signals was common practice. Traders would only use a single indicator (the %D) called a "signal line."

Because the %D in the "fast" oscillator was used to create signals, it stands to reason that the "slow" oscillator was used to take advantage of this feature. The slow oscillator used a three-day SMA to "soften" the %K.

The basic formula for the stochastic oscillator is:

%K is 100 X [Closing Price - Lowest Price of N time periods] / [Highest Price of (N - a lesser number) time periods]

This equation determines the range between the high and low prices over a specified period of time. The currency pair's price is shown as a percentage of that range with 100% representing the top limit and 0% at the bottom.

The Fast Stochastic Formula

Fast %K = the basic %K calculation

Fast %D = a three-period simple moving average of Fast %K

The Slow Stochastic Formula

Slow %K = Fast %K softened by applying a three-period simple moving average.

Slow %D = a three-period simple moving average of Slow %K

The Full Stochastic

Full %K = Fast %K softened by an N-period simple moving average

Full %D = an N-period simple moving average of Full %K

In many cases, the values used for the "N" in the formula are the time periods of 5, 9, or 14 units. Some traders set N at 14-time periods so that they can get enough data to sample more meaningful calculations. There are no hard and fast rules in this regard and you're free to experiment with any time period you choose.

The Dual Stochastic Trading Strategy

Now that we understand the single stochastic trading strategy, it will be easier to grasp the fundamentals of the Dual Stochastic Formula, which works in contrast with the formulas listed above.

This strategy is based on a combination of the fast and the slow stochastic while waiting for opportunities when the two indicators are at opposite ends of the spectrum. The only other indicator needed is the 20-EMA, and that's only if you really need it. Here are your parameters:

For the Fast Stochastic

1.   %K period is 5
2.   %D period is 2
3.   Slowing is 2
4.   Fixed minimum is 0
5.   Fixed maximum is100

For the Slow Stochastic

1.   %K period is 21
2.   %D period is 4
3.   Slowing is 10
4.   Fixed minimum is 0
5.   Fixed maximum is 100

Enter the results of both in the same window on the MetaTrader chart and enter your settings in the dialog box.

When to Enter and Exit a Trade

1.   This type of strategy, while simple, is best used with a mechanical trading system that has been programmed to identify trailing stops and stop-losses to ensure that you can ride the wave for as long as possible.

2.   It also works best with the shorts.

3.   Place the stop-loss order at 20 PIPs above the entry point. This will move the trailing-stop order behind the current price level in successful trades at about a distance of 10 PIPs.

Chapter 17: Types of Traders

While we've been hearing stories of many millionaire traders who did very well in the market, there are many other people who run into huge losses. If you want to succeed in the financial market, you have to develop a trading plan and then use that plan as a yardstick to guide all trading activities.

Generally speaking, you can either be a trader or an investor. Even though both traders and investors play in the same market, they do it differently. Warren Buffett, the Oracle of Omaha has been recognized as the richest and most successful investor of all time. George Soros is also a success in the stock market, but he plays the game in a different way.

Usually, investors have a long term view. This could be a year, a decade or three decades. They analyze and evaluate a stock, buy the stock and hold the position for a very long time to collect dividends. The game of the investor is dividends. Investors want to compound their monetary value over a long term period. Therefore, they evaluate a company, buy their stock and hold it for many years. The investor is not worried about the rise and fall of a stock price. The main income-generating stream of the investor is an inflow of annual dividends.

There is another way of playing the game. Instead of buying a position in a company and then holding it for years to collect a dividend, you can choose to buy the position at a lower price and then sell it at a higher price to make a profit. This form of playing in the financial market is known as trading because it focuses on buying securities at one price and then selling them at another price to make a profit. The accumulated profit over a long period of time tends to yield a greater return. This is where many people are entering the financial market.

Today, millions of people are becoming security traders by learning about volatility, price trends, and patterns in the market and how to play the game to win. The securities traded in the financial market include options, stocks, index, commodities, futures, and currencies. Each financial instrument varies from the other, therefore, the trader needs to learn and understand the fundamentals of each market and the best way to approach. Once you get to know the securities and where you want to focus your time and attention, you need to then develop a trading style. This is where swing trading, trending trading, day trading, scalp trading, and all others come in.

When people refer to retail, 'stay-at-home' traders they often call these people day traders. Retail traders can fall into many different categories depending on the type of strategy they employ. But what is the difference between a swing trader and a day trader? Is there a difference?

If you are a retail trader, then there are three categories that you could fall in to. Traders can either be classified as day traders, swing traders, or long-term position traders. You might even fall into more than one of these categories. You could use a mix of all three. The key difference is in the time frame of the position that these three types of traders will use. The three types of trades also require traders with different mindsets and strategies. They require a different degree of focus on the market, and some types of trades require a more active trader.

We talked earlier about the different types of trends, and how long they last. The trader who works with the shortest time frame is the day trader. The day trader looks to ride small, short term fluctuations that last less than a day. A day trader will be less focused on the overall trend in the market, and more focused on the small adjustments that happen throughout the market during a single given trading day. When the market opens, the day trader will have no positions from the day before. Instead, they will choose all new positions. By the time the trading day ends, the day trader will have exited all the positions they chose at the beginning of that day. Day traders can utilize short selling, options, and bullish techniques to make a profit.

Day trading tends to lean heavily on technical analysis. A day trader might be less concerned with the actual company than with the patterns in the company's stock on a given day.

The downside of being a day trader is a time commitment. Most day traders use day trading as their main source of income; spending the entire day from market open until close watching movements in the stock market. You can't really be a passive day trader. In order to day trade successfully, you need to have enough time on your hands that you can monitor your positions minute by minute and make decisions as things unfold in the market.

Because the movements in day trading are typically small, the profits are also small. This means that a day trader relies on a high number of smaller successful trades. Hopefully, when you add up all your trades, you will have enough money to pay the bills. This means that a day trader must have a larger amount of starting capital in order to make the profits of day trading worth it. If you don't have a good amount of capital and a willingness to quit your day job, day trading isn't the most practical option. In fact, I recommend that people shouldn't even consider day trading unless they have a healthy amount of experience in the stock market. Most people who attempt to become day traders will fail.

Sure, it is possible to make a lot of money very fast as a day trader. But that means its also possible to lose as much money, just as quickly. Day trading isn't a safe way to get rich, and its not a trading strategy for novice traders. It requires an in-depth understanding of the intricacies of the stock market, and the discipline to study and make high-stress decisions.

If you imagine day trading to be a laid back, work from home type of job, then you'd be mistaken. Day trading is a high-risk pursuit. Day traders must make decisions in a matter of minutes, or even seconds, about high volumes of their hard-earned money. The job does have its benefits; you can work from home and make your money independently of a boss. You don't have to commute to an office every day and you can take a day or two off without getting approval from HR first. These benefits are attached to a job that can be high risk, with a high degree of day traders burning out not long after their first trade.

But there is an alternative option. The risks and the rewards are slightly lower, as is the required investment of time and money. If you picked up this book, then you probably already know that day trading may not be the most feasible option for you as a trader. As a swing trader, you can still maintain a day job if you have access to a smartphone or a computer intermittently throughout the day. For a trader who is still learning the ropes, swing trading gives you more time to consider your positions which mean that the stress factor is slightly lower for a swing trader. Rather than being forced to make a guess on a position in a matter of a few minutes, swing traders can consider their next move over the course of a few hours or an entire day before they decide.

If you picked up this book, then you're interested in the second type of trading. Swing trading is like day trading; you're watching for short- and medium-term positions dependent on smaller adjustments in the overall trend. Swing traders have more time. The medium-term trends tend to move more which means that a swing trader will have the opportunity to profit more from one trade, but they will make fewer trades than the day trader. Slightly larger margins mean that a swing trader doesn't need quite as much capital when they initially invest.

If you want to trade actively, but you don't have the experience or the capital to trade full time, then swing trading is a good option. If you can monitor your portfolio from your phone or work computer, then you should be able to operate as a swing trader. The biggest factor in choosing what type of trader you want to come down to the lifestyle you want and skill level you possess.

The third type of trading that people employ is long term and position investing. While this type of trading doesn't really fit within the scope of this book, many swing traders and day traders will choose to hold these types of positions in order to diversify their strategies. A position investor will plan to hold on to a stock for a significant period; choosing a stock that they think is undervalued or has the potential for growth in the future. Fundamental analysis is the most important thing to a position investor. If you are interested in a company over a long period of time, then you will analyze the fundamentals of stock before deciding to invest. A position investor will probably expect to hold their position for years, using their investment as more of a savings tool than an active trading tool.

Position investing is considered the lowest risk form of investing. If you have a well-diversified investment portfolio then the average of all your stocks should go up over time. If you hold onto those investments through all the dips and peaks, then your initial investment will hopefully have grown.

The most important consideration for choosing which type of time frame strategy you want to use will be dependent on your personality. What is your temperament and ability to handle stress, and how much time do you have to commit to trading? There is nothing wrong with choosing the lower risk route of position investing with the occasional swing trade. In fact, most retail investors and traders fall within this category. For many people, this is the right place to be. If you are more risk-averse, then the stock market may serve better as a savings tool than as an active source of income.

There is a whole spectrum of trading that you can take part in, from position investing to day trading. The trick is to find the strategies and the level of participation that suits your life and your willingness to take risks. If you figure out what type of strategies suit you then you will be more likely to stick with trading and less likely to suffer from the burnout that is common among new traders who bite off more than they can chew. It's not a bad idea to start trading with simpler strategies and slowly move towards more active types of trading. Most experienced traders will have a portfolio that contains a mix of different types of investments with different time-oriented strategies. You can be a swing trader and a day trader and a position investor all at once. Just make sure you know what you're doing so that you don't overwhelm yourself.

There is also a difference in the amount of capital required to begin trading with any of these strategies. Day traders require the most amount of capital to begin. Most day trading accounts require a minimum investment of $25,000. This is not a small amount of money, and more than most beginner investors are willing to use. They require more money because their margins are smaller.

Swing traders require less. You can start a swing trading account with as little as $5000. It would be difficult to swing trade with any amount of capital much lower than that. Some people manage to swing trade with accounts that are as small as $1000, but this makes it difficult to diversify. If you're a long-term position investor, then there is really no minimum threshold. However, the same problems exist for long term investors; with less money, it will be more difficult to diversify, especially if you are managing your portfolio independently.

Levels of Traders

There are various levels for traders in the financial market: beginner, intermediate and advanced. Your knowledge, experience, and profits over time enable you to determine your level of trading ability. Most brokers would want to know your level of trading to enable them customized offering to meet your needs. Thus, before you learn about the swing trading overview, you might want to look at the three kinds of traders in the financial market and know where you belong.

Beginners

A beginner trader in the financial market is looking for ways and means to make a profit in the market by minimizing losses and without risking so much investment capital. Many beginner traders, today, prefer options trading because of the flexibility of enabling them to own options to buy particular security without bearing the risk of buying it upfront. Many of these beginner traders have their own jobs, buy study and learn about the financial market to develop a second stream of income through capital gains.

Intermediate Traders

These people have a certain amount of experience and knowledge in the financial market. They understand the game and have a way of analyzing securities. The intermediate traders may trade stocks, commodities, and options. They know how the market works, understand how to time the market and have made a considerable amount of wins in the market. The intermediate trader may not be the one with the millionaire portfolio account to manage, but they are people how to understand and know what they are doing.

Advanced Traders

These are the professional traders with sophisticated methods, strategies, and schemes of analyzing the market developed through years of trading activities. They manage a high amount of money in their portfolio, therefore, they seem to take much more calculated risks than the intermediate or the beginner traders. Some of these advanced traders may engage in day trading or even trend trading for a while. They are professionals who even trade full time in the financial market, either for themselves or on the behalf of their clients.

Is Swing Trading Right for Me?

If you are looking to make some money in the stock or any other financial market, there are various ways of doing that. Even though swing trading has become a popular trading style of the majority, you have to analyze yourself and see if swing trading is right for you.

The punchline is that you don't have to follow the masses and do what everyone else is doing. You need to do a good analysis of yourself and choose a trading style that works best for you. It should come from a good analysis of your trading & exit plan and your temperament. There are various trading styles you can adopt to increase the value of your portfolio in the stock market.

But you need to make sure what you have chosen meets your personality, temperament, knowledge, experience and trading plan. If you choose what works best for you, it will ease of trading and moving forward even when the going gets tough. You need to understand the level of emotional intelligence required to be successful with each trading style.

Typically, investors always want to hold the position of stock for years and decades. These people tend to be "emotionally immune" to stock price fluctuations in the market. They don't really care about the interest rates and the demand forces increasing or decreasing the value of their stock holdings. They look to the company which sold the stock to generate returns for their investments. They learn to stay calm and be emotionally stable in an upward market and a downward market.

On the other hand, if you are looking to get into day trading, swing trading or even trend trading, you need to watch your emotions. Temperament and emotional intelligence play a big role in being successful with any trading style. If you are fearful and risk-averse, you might be looking for a more safer trading style that meets your personality.

Also, if you are risk-tolerant and risk-loving, you might want to look for a trading style that will maximize your strength. Whichever way, you need to make sure you look at the downside of each trading opportunity before making a move. Always try to make sure you know an understand the trading style you want to use and how it matches with your goals, plans, and aspirations.

Day Trading

As the name implied, day trading simply means a financial trading style that does not get overnight. A day trading lasts only for a day. Traders are looking for volatile stocks they are observing or experiencing price movements to ensure that they achieve a considerable amount of success. Usually, day trading lasts from a few seconds to hours in the day.

The trading session closes with the close of each business day. Traders do not get the chance to hold their financial positions overnight. These are where many options, volatile stocks, currencies, and commodity trading comes. To be successful as a day trader, you need to have a keen eye on the market and mapping the trend and price patterns of financial securities.

You need to also be very good in the use of technical analysis to forecast and predict new price movements in the financial market to be able to earn a substantial amount of profit. You also want to make sure you know how to read the daily charts, 60-minutes charts, 30-minutes charts and all other charts to gain better insight into the securities in the marketplace.

Swing Trading

While day trading expires after each business day, swing trading continues for days and even several weeks. You can say that the next step in the time horizon ladder of trading is the swing trading. The time structure in this trading style reveals the fact theta the underlying financial security will have to take time before experiencing a swing in stock price to realize a profit.

Some swing traders who seem to be fundamental analysis inclined realizes that when the underlying company makes corporate changes or alterations, it may take a few days or weeks for it to reflect on the price of the stock. Therefore, a swing trader needs to read the stock trends and patterns and also follow the fundamental news to gain better insight into when and how the stock price might go up in order to experience a profit on the trade.

Swing trading involves more than one trading session. By analyzing the profit trend of the stock, you get to know when and how to make moves in the stock market in order to realize a profit. The main focus in swing trading is to keep an eye on a trend of stock price direction and make profits when the movement experiences a sudden change.

Position Trading

While day trading and swing trading deals with the now, position trading deals with the future. People who use position trading style buy and hold for a long period of time, expecting that the value of other stock holdings will increase with passing time. Well, while this can yield substantial profits when the underlying stock or financial instrument experiences an increase in shareholder value over time. Position traders may decide to hold their position for several months and years until they have attained their desired target profit where they think they can move on.

618

Long term investors are known for their ability to buy and hold for several years. After long term investors, position traders tend to be the next group on the line with the ability to buy and hold stocks for a long period of time to yield the desire share per price value. They operate with the belief that when the trend starts, it will continue for a long period of time. Based on this belief, they lunch their position trader style which yields good returns based on the trend and direction of the stock over time.

Position traders are usually passive when it comes to stock trading; they buy one stock and then hold it for a long time until it yields the maximum results where they choose to sell their position and move unto the next thing. But to do well in position trading, it requires that carefully fundament and technical analysis to be made before taking the hit. If price reversal takes place, position traders may lose a high value of their stock or financial asset's value.

Risks of Swing Trading

Swing trading is a jeopardy adventure that requires keen consideration and a lot of dedication. With swing trading, you have to monitor the market by every passing hour. This is in a bid to take advantage of any shift in the market. When you are a swing trade, you sticking to impressive financial management is what will make you thrive. The perception about swing trade has been that you will expose a lot of your money to jeopardy an, in turn, make peanuts as profits. Another school of thought has it that swing trade involves a combination of the worst aspects of day trading and those of position trading.

As compared to day traders, swing traders tend to thrive at night when most of the day trading has been closed. The special margin provisions are what they focus on. The problem that arises with swing trading is that their exposure to tax is severe as compared to day trading. In order to make it in any other type of business venture, you need to take into account how you respond to your risk. Failure of anticipation of this risk is like planning to fail altogether. Risks form every part of our daily adventures, not only in the business world. How best we anticipate them is how best we will conquer them.

Levies

Levies are the drawbacks of almost any type of trade. With levies, the effect is often felt by those traders who trade in full time. With day traders, they are exempted from this type of tax. The tax cuts across in that you are taxed even for the hardware that is used for business. This takes a larger toll on full-time traders. With tax, there is a demand that losses and gains in the capital have to be converted to ordinary losses and gains. There is a type of schedule in which gains and losses have to be reported. There are wash-sale thresholds that need to be met. Reporting your expenses as a deduction from the business may also be a subtle adventure.

These special tax qualifications make it subtle for some swing traders to trade every day. This is because they do not meet the requisite qualifications. Failure of qualification to be a swing trader will lead to you being taxed in the same manner as any other person who is investing

Day Trading, Swing Trading or Position Trading - A Comparative Analysis

Having understood the three styles of trading in the financial market, which is best of you? Which meets your goals, dreams, plans and personality style? Which will best work for you in attaining your portfolio dreams and profit margins? Before you consider making any decision, you need to know that all the three types of trading styles have the potential to generate a huge profit over time.

If you trade conservatively and wisely for a period of time, you are most likely to make more money in the market either you have been using day trading, swing trading or position trading. It is also very important that there is no free lunch in security trading. There are risks involved in any trade. You must do your risk/reward analysis before taking any trade decision.

Always endeavor to trade what you can lose. While the margin is good to use in stock or financial trading, you might jeopardize your financial life if you take all your money and bet it all on one stock. Make sure you have done your analysis and taken a considerable amount of time to shield your profits from much loss.

Now, let's take a closer look at how the three trading styles work and compare with each other, consider the following in-depth analysis. Knowing the difference in the trading approach will know what you need to do well and how you should strategize to excel in any type of trading style.

•Frequency of Trading: trading positions are held for minutes or hours on a business day. Traders can profit from trading financial securities by trading highly volatile stocks that will fluctuate on a working day to generate a profit on share per profit. Keeping track of multiple portfolios can become a challenge of the day trader.

•Commitment: Generally, day trading involves more commitment than any other form of trading style. The lower the time frame of the asset to increase or depreciate in value, the higher the monitoring and feedback required to make a win in the market. This can increase stress levels when other responsibilities are involved.

•Trading Method: If you choose to use a day trading method to play the game of the financial market, then you need to be actively engaged in the management of your portfolio. Day traders are highly immersed in the game, they follow the market and trend to make a good trading decision. They focus on buying or selling highly volatile stocks so that they can make profits.

•Liquidity: For those using a day trading method, you need to be liquid. As a day trader, every day is a trading day, but you can choose to place an order for a trading decision if you want. When you are day trader, you're liquid since you sell positions to make profits. Buying and selling are done daily, therefore your money is locked up in a stock or any other financial security.

•Trading Expenses: Generally, the shorter the trading time frame, the higher the trading expenses and the accompanying profit to be made in the trade. In a day trading, you are required to get all the financial data to make buying and selling decisions. That means bearing costs such as trading charts, insider trading news, brokerage commissions and paying for ongoing trade alerts.

•Leverage & Start-Up Costs: Usually day trading have high start-up costs, but you get to use leverage to maximize returns for each individual trade. By contacting your broker, you can get access to a host of margin that can be used to increase the return on each trading session. But you need to aware of the risks associated with margin.

• Competition: Many top-notch traders like the hedge funds and sophisticated trading institutions using computer program tend to play the day trading game. These people have a lot of cash at disposal, spending millions of dollars to manage multiply portfolio. As a day trader, you will be competing with these organizations in trading. Using smart tools and strategies is important to excel in the game.

• Risk Analysis: Sometimes, the stock price may fail to move or change as implied by the financial media and this could lead to potential losses in trading. A day trader might be exposed to a lot of risk in options trading when the option does not have enough time value to get "in the money" and earn profits from the trade.

Swing Trading

• Frequency of Trading: Swing trading generally involves a short time frame, a couple of days and weeks of holding and selling stock positions. Due to the low frequency of trading as compared to day trading, many corporate executives and buy professionals or beginner traders tend to enter the market through this trading outlet.

• Commitment: Even though you get to place several trades in a month, you need a considerable amount of commitment to excel as a swing trader. To do well in swing trader, it is very important to invest an hour or so to study the financial market, especially the stock market. You need regular daily or weekly monitoring some few minutes of the day through charts and platforms to stay on top of the game.

623

•   Trading Method: The aim of the swing trader is to identify the next move in stock prices, and then capitalize on the move to earn huge profits. Thus, the swing trader seeks to find volatile stocks, but the position and hold it for a couple of days or weeks, sell the position and earn profit from the price variance. Swing traders make money when they sell, but expend money when they buy positions.

•   Liquidity: As a swing trader, you may not be as liquid as a day trader. Since the trading activities are done either within the week or month, your funds may be locked up in your brokerage account while awaiting the underlying stock or financial security to swing for profit maximization. Having funds to take advantage of new stocks with potential price swings is very important.

•   Trading Expenses: A swing trader is not engaged in day to day trading activities, therefore there is not enough monitoring of the market. Most of the charts used by swing traders are free and involves only minutes of checking or monitoring to stay on track with the market. This is why swing trading seems to be favorable for beginner traders in the stock, commodity, and Forex trading market.

•   Leverage & Start-Up Costs: As compared with day trading, swing trading involves less trading capital to get started. Most swing traders tend not to very active with the management of their positions, requiring less trading capital to make swings and profits in the game. However, there are leverage packages with brokerage firms for swing traders; amounts provided may be as much as those involved in swing trading.

•   Competition: Swing trading does not involve a high barrier of entry and stiff competition like the day traders. Notwithstanding, there is an amount of tracking, analysis, and evaluation required to place any trader. There might also be competition regarding the trading of a particular stock as well as the market conditions regarding the volume of the stock.

•   Risk Analysis: Stock prices can change overnight and result in losses. This is why it is very important to take a closer look at the financial position of a stock or any financial instrument before placing a trade. Always make sure you do the required technical and fundamental analysis before swinging a trade.

•   Frequency of Trading: Position trading involves a long term perspective. You are not thinking of the next swing or change in prices to make a profit. Position traders buy and hold for a long period of time until their stock holdings increase in value. The time frame for position trading may be in months and even years, as long as it takes to reach the expected to earn potential of stock before selling.

•   Commitment: Position traders are the most passive traders. While day trading requires more activity in terms of constant monitoring and watching live stock price fluctuations to make a better trading decision, a position trader may check the charts and market status from time to time. There may be ongoing technical and fundamental analysis to make evaluation prior to a trade, but not as involving as a day trader.

•   Trading Method: Position traders buy and hold for a very long time and then sell when they have reached the expected profit-earning per share or when the market is expecting a huge change. Their trading philosophy requires that they don't worry about daily price changes of an underlying security, but rather make money from the long term valuation and price trend following.

•   Liquidity: A day trader sells and buys positions daily to earn profits, but a position trader has to wait for a long period of time before cashing in. After a position trader buys a position of the stock, the trading capital will be locked in for a period of time the trader is awaiting the appreciating of the stock to sell and realize the capital gains.

•   Trading Expenses: As a position trader, you place only a few trades per year. Therefore, your expenses are limited. You don't get to bear the costs of paying for constant changes in prices of securities to make a profit. Usually, the position trader focuses on making profits using a long term approach, this lowest amount paid in commissions and portfolio management as compared to swing and day trading.

626

• Leverage & Start-Up Costs: To be successful in position trading, you have to make sure that you have cash available for other things. Your trading capital may be locked up one stock for a long period of time. This is why it is important to analyze and look at your financial capabilities before using a position trading style to make profits in the stock market.

• Competition: As compared to swing and day trading, there is a relatively low amount of competition in position trading. You look at various publicly traded stocks in the financial market, you take your time to do the underlying technical and fundamental analysis and then buy the stock. You hold the position and sell when everything turns green or to minimize losses in a down market.

• Risk Analysis: The main risk in position trading is when the wind moves against you. When there is price reversal and the market moves contrary to your prediction, you might suffer losses. However, you can use a protective put option to protect the downside when your high earning stock seems to be going down in value.

Chapter 18: How to Buy and Sell Stocks

In order to buy and sell stocks, we must go through someone called a broker. A broker's job is to connect buyers and sellers on the stock market. If you've ever seen videos or pictures of the New York Stock Exchange, you've likely seen brokers moving around between the screens talking on the phone and brokering deals between traders.

You and I can't go to the New York Stock Exchange and start buying and selling shares independently. We must go through a licensed brokerage. With the advent of the internet, the cost of finding a brokerage has gone down and there are more options available that are more attractive to smaller retail traders. This has opened the door to new strategies and has made retail trading more accessible to anyone with a computer and internet access.

It doesn't take a large amount of money or an expensive broker to make some money on the stock market nowadays. The only requirements are the willingness to take on some degree of risk and the ability to read a few different types of charts. A good predilection to market research and financial analysis will also help. All the information you need to be an effective trader is available through your phone or home computer.

There are many different types of brokerages available through the internet, where you can manage your portfolio and make trades in one place. The type of brokerage you choose will depend on the amount of money you're investing as well. We'll talk about this later on in the book, but choosing a brokerage is the first step in trading or investing and it requires some thought and research once you've learned a little more about the different types of trading strategies and what sort of features you consider to be the most important.

When you are looking to buy a stock, you will see two different prices. The first price is called the asking price. It's a little like the 'buy it now price'. As an alternative, you can also buy a stock at the bid price. The bid price will be lower than the asking price which means you can get a better deal on the stock if the broker is willing to part with the stock at that price. Just like any time you make a deal, whether on the stock market or at a garage sale, offering a lower price means that there is a chance you may not get the stock you're bidding for. This means that if you're trying to quickly enter the market in order to capitalize on a trend, you might miss out if you bid and don't get the stock.

Whether a not a broker will sell you the stock for the bid price is dependent on many factors. The stock market is an experiment in the laws of supply in demand which means that a broker will make his or her decision based on these laws. If the stock is in low demand, you may be able to buy it for a price much lower than the asking price. If not, many people are buying the stock then the broker will be much more willing to part with it for a low price.

On the other hand, if the market indicators show that a stock is quickly on the rise and traders are seeing an opportunity forming, then the demand for that stock is probably going to increase. If you offer the broker a bid that's too low, then he'll probably turn it down because he can find someone to pay more for the stock.
Keep this in mind when you are going to purchase a stock. You might be able to save some money by buying a stock below the asking price. But if you have a feeling that the stock is in high demand, don't try and low-ball the broker because they will probably find a more willing buyer and you will lose the stock altogether and miss out on whatever trend you're following.

As traders, we can trade with two different kinds of accounts. When you sign up with a broker you will have the option of choosing one or the other. Most brokerages will give you a choice between the two. For many new traders, they open their account and are asked whether they want to open a cash account, or a margin account and they don't know the difference.

The main difference between a cash account and a margin account is the way they allow you to use your available funds. If you went to a bank and asked to get a card, you'd be given the choice between a debit card and a credit card. If you choose to get a debit card, then the card acts much like a regular wallet. You can only spend the money that you have in your wallet, you can't spend money you don't have on hand. If you choose to get a credit card then you have the option to purchase things, pay the bank back later. When the brokerage gives you the choice between a cash account and a margin account, your options are similar.

If you open a cash account and deposit $10,000 dollars, it means that you can buy $10,000 dollars' worth of stock. It's like a debit card. You can buy as much stock as you want, splitting your account however you want, by purchasing the stock with the cash available in your account.

This is the most straightforward way of managing your money whether you are getting a bank card or opening a brokerage account. However, there is a reason that people decide to get credit cards. With a credit card, you have more flexibility. If you have a bill to pay now, but your paycheck comes next week then you're able to pay the bill and cover it later.

By opening a margin account, you receive flexibility from the broker, who is extending credit to you so that you can buy stocks and pay later. If you open a margin account with $10,000 dollars, you can use the broker's credit to purchase stocks while the $10,000 acts as leverage for the credit.

Let's say that your $10,000 is tied up in stocks that you can't sell at the moment, but an opportunity has popped up that you want to take a position on. You don't have the cash on hand immediately, but you know that in a few days you'll have the cash so you can pay the broker back at that time. The added flexibility of a margin account means you can take advantage of opportunities even when you don't have cash on hand.

The flipside of the margin account, just like with a credit card, is the added risk of borrowing money with the intention of paying it back later. If you leverage your $10,000 to purchase more stocks on credit, then those stocks go down in prices then your losses are more than if you had just purchased the stock in cash. You'll lose on the stock dropping in price, but you'll still need to pay the broker back for the full price. Your broker might also get nervous that you won't pay them back. The broker might make you sell those stocks you have as leverage, and if you are selling them at a bad time then your losses will be even worse. You'll lose not only the money from the bad trade, but you'll lose the stock and the potential earnings from the shares you purchased in cash.

If you want to minimize risk as much as possible, then the best choice is to choose a cash account. This is often a good idea for newer investors. But if you avoid the risk by choosing a cash account then you will also lose out on the added benefits of using a margin account. Some swing trading strategies require a margin account, so you'll be unable to apply these strategies. There are ways to maintain a credit card in a safe and conservative manner, while still enjoying the benefits of having credit. Margin accounts can also be used safely if you minimize the amount of leverage you use and limiting your use of credit to certain scenarios.

Before choosing between a margin and a cash account, make sure you read the terms that apply to your brokerage. Many brokerages have rules for how much you can leverage and minimum amounts for opening a margin account. Once you've finished reading the rest of this book you will have a better idea of what types of strategies you want to use, and which account will be the most suitable. If you want to keep your trading simple and minimize risk when you are first starting out, then consider opening a cash account. But keep in mind the added flexibility and the ability to capitalize on opportunities when you don't have the cash immediately available. A higher potential for profits always comes with added risk, and vice versa.

Once you've opened your account, you'll start to watch the market, maybe even picking a few specific stocks to watch. You're watching in order to choose a good position. When traders refer to a position, they are talking about the stocks that they decide to buy or short in anticipation of the stock moving up or down. The most basic example of a position is buying a stock anticipating that the price will go up in the future so that you can sell it at a higher price.

While it may seem obvious that people make money on the stock market when the prices go up, there also traders whose strategies depend on the stock market going down by using a method called shorting. It's a higher risk strategy that is quite common among day traders and swing traders.

Short selling works like this; a trader has a gut feeling that the price of a stock will drop soon. They've seen the indicators and they think the stock is overvalued for whatever reason, and they anticipate a decline in the price followed by a high volume of traders offloading the stock at the same. But how can a trader profit off this scenario?In this instance, the trader doesn't own any of this stock. So, in order to short sell, he or she borrows shares of that company from the broker and then sells them. Remember that this trader anticipated a drop in the price of this stock. Now that they've sold it, they wait. Eventually they will have to pay back the broker for the borrowed stock. If they were right about the stock price plummeting, then by the time they pay their broker back for the shorted stock they will only have to pay back a fraction of what they bought the stock for. They make their profit in the beginning by selling high and buying low, rather than the ordinary trade which happens in the reverse.

The risk with short selling, of course, is that the price of the stock might go up instead of down. It might turn out that the gut feeling you had about a stock being undervalued was wrong; instead of the price plummeting as you expected, it just keeps going up. No matter how high it goes, you will have to buy the stock back for your broker. If I short $200 worth of shares hoping that tomorrow they will go down, but instead they are suddenly worth $300 this means that I'll have lost $100. You might consider waiting, maybe you mistimed the drop, but the shares might still go down. You wait a few days and now the stocks you shorted are valued at $400. So, you received $200 from short selling, but you owe your broker $400. The dangerous thing about short selling is that you have no idea how high a stock price can go up. If the stock is overvalued and the price has been rising, then there is a chance that it could continue doing that and it may not stop in foreseeable future. With short selling, it's a lot trickier to turn the boat around and minimize your losses.

The advantage of short selling is that when you rely on the stock price going up to make money, you usually must wait much longer to see the price rise. When the price of a stock rises, it usually increases slowly over time which means that someone anticipating a stock price increase must wait longer to see the same profits as a short seller. When the price of a stock drops, it drops quickly due to market psychology. You can make a quick profit with short selling.

Some people question short selling, saying that it poses a moral hazard. Profiting off a market that is going down, or a business that is doing poorly. The questionable ethics of short selling have led to regulation of short selling which means restrictions on the times that traders can short stocks. For example, you can short sell in a market that's already in recession. The market has been moving upward for a trader to engage in short selling.

In the early days of the stock market, people who try to make money by instigating a price drop. A large group would short sell a stock at the same time. A high volume of short-sellers at once would cause the market to panic and people would start to sell their own shares creating an artificial drop in price.

Proponents of short selling argue that they are doing the stock market a favor. They are helping to predict downturns and warn the public about overvalued stocks. In 2008, short-sellers made billions of dollars by anticipating the collapse of the housing market, short selling a large volume of stocks right before the Great Recession.

Short selling is an important tool because it gives us a method of profiting in all kinds of situations. You don't need to wait for a stock to go up in price in order to make money. You can make money off a stock whose price is going up; known as a bullish stock. You can also make money short selling on a bearish stock. The bull and the bear are classic wall street symbols for the different types of market trends. A bull market is named after the way a bull attack by thrusting its horns up, so a bull market is moving up. The bear market gets its name from the downwards swipe of a bear's claws when it attacks. Financial analysts often refer to stocks being bullish and bearish, while the market might be a bull market or a bear market. For a market or a stock to qualify as being bearish, then we need to see a downward trend over a given a trend over a period. Not every downward movement in the price of a stock makes the stock bearish. If analysts start referring to a bear market, the stock market would have to have experienced a loss of 20% or more of its overall value. A bear market must occur over an extended period. In 2008, when the stock market experienced a great recession, stocks were bearish for over 17 months.

A bear market is often, but not always, correlated with an economy that is not doing well. When growth starts to slow down in the market, investors begin to feel less confident about the economy. After all, what goes up must always down?

Investors see the slowing growth and anticipate a drop. They'll either start investing less or selling off investments to protect themselves from the drop that they anticipate.

When a significant number of investors begin to act this way then the demand for stocks will go down, which means the price of the stocks will go down and the drop will be exacerbated by the collective panic. Many investors begin to fear a bear market when the prices for stocks are peaking but the outlook for the companies, they are investing in begins to drop. The market will remain bearish until investors anticipate it to turn around again.

A bull market happens when the value of the market is increasing over time. Not every increase in the market is bullish, but like bear markets, the market value needs to be increasing for a good amount of time for it to qualify as a true bull market. When the market is bullish, investors will see this as an opportunity. They expect the prices will continue to rise, so they buy stock in order to make some money from the increase.

So, with swing traders buying and selling a stock, they have an opportunity to make money off of the market in a variety of conditions. The simplest approach is buying low and selling high. Making money on a bullish market is less risky, and the most straightforward. It's also the way an investor will make their money if they are waiting for a profit from a long-term investment. If you want to make money on a bullish market, then the best time to buy a stock is often during a bearish market. If you use this approach, you will have to be willing to wait for however long it's necessary for the market to turn around and move upwards again.

The short-selling stock has the potential for quick profits, but they come with higher risk. Short selling is one of the most common methods of swing trading. Unlike buying stock and hoping for a bullish market, short selling requires less patience because the time frame is shorter. You must be aware though, that this means you can lose a lot more in a shorter amount of time. Short selling is a more active swing trading strategy that requires an astute trader who is willing to keep up with market trends as they unfold.

Keep in mind that some brokerage companies, especially for small-time traders, don't offer short selling. For example, Robinhood is a popular app for many beginning investors because it has no trading fees which mean that you can trade with even a small amount of money without your profits being eaten away by fees.

This brings us to our next section where we will discuss the different types of swing trading. Knowing a little bit about these strategies will help you choose a broker. You can identify which brokers have these tools available. An important factor to consider is the fees that the broker will charge. Depending on the amount of money you are trading with, these fees will quickly add up if you're making multiple trades. If you're only using a small amount of money, then you'll spend more money on fees than you'll be profiting. Therefore, it's important to think about the strategy you want to use when you're swing trading before you choose a broker. Different brokers will come with different features and will enable different strategies. The amount of money you start with will also be an important consideration.

Once you've chosen your broker, you will have to decide which type of account is best for you. Whether that's a margin account or a cash account, you will have different advantages depending on the one you choose. Of course, your skill level and your level of experience should be an important factor when you're considering a broker. A margin account might give you more flexibility and might make it possible to achieve higher profits, but the risk will be higher. How much do you want to risk when you are first starting out? There are a lot of things to watch for when you're trading stock; sometimes the best solution is keeping your trades simple when you're first starting out.

We mentioned Robinhood as a popular choice for beginning investors. You can trade with a smaller amount of money because there are no commissions for trades. The biggest downside to using Robinhood is the fact that they don't allow you to short. If you are a beginning investor only interested in trading bullishly, then this won't be a problem. If you're a more experienced investor and you want to tap into the profits from short selling and use strategies that only work on a bearish market, then opening an account with Robinhood will be limiting. There's nothing wrong in starting with simple strategies and smaller amounts of capital. For this, there is nothing wrong with choosing a service like Robinhood while you learn the ropes and do your first trades. You'll save money on commission fees and you will have a relatively simple setup to begin trading. You might read this book and think you've got a pretty good grasp on swing trading and jump right into using multiple strategies on a complex platform. The truth is, once the ticker starts moving and you must make decisions, a lot of the information you retained will be lost in the heat of the moment. Remember, there is nothing wrong with starting out using simple strategies.

You'll also want to think about what the brokerage platforms will provide in terms of technical assistance. Most decent trading apps will give you the ability to monitor your portfolio in real-time, but there are added features that can be helpful when you start using more comprehensive strategies. In order to streamline the process, buying and selling stocks should be as easy as possible through your brokerage account.

In addition to that actual trading of stocks through your broker, many apps offer a comprehensive analysis in real-time. Many apps also offer the added benefit of access to market research and in-depth coverage of certain stocks. This by itself shouldn't be the only selling point. Most of the research provided can be found on your own. If you want to have the research available in one place, then using an app that provides this will be useful but not totally necessary.

What is more useful is finding brokerage fees that can send you text and email alerts about a stock movement. If you're a swing trader then you probably aren't monitoring the market during every minute that it's open, but you should be able to keep close tabs on it especially if you are anticipating a movement. If you are waiting to decide on a position, your brokerage can send you text alerts when the price of a stock goes up or below a certain alert price. This enables you to keep track of your stocks or potential opportunities even while you busy at work or running errands. You never know when an opportunity may present itself.

Stock Options

Another way to add flexibility to your trading strategy is by using stock options. Stock options are especially popular in recent years because they can be an effective way of lowering risk while also giving you the ability to hedge several positions at once without tying up your capital until you know you want to make a move.

Options consist of puts and calls. When you buy a stock option, you are paying a broker to hold a stock a certain price for you. Let's say a new kid moves into the neighborhood, he has a trading card that you think is worth a lot of money. You want to wait to buy it, but you think that other kids in the neighborhood will want it as well. You tell the new kid that you think that trading card is worth $7, and you offer him $2 to hold the price at $7. The next day, the rest of the kids in the neighborhood see the trading card and offer him $10 for it. But you've already made a deal, paying him $2 to hold on to the card for you at a fixed price. You buy the card for the fixed price you've agreed upon, and then turn around and sell it to the kids offering $10. This is essentially how an option works.

When you buy a stock option, you are purchasing the option to buy it and sell it at a higher price later down the road. Let's say instead that you give your neighbor $2 to hold the price at $7 for you. Tomorrow the kids in the neighborhood show up, but they don't think the card is as valuable as you do. They only offer him $5. You decide in that case, not to buy the card from him at $7, because it's not worth as much as you thought. Instead of being out $7, you are only out $2 because you didn't purchase the card outright. You just paid the cardholder to hold it for you at a certain price.

With stock options, you're paying the broker to hold it at a fixed price. If you see a stock that you think might go up, you can buy an option from the broker to hold it at the current price. If the stock goes up, then you will make a profit because the broker will still sell it to you at the discounted price. If it goes down, then you'll only lose the option fee rather than the entire price of purchasing the stock. Stock options allow you to set a price for yourself without committing the amount of capital it would take to buy the stock outright.

The fee that you pay the broker to hold the stock at a price is known as a strike price. In options trading, if the stock doesn't do as well as you'd hoped then ideally you will only lose the strike price rather than the entire price of the stock. If your broker is sitting on a stock valued at $15, you can pay them $3 in order to hold the stock at that price. If the value of that stock goes up to $22 next week, then you pay your broker $15 and then sell the stock. Your call on this option will have made you a $4 profit. What if, however, you pay your broker $3 to hold the stock at $15. Next week the price of the stock drops to $10. If you had bought the stock outright then you would have lost $5. By buying an option on this stock, you instead will only lose the $3 you paid for the strike price.

Typically, options have expiration dates. You can't buy an option and hold onto it indefinitely; the broker will set a day and you must choose to exercise the option by that day. Brokers will usually sell options in sets, with 100 shares per set. It allows you to gain an advantage in several opportunities, without committing to the risk of tying up too much capital. Trading options are a way to keep your portfolio flexible and react to the market, rather than being fixed to a position. It's a way to make your portfolio more diverse even when you are working with a smaller amount of money.

There are major advantages to shifting your strategy towards trading options. On the flip side, they are also more complicated than normal trades. It requires a good amount of organization to manage your options, which is usually done the best when you have some experience as a trader. When you own a stock, then you know what price you bought it for and what you stand to gain or lose at any given time. When you own stocks, there isn't any confusion when you look over your portfolio. If you trade options you will have to pay closer attention to your buy and sell price, as well as your strike price. You must not only sell for a profit but sell for a profit that is large enough to cover the cost of your strike price. Choosing to use an option and selling a stock too early can result in a negative result, even when the trade was positive. It's an easy mistake to make when you are first learning how to trade options.

Another advantage of option trading is the number of opportunities at any given time. Options traders can be flexible where regular bull and bear traders become fixed in a position once they've entered it. For beginner traders, I recommend spending some time using simpler strategies before you start to try options trading. While options trading has an added degree of flexibility, it is much more complicated. There are entire books devoted to different options trading strategies, with strategies much more involved than swing trading strategies. Its good to understand what's out there in terms of potential strategies, so you can plan and choose a broker that will enable you to use these strategies in the future. Like any type of trading, options traders need to be diligent and focused in order to be successful. Passive beginner traders should probably shy away from options trading when they first start.

Exchange Traded Funds

Another way for small-time retail traders to diversify their portfolio is by using exchange traded funds. If you are a beginner and you don't have a lot of initial capital, then exchange traded funds are a good way to stretch your money to create a more diverse array of investments. They are easy to buy and sell and they don't require a large degree of capital to invest in, so they are simple to use and a good way to learn the stock market.

The diversity of exchange traded funds is their main advantage. The spread between the bid and ask price is typically lower so buying and selling are straightforward. Exchange traded funds are a combined list of stocks within a given sector. If you were smart, then you'd choose a sector where you already have a good amount of knowledge. That way you'll know what pieces of information to watch for. Having some technical knowledge about the companies you own share in gives you an advantage because when you are doing market research or research on specific companies, you might notice things that someone else would overlook. Just like if you were to buy a business, you would have more success if you bought a business where you understood the product and the relevant market. You'd know what companies to watch for and what new technologies might cause a change in the market. I recommend that as a beginning investor you pick ETFs in a sector that already interests you, where you won't mind doing research.

Diversification is one of the most important ways to minimize risk. The value of some stocks may drop, but overall the value of a well-diversified portfolio is more likely to go up. If you want to diversify your portfolio as a new swing trader, then this is the cheapest way to do it. ETFs can also be traded using the strategies we've already mentioned, such as short selling and options trading. It's worth reading up on exchange traded funds if you are a new investor and you want to add a little more horsepower to your trading strategies.

Chapter 19: Read the Market

By now we have talked about a few different types of trades that a swing trader can use. All these types of trades, whether you are using short selling or options or buying bullish stocks, require you to examine market factors to determine where you are most likely to make a profit. But there are thousands of stocks available on the market which you could take a position with for swing trading, so how do you know which stocks are worth watching? What types of indicators do successful traders look for?

In this chapter, we focus on the tools used by traders and investors to study the value of a stock and to make predictions about our expectations. As traders, we use two different types of analysis to make predictions or guesses about the projected value of a stock. The first type of analysis is called fundamental analysis and when we do fundamental analysis, we are looking at the actual business indicators relevant to stock, like the way we would evaluate the health of a business we were going to buy.

The second type of analysis is called technical analysis. When you look at a financial website like Finviz, you will see dozens of different numbers and indicators as well as numerous charts, all tracking different parts of the stock market. We call these technical indicators. Traders look for patterns and trends in technical indicators to make predictions.

Fundamental Analysis

Fundamental analysis is a way for traders to get insight into the performance of a business over time. Recall that we compared buying stock to buying an actual business. If I wanted to purchase a brick and mortar store, I'd be interested in looking at the numbers of how the business is performing. Fundamental analysis is very similar to the type of analysis you would do if you wanted to buy a business. You'd probably want to know things like how much profit the business is making, or how much debt the business has.

These indicators would give you a good picture of how the business is performing so that you could make a prediction about its long-term prospects. Is common sense that buying an unprofitable business would be a higher risk than buying a business that was doing very well? But it follows that the profitable business would be much more expensive to buy. We use fundamental indicators to determine whether the price of the stock matches what we think the stock is worth based on our fundamental analysis.

If we wanted to know the profits that a business is making, then we want to know the profit that a stock will get us. The first fundamental analysis measurement is called earnings per share. When we buy a stock or a share in a business, we are only buying a small percentage of that business. With earnings per share, we are calculating how much of the profit we will get for our own in the company. You can find the earnings per share of a company by taking the profit of a company and dividing it by the number of shares that a company has issued. The better the earnings per share are, the higher the value it is given by the market. A stock with high earnings per share is seen as valuable because people expect the company to continue to make profits.

The next thing you would want to know about a business you are buying would be the prospects for earning in the future. A company that is profitable today still needs to innovate and compete in the market so that it can continue to be profitable tomorrow.

If you wanted to see how business was growing, you would look at its growth over time. Has growth been stagnant? Has there been a decline in growth over the past few years? By looking at growth over time, you might have an idea of what the prospects look like for the company. Traders and investors use what's called projected earnings growth to determine the prospects for growth of a company so that they can find the value of the company. To find the projected earnings growth you would divide the price of the stock by its earnings per share, and then divide that value by the growth of earnings per share.

Not every analyst will use the exact same formula for calculating projected earnings growth. While this information is typically free to access companies' earnings reports, different companies may use slightly different methods of calculating projected earnings growth. Keep this in mind when you are looking at projected earnings growth so that your comparisons are made using consistent data.

Projected earnings growth is a useful tool when combined with earnings per share. Of course, if you see high earnings per share but a low price for the stock, you might think you are getting a good deal. If you take a closer look and see that the projected earnings growth is low or declining, then that might explain the reason why the stock is discounted.

While you might think you are getting a good deal based on earnings per share, the project earnings growth is a good tool to double-check and evaluate whether the prospects are good for the company and whether that high earnings per share will continue.

The same applies to stock with the opposite fundamentals. Maybe you see a stock that has low earnings per share, or the price for the stock seems too high relative to the earnings that you'll receive. Based on these fundamentals you might conclude that the stock is overvalued. However, a high projected earnings growth might give you enough reason to suspect that the prospects for the company look very good, even if their actual earnings per share are low now. After all, if you are long term investment then you will be looking for companies that will grow over time. You could argue the projected growth earnings are equally important as earnings per share for a long-term investor.

A company can evaluate the value of its own stock, which might be different from what the market will pay. This is known as the price equity ratio. A company uses its own fundamentals to determine the value of its stock and then compares it to the value given by the market. Using this ratio can help you determine if a company is undervalued or overvalued. A company with a high price equity ratio may be overvalued, while a company with a low-price equity ratio might be undervalued.

Another way to earn money through owning stocks is in dividends. Dividends are returns paid by the company for the shares of that company which you own. It's like the company giving you a small piece of their profits in return for owning some stock. Some people choose to reinvest their dividends in order to extend their ownership of a company. Not all the company's income is paid out in dividends though. A good percentage of the money earned by a company goes back into the company to pay expenses and grow. Another fundamental that traders can look for in a company is the dividend payout ratio. This amount of income that goes back to the shareholders, relative to the total income with the dividend payout ratio you are basically finding out; how big of a cut am I getting, relative to the entire pie?

Some companies will have higher dividend payout ratios, so this is another type of fundamental. Obviously the higher the price, the higher you would hope to get in return for the dividend payout. If you want to know how much you are making in dividends relative to the price you are paying for the stock, you would look at the dividend yield. You can use the dividend to compare the amount you will get in dividends relative to the price, and then compare this across companies. If the dividend yield is low compared to stocks at similar prices, then this is a negative indicator.

Companies need to own assets in order to function. Assets can be anything from machinery to materials, to intellectual property. Assets cost money, which means that the return on these assets is important to shareholders. You want to know that the assets are not only being paid for but that they are paying for themselves. If a company has a lot of assets, but their income is low relative to these assets, then this might be a red flag as a potential investor. The company is spending a lot of money on these assets, but the returns aren't that impressive relative to what the company has invested. The fundamental used to determine this is known as return on equity. To find equity, take the cost of the assets less the debt incurred to buy those assets. Then divide the company's income by that number. This will provide you with a return on equity.

Keep in mind that what is considered 'good' return on equity will depend on the industry. Different industries will require different assets, so the cost of operating the business and the margins will be slightly different. The overhead costs in one industry will be completely different from one type of company to the next.

An airline may have very expensive assets with smaller margins than an insurance company. Don't confuse yourself by comparing the return on equity of two companies in totally different sectors, because the comparison won't mean much. Instead, compare the return on equity for similar companies. If you are looking at buying stocks in Northwest Airlines, compare their return on equity to that of Lufthansa. Then you can compare the efficiency of two companies that provide the same service which requires similar assets.

On the other side of equity, a company also will manage some level of debt. While debt may seem like a dirty word to the individual, it is a tool that corporate managers can use to leverage their capital in order to grow and expand. Companies will take on debt in order to buy equipment or hire specialists to design a new product line. It's not unusual for companies to have some amount of debt for a variety of reasons. If a company manages its debt effectively, then they can drive expansion.

If you were going to buy a business, you would want to know if that business was in debt and why. You'd also probably ask if the company had an effective plan to pay off the debt. How much debt does the business have, relative to its assets and earnings? If we are planning to trade, we would ask the same question about a company whose stock we considered taking a position on. In order to make an assessment on a company's debt management, we would look at the fundamental known as the debt to equity ratio.

How much does the company owner in assets, and how much are those assets worth? What is the ratio of this equity to the level of debt the company has taken on? The debt to equity ratio will help us answer these types of questions. For the most part, it's a good sign if a company has less debt than equity.

The next fundamental and the one that brings us back to our first point will help us determine whether the company is profitable or not. If I want to buy a bike shop, the obvious questions would be; how many bikes do you sell per month or per year? How much money do you make on repairs? Now apply those questions to a stock purchase. How much product has the company sold, be it goods or services? Multiply this by the value of all these goods or service, and you will end up with total revenue.In short, you're looking at how much money the company is taking in. Ideally, you'll be looking for a company whose total revenue is steadily increasing if you're interested in a long-term investment. Conversely, if a company has shown a steady decline then the stock price will also decline.

Why is Fundamental Analysis Important

To summarize; if you're a swing trader then you should take an interest in fundamental analysis. Knowing the health of a company that you want to buy a share of is the first step to investing and trading intelligently. Just like buying a business, you would want to know how that business is doing, and how it will do in the future.

With the accessibility of the internet, these fundamental indicators should be easy to find. Publicly traded companies should have earnings reports, investor reports, or financial reports which are tailored towards prospective investors doing research on the health of their company. While at first, it might seem daunting to look through these extensive reports, it is invaluable to you as a trader. Now that you understand which fundamentals to look for, you narrow the scope of your research and study important indicators more efficiently.

Fundamental analysis is also helpful because you will be able to compare the health of companies within the same sector. When you limit your research to a sector then the fundamentals will have appropriate context. With fundamental analysis, you are acknowledging that the price of the stock does not tell the entire story on its own. Look at the health indicators of a company, as well as the macroeconomic influences. The see how other companies are performing in the same circumstances. Try and give yourself a complete picture of the business before you decide to buy stock in the company. At the end of the day, treat it as if you are buying the entire business. What sort of questions would you ask the previous owners before risking your hard-earned capital?

Market Psychology

Market psychology generally refers to the predominant sentiment of participants in the financial market at any given time. The sentiments of investors can, and usually steer the performance of the market in directions that are atypical of fundamentals. For example, if investors abruptly show a lack of confidence and make the decision to pull back, the chances are that markets will fall.

The behavior of consumers or how people purchase and use goods as well as services is a vibrant field of psychological research, especially for companies and organizations seeking to sell their goods and services to as many consumers as they can. Taking into consideration what people purchase-and the reason behind their purchases, it affects various aspects of their lives, research into the behavior of consumers connects issues of communication (how various people react to marketing and advertising), identity (do purchases reflect personality), decision making, status in the society and physical and mental health.

Nonprofit organizations, corporations, and political campaigns all consult about the behavior of consumers before determining the most effective and efficient way to market their products, political candidates as well as any issue they may want to sell to the consumers—in some instances by manipulating people's worst behaviors, their fears as well as their healthy behavior. However, most of the consumers are not powerless: understanding the various techniques that companies employ and the psychological explanation behind the reason why people make confusing decisions of purchase can help them rationally determine what to purchase, where to purchase it, when to purchase it and why.

Behaviorism

This aspect of psychology is of the idea that the way people act is controlled by external stimuli. Simply put, we are always convinced to do something because of outside influence. John Watson, a psychologist, was the founder of the perspective of behaviorism. According to him, every reaction is regarded as behavior. Therefore, all your actions, feelings, and thoughts are behaviors, and they are a result of external stimuli. This means that if you have a certain attraction to a brand of soap and the

649

soap commercial features a singer who reminds of somebody you love, chances are you are likely to buy this brand of soap.

Cognitive Approach

This approach suggests that our behaviors are mostly affected by processes that go on in our minds. Cognitivism acknowledges the power of external stimuli like brand loyalty or packaging has the power to influence, but they do not think it is the most important aspect. Therefore, you might listen to the same soap advertisement and might be influenced by the singer, but from a Cognitive point of view, the interaction between the external factor and your logical thinking, as well as the mental processes in your mind, are what lead you to buy something.

Rational Benefits

For quite some time, it was believed that people made their decisions based on their usefulness. Just the same way Jeremy Bentham wrote over two centuries ago: "Nature has forced human beings under the command of two supreme masters. It is up to them to independently decide what we ought to do, and also make a determination on what we shall do.

The idea here is very simple, maximize the pleasure as you subsidize the pain. Make sure that you get the best value for your money. In other words, choose to do what will be most beneficial to you. This principle has been given a thumbs up in a myriad of domains ranging from legislation to most importantly, in this case, the hypothesis of efficient marketing in economics.

In the marketing field, the idea exhibited itself in the belief that good selling is largely contributed to by "rational benefits." Nonetheless, it is very clear that there is more in relation to marketing in comparison to rational benefits.

Share of Synapses

Neuroscientists have found out that our feelings contribute more to how we choose to make decisions than the way it was previously thought. Scientific research found out that clinical patients whose emotions were subsidized by sickness found the process of making decision proving to be difficult for them. They were aware of the facts, but they did not have the ability to gauge them.

Even more fascinating is the findings of Joseph Ledoux, who discovered that emotions are instrumental in achieving effective learning by releasing chemicals that generate connections in our brains, referred to as synapses. In addition, as soon as those connections are established, they regularly ignore the rational region of our brains, for instance, when we jump away to create space for a car only to come to the realization that it happened later on.

Therefore, when we indulge in the issue of brand associations-cultural memes, archetypes as we; as brand experiences, we are merely talking about synapses that have been created in the brains of consumers. Strong brands have created stronger synapses that identify with a series of positive things. Weak brands, on the other hand, have relatively weaker synapses that reflect very little.

If we really desire to improve market share, we must begin by building a share of the synapse.

A Tale of Two Systems

Daniel Kahneman, who founded behavioral economics, has made similar conclusions in his work. In one of his books, he gives us a description of the two systems in charge of leading us to action. The first one is highly automated and extremely emotional. It depends on the rules of the thumb, generally referred to as heuristics, that give it the ability to react rapidly.

Simply put, it is fast and thrifty. The second one is extremely rational, and it gauges facts. It makes complicated calculations and requires more effort and time. We only resort to the second system when the first fails to meet our expectations.

Our dependence on one system results in some peculiarity or singularity in our behavior. For example, research indicates that consumers who are given discounts are likely to enjoy the product less in comparison to those who have been exposed to a brand marketer. We opt to pay more to counter a problem rather than have a chance to get a similar amount. We emphasize more on the information that we can see first.

Irrationally Digital

The maiden launch of the consumer internet made many people think that it would make buying decisions to another level of rationality. Purchasing in an environment that is rich in information would enable consumers to conduct extensive research on purchases as we as make comparisons of different products. To a certain degree, that has been true.

Nonetheless, e-commerce has also smoothened the path to purchase, making it simpler to purchase on an impulse. This favors the first system that is frugal and first over the second system that is lazy and slow. In a real sense, there is a high chance that consumers will depend on brand relations that were put into place before they declared the intention to buy than of information availed at the time of purchase.

Brands will be strengthened more in the digital era. Purchases will involve more emotions than rationality.

Technical Analysis

We mentioned earlier that there are two different types of analysis that swing traders apply when they are trying to

652

evaluate potential positions. Now, you have learned how to research the performance of a company, and how its internal indicators can influence your decisions on trading. That is the basis for fundamental analysis.

The second type of analysis is called technical analysis, and it involves the study of patterns in order to make decisions about trading positions. Technical analysists use historical data and statistics to examine patterns in the stock market. While these patterns may have variations, there are some patterns which are consistent and knowing how to recognize characteristics of these patterns will enable you to anticipate movements and make judgments about the psychology of the market.

While you are anticipating movements in the market and trying to determine your own positions, there are millions of other traders trying to do the same thing. Around the world, many of these traders are watching the candlestick charts and trying to make the same predictions that you are trying to make. All these traders are competing with the same thought in mind; making a profit.

Chapter 20: The Swing Trader

With some understanding of technical analysis and fundamental analysis, you will already be ahead of most beginner traders when you enter your first trade. Beyond the research you can do, there are a handful of other aspects of trading that often get overlooked but that will become obvious over time. These things fall into the category of "stuff you wish someone had told you when you started swing trading". Luckily, this book is here to help.

Swing trading is like a test that requires constant studying a revision. You should treat it like an important test or an important paper that requires good research. If you research effectively, then you will profit. If you get lazy with your research, then you might miss obvious signs that would have led you to make a different decision in the first place.

On the flip side of that, don't get slowed down by trying to find a position that ticks all boxes of a perfect bet. You should be detailed with your research, but ultimately there are some trades where you will need to trust your gut above all else. This is a skill that is developed over time, and so you will get better at it. But you won't be able to analyze every technical and fundamental element on every trader.

This is where things like organization and good record keeping come in to play. As you enter more and more positions, you will notice certain indicators that will match your mindset and your strategy better than others. Sure, there are no indicators that are 100% foolproof, so don't try to look for those either. But your mindset and the type of trading you engage in will make some indicators more important than others. As you learn to trade more efficiently, you will know which indicators to look for right away based on the characteristics of a certain company. Don't forget about all the other indicators, but in some instances, there are certain indicators which she is highlighted about the others. If things don't line up with your strategy, don't force yourself to take a position just for the sake of trading. Start out with fewer, smaller trades and slowly expand your trading as you learn and practice. Stay organized and focused and eventually it will come together.

If you choose to participate in swing trading over other types of trading, then you are probably most interested in the time frame that swings trading presents. You are more flexible than both a day trader and a long-term position investor. If things are going well, you don't have to remove yourself from a position the way a day trader will. If things are going poorly then you don't have to ride out the roller-coaster cycles the way a position investor has to. Your advantage over the long-term investor is to seek opportunities that look good at that moment, rather than keeping your capital tied up in long term prospects.

In addition to these advantages you are also susceptible to risks that are unique to a swing trader. Because you hold your position longer than a day trader, the effects of a bad trade will be drawn out and may result in higher losses. The day trader can respond to any movements or price changes because all their positions last less time than a day. A swing trader is more likely to hold a position overnight. Even though the stock market closes, the price of stocks can change after hours. If this happens then you are stuck holding your position whether that position is a good one or not.

Remember that the stock market represents shares in companies that operate and exist outside of the stock market. Business news and company developments don't turn off for the day just because the stock market closes. A company could put out a press release that significantly affects the price of stock even after the market has already closed, leaving investors nervously sitting on their hands until the market opens again. Examples of events that could shape stock price after hours include secondary offerings and financial releases. You will have to be aware of the impact these could have on your position.

When a company issues stock, it usually doesn't release all the available shares at once. The company will hold on to a certain number of shares in the case it needs to generate capital in the future. By selling more shares later, the company will generate extra cash. This is common if a public traded company is trying to expand a product line or invest in a new development. By introducing a secondary offering at the right time, the company can get cash on hand fast.

If you're a shareholder though, the secondary offering may damage your portfolio. We've established that the price of a stock is the result of interactions between supply and demand. When a company releases a secondary offering, then the supply of the stocks will increase. An increase in the supply of something typically results in a decrease in price to find the equilibrium price point between supply and demand.

The impact of a secondary offering will depend on the position you've taken as well as the number of shares released. Sometimes the secondary offering won't be large enough to impact the price of the stock in any significant way. A small increase in the percentage of shares available may not make a big difference. But if the secondary offering is quite large then it can significantly devalue your position.

The problem is, you can't anticipate a secondary offering because companies won't announce it ahead of time. Sometimes you think you have found a good position and the company will announce a secondary offering out of nowhere. But, its an added element to be aware of if you keep a good eye on the fundamentals of your company. If a company is struggling to bring in revenue, but they are talking about expanding certain lines of their business then this company is more likely to make a secondary offering. Again, there is no way to know for sure but there are warning signs that lay in the fundamentals of a company, and now you know to keep your eyes peeled.

The next thing to watch for is financial releases or statements about the company's earnings. The good thing about these is that the company will announce them ahead of time, so you can plan around them. They always happen after the market is always closed but they still impact the way your position opens the following day. If the company announces their revenue and they are showing signs of growth, then you'll be happy you were holding a position in that stock. If the company announces stagnant growth or a decline in growth, then the results of that announcement will be reflected in the price of the stock on the following day. You can either see this as an opportunity or avoid holding positions during financial announcements, depending on your confidence in the company. Either way it's something that's worth knowing about if you plan on becoming a swing trader.

You should pay close attention to what analysts say about a stock, before and after you buy it. What they predict may come true but more importantly, what they predict may encourage certain movements among investors. They may also make predications after the market closes that will affect the value of your positions on the following day. This could either be a benefit to you or it could hurt your portfolio; keep yourself updated on what the analysts are saying so you don't wake up to any surprises when the market opens.

Types of Swing Traders

All types of trading styles involve the use of technical and fundamental analysis to analyze stock price movement and then entering the market to capture profits based on key indicators. Even though swing trading focuses on making a profit by capitalizing on an impending, sharp change in stock, there are two types of swing trading methods.

1.   Short Term Swing Trading:
In this case, the holding time for a swing trader is a couple of days. It may be two days of three days. The swing trader is

looking for an opportunity to capture some profits in the marketplace by analyzing the price volatility, trend, and direction of stocks in the financial market. A short term swing trader may focus on analyzing the market by reading daily or 60-minute charts.

Apart from the time frame for the swing trading being short, many of these traders seem to hold a smaller position. For example, a trader may choose to swing a stock for $ 34 with only 200 shares. Due to the risks associated with some of these short term trading techniques, many traders tend to hold smaller positions while looking to maximize gains through sudden price fluctuations.

2.   Long Term Swing Trading:
In this swing trading, the focus is a little bit wider than just a couple of days. The swing trader is looking to make money in the price swing of an underlying asset over a week or more. The trader studies and analyze the financial market using daily and weekly charts. This enables them to have a long term perspective about the market and then know when to enter and exit.

A swing trader can decide to trade for the short term and also for the long term. There are no hard and fast rules about it. Swing trading generally involves finding ways to make shorter or immediate term profits by finding sudden, potential price changes in the stock market of publicly traded companies. Generally. Swing traders are either intra-day, intra-week or even intra-month stock traders. The focus is not about the holding time but finding the entry and exit points on a stock price movement to capture profits.

The Basic Concepts of Swing Trading

Once you settle on swing trading, you need to have a good overview of swing trading and how it works to do well in the long term. Your knowledge of swing trading and how to play to win in the game will give a greater edge in the financial market. As they say, "To a man with a hammer everything is a nail." As long as you study the swing trading and the fundamentals, you can apply the swing trading strategies and techniques to any kind of stock, option, or financial instrument. To be successful in swing trading, you need to develop the mindset and thought patterns of the successful traders.

When you see how the game works, you can plan how to make the move to ensure most of your swing trading moves yields better results: The following are the basic concepts you have to keep in mind when executing any swing trading strategy:

1.   Use technical and fundamental analysis to look for price trends, directions, and movements of stocks so that tactical plans can be put in place to know when to make a move. This forms the basis for selecting the right stocks for swing trading. Success in swing trading has a lot to do with picking and selecting the right stocks from the beginning.
2.   Identifying the stock market and looking for where the price of a particular stock is most likely to move in the next few days or weeks. Entry and exit points are crucial in swing trading. There is a time to enter and exit the market to capture the profit. That is why timing and regular market monitoring of the market is very important.
3.   Making Risk/Reward Ratio Analysis. Before each swing trade movement is made, a seasoned swing trader wants to know what amount of risk should be borne and what amount of reward can be reaped from the trading activity. This helps in using mechanisms such as stop loss and profit target for better trading experience.
4.   Entering the market by buying a position of a stock with a potential price swing movement in the near future to yield a considerable amount of profit. Once stock and risk/reward analysis has been done, a specific swing trading strategy can be executed to ensure the best outcome is obtained from the underlying trading activity.

5.   Holding the position for the short term. It can be a couple of days or weeks and then looking for where a surge in stock price is likely to take place. Regular monitoring and analysis of the stock market to get an update on the underlying position are very important for a successful swing trading.

6.   Capturing profits and gains from stock price movement. The game of swing trading is looking for avenues to make immediate gains by looking at the volatility and price and trend of an underlying stock. Once the market moves, profits can be realized by making a swing through selling a position to make profits from the trading activity.

7.   Evaluating the trade and profit/loss made. A good swing trader wants to learn from every single trade and improve the application of strategies and techniques over a period of time. After each trade, either a win or loss, the successful swing trader wants to evaluate and study the trade to glean lessons which would be used to make the next trade very successful.

8.   Moving unto the next trading opportunity. A swing trader analyzes the market to find entry and exit points, captures profit through the swing and then moves on to the next trading opportunity. There is no need worrying or brawling about a position that has been lost due to missed predictions and analysis. You move to the next trading opportunity.

The whole concept of trading is about buying and selling to make a profit. You buy low, sell high and then make a profit. You can also sell a position before the market price of that security goes down in value so that you can profit from a downward market. To do very well trading in the financial market, you have to decide on the security and the trading style you want to use to play the game.

What Makes Swing Trading So Popular?

Swing trading has taken on a nosedive in recent times. Many people are taking advantage of swing trading due to their flexibility, profit/loss structure and the minimum amount of engagement required to be successful in the trade.

While all the three types of traders can engage in swing trading, it seems to be a favorable and suitable medium for beginner traders. Both intermediate and advanced traders can use swing trading to increase the value of their portfolio, but swing trading seems to be suitable for beginner or non-active traders.

Swing trading does not involve keen oversight and insight into the financial market to make profits. It involves holding positions for a few days or weeks to make a profit. Regular feedback and monitoring are needed to do well in swing trading. Nonetheless, with just a couple of hours per day, any individual can start studying the financial market and get started with swing trading.

To do well in swing trading, you need to dedicate regular and ongoing time for studying the market. The more you study the market, the better your insight about what is going on and the ability to predict trends to capture quick profits in the market. The game of swing trading is all about knowing where the market is going and then finding ways and means to capitalize on that move and make short term profits.

Even though there are risks associated with swing trading, it is less time consuming and engaging as compared to other trading styles. If you're looking to start trading in the stock market, swing trading is one the best ways to get in the game. As compared to day traders who need to have a deeper understanding of various technical and fundamental indicators that influence the price of a security, you don't have to worry too much about these times. With just a couple of hours per day and a trading capital, you can start with swing trading.

661

Chapter 21: Swing Trading for a Living

When you are employed by a traditional boss, you are given a job description. You do your job and get paid what you have done. You also get to risk sick leave, bonus and pension plan for your retirement. If you quit your job for swing trading, you need to know that you will be losing the perks that come with having a job with a corporate body.

The rules for success are not the same. You can be a successful employee at an organization, but the mindset and the training required for you to do very well is not the same trading in stocks. You need to learn and readjust your strategy and mindset if you're going to survive and thrive in swing trading. Always see yourself as being in the business of swing trading as compared to adopting an employee mentality.

According to experts, many traders lose money in the long term. To be on the other side of the game, among the successful traders who buy big houses, drive nice cars and build an amazingly wonderful portfolio, making at least six-figure income each year, you need to know and understand the tricks of the game to succeed.

Instead of blindly quitting your job and then going straight into swing trading, the best strategy will be to keep your day time job, swing the market and gain the skillset and experience of professional traders. With the newly develop mindset, skillset, and experience, you will be in a better position to begin earning a steady stream of income, regardless of minor trade losses to do well in the game.

The following tips will guide you on starting and building your own swing trading business:

1.   Have Savings Set Aside

Before you get started, make sure you have at least 6 months to one-year living expenses in cash. Yes, you need at least 6 months to one-year living expenses in cash. Some of you might be saying that's just too much. Well, it might be true! But the fact is that if you don't have enough savings aside to serve as a cushion against unforeseen circumstances, you will find yourself worrying about money for everyday life and that will take your mind off the game and kill you alive.

2.   Start Small and Learn

A typical mistake of many people is putting much of their risk capital into one trade. You have to learn to diversify your trade strategy and trading activities to offset losses in the long term. Build and develop a trading plan that is consistent with your trading style and personality and then use that as a framework to start small and learn as you progress.

3.   Set a Monthly Income Target

If you want to do swing trading for a living, then your goal needs to be to have a regular, predictable stream of income that covers all your living expenses with enough surplus set aside for long term investing. How much do you need for your monthly living expenses? Based on that amount, you can then plan and develop a strategy to achieve revenue and profit goals.

4.   Develop a Winning Process for Trading

Once you have set your revenue goal, you have to develop a winning process to use to achieve the set target for each month. Even though you need an amount of luck to do well in swing trading, you have to make sure you develop a predictable, winning process for analyzing trades, placing trades and evaluating performance. Instead of basing trading on happenstance, have a steady winning system to manage all your trading activities.

5.   Be Cautions and Careful With Everything

Sometimes, when everything is going your way and you are getting many wins per trade, you can forget to take caution. Swing trading involves risk and you can risk blowing off all your trading capital in a split second. Therefore, you need to be conservative with your trade. Analyze and access the amount of risk you are exposing yourself to before engaging in any kind of trade.

6.   Focus on one market at a time

Some people want to be trading in forex, stocks, options and any other financial instrument at the same time. That will not work. You have to keep your trading efforts and energy in one single market. If you want to do well in stocks, focus on stock trading. If you want to do well in EFT, stay focus on EFT. If you want to ensure you do well in options, then focus. Successful focus on one market and become an expert at one time before moving to another.

7.   Aim at Being Excellent

Brain Lund, a seasoned stock trader said, "Being able to day trade for a living successfully means reaching a level of excellence that most people will never achieve, no matter what career they choose. It's the difference between being a movie extra and an Oscar-winning actor." To earn a living in swing trading, you have to go above average. You must be willing to go the extra mile to be excellent at what you do to be successful in the trade.

Setting Goals, Objectives & Strategies for Trading

It is possible to survive and thrive in swing trading. There are many people who are doing it and you can do too. You should know that successful traders are not smarter than you, they might only be more committed and dedicated than you. If you can give your swing trading the same dedication and commitment, you will find your trading account souring with a high amount of profits.

Brain Tracy said, " Success is goals, all else is commentary." To be successful in swing trading, you need to set your yearly, quarterly, monthly and weekly trading goals. Those goals must be translated into plans and strategies which will be executed to achieve the intended results.

Execution and evaluation are very important because you can plan all you can but the only thing that counts is your ability to execute on your goals and achieve the desired outcome. Use the following steps to start setting goals and planning strategies for an effective swing trading:

1.   Clarify Your Goals

It all starts with being clear about your goals. Some people claim they have goals, yet their goals are not clear enough for them to achieve them. You need to make sure you have clear goals and objectives trading. How do you start clear goals? Make them specific, measurable, attainable, realistic and time-bound (SMART). For example, " I grow my entire portfolio by 20% in six months." This goal is clear, concise and succinct. It can set you on the path of success.

2.   Clarify Your Motivations

Even the best goals fail for lack of motivation. Motivation is the fire that drives you to work tirelessly in pursuance of your goals. Therefore, you need to make sure you have determined and clarified the goals you want to set for your trading activities. Why do you want to achieve want? What will make you keep going even when the odds are set forth against you?

666

3.   Determine Your Time Commitment

Your goals are not going to achieve themselves. You have to invest the time, energy and resources to work hard towards their achievement. Therefore, determine your time commitment per day, week and month for your trade. Make sure you are investing the right amount of time to analyze, study and evaluate and execute your trading strategy to do well in the trade.

4.   Determine Your Knowledge Requirement

You need knowledge if you are going to do well in swing trading. You need to be a committed learner. You have to be continuously learning about the market and using various means to get smarter in the game. The more you learn and acquire experience in swing trading, the clearer your vision becomes and the lower your risk.

5.   Determine Your Risk /Reward Ratio

What is your predetermined risk/ratio? How much money do you want to risk in every trade to achieve your trading income goal? Ideally, you might set a trading goal of 1: 3, but that will be dependent on your risk assessment and risk management ability. Know the amount of risk you want to entertain in your trading and projected reward to obtain from it.

6.   Determine Your Trading Strategy

A trading strategy is a way to initiate and execute a trade to achieve your profit goals. What kind of approach do you want to use? A bearish trading strategy or a bullish trading strategy? Understand the various trading strategies and then start using one. Once you find something that is working for you, stick to the plana and use that formula to earn a lot of swing trading income.

Swing Trading Rules for Making Money

If you want to make money in swing trading, you have to make sure you have set rules and regulations for trading. You can't just be like everyone else. You need to distinguish yourself by being a professional swing trader. Choose your swing trading style (short term or long term) and then make sure you have set rules to guide you in executing your trades.

1.   Always have a clear trading plan before placing a trade

There are many people who have this whole idea of buying on impulse. They have cultivated and developed this buying habit for a very long time. The problem is that they transfer their impulse buying behavior to swing trading and this causes a lot of problem for them.

You can't be successful with swing trading with an impulse buying mentality. You need to keep a close eye on the market, watch a groud of stock consistently until you develop a good instinct about new price movements. This is when buying decisions should be made. Set up a stop-loss order, establish a clear target and limit for each trade and carefully analyze a trade before committing funds to it.

2.   Learn to control your emotions

When it comes to swing trading, fear and greed are the top emotions that run the actions of many traders. When they are fearful of market conditions, they execute a bearish trading strategy. At another time when they are greedy about market conditions, they execute a bullish trading strategy. Following the masses can cause a bit hit to your trading capital.

You have to preserve your trading capital from losses. That means you should master your emotions. Control your emotion of greed and fear by taking a deeper look at securities before trading. Always make sure you use a combination of technical

668

indicators to look at whether a financial instrument is a viable trading opportunity or not. Stay objective and do your fundamental and technical analysis before trading. Evaluate your trades and learn from your experiences.

3.   Always follow a group of stocks closely for a period of time

You have to keep an eye on multiple numbers of stocks daily to be able to spot an entry point for a trade. The best time for this pre-market hours. Before the marketing opens, you can decide to look at the financial news, charts, earnings reports, stock price movements, and all others.

Reading articles from trusted websites is also very important to keep a close eye on the market. Always make sure you are tracking a group of stocks at the time to launch a trade. Check highly volatile and highly traded stocks. Look for trends and volumes for trading.

4.   Use multiple technical Indicators

When it comes to technical analysis, many traders simply rely on one technical analysis to forecast stock price movements. But that is not the best practice of the trade. Endeavor to use multiple technical indicators such as to find entry and exit points such as double buttons, moving average crossovers, flags and pattern tracking to find entry and exit points before placing a trade.

5.   Don't rush into a trade, be patient

The problem of some people is analysis paralysis. They over-analyze and fail to take action at the eright right entry points to make wins. For some others, it simply sheer rushing into a trade because of their quest to make profits. You need a perfect balance between two. You have to know when to wait, enter and exit a trade.

Again Charlie Munger's quote says it all, " The big money is not made in the buying and selling, but in the waiting." You have to learn to wait patiently to see clear indicators of a financial instrument before moving to trade. Because some people call themselves day traders, they think they need to be placing a trade every day. Exercise patience, watch the market, invest time to due diligence before trading.

6.   Always Trade with Money You Can Afford to Lose

After you have done your analysis, determined your risk/reward ratio and found the best entry points for your swing trading, one thing always comes to mind. What's that? The cash. Before you use your risk capital in any trade, ask yourself if you can afford to lose that money if the trade goes against you. Avoid being overconfident about the market.
Sometimes, the market crashes against us the most when we are too overconfident. Analyze the trade and check if you can afford to lose the money you are expending to place the trade. This will help you to be reserve and conservative with your trading.

Financial Instruments for Swing Trading

After all, is said and done, the last thing remains: getting into the game. You need to trade before you can experience any wins or make any profits. But just because you have to trade does not mean you should launch a trade into any market. Look at the financial instruments that you can start swing trading with. Take one at a time and learn to focus.

The seasoned swing traders always focus on one financial instrument and then becomes the best at it, before moving to something else. If you are looking at some financial instruments to start your swing trading, check the following: stocks, bonds, options, mutual funds, indexes, ETS, currencies, cryptos, and many others. Know your trade and focus on one financial instrument one at a time.

When you set out to start swing trading, one of the challenging decisions to make is the kind of financial instruments to get started with. You can get overwhelmed with a host of information out there about each financial instruments and that can literally get you frustrated. It is also very important that you avoid dabbling in many financial instruments.

Jason Bond, the American stock trader said, "Call yourself a trader when your portfolio reaches $10,000. With $10,000, a swing trader can start to diversify. That means spreading out funds across picks to hedge your risk – protecting against small losses along the way. The sniper does not have this luxury." Before you reach that goal, you need to focus on one financial instrument.

Usually, when most people think about swing trading what comes to mind is stocks trading. But you need to know that swing trading is just a method of trading securities, not just stocks. You can use swing trading method to trade stocks, options, EFTs, crypto, and forex. The principles of swing trading apply across all the financial instruments, but there are pros and cons of each financial instrument.

Before you choose and select any financial instrument, you need to know how the market works and how to leverage fluctuations in pricing to make profits. Always remember that the goal in swing trading is to find a swing in the price of a financial instrument and then move in and out of the market to make a profit. If you have the right mindset and skillset, then trading any market will be a lot easy.

Swing Trading EFTs

Exchange-Traded Funds (EFTs) have become one of the best entry points for swing trading. The stock market has become very competitive and highly dominated by market players. This has paved way for many people to move unto EFT trading. Since there are over 1,400 exchange-traded funds all across the US, you can get to select various EFTs to trade.

As with every financial instrument, there are rules of the game. To succeed in trading EFTs, you have to follow simple rules of trade. One thing you have to know is that just like there are sedate and volatile stocks, there also volatile EFTs and volatile EFTs. To increase the probability of making profits in the trade, you have to avoid sedate EFTs and then focus your attention on volatile EFTs that have a fluctuating price and high volume of trade.

Weak trends can lead to EFTs failure to yield profits during a considerable period of time. That means it is very important that you look at the charts and trends to select the best entry and exit points of EFTS before making a decision. Always make sure you have a selected number of EFTS to execute well-calculated trades o earn profits.

Look for pattern-breaking stocks that have the potential to be increasingly volatile for a period of time. A good practice for all EFT traders is to develop an EFT Swing Trading strategy. For example, you can choose to look for an upward trend and then buy EFTs that are increasing in their price as the chart moves upward. As the price moves upward to sell your EFT to pocket a decent profit.

Swing Trading Options

The beauty of swing trading options is that it can enable you to trade high priced stocks without necessary expending a lot of cash. Instead of buying the stocks at once from the stock market, you can buy an existing option of the underlying stock. To play the game of swing trading in options, it is very important to understand the fundamentals of the trade and how options work.

Options trading is simply the act of buying or selling the contract to an underlying stock sold at a strike price and set to expire at a predetermined period of time. Swing trading is a short-term way of earning profit in the financial market. While you can trade options for a longer period when you are swing trading options, your goal is to find the right stock, get in and out of the game in a couple of days or weeks.

The expiration date of the option sets the tone for the swing trading. To ensure you are doing swing trading, you need to make sure you study the asset class and pick the right expiration date and strike price to earn a profit. Ideally, you have to look for "out of the money" options which are not far off, then pick a strike price that will enable the stocks to get "in the money" in a couple of weeks to earn a profit.

For those with a small amount of trading capital, options are the best place to enter the market. You can pay a premium to buy call options of high priced stocks and earn a decent profit when the market is taking an upward swing. You can also choose to buy put options of stocks that are taking a downward swing and earn money from the difference in price movements.

There are bullish and bearish trading strategies to use in options. Depending on the type of market you are dealing with, you have to make sure you are using the right strategy. Apart from the call and put options, there are other options trading techniques to use to limit your losses and maximize your gains. It is also very important that you focus your time and effort on analyzing the stock market to know the right type of stocks to select for options.

Swing Trading Stocks

For many beginner traders, you might not have the money and leveraged facility to buy many high priced stocks. But if you were to be using options, you can trade the stocks with a minimum of capital. In this case, it is advisable to go for "penny" stocks that re less than $ 10. With just $ 100 you can start swing trading stocks directly without using options.

When trading stocks, you have to define your winning strategy. You have to know that you can make thousands of dollars in cash and lose all of them in a couple of days if you fail to look at the downsides and develop a strategy for your trade.

Your goal in swing trading is to have a consistent income stream that will cover your living expenses and provide a surplus for future investments. To achieve this target, you must choose either a bullish or bearish trading strategy or both to help achieve your desired goal. You need to keep an eye on the stock price movements of you are using low cap stocks.

Swing trading favors liquid, volatile and high volume stocks that are readily available in the market. Using technical indicators you can choose to find an uptrend, then buy the underlying stock. Hold it for a while and when you see the trend continue, sell. That may mean leaving a lot of money on the table. But, it's better than the marketing crashing and losing so much money in the down market.

Swing Trading Crypto

We all know how volatile crypto currencies are. Many people have amassed fortunes in the cryptocurrency trading market. They bought cryptos at a very low priced, held it for a while and then sold it to make a huge amount of profit. But there are a lot of digital currencies in the market today, you have to decide on the ones you want to focus on.

While Bitcoins and Ethereon are the most popular ones. You can get your hands on a few cryptos as possible. Always endeavor that you stay up to date with current news and alerts about the crypto market. Things sort of change and turn very fast and you can stand the chance of getting big losses if you take your eye off the ball.

Many people bought bitcoins and held it in the e-wallet. They kept it for far too long until the value went down and then ended up losing a lot in value. The goal of swing trading is not to buy and hold for along term. You want to but an asset class, hold it for a while and when the market is favorable, sell it and then move onto the next opportunity.

The high volatility of cryptocurrencies stirs up fear and worry in many swing traders, therefore, many don't tend to swing trade cryptos. But, you don't have to worry. The same principles apply for crypto swing trading. Buy currencies at low prices, look for favorable times and then sell to make a profit and move unto the next thing.

Some brokers don't have crypto trading on their asset class. Therefore, make sure you know what the broker deals with and use a brokerage service to provide a trading opportunity for cryptocurrency swing trading opportunities. Always make sure you study the market, know the tends and the prices before placing a trade.

Swing Trading Forex

The game of forex trading is merely a game of technical analysis. As in the case of stocks where the performance operation of the underlying company can affect the stocks, their situation is different in forex trading. Therefore many forex traders use technical analysis to analyze the market and predict the new price fluctuation in international currencies.

Some of the technical analysis used in forex trading include the Elliotte Wave Theory. You have to study the trends and waves in the currency market to know where the next change is going to turn. Then you can comfortably bank your trust and plan a trade that will earn your profit. The forex market is affected by the news media, the global commodity market, and many others. Therefore, it is also very important to keep an eye of the forex market in order to get prepared to make a sale.

Common Money Management Mistakes

Some people struggle with basic money management; they never set aside emergency funds and don't save for retirement. Most of them live from paycheck to paycheck, and at the same time, are still struggling with debt. Without further ado, let us look at the common mistakes that hurt your ability to manage your money.

•   Big annual tax refund
A tax refund is good, and only you can save the whole amount or use it to reduce your debt. The problem with this 'saving' method is that you don't get a chance to earn any interest from it, and you don't have access to it in case of an emergency.
•   Recording your expenses in your head
Some people only have a rough idea of their spending in their memory. To know your actual spending, you should go through your credit card and bank bills. You will be surprised to see where you direct your money and how much. The best solution is to have an applicable method to track your actual spending. You can choose among the different free online sites that are meant for that.

•   Assuming the non-monthly spending
We easily forget expenses like vacations and holidays. To include them in your budget, you turn to take the annual amount that you spend on them and divide them by 12. By doing that, you will make the monthly expenses and include them in your budget. You should save that amount so that it will be there when the time comes for a vacation. It is true that the interest you will earn on that amount is little, but isn't it better than paying interest on the debt?

•   Overspending
Recording your expenses makes it easier for you to know how much and where you spend your money. You should aim at reducing some expenses that you can do without.

676

Cancel subscriptions and memberships that you do not use, carry your lunch to work, compare costs of things like insurance policies, groceries, and mortgages; these are some different ways that you can avoid overspending. These small changes will add up, and with the time, you will see a difference in your money management.

- Directing an extra amount to clear your debt

Paying your debt on time and the required amount is good, but wouldn't it be better to put in an extra amount to help you to pay your debt faster? Plan to implement this, giving priority to the debts with a higher amount of interest rates. Once you clear one, you move to the next one with the highest rate till you clear all your debt.

- Living from salary to salary

By now, we should know that the unemployment rate is high; therefore, utilizing all your salary monthly and waiting for the next one is not a smart move. Train yourself to save money towards retirement and have an emergency fund. You can also invest in investments that are safe and easily accessible.

- Saving after spending

You should plan for your savings to be deducted automatically immediately you receive your payment and before you get a chance to spend it. If you plan on saving what will be left after spending, it is not a wonder that you will never save at all.

- Overlooking a chance to borrow from your home equity

I know it sounds bad to put your home in line, but trust me, it isn't if there exists a chance of being unable to make the payments. You can get a home equity loan to refinance a high-interest debt. It will reduce your monthly interest obligation, and it is also tax-deductible.

Defining and Building a Trading Routine

You have your goals, plans, and strategies all set. What's the next thing? Your trading routine. The trading routine is the day to day activities and time commitments that will be required in working to achieve your trading/portfolio goals for each month and year. Once you define and build a trading routine, be sure to stay focused and work on it to reach your goal.

Pre-Market Hours: This is the first part of your trading time. Before the financial market opens, what do you want to start doing? What do you want to start engaging yourself with before the market opens? Well, the best thing to do with your pre-market hours is to plan, prepare for the trading day.

Consider using the news media to look at current holdings, sector, and overall market sentiments. You should also create a watchlist for opportunities and trades in the day. CNBC, Market Watch and the other trade journals are good for your pre-market hours.

During-Market Hours: What do you need to do during market hours? You have to stay alert and vigilant. Don't get into the game of trading because everyone is doing so. As Charlie Munger said, " The money is not made in buying and selling, but waiting." Market hours are the time to enter and exit trades, but only places trades after you have waited, studied and carefully analyze a particular stock or financial instrument.

Post-Market Hours: When the market is over, you want to evaluate and measure your progress. Every day is a day for you to work towards the achievement of your trading goals and plans. Once the market is over, take the time and review what happened in the day. This can take you a couple of minutes or hours, depending on what you want to evaluate. Look at the financial market at the close of the day, monitor fluctuations and various trade indicators. Keep your eye on looking for the next upcoming swing.

You've probably been reading this book and wondering at what point we will start to talk about swing trading strategies. After all, you are probably most interested in the actual strategies that you can apply to make money swing trading. You can see though, that there is a lot to learn before you can start to understand the strategies that people use to swing trade. The market has many factors at play, and you need to understand the tools used to assess companies and their technical movements. You won't be able to use the same strategy in every situation, so knowing how to read the market is the first step before learning strategy.

The indicators that you are looking for will depend on the type of strategy you are using, so pay close attention to the fundamental characteristics of companies and you'll start to recognize similarities amongst different opportunities.

The first step is to make a habit of mining for opportunities. There are a lot of fascinating economic and business journals available on the internet that you can peruse for information about current events and finance news. You never know how you will identify your next opportunity. An article about energy companies in Texas may inspire you to research energy contracts in the American Southwest, and which companies to watch for. An article in a tech news magazine might send you on a hunt for publicly traded companies developing a certain type of computer hardware. If it intrigues you, then let yourself be drawn in for further research. The important thing is to spend a little time each day reading and identifying possible opportunities. Once you've noticed an opportunity, dig a little deeper and review the company's involved and check out their fundamentals. How have these companies been performing? Is it worth taking a position?

You can do this research by looking at the market sector by sector. Find indexes that represent different sectors you are interested in and check up with them every day. It's good to have a relatively broad field of interests from which you can identify options. One sector might be ripe with opportunities while another sector lags on the same day. Being able to switch gears and focus on the place where opportunities are happening will make you a more effective and well-rounded trader.

The type of strategy you use will also affect what characteristics you'll be looking for. If you are willing to take on a little more risk and you want to try swing trading, then you will be looking for stocks that show signs of a moving downwards. With the uptick rule, you will have to find stocks that are moving up now, but you have reason to believe that they will continue to drop in the future.

If you want to buy a stock and hang on to it and make a profit, then you'll be looking for stocks or sectors that are healthy and have continued and consistent growth. The earlier you enter a position, the better. Look out for signs of reversals as both a short seller and a bull trader. The sooner you enter a position after a true reversal, the more you can earn.

Remember the tenet of Dow Theory that states that the average of all the stocks in the index should confirm each other. You may just take a position on one or two stocks, but its good to have a picture of the entire sector. This will tell you whether you will be swimming upstream or downstream. It's OK to swim upstream as long as you feel like you have a compelling reason. When you have identified a stock that balances risk and reward ratio, decide what price you'd like to buy-in. This will require some research into the fundamentals of a company so you can evaluate whether you are overpaying or underpaying.

One strategy that you can employ as a swing trader is known as gap trading. In the last chapter, we discussed gaps that can open between trading days. A gap is when there is a significant difference between the closing price of a stock today, and the opening price of that stock tomorrow. As a swing trader, you can try and take advantage of these gaps by anticipating that gap and choosing a favorable position. There are instances when the gap could go against you; like with a secondary offering or a bad financial report. But there are just as many instances when you can try to predict a gap.

Swing traders have an advantage over day traders because they can use this gap. Day traders are also less susceptible to the risk that the gap creates. Depending on your outlook and your strategy, you may see the gap as either a good thing or a bad thing. Unfortunately, with gap trading, you don't have much control if the stock price moves against your position. You just must wait for the market to open the next day in order to react.

Gaps could open in several ways. A company could release a statement of earnings, and as a result, the price of the stock could drop or go up significantly in a short amount of time. Unfortunately, it's hard to anticipate a company's earnings report in order to make an educated guess on a good position. Most investors consider it to be too risky to play the gap on an earnings report because it's too easy for there to be a surprise when the company releases its statement.

Another way to take advantage of a gap is by researching companies that are developing new technologies. This type of stock can be very volatile, with attitudes changing swiftly about the predicted success or failure of the product. The volatility could be an opportunity for the swing trader if they timed it right. Just be aware of the way the market can respond to an announcement about new technology. The stock price may shoot up to unprecedented levels as a result but often, things will settle down shortly after. Knowing how to time a position during a product announcement will be a major factor in whether you stand to make any money.

Remember; not all products succeed either. Sometimes a new product can hurt the company, in the long run, more than it helps them in the short run. Imagine an automotive company that announces the release of a new model. For a while, the model could increase anticipated earnings and investors might flock to the company. But the first model of the car might have

681

more issues than expected, and the safety rating may be lower than normal. Remember that Dow Theory says that every action results in a reaction on the market. A product that performs poorly can do just as much harm as a product that performs well. Keep track of the progress of the companies in your portfolio, and make sure you time your positions well.

Another way a swing trader can ride a trend is to seek industries that are experiencing booms. Look for industries that are 'trendy'. Right now, the marijuana industry is experiencing a major boom and investors who recognized the possibilities of this trend early are enjoying a growing portfolio. With the legalization of Marijuana in Canada and many states in the US, there are new companies popping up all over as demand for the product is growing. Eventually, there could be a bubble once the expansion adjusts. But trends like these present opportunities for swing traders. Whether or not you decide to invest in the marijuana industry, its an example of a rideable trend. Who knows how it could play out?

These opportunities that exist in trends don't come around too often, and a swing trader must be patient in order to identify them. Usually, though, all one needs to do to find out about these trends is read the newspaper. Trends come and go and the window for making a real profit is limited. But if you're patient then there will always be another trend around the corner. The trick is to keep your ears to the wind so that you know when an opportunity has arrived.

Just like any swing trading strategy, a lot of it comes down to timing. A good example of a famous trend is the dotcom bubble in the 90s and early 2000s. A lot of people made big off the rise in internet technologies and computer companies. Eventually, though, the trend took a major dip and there were just as many losers from the dot-com trend as there were winners. Just remember that the stock market works in cycles and patterns, and these patterns often repeat themselves. Monitor your positions and stay up to date on news cycles.

When it comes to deciding on a position, timing is important. This means not only timing your exit but also timing your entry. It's better to be patient and wait for a good opportunity to buy when the stock price is low than to try and rush in out of impatience.

Before you open a position decide how much you are willing to pay. This is important because when you have a target price you can calculate exactly what you are risking before you even take on a position. Again, it's better to figure this out before you even take the position. Once you've determined an entry point then you must be patient. Wait for the price of the stock to match your ideal price. If it doesn't, then move on. Never forget that being a good trader requires discipline, which includes knowing when you should take an opportunity and when you should look at other options.

There are ways to track the price or set entry points without the need to constantly monitor the market. For example, a lot of brokerages offer alert services where you can receive notifications when the price of a stock has reached a predetermined target. You decide on an entry point and go about your day, then you receive a notification from your broker. You can even give them a limit order, which tells your broker to buy the stock for you once it hits that target. These notifications are also available for sale targets, so your broker can let you know when the stock has reached that target. They can even sell it automatically for you.

You've read about setting an exit point by now, and how sometimes you'd like to leave some flexibility in case the stock price continues to move in your favor. One way to do this is by not exiting your position all at once. Let's say you a buy a stock and the price of that stock has risen beyond your exit point and it is still moving. You want to preserve some of your earnings, but you are also curious about how high the stock might go. You take to exit your position with only a portion of your money while leaving the rest in. You slowly withdraw your position in increments, but you maintain some percentage of your position until you are completely ready to withdraw. This technique is called scaling out.

Routines and Fundamental Principles of Swing Trading

Swing trading can be a daunting task for the normal retail trader. Professional traders have more information, leverage, experience as well as lower commission rates: nonetheless, they are significantly limited by the items they are allowed to trade in, their enormous amount of capital, as well as their ability to face the risks that come their way. (Large organizations trade in enormous sizes that are difficult to move in and out of stocks speedily). Here, we take a look at what an efficient daily swing trading fundamentals and routine looks like as well as how you can equally be successful in your trading ventures.

Pre-Market

Usually, the retail swing trader will start his day before the securities exchange opens its doors for its routine day-to-day trading period, usually referred to as the opening bell. The time that leads up to the opening is important for getting to experience a general feel of the market that day, coming up with a day-to-day watch list, doing an inspection of any existing positions as well as locating potentials of trading.

Market Overview

The most vital undertaking of the day is to draw level with the latest developments and news items in the market. The swiftest way to involve using cable television channels like Consumer News and Business Channel (CNBC) or markets that have good reputations like a market watch. Market watch is primarily an American-based website that contains financial information and is tasked with giving trades business news, as well as how the stock market looks like on different days. The trader needs to direct his focus at three crucial things:

1.   General market sentiment. This is used to refer to major economic reports, currency, overseas trading sessions, inflation, among others.
2.   Sector view/sentiment (growing sectors as well as hot sectors)
3.   Present-day holdings- This may include the securities and exchange (SE) filings, earnings, and news.

Find Potential Trades

Thereafter, the trader will look for probable trades for the day. Normally, swing traders will opt for a position that has a basic catalyst and exit or manage the position with the help of technical analysis. Finding basic catalysts depends on the two ways described below:
1.   Special Opportunities – Usually, these are the best findings, and they can be found through SEC filings and, in some instances, headline news. These types of opportunities may involve bankruptcies, initial public offerings (IPOs), mergers, takeovers, acquisitions, and restructurings, among other similar events. Ordinarily, these are usually located by monitoring certain filings from SEC, such as 13D and S-4. These can be executed easily with the help of sites like SECfilings.com. It will do so by sending a message as soon as a filing of that sort is made. Usually, these types of opportunities carry a significant amount of risk, but they bring forth numerous rewards for people who take time to conduct research on each opportunity. These sorts of plays usually involve the swing trader buying when most people are selling and opting to sell when everybody else is on a buying spree. They usually do this as a way of "fading" overreactions to events and news. Fading, in this case, refers to a contrarian strategy of investment that had a tendency of trading against the predominant trend.
2.   The sector plays – The most efficient way to find these is by doing an analysis of the news or consulting well-known websites that contain financial information to find out which sectors are doing well. For example, you can come to the conclusion that the energy sector is hot by looking at a popular

energy exchange-traded-fund or analyzing the news to see whether the energy sector will be mentioned. Traders in search of higher risk and consequently higher returns may opt to seek out more unclear areas such as titanium or coal. Ordinarily, they are very hard to analyze, but the returns they bring forth are so much greater. This sort of play involves the swing trader taking up trends ant opportune times and focusing on these trends until there are indications of retracement or reversal. Chart breaks are also another opportunity that swing traders can take advantage of. Usually, they are stocks that have been traded in heavily and that they are close to key resistance or support level. Swing traders will seek a variety of patterns specifically designed to foresee breakdowns or breakouts such as channels, triangles, Fibonacci levels, Gann levels, Wolfe waves, among others. It is important to note that chart breaks are only important if there are enough dividends in the stock. This kind of plays involves the swing trading purchasing after a breakout and then opting to sell again after a short while at the next level of resistance.

Make a Watch List

The next thing to do is come up with a list of stocks for that day. Basically, these are stocks that possess an important catalyst and have a chance of being a good trade. A section of swing traders ensures that their trading stations have a dry-erase board with a cataloged list of opportunities, target prices, entry prices, as well as stop-loss prices.

Check Existing Options

Lastly, the trader should make use of the pre-market hours to do a review of the news, evaluate their existing positions to ensure that no sort of material thing happened to the stock the previous night. The material, in this case, is used to refer to something that affects the securities of the stocks. This can easily be done by just typing stock symbols into any news service search like Google News, for instance. Thereafter, traders seek to find out if there have been any filings that were made through a process that involves searching the EDGAR database of SEC. If they figure out that the existence of material information, they go ahead and analyze it to figure out whether it has an effect on the current trading plan. In addition, as a result, a trader may be forced to make adjustments to their take-profit points or stop-loss.

Market Hours

These hours are for observing and trading. Majority of swing traders review level ii quotes that enable you to have a look at who is selling and buying and at what rates are they trading. Traders that come from the day-trading world usually seek to find out which market maker is making sales (this has the ability to give the traders a hint of who is controlling the market maker's trade), to also take note of head-fake bids as well as asks that have been placed to mix up retail traders.

As soon as traders find a feasible trade, they commence the search for an exit. Typically, this is carried out through a process of technical analysis. The majority of swing traders prefer to use Fibonacci extensions, price by volume, or simple levels of resistance. Ideally, this takes place even before the trade being placed. However, a lot will solely depend on the trades of the day. Moreover, there may be a need to make adjustments later on contingent to future trading. However, there is an overall rule that you should completely avoid adjusting a position to face more risk — for example, adjusting levels of stop-loss upwards with the aim of locking in profits, only adjusting levels of profit-taking if trading goes on to look hopeful or optimistic.

Getting into trades is usually more artistic than scientific, and it has a tendency to depend on the trading activities of the day. On the other hand, the management of trade as well as exiting should constantly be a specific science.

After-Hours Market

Scarcely do you ever find traders trading during after-hours simply because, during this period, the market is in a state of illiquidity, and in most cases, the spread is usually too much to give justifications for? The most crucial aspect of after-hours trading is evaluating performance. It is crucial to make a record of all trades as well as the ideas for both performance evaluation and d tax purposes. Performance evaluation basically refers to taking a look at all trading activities and taking note of things that need to be improved. Lastly, a trader should do a review of their open positions one more time, particularly paying attention to earning announcements that usually take place during the after-hours or any other material happenings that may have an impact on holdings.

Use Multiple Timeframes

Traders have a chance to really gain a competitive advantage when they learn how to use multiple time frames at the same time. The lengthier time frame is the basis of identifying the trend, whereas the lower time frame is used in case you are in the search for short-term reversals in the trend's direction. Considering that the weekly chart represents an uptrend, then you need to be patient until there is a down wave on the daily charts that go back to their original state then put this into use as a lengthy entry.

Types of Trade

a) Retracements
i.   Measuring a pullback
•   Consider using an oscillator
•   Do a subtraction of an average tune range [ATR] from the wing high that you did last

- Find a price to reconstruct under a less lengthy period moving average.
- Find the price that you will use to retrace a percentage of the preceding swing. For example, 50%

ii. Trade-offs in the period used to set the oscillator
- The longer the period used in setting the oscillator, the lower the number of possible trade setups. However, the signals become weaker.
- Period of low cycles has a tendency of coinciding with a more profoundly exaggerated reading. Usually, trades that have been established during a period of low cycles can normally be held for lengthier periods of time.

b) Tests

1. Failure test
This takes place at the end of a trend that has been sustained when the market is crippled from making a leg down or up. It represents a loss of driving power but is not an indicator of a change in trends in and of itself.

2. Box
It usually takes place in the trading range environment. Whenever the market permeates one side of the range of consolidation but in turn clenches inside the rage, the possibility is that it will have a taste of the other part of the range.

Trade Management
Swing traders do not engage in trade if the conditionals are marginal because they need to secure their profits and avoid giving them back. They try as much as they can to ensure that their trades are very close to their initial support or levels of assistance.

They practice stop management which basically involves:
- Placing stops at points of logic like above the resistance or under support where your earlier analysis would be disregarded.

- Whenever the trade depicts that the profit is enough, they relocate the initial stop with the aim of the breaking-even level.

Traders leave whenever they detect any indication of instability or adverse movements in opposition to the position. They opt to cut down the size of the position if there is any sort of uncertainty or when it is not in a working condition.

Always Have Your Main Resistance/Support Lines Drawn In

Traders always ensure that they draw in their lines of resistance in such a way that they are very relevant to the price levels at the moment. Usually, you are advised to draw in a minimum of two major lines. Otherwise, three or four lines is the recommended standard.

The Bottom Line

Taking a look at the principles and daily routine of the normal swing trader, it is clear that the pre-market routine is very important to achieve well-wheeled trading. This is the only time that offers traders numerous trading opportunities, and the day is well planned for. Market hours can simply be summarized as a time to enter and exit positions and not coming up with new plans. Finally, after hours is merely a moment to take a look at the day's trade and consequently carry out a performance assessment. Adopting this kind of daily trading routine consequently beats market returns. All that it takes is preparation and proper planning, as well as some valuable resources.

690

Chapter 22: Protect Your Capital

There is no way around it; if you want to get involved in swing trading then you will have to put up some of your hard-earned money, risking it in the hopes that you make a profit. In order to play on the stock market, you have got to be willing to take some risks. If you are totally risk-averse, then swing trading isn't for you. It's healthy to be afraid of risk. You never want to lose your money, even if you're willing to put up with some risk. The trick to being a successful trader knows how to evaluate risk levels. When is the risk too high, and when should you cut your losses?

Before you even open an account, you should take time to consider how much risk you are willing to take. You should never put money in the stock market that you can't afford to lose. If you have a bad trade and your portfolio takes a hit, there are still bills to be paid and mouths to feed. Assess how much money you are willing to put into your account when you are first starting.

There are dozens of strategies and tools to help you make money on the stock market, and we've already discussed many of them in this book. There are just as many strategies which are crucial to minimizing risk and minimizing losses. Before you even begin a trade, you should establish an exit point so that when a trade results in a loss, you keep the loss to a minimum. After all, the money you lose is less money you will have to invest with later.

One of the most challenging aspects of investing in the psychology of defeat. You did your research, chose a stock, and decided on a position. After using some of your cash to pay for that position you began to see that the stock market moved against you. You were confident about your bet, but now as the market moves you are losing money. It could turn around, maybe you should wait it out. But if you wait, then you might just lose even more money. If you continue to wait your losses

691

have only really occurred 'on paper'. But once you exit a position on a loss, you are making that loss real. When you finally decide to exit, you exit the position with less money than you started. If you keep waiting though, the market could continue to move against you and your stubbornness will only make it worse.

It's one of the most difficult parts of being a trader, acknowledging that you were wrong and backing out and moving on. In order to combat this, you must be disciplined and create an exit strategy for yourself. This means setting a stop-loss point where you commit to exiting before the trade even begins. If you buy a stock at x amount, deciding that if the stock price drops so many percentage points below x then you will cut your losses and leave the position.

If you start swing trading after reading this book and you stick with it, then there is no doubt that will incur a loss at some point. It's a part of swing trading that you should accept before you begin. If you accept this now, then you are more likely to take a step back and recognize when you decided on a bad position. But in the heat of the moment, the frustration of a loss might take over and you may find yourself struggling with what to do.

Most traders will set a stop loss point that is 6-8% below the price they bought the stock for. Choosing a stop loss point between 6-8% is ideal because it's not a huge amount to lose. If you lose 6-8% of your invested capital in a bad position, it's not hard to make that amount back on a good trade. If you let the loss become much more than that, you will have a hard time gaining that money back. You'll have to have an even more profitable trade in the future in order to just get back to where you started. I often choose 6-8% as a stop loss point because I am confident that I can make that amount back with just a few successful trades. The key is to keep your losses low enough so that you can keep trading and make that money back.

It can be difficult to force yourself to stick with the stop-loss plan. Being a good trader requires a cool, disciplined head especially in times of a loss. If you have these personality traits then you are more likely to keep your head down when things aren't going well and stick with your original plan, which means you'll be in a better position to trade again later and hopefully have profitable trades in the future. Remember that this is what makes swing trading advantageous for a beginning trader. While things may unfold quickly for a day trader, things move slower when you are swing trading.

The other question to ask before you enter a position is how much you can make, and how much can I lose. If I see an opportunity to make $100 that requires me to take a position that costs $200, then this position isn't worth it because I'm risking twice as much money as I can make. Most trades will consider the risks compared to potential rewards when picking up a new position. For any type of trader, you should only take positions where the inverse is true. If you have the potential to make twice as much as you stand to lose, then this is a better bet and the risk is more worth it.

Evaluating the risk of any given trade is the first thing any trader should do before taking a position. How volatile is the price of the stock you are taking a position on? Volatility is the frequency at which the stock moves up and down, and it can be a good indication of the risk involved with investing in that stock. If a stock has a lot of upward and downward movement then there is the potential that this stock may result in profits, but it also comes with a higher degree of risk. The more volatile a stock is, the higher the risk associated with trading that stock.

If you choose a position, and things are working in your favor, then you will need to consider how long to ride the trend in order to maximize the profit you make on that position. If you buy a stock and the price keeps rising, how long should you hold onto it before you sell? You might choose a target for your profit but get cold feet and back out before the stock price hits that level, fearing that if you wait too long then you will miss out on what you've already gained. After all, when the stock price is moving in a favorable direction for your position, you have only made money 'on paper' until you exit the position.

So, you should pick a target to exit, even on a positive trade. You should stick with your plans and choose your stop-loss and exit points carefully. But in the case of an exit point on a profitable trade, there is, of course, more flexibility. If you are willing to keep monitoring the stock and continuously reevaluate then you can be more flexible with your exit target. If you have a good reason to believe that the stock will continue to go up beyond the exit point you've chosen, then you should plan to ride it. Just be ready to exit the position quickly, and make sure you're able to stay close to a chart.

Remember that in these moments a lot of the decision comes down to our fundamental and technical indicators. This means that you must stay up to date with the goings-on of a company whose stock you've chosen a position on, and you should be able to read a candlestick chart to look for signs that the market perception of that stock is about to change. Anticipating the moves of other traders will help you decide when you think a trend is about to reverse, and when it's a good time to exit.

The last major part of managing risk involves knowing how much you should stake in a certain position. We've already talked about managing the risk/reward ratio on a potential position. But what percentage of your total capital should you stake on any one position? It's generally a bad idea to risk your entire capital by putting all your money in one position. This is a key part of diversification. Not putting all your eggs in one basket is the golden rule of trading and the most important part of managing risk.

It's true of swing trading that some of your trades will make you a profit, and some trades will end in a loss. So, it makes sense that diversification is the best way to making a profit overall on the aggregate of all your positions.

Most investors choose to use what is known as the one percent rule. You should never put more than 1% of your total account on any single position. If I had an account with $100,000 then I should never risk more than $1000 on any one position. Unfortunately, following this rule can be very difficult if your investment capital is much smaller. If you only have $5,000 in your account, then you can only put $50 on any one trade. So obviously this rule will be easier for traders with larger accounts.

Sometimes a trader may feel especially confident about a potential opportunity that they've identified. They might decide that in a certain case, it's worth it to break their own rules. It can be easy for investors to get caught in this trap, thinking that they've found a path to easy money and as a result they put more than they should have into one position. But the market often goes against what we expect. There is always the chance that something that appeared to be a sure bet turns out to be a lemon. The overconfidence that easy money could be had results in heavy losses.

Always remember that risk is a factor in every position. A wise investor will try to mitigate the damage from risk, rather than avoid it altogether. But a major distinction between traders who fail and traders who succeed is the fact that successful traders have a better understanding of the risks at play in the market. A seasoned trader will rarely break the rules as a result of overconfidence.

Being a profitable trader is not about hitting it big on investments where you outwit the market and discover some massive untapped opportunity. That idea may get popularized in movies like The Big Short, where traders made a fortune off one good position. This type of opportunity is actually very rare. Good traders are people who can manage many smaller positions at once and who have a higher number of profitable trades than trades resulting in a loss. A caveat to that is knowing how to minimize the damage when you do incur a loss and doing their homework to study the market and find several good opportunities at once.

Something that helps many successful traders is keeping a detailed record of all the trades you participate in. It not only will help you keep your position straight in your mind, but it will also give you something to refer to. You'll be able to see what worked and what didn't. If you can keep an organized and detailed record of your trades, then you can iron out your strategies with different types of stocks.

For every trade I participate in, I will take note of several things. If I rely on fundamentals to identify opportunities with certain stocks, I will make a record of which stock I was studying and what the fundamentals looked like when I took my position. I'll probably even make a note of technical details and the performance of the stock throughout the time that I held my position; opening and closing prices, as well as the trading volume of the stock that I held.

You may pick stocks for a variety of reasons. The reasons may be purely formulaic; you choose a stock based on certain fundamental indicators or based on the technical characteristics of the stocks price movement. Whatever means you use to choose a stock; you will be making a bet on that stock's future performance. So, for every stock you take a position on, you should record why you chose the position you did in addition to the performance of the stock. Did it match your expectations? If the stock didn't perform in the way that you expected, were there factors that you overlooked that would have affected your decision to take on a certain position? Do you believe there were any external or internal factors which affected your success on this trade? If there were external or internal factors, what were they?

Over time you will begin to get a feel for what indicators matter the most, and which ones fit the best with your strategy. If you keep a record of your trades, then you might notice patterns with certain kinds of stocks or certain fundamentals. The best education for a trader experiences, so you should try to get the most out of your experience by paying close attention to the factors which affect the success of your trades.

Of course, your trade journal should also include a record of which trades were successful and which trades were not, as well as your profits. How much did you pay for a position, and at what price did you exit the position? You'll start to see what your success record is. If you want to be a profitable trader, then you need to have more successful trades than trades that resulted in a loss.

The best day traders will be organized and detailed. Remember, this is real money you are investing in. Like treating stock as if you were buying the whole business, you should approach trading as if it is a serious job. It requires diligence and clear thinking as well as an organized and rational approach to your decision-making process. The better your research is, and the better your records are, the more likely you will be to learn and improve as a trader.

If you maintain an organized and logical manner of trading, then you are less likely to succumb to the stress that is associated with trading. Trading requires you to think on your feet and make intuitive decisions with limited information about the perceived outcomes. If you are organized and diligent then it will be easier to make these decisions with confidence, rather than in a state of stress.

While you must be able to accept the risk, you should go into every trade with the intention of making money on that trade. You should never enter a trade with a reckless you-only-live-once type strategy. You might make a good profit on one or two trades if you use this method, but most of the time you will lose because you didn't do your research, or you were overconfident in a position.

The stress from potential or real losses and the quick thinking that is required of a trader can make it easy to burn out in this job. People who thrive under pressure are more inclined to succeed and stick with it because they will accept the job for what it is and make decisions without dwelling too much on fear or doubt. There is risk, and some fear of risk is healthy. You should never accept risk blindly or just for the sake of taking a risk. The risk should serve a purpose or have some potential for a positive outcome.

Glossary

Anticipation - it is the act of a stock trader predicting about the security market future before either buying or selling of his or her stock.

Asking Price - an initial price at which the security can either be sold for by the investor in the security market
Bearish Stock; a form of stock that is anticipated to decrease in value over a specific time by a stock market trader.

Assignment – this is the process of issuing an option seller or writer with an exercise notice instructing him to sell or buy 100 shares of particular equity at a stipulated amount as the strike value.

At the Money – an 'at the money' option is one that has a cost that is equivalent to the equity's value.

Automatic Exercise – this refers to the process where options that are in the money are exercised automatically, if still in the money during expiration.

Breakeven Point – the point at expiration where an option strategy returns zero profit and zero loss.

A Bearish – market expectation that the value or price of an option will decline over time.

Bear Market – when the overall prices of a market are on the decrease.

Bear Spread – a spread that aims at generating profit from bearish price movements.

Bid Price - it is the highest price of securities such as stocks in the security market a dealer is willingly prepared offer in exchange for the securities.

Bid-Ask Spread – the value obtained from calculating the difference between an option's ask and bid prices.

Black Scholes Pricing Model – model that uses factors such as the value of the underlying security, strike price, time value, and volatility to estimate the price and profits made from options.

Broker – (*definition 1*) a person or organization that processes option contract orders on behalf of traders and investors.

Broker - (*definition 2*) the professional who is responsible for either buying or selling of securities such as stocks for his or her clients.

Brokerage - an individual or a firm responsible for arranging transaction of buying and selling of securities for the sake of getting commission after the exchange is successful.

Bullish – a market state defined by the possibility of the cost rising in future.

Bullish Stock - a type of stock that is predicted to rise in value over a certain period of time by a stock trader in the security market.

Bull Market – state when the overall market prices are increasing.

Bull Spread –trading spread established with the aim of generating profit from bullish stock and market movements.

Buy to Close Order – an order generated when a trader wants to close an existing call position. This is achieved through purchasing contracts that you previously sold to other investors.

Buy to Open Order – this is an order that you place if you want to enter a new position of purchasing contracts.

Call Option - the kind of option that gives a buyer some authority to buy 100 shares for given equity at predefined prices and expiration periods.

Carrying Cost - the cost incurred when using capital to buy options based on the interest received from borrowed capital.

Cash Account - one of brokerage accounts where an investor is required to make full payments of the securities he or she has purchased.

Cash-Settled Option – an option where profits are given to the holder in terms of cash, not in the form of shares.

Close – end a trading position. Also refers to the time of the day when the market stops to operate and the final option prices are determined.

Closing Order – an order that you raise to end a contract that is already in existence.

Combination Order – an order that comprises of more than one basic order.

Contingent Order –an order that allows you to set customized parameters for entering or exiting options contracts.

Contract Range –the highest prices of a single contract minus its lowest prices.

Contract Size – the number of share units covered by individual contracts. In options trading, the default size is 100 shares.

Covered Call - a trading strategy used to make profits from existing contracts when the market is neutral.

Covered Put – a trading strategy that works together with short selling to make profits from existing positions. This strategy protects your investment from short-term price increments.

Currency Option – a form option that has currency as the equity.

Commission – money you give to brokers or brokerage companies for their services.

Credit – the amount of money you get in your account for selling an option.

Day Trader - A person who purchases or sells securities in the security market within a span of a single day.

Debit – the amount of money you give out when purchasing an option.

Derivative – an instrument, which obtains its value from other financial instruments. For example options and futures.

Discount Broker – a broker that only carries out basic order processing for options traders.

Discount Option – an option that sells at a price that is less than the intrinsic value.

Dividend Yield - a form of dividend that is illustrated in form of percentage of the present share price.

Dividends Pay Out Ratio - it is the relative amount of the total revenue that a company pays its shareholders.

Dividends - these are the returns that are paid by a company which an individual owns shares in it.

Early Assignment – when a contract seller fulfills the requirements of the contract before its expiration period.

Early Exercise – the process of closing contracts before they expire.

Earnings Per Share - The portion of the profit made by a firm which is allocated to each share that is out standing in the firm's common stock.

Equity Ratio - A ratio that portrays of how much assets in a firm are being funded by the equity shares.

Exchange Trading Funds - Funds invested for trading in the stock exchange trade.

Exercise – buying or selling an options contract at a specific strike price and time period.

Exercise Price – the price of each share at which it is sold or bought at expiration. This is another name for the strike price.

Expiration Date – The date when a contract stops to exist or expires.

Expiration Month – the month in which expiration takes place.

Expire Worthlessly – a contract that expires worthless is one that returns no profit at the expiration date.

Extrinsic Value – those aspects of an options pricing that are determined by factors not related to the cost of the equity or security.

Fundamental Analysis - a method of analyzing the intrinsic value of a financial instrument in the stock market and its price value in future.

Hedging – the process of investment that seeks to minimize the risk of trading tour investments.

Historical Volatility – measures an equity's volatility levels through studying past price movements over a period of time.
Horizontal Spread – spread created from several contracts that feature the same strike price and different expiration dates.

Implied Volatility – an estimate of an underlying security's future volatility levels based on current prices, using pricing models.

Index Option –a contract on the options market whose underlying asset is not stock but an index.

In the Money – contract whose stock value s more than the current cost in case of a call position, the opposite is true for a put contract.
Inflation Rate - the percentage in change of either the rice or fall of prices of securities in the stock market.

Inflation - a moment where the prices of securities can either experience a sudden rise or an impromptu fall.

Interest Rate - an amount of interest that paid after a certain amount of time to a stock trader for the money he or she has invested in the stock market.

Interest - this is the amount of money an investor in the stock market receives in turn from the money he or she invests in the stocks purchased.

Intrinsic Value – a contract whose equity value is higher than the strike amount.

Investor - an individual who willingly allocates his or her capital in the stock market with an aim of getting profits in return after a certain amount of time.

Long Position – a position that is created when you purchase a call or put contract.

Leg – individual positions that form up a contract comprising of several positions.

Leverage – the process of using options to obtain more payoffs from the options market.

Limit Order –an order that allows you to trade options at the specified minimum and maximum strike prices.

Limit Stop Order – an order that instructs positions to close when certain prices are attained.

Liquidity - the level of availability of a certain financial instrument. In other words, this is a measure of the level of ease that a certain instrument can be bought or sold without affecting the prices.

Listed Option – an option that is listed on the options market.

Margin Account - a type of brokerage account that an investor give an investor ability to lend cash to customers for them to purchase securities or other financial instruments.

Margin Requirement –this is the amount of money that a trader deposits in his brokerage account to cover for naked option positions. These acts as collateral for the brokerage firm to purchase or sell options on behalf of the trader.

Market Bubble - a situation where prices of stocks are escalated above their actual value by traders.

Market Indicators - formulas and ratios that are able to illustrate the gains and losses in the indexes and stocks.

Market Order – one used to buy or sell a contract at current market prices.

Market Stop Order – the order that closes a position when certain market prices are attained.

Moneyness – a technique used to define the correlation between an equity is underlying cost and the strike amount of an option.

Morphing – the process of creating synthetic positions, or transitioning from one position into another using a single order.

One-Sided Market – market state when buyers are significantly more than sellers, or sellers more than buyers.

Online Brokers – a broker that allows you to process your orders through an online platform.

Opening Order – an order used to create new options contract positions.

Optionable Stock – stock that acts as underlying security for certain options.

Options Contract – a right to purchase or sell shares at specified strike prices and expiration times.

Options Holder – the person who owns an options contract.

Options Trader – a person who buys and sells options.

Out of the Money – an option gets out of the money when the cost of the equity of the underlying security is not favorable to the trader based on the strike price. A call option can become out of the money if the value of the underlying equity is below the strike charges. On the other hand, a put option becomes out of the money when the cost of the underlying equity is higher than the strike charges.

Over the Counter Options – options that are traded over the counter and not through online exchange platforms.

Over Valuing - an occurrence where a stock market trader estimates the prices of stocks to be higher than the actual value in the market.

Portfolio - a grouping of several financial assets such as currencies cash, bonds, stocks and other cash equivalents which are owned by an individual or an organization.

Pricing Model – a formula that can be applied in the determination of the abstract or theoretical value of a given options contract using variables such as the underlying security, strike price, and volatility.

Premium – the amount paid to acquire an option in the options market. Premiums are often quoted as price per share.

Profit - it is the excess revenue a stock trader gets from either buying or selling of stocks in the stock market.

Physical Option – the kind of option that has underlying equity in the form of physical assets.

Put Option – an option that allows you to write or sell underlying equity at a specific strike amount and expiration times.

Realize a Profit - making some profit when you close a position contact.

Realize a Loss – incurring a loss when you close a position contract.

Retail Trader - a person or an organization that is focused in investing their capital in futures, options, bonds and stock.

Risk - it is an unforeseen factor that can lead a stock trader to experience losses while trading in the stock market.

Scaling Out - situation in the stock market where a trader get out of his or her position so as to either buy or sell his or her financial instruments.

Security Index - an indicator in the security market that uses statistical data to analyze the changes that are experienced in the securities market.

Sell to Close Order – order placed when closing a long position that is already in existence.

Sell to Open Order – order placed when opening a new contract position.

Settlement – when contract terms are finalized after exercising a position.

Shares - indivisible form of capital that is used to signify a person's ownership to a certain company.

Short Position – the state attained when you sell contracts.

Short Selling - A phenomena where a stock market investor borrows securities which he or she sells later in the stock market with an aim of making profit by buying them later.

Spread – a position made from selling several contracts belonging to the same underlying security.

Spread Order – an order that instructs a broker to create a spread of several positions that are transacted simultaneously.

Stock Market - a loose network of several traders who willingly buy and sell stocks which represent ownership of certain business.

Stock Options - an agreement agreed by the stock market investor and his or her broker granting the broker exclusive rights to buy or sell shares at a predetermined price.

Stock Trader - an individual or a firm involved in the trading of stocks.

Stock - it is a type of security that gives an individual ownership to certain company and it is sold at a particular market price.

Stop Loss Point - points where a stock trader gives instruction of certain stocks to either be sold or bought when they attain a certain price in the stock market.

Stop Order – An order implemented to close positions from the market when certain price parameters are attained.

Strike Price – the amount of money given or received when a contract holder decides to close a contract position .

Swing Trader – (*definition 1*) a stock trader who holds his or her financial instruments such as stocks for a long time before he or she trades them.

Swing Trader - (definition 2) An individual who either buys or sells securities in the market for a period of several days or weeks so as to capture the gains of the market.

Synthetic Position – a trade position that combines options and stocks in a single contract to emulate another option position.

Synthetic Long Call – a synthetic position that allows you to own calls. It entails purchasing puts as well as their related underlying assets.

Synthetic Long Put – a position that allows you to own puts. It entails purchasing calls then short selling the underlying security related with the call.

Synthetic Short Call – a position that is similar to purchasing short calls. Entails selling stocks and selling put options associated with the stock.

Synthetic Short Put – a position that similar to trading short puts. It entails purchasing stock then selling call options associated with the stock.

Synthetic Short Stock – this is a synthetic options position that is similar to going short on stocks. It entails writing one call contract at the money than purchasing one put option that is also at the money for the same underlying stock.

Technical Analysis – a technique used to predict the price of financial instruments such as stocks through analyzing the historical price data of the underlying security.

Theoretical Value – refers to the cost of an option position derived using pricing models and mathematical formulas.

Time Decay – the period when the extrinsic value of an option decreases as it approaches the expiration date.

Trading Plan – this is a plan that traders create to outline how they will carry out transactions on the options market. The plan always contains objectives, trading methods and strategies to be used.

Trailing Stop Order – this is an order whose stop price is a percentage change from the best price ever reached by a given position.

Trading Style – the method used by a trader when transacting on the options market.

Trend – a continuous movement or change in the price of options or market patterns.

Time Value - the time value of any call contract or put contract is the section of the premium that is more in value than the quoted intrinsic value.

Underlying Stock – the kind of security upon which the value of an option is derived.

Under Valuing - a situation where prices of stocks are estimated to be lower than the actual market prices by a stock market trader.

Volatility – the level of rising or falling of the cost of a given option.

Vertical Spread – a combination of options positions established from multiple contracts that feature diverse strike amounts with similar expiry dates.

Volatile Market – an exchange platform that has prices or conditions that keep changing in an unexpected manner.

Volatility Crunch – sudden decline in an option has implied volatility.

Volume – the number of transactions carried out in relation to a certain option or underlying security.

Weekly Option – an option that expires within one week.

Writer – the person who creates contract positions for selling options.

Writing an Option – the act of selling an option contract.

Conclusion

With the information you've gained from this book, you are hopefully interested in starting your own account and beginning the process of researching your own trade opportunities. By now you have some foundation from which to do your research as well as a clearer picture of what to expect when choosing a broker and entering your first position.

The research required to be a successful swing trader won't stop when you finish reading this book. Every trade you enter will require another round of reading and studying so that you can choose a position with confidence. Remember what good research consists of; look at the fundamentals of a stock and the history of its performance over time.

Decide if you want to choose a strategy based on the stock or the other way around.

Keep your efforts simple at first, take your time to learn how the market works. As you gain experience your trades will go smoother and you will learn what works and what doesn't. Keep a record of how your trades go. If you continue to swing trade, then over time you will participate in a lot of trades and hold a lot of positions. To learn from them effectively you have got to take notes ad keep track of your progress. You will learn faster if you keep a record.

The amazing thing about trading and competing in the stock market is the sheer number of opportunities available. At any given time, there are new profitable positions that are waiting to be discovered. If you genuinely enjoy reading about new companies and current events, then it will be easier to identify opportunities as they appear.

The other advantage you have currently as a swing trader is the vast network of information available to you. Your stock research is no longer limited to what you can find in a public library and keeping track of the stock market in real-time doesn't require you to be attached to a landline phone. The trends that are hard to reach are more available. Imagine trying to find promising new companies to invest in before the age of the internet. You would have to hear about stock opportunities through sheer luck or knowing the right person.

Now anyone can have access to the information. This means that the market is a lot more competitive, but it also means that there are a lot more opportunities. The internet also provides endless resources to learn strategies and hear what analysts are saying. At the end of the day, take a lot of the noise with a grain of salt. The money you are risking is your own, and you should be leery of the way that certain analysts' opinion can be regarded as fact. Use the information to learn, but always fall back on your own research and intuition at the end of the day.

If you can learn how to trade profitably then you'll be able to enjoy the fruits of a rewarding job. Maybe you will decide to trade more actively and become a day trader. There is nothing wrong with maintaining a balance and swing trading in addition to your normal job. Be honest with yourself about the needs of your lifestyle, and whether your personality is a good match for that kind of path.

Whichever way you choose; whether you decide to continue swing trading or day trading, you'll gain the additional freedom that comes with being your own boss and making money independently for yourself. This is the main reason why people choose to get involved in swing trading; the added flexibility it can offer your life. But, just like any job, it requires work and dedication. Don't be frustrated with yourself if you don't see results right away. Don't think of yourself as a failure or a bad trader if you have a few bad trades. It happens to all of us when we first begin down this path, and it's a part of the learning experience.

The next step is to stop reading already and to get ready to get started taking advantage of the benefits that are unique to a swing trading strategy. While it may not be exciting, what this means in practical terms is that it is time for you to get down to business and start doing your homework. While you might want to avoid all of that and jump right in, as previously mentioned all this is likely to do is to nip your trading career in the bud before it even begins.

The game of swing trading is a mental game. Therefore, above the technical skills and experience, you need to succeed, you need to make sure you exhibit the right attitudes. As they say, " attitude is everything." If you put forth the right attitude and learn the tricks of the game, you will do well that those who do not.

Be conservative. While you can make huge profits in swing trading, avoid the "get rich quick" attitude. Don't be lured by the success stories of those swing traders who buy big houses, big boats and go for amazing vacations through their income from swing trading. Success takes time, dedication and experience.

Another thing you have to take note of is your mindset. There are many success stories of people who are making it swing trading. Avoid dealing with negative, bitter people who have been hurt in the trade, Remember that that you will become who you associate with. Therefore, associated yourself with seasoned, experienced and successful swing trader in every financial market and learn their mindset. There's always something to learn every day to get better in the game of swing trading.

If you are still nervous about the prospect of risking your hard-earned money on the stock market, there are other ways for you to gain practice and experience as a trader without risking your money.

Investopedia hosts a stock market simulator that is free to use and available online. When you sign up, the simulator gives you $100,000 of virtual money to use for trading securities. The simulator tracks real stocks from the New York Stock Exchange and all the major stock indexes. The simulator is updated every fifteen minutes so that you are essentially trading in real-time with the stock market simulator.

The simulator even considers the fees charged by brokers, as well as the commissions. When you trade regularly, whether, with real money or virtual money, you will have to keep track of how these fees are affecting your margins. The fees charged by brokers will affect your decision making, as they will always be a factor in the profitability of your trades. The stock market simulator will give you practice in managing these fees.

The only thing missing from the stock simulator is the psychological challenge of dealing with real risk. You will never know how it feels to truly manage risk until you are trading with real money. The main advantage of using a stock trading simulator is that you will be learning the mechanics of trading. This is just as important to be a good trader, and stock market simulators are something you should look into if you are interested in gaining some free experience.

So, if you have a hunch about a company or you can feel the air changing in the stock market but you don't have the capital to invest right now, you can use a stock market simulator to test your theories and learn in the meantime. Learning how to manage trades will give you confidence when it comes to putting your real money to work.

The more you practice and prepare to start swing trading with real money, the more likely you will be to succeed. The reality of swing trading is this; most will fail to make any profits, or they will quit before they have any success. Swing trading is difficult and competitive. You will be in a much better position to succeed if you can continue to research and learn, practicing and solidifying strategies.

You should be constantly reading about the economy and the stock market. Publications like The Economist, the Wall Street Journal and MarketView will be good resources for learning how economic news and developments will impact the performance of the stock market. They will give you a place to start your research on identifying opportunities in the current market conditions. Current events will steer investor confidence and subsequently the movements of stock prices. Even if you don't open an account right away, get in the habit of keeping up with current events and financial news.

Remember that the best way to find opportunities is to research stocks and sectors that you already have a personal interest in. The knowledge you have already is a useful tool for staying ahead of the market. If you have an interest in cars, then you'll probably enjoy reading about automotive companies; what new car models are being introduced and how do you think they will perform? If you have an interest in computers and tech; what types of technology have you read about that you think could be groundbreaking? Out of all the new companies producing these technologies, which ones have the most promising fundamentals, and are more likely to succeed? If you approach to research this way, then you'll no doubt find opportunities for stocks to trade and invest with.

With all of this in mind, I hope that it is clear to you at least that swing trading is not a passive or easy way to make extra money. You must do your research. But if you find sectors that interest you, and you have a natural interest in current events and a keep an eye for opportunities then you will succeed.

CPSIA information can be obtained
at www.ICGtesting.com
Printed in the USA
LVHW010809211120
672146LV00001B/12